This book provides a new quantitative view of the wartime economic experiences of six great powers: the UK, the USA, Germany, Italy, Japan, and the USSR. What contribution did economics make to war preparedness and to winning or losing the war? What was the effect of wartime experiences on postwar fortunes, and did those who won the war lose the peace? A chapter is devoted to each country, reviewing its economic war potential, military-economic policies and performance, war expenditures, and development, while the introductory chapter presents a comparative overview. The result of an international collaborative project, the volume aims to provide a text of statistical reference for students and researchers interested in international and comparative economic history, the history of World War II, the history of economic policy, and comparative economic systems. It embodies the latest in economic analysis and historical research.

The economics of World War II

Studies in Macroeconomic History

Series Editor: Michael D. Bordo, Rutgers University

Editors: Forrest Capie, City University Business School
Barry Eichengreen, University of California, Berkeley
Nick Crafts, London School of Economics
Angela Redish, University of British Columbia

The titles in this series investigate themes of interest to economists and economic historians in the rapidly developing field of macroeconomic history. The four areas covered include the application of monetary and finance theory, international economics and quantitative methods to historical problems; the historical application of growth and development theory and theories of business fluctuations; the history of domestic and international monetary, financial and other macroeconomic institutions; and the history of international monetary and financial systems. The series amalgamates the former Press series **Studies in Monetary and Financial History** and **Studies in Quantitative Economic History**.

Other books in the series:

The economics of
World War II

Six great powers in international comparison

edited by
MARK HARRISON

 CAMBRIDGE
UNIVERSITY PRESS

PUBLISHED BY THE PRESS SYNDICATE OF THE UNIVERSITY OF CAMBRIDGE
The Pitt Building, Trumpington Street, Cambridge, United Kingdom

CAMBRIDGE UNIVERSITY PRESS
The Edinburgh Building, Cambridge CB2 2RU, UK   www.cup.cam.ac.uk
40 West 20th Street, New York, NY 10011–4211, USA   www.cup.org
10 Stamford Road, Oakleigh, Melbourne 3166, Australia
Ruiz de Alarcón 13, 28014 Madrid, Spain

First published 1998
First paperback edition published 2000

Typeface: Monophoto Times 10/12pt   *System*: QuarkXPress [SE]

A catalogue record for this book is available from the British Library

Library of Congress cataloguing in publication data

The economics of World War II: six great powers in international
comparison / edited by Mark Harrison.
        p. cm.
    Includes bibliographical references.
    ISBN 0 521 62046 5 (hardbound) – ISBN 0 521 78503 0 (paperback)
    1. World War, 1939–1945 – Economic aspects.   2. Great Britain –
Economic conditions – 1918–1945.   3. United States – Economic
conditions – 1918–1945.   4. Germany – Economic conditions – 1918–1945.
5. Italy – Economic conditions – 1918–1945.   6. Japan – Economic
conditions – 1918–1945.   7. Soviet Union – Economic
conditions – 1918–1945.   I. Harrison, Mark, 1949–
HC58.E36   1997
940.53'14–dc21   97-10264 CIP

ISBN 0 521 62046 5 hardback
ISBN 0 521 78503 0 paperback

Transferred to digital printing 2005

Contents

7 The Soviet Union: the defeated victor 268
Mark Harrison

Figures

Tables

Contributors

Werner Abelshauser (Faculty of History and Philosophy, University of Bielefeld)

Stephen Broadberry (Department of Economics, University of Warwick)

Akira Hara (Faculty of Economics, University of Tokyo)

Mark Harrison (Department of Economics, University of Warwick)

Peter Howlett (Department of Economic History, London School of Economics)

Hugh Rockoff (Department of Economics, Rutgers University, and the National Bureau of Economic Research)

Vera Zamagni (Department of Economics, University of Bologna)

Preface

The purpose of this book is to provide a new comparative evaluation of the wartime economic experience of six great powers: the UK, USA, Germany, Italy, Japan, and the USSR. It asks: what contribution did economics make to these countries' war preparedness, and to winning and losing the war? What was the effect of wartime experience on the postwar fortunes of the great powers? It aims to provide a text for students of international and comparative economic history, the history of World War II, the history of economic policy, and comparative economic systems, and a work of reference for scholars engaged in research in these fields.

The scope of each chapter includes each country's economic war potential, military-economic performance, war expenditures and losses, and the long-run impact of World War II on each country's economy. Each country's prewar size and development level, economic system characteristics, and military-economic policy are considered in relation to the part they played in the war effort of their respective coalitions, and in the outcome of the war as a whole. Existing interpretations of wartime economic performance are reviewed and revised: what does the wartime experience tell us about the capacity and durability of different economic systems, the effectiveness of regulation by quantities versus prices, the social and economic limits on resource mobilization, the policy and practice of rearmament 'in width' or 'in depth', and the role of foreign resource transfers? Hypotheses about whether the war helped to remove or entrench institutions hindering long-run economic development are also reappraised.

Three things make this the right moment for such a reappraisal. First, there is a sense in which we are no longer living in the 'postwar period' and have passed beyond it. The defining moment of the era in which we live now was the ending of the Cold War in 1991, not the ending of World War II more than fifty years ago. Indeed one result of the end of the Cold War has been to present scholars engaged in international and comparative economic history with new research on World War II, and new collaborative opportunities, not least in Russia and with Russians.

At the same time there is a deeper sense in which the terrible events of World War II continue to shape our contemporary world. Consider the range of issues today confronting the countries which led that struggle – problems such as the difficulties hindering Europe's economic and monetary unification; the bloody ethnic disintegration of Yugoslavia; the attempt to reassert international jurisdiction over war crimes in Bosnia; Italian, German, and Japanese reassessments of their wartime leaders and roles; Japan's search for a world role commensurate with its economic status; its regional difficulties in relation to the two Koreas and the two Chinas; its unresolved territorial dispute with Russia; Russian nationhood in the process of its redefinition in terms of military and Slavophile ethnic values; American engagement and disengagement with European security and the rebuilding of eastern Europe. As we face up to these issues, we cannot help hearing the *motifs* of 1939–45 being orchestrated over again, often by men and women (but in fact they are nearly always *men*) of the postwar generation who think, wrongly, that these are their own new tunes, and that they are playing them for the first time. Therefore it remains important for us to see World War II as it really was, so that we can learn to see today as it really is.

Second, contemporary economic problems – ranging from the rebuilding of eastern Europe to adjustment of the western European economies to new centres of economic power on the Pacific Rim – have brought renewed interest in the processes of post-World War II reconstruction. But investigation of postwar reconstruction requires the background of a well-founded account of the war itself – of such aspects as the degree of mass participation in the war effort, the social and economic limits to mobilization, the degree of continuity of market and administrative institutions, the entrenchment or destruction of interest groups, and the true extent of war damage to human and physical assets. Only if we first understand these will we go on to understand how our world remade itself afterwards.

Third, the war offers an experience of intrinsic interest to present-day economists in terms of government versus the market. With the end of the Cold War, our understanding of economic systems is moving away from an oversimplified contrast between free-market capitalism and bureaucratic state socialism. But this demands a deeper analysis of the social relationships and government institutions which make markets work. It is commonly observed of the twentieth century that when war broke out, markets broke down. To explain this several hypotheses are traditionally proposed: market allocation was insufficiently slow to mobilize resources through the operation of price signals and incentives, the potential redistribution of income towards profits in war industries was threatening to social stability, individual households and firms left to themselves pursued a strategy for defeat (i.e. to wait and see, to look for a free ride on the back of others' efforts, to conserve peacetime priorities, occupations, and relationships, and not to accept temporary mobilization). As a result, the war everywhere saw an enormous growth of government at the expense of private uses of resources, and a displacement of market forces by government allocation.

At the same time it is far from clear that the corollary of market failure was necessarily government success. There were some problems which markets might have solved anyway (such as the restriction of private consumption) on which government expended considerable efforts. There were other problems which government sometimes made worse (e.g. by overmobilizing resources). There was also a third group of problems which could not be solved either by markets or by government (e.g. an overall deficiency of resources). While the authors of this book adopt a variety of perspectives on the central issue, a common theme of their accounts is the significance of constraints on government action, and the importance of finding a balance between market forces and administrative force in their social context.

This book does not just dwell on failure. Another often-repeated theme of the chapters which follow is that of economic miracles. At the time, the successes of German and Japanese recovery from the 1929 slump, the American, German, and Soviet productive efforts in World War II, and the German, Italian, and Japanese postwar recoveries were all described as 'miraculous' from one point of view or another. A central concern of the authors is to show that, on closer inspection, there were no miracles – and no irrational disasters, either. There was nothing special about being American, German, Italian, Russian, or Japanese (it is more than 200 years since the last British 'economic miracle' of the Industrial Revolution, and even that is disputed nowadays). There *were* rationally understandable, successful combinations of luck, judgement, force of will, inherited resources in the right place at the right time, and the institutions to set them to work, giving them moral as well as economic force – just as the economic setbacks and disasters of this period can be rationally understood as the result of bad luck, bad timing, defective institutions, and lack of resources.

Perhaps that makes everything sound too simple. According to Clausewitz, who founded modern strategic studies in the years after the Napoleonic wars, 'Everything is very simple in War, but the simplest thing is difficult' (*On War*, 1968, ed. A. Rapoport, Harmondsworth). The imperatives of war appear to simplify everything down to a few basic requirements, but to attain them in the 'resistant medium' constituted by danger, shock, surprise, excitement, fear, hunger, exhaustion, wounds, bereavement, boredom, isolation, ignorance, deception, self-interest, and indiscipline, turns out to be a process of endless complexity. In World War II the process of applying violence to the army of the adversary also required societies and economies to undergo violent alteration. Because of this the world changed and was never the same again. To understand the result is the authors' common purpose.

Acknowledgements

The contributors to this volume are members of the international workgroup on the economic history of World War II. Our workgroup was formed in 1991, and met on two occasions, at the Universities of Bielefeld (Germany) in May 1993, and at the University of Warwick (England) in September 1994.

The contributors are deeply indebted to the other participants in our two meetings, especially Vladimir Busygin (Novosibirsk), Nick Crafts (LSE), Grigorii Khanin (Novosibirsk), Stephan Merl (Bielefeld), Avner Offer (Oxford), Richard Overy (London), Rolf Petri (Florence), and Bryan Sadler (Warwick), and also to the secretaries to the workgroup, Iris Kukla (Bielefeld) and Jenny Penfold (Warwick) for their efforts on our behalf. They also wish to express their appreciation to the Universities of Bielefeld and Warwick for their hospitality.

Werner Abelshauser thanks Eamonn Noonan, and Akira Hara thanks Mitaka Ltd for their respective translations.

Finally, the generous financial support of the Volkswagen Foundation under the programme *Diktaturen in Europa des 20. Jahrhunderts: Strukturen, Erfahrungen, Überwindung und Vergleich* was indispensable for the final success of our project. We are duly grateful.

Mark Harrison

Abbreviations

ABB	Amt für Berufserziehung und Betriebsführung (Germany)
ACS	Archivio Centrale dello Stato (Italy)
ADGB	Allgemeiner Deutscher Gewerkschaftbund (Germany)
AM-lire	lire issued for expenditure by the Allied powers (Italy)
Ammassi	compulsory pooling of basic foodstuffs (Italy)
ASBI	Archivio Storico della Banca d'Italia (Italy)
ASKI	Ausländersonderkonten für Inlandszahlungen (Germany)
BA	Bundesarchiv (Germany)
CIA	Central Intelligence Agency (USA)
CNR	Consiglio Nazionale delle Ricerche (Italy)
Confindustria	Confederazione Generale dell'Industria Italiana (Italy)
CSO	Central Statistical Office (UK)
CSVI	Consorzio Sovvenzioni su Valori Industriali (Italy)
DAF	Deutsche Arbeitsfront (Germany)
DINTA	Deutsches Institut für Technische Arbeitsschulung (Germany)
ESB	Economic Stability Bureau (Japan)
GARF	Gosudarstvennyi Arkhiv Rossiiskoi Federatsii (the Soviet Union, Russia)
GATT	General Agreement on Tariffs and Trade
GDFCF	gross domestic fixed capital formation
GDP	gross domestic product
GDP(E)	gross domestic product (expenditure)
GHQ	General Headquarters of the Allied Powers (Japan)

GNP	gross national product
GOPO	government owned, privately operated capital (USA)
Goskomstat	Gosudarstvennyi komitet statistiki (the Soviet Union)
HAFRABA	Verein zur Vorbereitung der Autostraße Hansestädte-Frankfurt–Basel (Germany)
IBRD	International Bank for Reconstruction and Development (the World Bank)
IMF	International Monetary Fund
IMT	International Military Tribunal (Germany)
IRI	Istituto per la Ricostruzione Industriale (Italy)
ISTAT	Istituto Centrale di Statistica (Italy)
IVMV	Istoriia Vtoroi Mirovoi voiny (Bibliography, the Soviet Union)
KSKS	Kanketsu Showa Kokusei Soran (Bibliography, Japan)
LTES	Long-term economic statistics (Bibliography, Japan)
Mefo	Metallurgische Forschungsgesellschaft mbH (Germany)
MITI	Ministry of International Trade and Industry (Japan)
MPS	Material Product System of national accounts (the Soviet Union)
NATO	North Atlantic Treaty Organization
NKVD	Narodnyi komissariat vnutrennykh del (the Soviet Union)
NMP	net material product (the Soviet Union)
NNP	net national product
NS	national-socialist, *or* Nazi (Germany)
NSDAP	Nationalsozialistische Deutsche Arbeiterpartei (Germany)
OECD	Organization for Economic Cooperation and Development
R&D	research and development
RAND Corporation	The United States Air Force think-tank (USA)
RDL	Regio Decreto Legge (Italy)
RGAE	Rossiiskii Gosudarstvennyi Arkhiv Ekonomiki (the Soviet Union, Russia)
RM	Reichsmarks (Germany)
RSI	Repubblica Sociale Italiana (Italy)

RST	Rossi-Sorgato-Toniolo (Bibliography, Italy)
SNA	System of National Accounts
SPD	Sozialdemokratische Partei Deutschlands (Germany)
SS	Schutzstaffel (Germany)
SVIMEZ	Associazione per lo Sviluppo del Mezzogiorno (Italy)
TsSU	Tsentral'noe statisticheskoe upravlenie (the Soviet Union)
UK	United Kingdom (of Great Britain and Northern Ireland)
USA	United States of America
USAF	United States Air Force
USSBS	United States Strategic Bombing Survey
USSR	Union of Soviet Socialist Republics (the Soviet Union)
WTB	the German trade unionists Woytinski, Tarnow, and Baade

1 The economics of World War II: an overview

Mark Harrison

Introduction: economic factors in the war

This book deals with two issues in the economics of twentieth-century warfare. First is the contribution of economics to victory and defeat of the great powers in World War II. Second is the impact of the war upon long-run economic trends and postwar institutions in the economies of the great powers.[1]

What was the contribution of economics to the outcome of the war? As far as this first question is concerned, the authors share a broad under-standing of 'economics', which comprises the national requirements of the war, the quantity and quality of resources, their availability and mobiliza-tion, and the institutions and policies which mobilized them for wartime purposes. As for resources, we understand them to include not only phys-ical resources such as minerals, materials, and fixed capital assets, and financial stocks and flows, but also the human resources represented by the working population, its health and literacy, its degree of skill, training, and education, as well as assets represented by scientific knowledge and technological know-how.

How important were these economic factors in deciding who won the war, and who lost? In answering this question it has always made sense to distinguish two periods of the conflict. In the first period, economic considerations were less important than purely military factors. This was the phase of greatest success for the powers of the Axis, and it lasted roughly until the end of 1941 or into 1942 (the exact turning point differed by a few months among the different regional theatres). In this first period, the advantages of strategy and fighting power enabled Germany and Japan to inflict overwhelming defeats upon an economically superior combina-tion of powers. The factors of strategic deception and surprise, speed of movement, skill in the concentration of forces and selection of objectives, martial tradition, and *esprit de corps* were all on their side.

1

Of course, economic factors were not entirely absent. If Germany or Japan had been poor, agrarian nations the size of Liechtenstein, neither would have launched war against the most powerful industrial economies in the world. Nonetheless, despite significant economic inferiority, the Axis powers made substantial progress towards their war aims and at times appeared to be on the verge of complete success. Their outstanding generalship and the combat qualities of their armies had created a catastrophic situation for the Allies; 'On the face of things', writes Richard Overy, 'no rational man in early 1942 would have guessed at the eventual outcome of the war.'[2] It was also largely the military failures of the Axis powers, not their economic weakness, which brought this first period of the war to an end without the decisive victory which had previously appeared within their grasp.

In the second period of the war, which began in 1942, economic fundamentals reasserted themselves. The early advantages of the Axis were dissipated in a transition period of stalemate. A war of attrition developed in which the opposing forces ground each other down, with rising force levels and rising losses. Superior military qualities came to count for less than superior GDP and population numbers. The greater Allied capacity for taking risks, absorbing the cost of mistakes, replacing losses, and accumulating overwhelming quantitative superiority now turned the balance against the Axis. Ultimately, economics determined the outcome.[3]

Population, territory, and GDP

The prewar balance

There is considerable evidence to support this view, but its scope must be nearly global in coverage and requires some explanation. A first balance can be struck for the alliance system which existed prior to the outbreak of the world war. Table 1.1 gives basic indicators for the prewar coalitions based on the frontiers of 1938 – population, territory, and GDP. The military-economic significance of GDP and population may be obvious; they set the upper limit on the production and personnel potentially available for war. Territorial expanse was also of importance; it helped to determine the quantity and diversity of available natural resources such as metallic ores and mineral fuels, and the degree to which each coalition could expect to form a self-sufficient economic bloc under conditions of wartime disruption of international trade.

On one side was the Anglo-French alliance system which, when the respective colonial empires are taken into account, comprised nearly 700 million people – one third of the globe's population – and 47.6 million square kilometres. On the other side were the powers of the Axis – Germany

Table 1.1. *Population, gross domestic product, territory, and empires of the Allied and Axis powers within contemporary frontiers, 1938*

	Popul-ation, million	Territory, sq. km		GDP, international dollars and 1990 prices	
		total, thou.	per thou. people	total, $ bn	per head, $
	1	2	3	4	5
Allied powers					
UK	47.5	245	5	284.2	5,983
France	42.0	551	13	185.6	4,424
UK dominions	30.0	19,185	639	114.6	3,817
Czecho-Slovakia	10.5	140	13	30.3	2,882
Poland	35.1	389	11	76.6	2,182
French colonies	70.9	12,099	171	48.5	684
UK colonies	453.8	14,994	33	284.5	627
Allied total	689.7	47,603	69	1,024.3	1,485
of which, great powers only (UK and France)	89.5	796	9	469.8	5,252
Axis powers					
Germany	68.6	470	7	351.4	5,126
Austria	6.8	84	12	24.2	3,583
Italy	43.4	310	7	140.8	3,244
Japan	71.9	382	5	169.4	2,356
Japanese colonies	59.8	1,602	27	62.9	1,052
Italian colonies	8.5	3,488	412	2.6	304
Axis total	258.9	6,336	24	751.3	2,902
of which, great powers only (Germany Austria, Italy, and Japan)	190.6	1,246	7	685.8	3,598
China					
(exc. Manchuria)	411.7	9,800	24	320.5	778
Allies/Axis	2.7	7.5	2.8	1.4	0.5
Great powers only	0.5	0.6	1.4	0.7	1.5
China/Japanese empire	3.1	4.9	1.6	1.4	0.4

Notes:
Countries and groups of countries are ranked under each subheading in descending order of their GDP per head. 'Colonies' include League of Nations mandates and other dependencies. Figures are given for territory within 1938 frontiers, except as noted below.
   UK dominions: Australia, Canada, New Zealand, Union of South Africa. Canada includes Newfoundland and Labrador.
   Czecho-Slovakia: including the Sudetenland (annexed by Germany in September 1938).
   French colonies: mainly in the Near East, Africa, and Indo-China.

Notes to Table 1.1 (*cont.*)

UK colonies (including joint Anglo-French and Anglo-Egyptian colonies): many countries in the Near East, south and southeast Asia, Africa, the Caribbean, and Oceania.

Germany: the geographical entity of the Versailles treaty, excluding the Sudetenland and Austria.

Japanese colonies: Korea, Formosa (Taiwan), and Manchuria.

Italian colonies: mainly Libya and Abyssinia (Ethiopia).

Sources:

Population

All figures from Maddison (1995), appendix A, except that Czech-Slovakia, Poland, Germany, China (except Manchuria), Manchuria itself, and various colonial populations, all within contemporary frontiers, are taken from League of Nations (1940), 14–19.

GDP

Population multiplied by GDP per head (for Czecho-Slovakia, GDP per head of 1937).

GDP per head

All figures from Maddison (1995), appendix D, except as follows.

UK dominions: for South Africa, the white population (20 per cent of the total, from League of Nations (1940), 14–19) is assigned the same GDP per head as the average for Australia, New Zealand, and Canada, and the black and coloured population is credited with the African regional average.

French colonies are divided among Indo-China, Algeria, and other (mainly African) colonies. The GDP per head of French Indo-China is based on that of Vietnam (see above), and that of Algeria is derived in the same way. France's other colonies are credited with a GDP per head based on the African regional average.

UK colonies are divided among south Asia, Africa, and other. The GDP per head of south Asian colonies is a weighted average of that for 1938 of Burma, India, Pakistan, and Bangladesh within modern frontiers.

The GDP per head of African colonies is taken as that of Maddison's African regional average, and that of other (mainly southeast Asian colonies, but also of those in the Pacific, and Caribbean) is based on the Asian regional average.

Italian colonies: the weighted average of GDPs per head of Libya and Ethiopia, derived as above.

Japanese colonies: for Korea and Formosa, GDPs per head are those given by Maddison for South Korea and Taiwan; that of Manchuria is based on his China average.

Territory

League of Nations (1940), 14–19. All figures are within boundaries of 1938, except that Germany excludes Austria and the Sudetenland; the frontiers of Czecho-Slovakia are those of the beginning of the year.

Territory per thousand

Territory divided by population.

(now including Austria), Italy, Japan, and the much smaller colonial empires of Italy in Africa and Japan in east Asia; these amounted to 260 million people and a little more than 6 million square kilometres. Thus the Allies outweighed the Axis by 2.7:1 in population and 7.5:1 in territory. In the Far East, Japan was also at war with China, the population and territory of which exceeded those of Japan and its existing colonies by 3.1:1 and 4.9:1.

For each country or region the table lists GDP as well as population and territory. Population and territory can be measured without much ambiguity, and the researcher need worry only about measurement error. GDP is different because it requires a complex process of evaluation of each country's real product in a common set of prices. For table 1.1 I rely mainly on Angus Maddison's historical time series which are expressed in present-day dollar values and extrapolated back over long periods. This in itself allows many opportunities for error. In addition many of the countries (especially the relatively poor colonial possessions) represented in the table are assigned GDP values on the basis of indirect evidence. Therefore the GDP figures may be taken as indicative, but not precise. According to table 1.1 the Allies of 1938 with their empires disposed of more than $1,000 billion of real product, compared with the $750 billion of Axis GDP, an Allied advantage of 1.4:1. China also outweighed Japan and its colonies in GDP by a similar margin. In every major respect, therefore, the Axis disadvantage was strongly marked, though less in GDP than in population or territory.

The potential advantage of the Allies was greater in population, and still more in territory, than in GDP. This is explained by the adherence to the Allied bloc of great low-income regions in Africa and Asia – the British and French empires. Thus the territorial expanse per head of the Allied population was nearly three times that available to the Axis population. But the average Allied income level was less than $1,500 per head, half the Axis level of $2,900. The same imbalance is present in the comparison of China with the Japanese empire: Japan was poor by west European standards, and its colonies were poorer, but China was poorer still, with less than half the income per head of the Japanese empire.

Suppose we narrow the focus to the great powers alone – the UK and France on one side, Germany (excluding Austria), Italy, and Japan on the other. When the lesser powers and colonial empires are excluded, the balance of size shifts against the Allies; although richer in resources and GDP per head, they were smaller than the Axis powers, with only half their population, 60 per cent of their territory, and 70 per cent of their GDP.

The balance in wartime

Under the impact of war, the balance changed. Two factors were at work. One was the accession of new allies to each side as the war became a global conflict. Between 1938 and 1942 the Axis powers were joined by Finland, Hungary, and Romania, the Allies by the USA and USSR. China, already at war with Japan in 1938, was also becoming an Ally, although one of doubtful military value, not least because of its internal civil war of nationalists versus communists. The Allies were the principal beneficiaries of globalization of the war – just in population, for example, the USA and USSR represented more than 300 million people compared with the gain to the Axis of the 28.5 million combined population of Finland, Hungary, and

Romania. The other process was the changes in *de facto* jurisdiction arising mainly, though not exclusively, from Axis expansion. By 1942 the Allies of 1938 had lost territories on which there had resided before the war some 260 million people. Partly on this account, and partly at the expense of previously neutral countries and colonial populations, the Axis powers had brought under their own control territories in Europe and Asia with a prewar population of nearly 350 million people. Indeed, to change the balance in their own favour was a principal strategic objective of Axis expansionism; each of the Axis powers aimed to achieve self-sufficiency within a colonial sphere expanded at the expense of the Allied and neutral powers.

The changing balance is illustrated in table 1.2, which recalculates the resources on each side within the boundaries of 1942 when the Axis empires had reached their greatest extent. However, for many regions wartime population and GDP indicators are unreliable or non-existent. Therefore, the table is based not on incomes and populations of 1942 but on the 1938 aggregates already used in table 1.1; it shows the purely territorial effect of change in the boundaries of control, holding GDP and population constant, and does not take into account the fact that by 1942, for example, the USA was much richer or the USSR much poorer than in 1938 within constant frontiers.

Table 1.2 shows that by 1942 the economic odds had shortened greatly in favour of the Axis. Using 1938 indicators, by 1942 the *ex ante* advantage of the Allies had fallen to 1.9:1 in population (but still 7:1 in territory, a figure reflecting the vast north American prairies and Siberian steppe) and only 1.3:1 in GDP. If China is excluded, the equivalent figures are 1.2:1 and 1.1:1. In other words, by 1942 the Axis powers were no longer economically inferior to the Allies, and were on more or less equal terms in overall GDP of 1938.

The assumptions underlying table 1.2, in particular the use of 1938 income levels, correspond in a certain sense with the expectations of Axis military-economic policy. Before the war German and Japanese decision makers looked at the colonial spheres of their adversaries and saw them to be rich sources of labour and materials, which they expected to be able to take over intact and exploit to the full. At the same time, when they looked at their adversaries' home territories, they did not anticipate any very vigorous economic mobilization in response to Axis expansionism. In short, they did not expect their enemies to become very much richer than before the war or their colonial annexations to become very much poorer in consequence of the war itself. In fact, however, wherever the Axis powers conquered, incomes fell and the difficulty of extracting resources from the conquered territory increased. At the same time their enemies mobilized their resources and became, on average, richer and economically more powerful than before the war.

Table 1.2. *National and colonial boundaries of 1942, showing populations and GDPs of 1938*

	Popul-ation, million 1	Territory, sq. km		GDP, international dollars and 1990 prices	
		total, thou. 2	per thou. people 3	total, $ bn 4	per head, $ 5
Allied powers					
Allied total, 1938	689.7	47,603	69	1,024.3	1,485
China, 1938					
(exc. Manchuria)	411.7	9,800	24	320.5	778
Net gain, 1938–42	93.8	20,401	—	724.5	—
Allied total, 1942	1,195.2	77,803	65	2,069.3	1,731
excluding China	783.5	68,003	87	1,748.8	2,232
of which, great powers only (UK, USA, and USSR)	345.0	29,277	85	1,443.5	4,184
Gains, 1938–42					
USA	130.5	7,856	60	800.3	6,134
USSR	167.0	21,176	127	359.0	2,150
US colonies	17.8	324	18	26.5	1,495
Near East and North Africa	38.6	6,430	167	52.1	1,351
Losses, 1938–42					
France	42.0	551	13	185.6	4,424
Czecho-Slovakia	10.5	140	13	30.3	2,882
Poland	35.1	389	11	76.6	2,182
Occupied USSR	62.4	978	16	134.2	2,150
US colonies	15.9	296	19	23.9	1,497
French colonies	70.9	12,099	171	48.5	684
UK colonies	23.2	933	40	14.4	621
Axis powers					
Axis total, 1938	258.9	6,336	24	751.3	2,902
Net gain, 1938–42	375.7	4,834	—	800.7	—
Axis total, 1942	634.6	11,169	18	1,552.0	2,446
of which, great powers only (Germany and Austria, Italy, and Japan)	190.6	1,246	7	685.8	3,598
Gains, 1938–42					
Denmark	3.8	43	11	20.9	5,544
Netherlands	8.7	33	4	44.5	5,122
Belgium	8.4	30	4	39.6	4,730
France	42.0	551	13	185.6	4,424
Norway	2.9	323	110	11.6	3,945

Table 1.2 (*cont.*)

	Popul-ation, million	Territory, sq. km		GDP, international dollars and 1990 prices	
		total, thou.	per thou. people	total, $ bn	per head, $
	1	2	3	4	5
Axis Gains (cont.)					
Finland	3.7	383	105	12.7	3,486
Czecho-Slovakia	10.5	140	13	30.3	2,882
Greece	7.1	130	18	19.3	2,727
Hungary	9.2	117	13	24.3	2,655
Poland	35.1	389	11	76.6	2,182
Baltic states	6.0	167	28	12.9	2,150
Occupied USSR	62.4	978	16	134.2	2,150
Bulgaria	6.6	103	16	10.5	1,595
US colonies	15.9	296	19	23.9	1,497
Yugoslavia	16.1	248	15	21.9	1,360
Romania	15.6	295	19	19.4	1,242
Dutch colonies	68.1	1,904	28	77.4	1,136
Thailand	15.0	518	35	12.5	832
UK colonies	23.2	933	40	14.4	621
French colonies	24.1	740	31	10.9	452
Losses, 1938–42					
Italian colonies	8.5	3,488	412	2.6	304
Allies/Axis, 1942	1.9	7.0	3.7	1.3	0.7
exc. China	1.2	6.1	4.9	1.1	0.9
great powers only	1.8	23.5	13.0	2.1	1.2

Notes:
The Allied powers
Between 1938 and 1942 the UK was joined by the USA, USSR, and China in the alliance which would eventually become the United Nations.

USA: including Alaska and Hawaii.

USSR: the territory of 1938, excluding the annexations of 1939–40 (eastern Poland, Bessarabia and northern Bukovina from Romania, a strip of Finnish territory, Estonia, Latvia, Lithuania).

US colonies: Philippines, Puerto Rico.

China: China, already partially dismembered by Japan, was a doubtful military asset, being as much a battleground (with its own continuing civil war as well) as a power. In the table, Allied totals are computed with and without China.

Allied gains and losses
Over the period between 1938 and 1942, the following changes transpired in terms of military defeat, occupation, and annexation.

Near East and North Africa: the British took effective control of the former Italian colonies as well as Egypt, Iran, and Iraq.

France, Czecho-Slovakia, and Poland were defeated and occupied directly or (in the case of Vichy France) incorporated into the German economic space.

The latter aspect of the war is captured in table 1.3, which shows the GDPs of the great powers from 1938 through to 1945 (see also figure 1.1). The table makes some allowance for the fact that both France and Italy changed sides during the war (twice in the French case), but the spirit of the table is to look at the changing economic strength of the great-power coali-

Notes to Table 1.2 (*cont.*)

Occupied USSR: shown here is only that part (see above) which had been subject to Soviet jurisdiction in 1938; the rest is counted elsewhere.

US colonies: the Philippines were lost to Japan.

French colonies: in wartime these fell technically under the jurisdiction of the Vichy regime, but (apart from French Indo-China, dealt with below) were mostly remote from the Axis economies and played little role in the war efforts of either side. In the same way, although the Allies were joined by the governments-in-exile of Belgium and the Netherlands, Belgian and Dutch colonies were either seized by Japan (the Dutch East Indies) or lost to both sides.

UK colonies: Burma, Borneo, Hong Kong, and Malaya were lost to Japan.

Axis gains and losses

Between 1938 and 1942, Germany was joined on the eastern front by Finland, Hungary, and Romania.

Germany and her allies conquered Denmark, Netherlands, Belgium, France, Norway, Czecho-Slovakia, Greece, Poland, the Baltic states and other Soviet territories, Bulgaria, and Yugoslavia.

Japan seized the Phillippines from the United States, the Dutch East Indies, Thailand, the British colonies in East Asia listed above, and French Indo-China.

By the end of 1942, however, Italy had lost its African empire.

Sources:

In most respects, as for table 1.1. However, some new countries enter the table, and some have to be taken in parts.

US colonies: the weighted average for Puerto Rico and the Philippines. For Puerto Rico, GDP per head in 1950 is interpolated on the South American regional average for sample countries in 1938 given by Maddison (1995), 212 (the same procedure, using the African and Asian regional averages, is used below for Zaire, Algeria, Vietnam, Libya, and Ethiopia, and in table 1.2 for Egypt, Iran, and Iraq).

Thailand: GDP per head and population are taken from Maddison (1995), appendices A and D.

Egypt, Iran, and Iraq: population and GDP per head, given for 1950 by Maddison (1995), appendix F, are interpolated on his African and Asian regional averages respectively for 1938.

USSR: 1938 population within contemporary frontiers is from Andreev, Darskii, Khar'kova (1990), 41 (converted to mid-year), and GDP per head as in Maddison.

In 1941–2 the USSR lost 1,926,000 square kilometres of territory occupied on Jan. 1, 1939 by 84,852,000 people (TsSU (1959), 39) – say, 84 million as of mid-1938. However, in 1938 other jurisdictions (Polish, Latvian, Lithuanian, Estonian, Romanian, etc.) had covered more than 21.5 million of the 84 million, who must therefore be excluded to avoid double counting. The same applies to 948,000 of the 1,926,000 square kilometres. It is assumed that the 1938 GDP per head of the occupied territories was the same as for the USSR as a whole.

Dutch colonies: the GDP per head of the Dutch East Indies is based on that of Indonesia.

Table 1.3. *Wartime GDP of the great powers, 1939–1945, in international dollars and 1990 prices (billions)*

	1938	1939	1940	1941	1942	1943	1944	1945
Allied powers								
USA	800	869	943	1,094	1,235	1,399	1,499	1,474
UK	284	287	316	344	353	361	346	331
France	186	199	82	—	—	—	—	101
Italy	—	—	—	—	—	—	117	92
USSR	359	366	417	359	318	464	495	396
Allied total	1,629	1,721	1,757	1,798	1,906	2,223	2,458	2,394
Axis powers								
Germany	351	384	387	412	417	426	437	310
France	—	—	82	130	116	110	93	—
Austria	24	27	27	29	27	28	29	12
Italy	141	151	147	144	145	137	—	—
Japan	169	184	192	196	197	194	189	144
Axis total	686	747	835	911	903	895	748	466
Allies/Axis	2.4	2.3	2.1	2.0	2.1	2.5	3.3	5.1
USSR/Germany	1.0	1.0	1.1	0.9	0.8	1.1	1.1	1.3

Sources: For 1938, see table 1.1. Other years are interpolated on index numbers as follows: UK, table 2.1 (col. 4); USA, table 3.1 (col. 4); Germany, table 4.1 (col. 1); Italy, table 5.1 (col. 3); Japan, table 6.1 (col. 1); USSR, table 7.7, part (A). Figures for the USSR for 1939 are interpolated on population within 1938 frontiers on the assumption that GDP per head remained unchanged compared with 1938 (for evidence on this score see Harrison (1994), 269; Maddison (1995), 200). For France and Austria see Maddison (1995), appendix B.

tions as they existed in 1942. The prewar GDP of the combined Allied powers exceeded that of the Axis powers by 2.4:1. Subsequently the ratio moved somewhat against the Allies, falling to 2:1 in 1941, because the Axis economies expanded while the resources of France, knocked out of the Allied coalition in 1940, became available to Germany. In 1941 Soviet GDP was also beginning to fall under the impact of German attack. But 1941 was the Allied low point.

From 1942 onwards the ratio moved steadily in the Allied favour. First, the United States economy, already by far the largest among the great powers in GDP terms, embarked on a huge quantitative mobilization drive; by 1944, US GDP stood at nearly twice its 1938 level. Second, the Soviet economy, although hit hard by invasion in 1941 and harder still in 1942, was subsequently stabilized and then mobilized to a higher level of output. Third, Italy was knocked out of the Axis coalition in 1943. Fourth, the

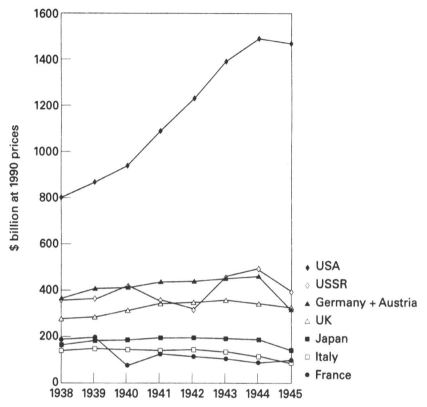

Figure 1.1 Real GDPs of the great powers, 1938–1945
Source: table 1.3

GDP of occupied France fell steadily year by year. Fifth, by the end of
1944, the German and Japanese economies were collapsing. Thus, in 1942
and 1943 the great-power economic balance moved strongly in favour of
the Allies and even before the economic collapse of Germany and Japan
had already reached 3.3:1 in 1944.

Only on the eastern front did the Allies not possess the advantage. The
Soviet Union had more than twice Germany's population and many times
its territory, but, with 1938 per capita income at 40 per cent of the German
level, was roughly the same size in GDP terms. Because the German
economy grew under the stimulus of increasing mobilization, while the
Soviet economy collapsed under the weight of German attack, by 1942
rough parity had been transformed into a substantial German advantage.
Still relatively untroubled by Allied bombing and the threat of a second
front in the west, Germany was able to devote nearly all of its military

resources to the war in Russia. The war in eastern Europe was therefore much more closely fought than in other theatres where the Allies always held the upper hand economically speaking. With recovery in 1943 the Soviet economy was able to reestablish a narrow advantage, but it remained a finely balanced thing until 1945.

In another respect as well the Allies retained an important overall advantage, even in the worst periods of setback and defeat. This lay in the bloc of trading partners available to each side, illustrated in table 1.4. Allied naval supremacy limited Germany and Italy to overland trade with their neutral neighbours and the neutrals adjacent to occupied Europe; together these constituted a zone with a prewar population of 70 million people and GDP of $150 billion. But this was little more than half the size of the bloc available to the Allies made up by the Irish Republic, the neutral neighbour of the UK, and the countries of central and south America, several of which eventually declared war on Germany in early 1945. Again, trade with neutrals principally benefited the western Allies, and was turned to Soviet benefit only indirectly through the medium of Allied aid to the USSR.

Table 1.5 reveals that by 1944 the five great powers still in the game were fielding more than 43 million soldiers (probably more than one-third of their combined prewar male population of working age), with two-thirds of them wearing Allied uniform. Thus the table also shows how the advantages of size were translated into numerical superiority of military personnel. Before the war the combined forces of the Anglo-French alliance just outweighed those of Germany, though not of the Axis powers taken together. In 1940 and 1941, despite the rapid war mobilization of the UK, the French surrender and Italian entry into the war ensured that the Allied (from mid-1940 to mid-1941 the British alone) forces became numerically inferior to their enemies. With 1941, however, German attention switched to the east. From 1942 onwards, despite Japanese entry into the war, with American mobilization now added to the Soviet war effort, the forces of the Axis were always outnumbered in the main theatres of conflict. By 1944 the Allied advantage stood at almost 2:1 on the eastern front as in the west and the Pacific.

The quantitative disadvantage of the Axis powers was even greater in munitions than in men, as the data in table 1.6 suggest.[4] The raw figures are summarized in table 1.7 which shows, first, the astonishing quantities of weapons produced in the period of most intense global conflict, 1942–4: nearly 50 million rifles, automatic weapons, and machine guns, more than 2 million guns and mortars, more than 200,000 tanks, more than 400,000 combat aircraft, nearly 9,000 major naval vessels. But by far the greater part of this vast flow emerged from Allied factories and shipyards. As table 1.7 reveals, in every broad category of ground and air munitions Allied produc-

Table 1.4. *The main neutral-country trading blocs of the wartime coalitions, showing population and GDP of 1938*

	Population million 1	GDP, international dollars and 1990 prices	
		total, $ bn 2	per head, $ 3
Allied trading bloc			
Ireland	2.9	9.2	5,126
Independent states of Central and South America	126.7	250.3	1,975
Allied total	129.7	259.4	2,001
Axis trading bloc			
Switzerland	4.2	26.4	6,302
Sweden	6.3	29.8	4,725
Spain	25.3	51.1	2,022
Portugal	7.6	12.9	1,707
Turkey	17.0	23.1	1,359
Portuguese colonies	9.5	7.0	735
Spanish colonies	1.0	0.7	714
Axis total	70.8	151.0	2,133
Allies/Axis	1.8	1.7	0.9

Notes:
Ireland, although neutral, could scarcely avoid a high degree of commercial integration into the British war economy. The only significant neutral trading partners of the wartime Allies were in Central and South America, but the colonial dependencies are already accounted for or otherwise dealt with in table 1.2, so only the independent states remain to be dealt with here: Argentina, Bolivia, Brazil, Chile, Colombia, Costa Rica, Cuba, Dominican Republic, Ecuador, Guatemala, Haiti, Honduras, Mexico, Nicaragua, Panama, Paraguay, Peru, Salvador, Uruguay, Venezuela.
   Spanish colonies: mainly Spanish Guinea, Spanish Morocco, and Spanish Sahara.
   Portugese colonies: mainly Angola and Mozambique, but also territories elsewhere in Africa, India, and east Asia.
Sources: As tables 1.1 and 1.2. Populations are taken from League of Nations (1940) where not given by Maddison (1995). GDPs per head are from Maddison (1995), except that, where not available for the territories specified, the regional average is assumed, weighted where necessary (as in the case of Portuguese colonies) by population.

Table 1.5. *Armed forces of the great powers, 1939–1945 (thousands)*

	1939	1940	1941	1942	1943	1944	1945
Allied powers							
USA	—	—	1,620	3,970	9,020	11,410	11,430
UK	480	2,273	3,383	4,091	4,761	4,967	5,090
France	5,000	7,000	—	—	—	—	—
USSR	—	5,000	7,100	11,340	11,858	12,225	12,100
Allied total	5,480	14,273	12,103	19,401	25,639	28,602	28,620
Axis powers							
Germany	4,522	5,762	7,309	8,410	9,480	9,420	7,830
Italy	1,740	2,340	3,227	3,810	3,815	—	—
Japan	—	1,630	2,420	2,840	3,700	5,380	7,730
Axis total	6,262	9,732	12,956	15,060	16,995	14,800	15,560
Allies/Axis:							
eastern front	—	—	1.1	1.5	1.4	1.9	2.3
western and							
Pacific fronts	1.2	0.8	0.9	1.1	1.9	1.9	1.6

Notes:
The Allied and Axis totals sum the preceding rows in each column; however, the Axis total is based on the average of the alternative Japanese series. The ratios of Allied to Axis forces on each front are calculated as follows.

Western and Pacific fronts: for 1939 UK and France versus Germany. In 1940, the French and Italian forces are included, each with a 50 per cent weight since Italy joined the war in mid-year, at the same time as the French surrendered. In 1942–3, USA and UK versus one-tenth of the German armed forces, plus Italy, plus Japan (the average of the alternative series), but in 1943 the Italian forces are given a weight of two-thirds corresponding to the eight months of fighting before the Italian surrender. In 1944–5, USA and UK versus one-third of the German armed forces, plus Japan.

Eastern front: USSR versus Germany, assuming that Germany allocated 90 per cent to the eastern front in 1941–3, but only two-thirds in 1944–5.

Sources:
USA, table 3.11 (col. 3).

UK, table 2.13.

France: according to Kedward (1995), 401, there were 'just under 5 million' in the French army after mobilization in September 1939, with 'a further two million possible soldiers available in the Empire', which I assume to have been mobilized by 1940.

USSR, as table 7.8.

Germany: Förster, Messenger and Petter (1995), 468.

Italy: personal communication (Vera Zamagni).

Japan, table 6.9 (the rounded average of cols. 1, 2).

Table 1.6. *War production of the great powers, 1939 to August 1945 (units)*

	1939	1940	1941	1942	1943	1944	1945	Total
USA								
No. of months	—	—	1	12	12	12	8	45
Thousands								
Rifles, carbines	—	—	38	1,542	5,683	3,489	1,578	12,330
Machine pistols	—	—	42	651	686	348	207	1,933
Machine guns	—	—	20	662	830	799	303	2,614
Guns	—	—	3	188	221	103	34	549[a]
Mortars	—	—	0.4	11.0	25.8	24.8	40.1	102.1
Tanks and SPG	—	—	0.9	27.0	38.5	20.5	12.6	99.5
Combat aircraft	—	—	1.4	24.9	54.1	74.1	37.5	192.0
Units								
Major naval vessels	—	—	544	1,854	2,654	2,247	1,513	8,812
UK								
No. of months	4	12	12	12	12	12	8	72
Thousands								
Rifles, carbines	18	81	79	595	910	547	227	2,457
Machine pistols	—	—	6	1,438	1,572	672	231	3,920
Machine guns	19	102	193	284	201	125	15	939
Guns	1	10	33	106	118	93	28	390
Mortars	1.3	7.6	21.7	29.2	17.1	19.0	5.0	100.9
Tanks and SPG	0.3	1.4	4.8	8.6	7.5	4.6	2.1	29.3
Combat aircraft	1.3	8.6	13.2	17.7	21.2	22.7	9.9	94.6
Units								
Major naval vessels[a]	57	148	236	239	224	188	64	1,156
USSR								
No. of months	—	—	6	12	12	12	8	50
Thousands								
Rifles, carbines	—	—	1,567	4,049	3,436	2,450	637	12,139
Machine pistols	—	—	90	1,506	2,024	1,971	583	6,174
Machine guns	—	—	106	356	459	439	156	1,516
Guns	—	—	30	127	130	122	72	482
Mortars	—	—	42.3	230.0	69.4	7.1	3.0	351.8
Tanks and SPG	—	—	4.8	24.4	24.1	29.0	20.5	102.8
Combat aircraft	—	—	8.2	21.7	29.9	33.2	19.1	112.1
Units								
Major naval vessels	—	33	62	19	13	23	11	161

Table 1.6. (*cont.*)

	1939	1940	1941	1942	1943	1944	1945	Total
Germany								
No. of months	4	12	12	12	12	12	4	68
Thousands								
Rifles, carbines	451	1,352	1,359	1,370	2,275	2,856	665	10,328
Machine pistols	40	119	325	232	234	229	78	1,257
Machine guns	20	59	96	117	263	509	111	1,176
Guns	2	6	22	41	74	148	27	320
Mortars	1.4	4.4	4.2	9.8	23.0	33.2	2.8	78.8
Tanks and SPG	0.7	2.2[b]	3.8	6.2	10.7	18.3	4.4	46.3
Combat aircraft	2.3	6.6	8.4	11.6	19.3	34.1	7.2	89.5
Units								
Submarines	15	40	196	244	270	189	0	954
Italy								
No. of months	—	6	12	12	8	—	—	38
Thousands								
Rifles, carbines	—	—	—	—	—	—	—	—
Machine pistols	—	—	—	—	—	—	—	—
Machine guns	—	—	—	—	—	—	—	125
Guns	—	—	—	—	—	—	—	10
Mortars	—	—	—	—	—	—	—	17.0
Tanks and SPG	—	—	—	—	—	—	—	3.0
Combat aircraft	1.7	3.3	3.5	2.8	2.0	—	—	13.3
Units								
Major naval vessels	40	12	41	86	148	—	—	327
Japan								
No. of months	4	12	12	12	12	12	8	72
Thousands								
Rifles, carbines	83	449	729	440	634	885	349	3,570
Machine pistols	—	—	—	—	—	3	5	8
Machine guns	6	21	43	71	114	156	40	450
Guns	1	3	7	13	28	84	23	160
Mortars	0.5	1.6	1.1	1.5	1.7	1.1	0.3	7.8
Tanks and SPG	0.2	1.0	1.0	1.2	0.8	0.4	0.2	4.8
Combat aircraft	0.7	2.2	3.2	6.3	13.4	21.0	8.3	55.1
Units								
Major naval vessels	21	30	49	68	122	248	51	589

Notes:
[a] Small calibre naval and aviation weapons accounted for roughly half this number.
[b] Including armoured cars.
Sources:
Ground and air munitions (SPG are self-propelled guns), except Italy: IVMV, vol. XII (1982), 168, 181, 183, 200, 202.
    Major naval vessels (excluding landing craft, torpedo boats, and other auxiliary craft), except Italy: Overy (1995), 1060.
    Italy, all figures: personal communication (Vera Zamagni).

Table 1.7. *War production of the great powers, 1942–1944*

	Rifles, carbines (thou.)	Machine pistols (thou.)	Machine guns (thou.)	Guns (thou.)	Mortars (thou.)	Tanks (thou.)	Combat aircraft (thou.)	Major naval vessels
The Allied powers								
USA	10,714	1,685	2,291	512	61.6	86.0	153.1	6,755
UK	2,052	3,682	610	317	65.3	20.7	61.6	651
USSR	9,935	5,501	1,254	380	306.5	77.5	84.8	55
Allied total	22,701	10,868	4,154	1,208	433.4	184.2	299.5	7,461
The Axis powers								
Germany	6,501	695	889	262	66.0	35.2	65.0	703
Italy	—	—	83	7	11.3	2.0	8.9	218
Japan	1,959	3	341	126	4.3	2.4	40.7	438
Axis total	8,460	698	1,313	395	81.6	39.6	114.6	1,359
Allies/Axis	2.7	15.6	3.2	3.1	5.3	4.7	2.6	5.5
eastern front	2.3	11.9	2.1	2.2	7.0	3.3	2.0	—
western and Pacific fronts	3.1	22.9	4.0	3.8	3.4	6.6	3.0	—

Source: Calculated from table 1.6. Two-thirds of Italian production between mid-1940 and mid-1943 is assumed to have taken place within the period 1942–4. For ground and air munitions, two-thirds of German war production are assigned to the eastern front. No account is taken of the contribution of the western Allies to Soviet munitions supply, or of the Italian contribution to Axis forces in Russia.

tion dominated by a margin of at least 5:2 (rifles, combat aircraft), and in some case by much more (3:1 for guns and machine guns, 5:1 for tanks, mortars, and warships, 15:1 for machine pistols). The Allies held the upper hand on every front – in the east almost as much as in the west and the Pacific. On both main fronts the Allied advantage was greater in every category of weapons than in men, reflecting the higher level of equipment per soldier of the Soviet, British, and United States armies.

Size and development

It would be a mistake to interpret these figures as meaning that size was the only economic factor of importance. Also of great significance was the level of economic development, which, for present purposes, we will measure by GDP per head.[5] Here again the picture is complicated. Thus table 1.1 showed that the advantage of the Allies was larger in population than in GDP. Average incomes of the prewar Allies were little more than half the Axis level. There was still a significant gap (although a smaller one) in 1942. But it is very important to note that GDP was distributed much more unequally among the Allied territories than within the Axis. By 1942 the Allies included the richest major power (the United States) as well as the poorest (China, or, if China is discounted, the USSR), in addition to the populous low-income colonial territories of the British empire in India and Africa. It is of great significance, therefore, that if we confine our attention to the core territories of each coalition, it was the Allies which held a roughly 1.2:1 advantage in prewar development level.

Development level could be regarded as significant in the following sense. The experience of two world wars showed that, when poor countries were subjected to massive attack, regardless of size, their economies tended to disintegrate. The exact mechanism of disintegration varied, but was typically already present in peacetime, in a low-productivity, poorly commercialized agriculture, and a general lack of resource diversity. The latter was influenced not only by lack of size, but also by poverty, since poor economies – even large ones – relied too heavily upon agriculture and could not afford a wide assortment of other activities. Mobilization disrupted trade internally and externally; the more industry was concentrated upon war production, the less was left to sell to peasants and foreigners alike in exchange for their food and oil, and the more rapidly imports and domestic food supplies disappeared from the urban economy. Poor countries also lacked the commercial and administrative infrastructure which modern governments could use to foster the objectives of wartime economic policy. Mobilization was therefore either ineffective or else self-limiting; if mobilization was achieved it could not be sustained, and tended if anything to accelerate economic collapse. In World War I this happened first to Russia, then to Austria-Hungary, finally to Germany itself – the poorest first, in inverse order of development level.

In World War II it was China which demonstrated first the weakness of a low-income great power. As table 1.1 revealed, China outweighed Japan in every economic dimension but GDP per head. Attacked by Japan in 1937, the Chinese economy disintegrated. China was saved from immediate destruction only because it was too large for Japan to swallow whole, while the part which Japan occupied was 'too poor and rebellious to exploit systematically'.[6] The USSR was another low-income power; the Soviet economy provides the exception to the rule because it did not collapse under massive attack in 1941, although every historical precedent suggested that it should have done so. Among the Axis powers Japan was the poorest, then Italy, with Germany at an income level comparable with the British. When it was the turn of the Axis powers to go down, defeat came to Italy in 1943, then Japan in 1945, in that order not because Italy was poorer than Japan, but because that was the order in which the Allies attacked them. Italy and Japan suffered most from disruption of external rather than internal supply, bringing deprivation of imports. In 1945 the wealthier German economy also collapsed at last, but only at the point when heavy bombing was combined with massive attack overland from both east and west.

Thus it may be argued that in general terms the outcome of the war was decided by size (the economically larger coalition won), but, nevertheless, if a large population and a large GDP were both highly desirable, a large GDP was better because of the developmental advantages which came with a higher level of GDP per head. The Soviet exception proves the rule, because it displayed a capacity for military mobilization characteristic of a much more highly developed economy, despite its relatively low income level.

Table 1.8 shows percentages of national income mobilized by the six great powers. Such percentages may be calculated at both current and constant peacetime (prewar or postwar) prices, and mean something slightly different in each case. The degree of mobilization measured in current values takes into account changing relative scarcities of guns versus butter and their current priorities relative to each other, whereas a constant-price measure reflects their changing relative volumes from a peacetime welfare standpoint. For present purposes constant prices are more useful, but are not available in every case. Nominal relative values are shown in the first part of the table for every country except the USSR. The second part of the table shows constant-price measures for the USA, Germany, and the USSR. For the USA and Germany the different standards of valuation make little or no difference, and we can infer that the same would be true for the UK from the fact that the British GDP deflator and retail price index (table 2.9 below) followed a nearly identical wartime path (i.e. the relative prices of consumption and non-consumption goods, most of which were war goods, did not change). For the USSR this would certainly not be true; as is shown in chapter 7, the cheapening of weapons and rise in food prices meant that the nominal defence burden fell far below the defence burden measured at prewar prices. For Japan and Italy there is no information on this point, and no way of knowing whether the nominal military burden may under- or overstate the real burden.

Table 1.8 shows that, however the military burden is measured, the Germans followed a path of ever-strengthening mobilization; nearly one quarter of German GNP was devoted to the war effort already in 1939, and this proportion probably reached three-quarters in 1944 before economic collapse ensued. In 1939 Japan's nominal share of national resources committed to the war (22 per cent) was similar to Germany's, although at that time Japan was confronted only by weak enemies. But in the next two or three years the Japanese struggled to raise this share by even a few percentage points until 1943, when its life-or-death struggle with the two most powerful industrialized countries in the world was already going badly. By 1944 Japan too was devoting three-quarters of GDP to the war, but Japan's final mobilization was much more of a sudden, last-ditch effort than Germany's, and ended the same way in economic collapse. As for the Italian mobilization, its failure is obvious by the fact that at its wartime peak it barely matched the prewar efforts of Italy's Axis partners, and stagnated or declined as the war turned against Italy.

The Soviet economy, although much poorer than the Italian, and comparable with the Japanese in terms of income per head, did not collapse despite its initial loss of wealth and income. It mobilized rapidly, shifting 44 per cent of GNP from civilian to military uses in two years (1940–2); maximum two-year shifts for other countries were 15 per cent for Italy, 29 per cent for Germany, 38 per cent for the UK (all in 1939–41), 31 or 32 per cent for the USA (1941–3), and 43 per cent for Japan (but only when it was too late in 1942–4). The Soviet economy went on to devote three-fifths of its national income to the war effort, a little below the German and Japanese peaks, but the Soviet peak came earlier in the war and proved more sustainable for a variety of reasons (including Allied aid). The Soviet success by comparison with other poorer countries was partly a matter of size; the Soviet Union was bigger than Japan or Italy in population and GNP, and far bigger in territory, and was already virtually self-sufficient before the war. But the precedents of disintegration and collapse of Russia

Table 1.8. *The military burden, 1939–1944 (military outlays, per cent of national income)*

	1939	1940	1941	1942	1943	1944
At current prices						
Allied powers						
USA	1	2	11	31	42	42
UK	15	44	53	52	55	53
USSR	—	—	—	—	—	—
Axis powers						
Germany	23	40	52	64	70	—
Italy	8	12	23	22	21	—
Japan	22	22	27	33	43	76
At constant prices						
Allied powers						
USA	1	2	11	32	43	45
UK	—	—	—	—	—	—
USSR	—	17	28	61	61	53
Axis powers						
Germany	23	40	52	63	70	—
Italy	—	—	—	—	—	—
Japan	—	—	—	—	—	—

Sources:
USA (per cent of GNP at current and 1958 prices): table 3.1 (cols. 3, 6).
  UK (per cent of net national expenditure at current prices): table 2.6 (col. 2).
  USSR (per cent of GNP at 1937 factor cost): table 7.11.
  Germany (per cent of GNP at current and 1939 prices): calculated from table 4.16. For war outlays at 1939 prices the same deflator is assumed as for government outlays generally; by 1943, war outlays accounted for 96 per cent of the latter.
  Italy (per cent of GDP at current prices): table 5.14 (col. 22) shows real military outlays divided by real GDP, both converted from current values by the same GDP deflator.
  Japan (per cent of GDP at current prices): table 6.11 (col. 5).

in World War I, and of China in World War II, remind us that size was not sufficient for economic survival under attack.

The success of the British economic mobilization testifies eloquently to the importance of development level by comparison with size and self-sufficiency. In terms of the scale factors shown in table 1.1, Britain was smaller than Japan in population and territory, smaller than Germany in GDP and territory, and the smallest of all the Allied powers by any measure. Being a highly open economy, exceptionally highly industrialized, the British economy also relied heavily on imported food and fuels. Despite being neither large nor self-sufficient, the British economy was comprehensively mobilized without major breakdowns of food or power supplies. Possessing the highly developed commercial, transport, and administrative infrastructure that comes with a high GDP per head, the British were able to expand the home production of calories, and ration fuel and energy efficiently. It was also easier for the British to supply their economy with food and fuels from across the world than for the Axis powers to exploit effectively the less industrialized, low-income colonial areas into which they expanded in the course of the war.

The link between development level and mobilization capacity is further illustrated in the contrasting results of German occupation in northwestern and eastern Europe. Northwestern Europe was the one high-income, industrialized region into which the Axis powers expanded. France provided Germany with as much food as all of the occupied USSR, *and* more industrial materials – an outcome which would have been viewed ironically from a prewar perspective, because it was the occupation of *eastern* Europe which was intended to make Germany self-sufficient in such deficit commodities, while the occupation of France was an accidental by-product of the evolution of the war.[7] German occupation policies successfully extracted 30–40 per cent of the wartime national products of France, the Netherlands, and Norway (and a similar proportion from the industrialized region of Bohemia-Moravia in the east), but obtained resources at much lower or negligible rates of extraction from the low-income, agrarian territories of eastern Europe.[8]

Part of the Allied success in mitigating simultaneously the British disadvantage of small size, and the Soviet disadvantage of low development level, lay in the pooling of Allied resources. The United States shared its capital-intensive, high-technology resources with Britain and the USSR (and Britain, at a lower level, also contributed to Soviet aid). The USSR and, to a lesser extent, Britain used their territory to provide forward bases for the assault upon Germany, and also bore the brunt of the fighting. In this way the Allied war effort formed an economically integrated whole – certainly in comparison with the war efforts of the Axis powers, each of which evolved independently, each relying on its own isolated colonial sphere.

The determinants of mobilization

Mobilization was essential to the war strategy of each of the powers. Nonetheless, understanding its importance requires a distinction between the different powers and the different theatres of the war. The Axis powers mobilized their economies first, before the world war broke out, aware of the risks of reliance on purely military advantage to bring easy successes. When the quick victories evaporated, they continued economic mobilization in a hopeless race with an economically superior enemy. The Soviets also began to mobilize in peacetime, in order to insure themselves against the likelihood of aggression, whereas the western Allies mobilized their economies only from the time when war was perceived as inevitable. Once this point was reached, the British, Americans, and Russians alike mobilized their economies knowing that only quantitative effort could neutralize the qualitative advantage of the Axis powers.

The precise degree of mobilization was much more important for the Russians than for the much richer British and Americans, and was more important to the outcome on the eastern front than in the Pacific and the Mediterranean. The Italian and Japanese GDPs were so small relative to combined Anglo-American resources that it simply did not matter that the Italians mobilized only 20 per cent or that the Japanese mobilized as much as 70 per cent of their national income for the war. Even a high percentage of a small quantity was still a small quantity. On the eastern front, on the other hand, the degree of mobilization was very important, because the German and Soviet economies were more evenly matched in terms of total output; if the Germans mobilized 60 per cent, and the Soviets only 30 per cent, then the Germans would win. On the western front the percentage of resources mobilized mattered less because the Anglo-American margin of superiority in combined resources over Germany was so great.

What underlying factors influenced the degree of mobilization? At one time most attention was accorded to two factors – distance from the main theatres of fighting, and the wartime economic system. Both rested on a rough comparison of the Soviet, British, and American experiences. As far as the first is concerned, these economies could be ranked in the same order both in terms of the degree of mobilization (from highest to lowest), and in terms of distance from the front line (from nearest to farthest).[9] It was the nearness of combat conditions, and the blurring of the distinction between the fighting front and the home front, which stimulated national feeling and promoted economic mobilization.

The other factor which received much attention was the wartime economic system. Again a comparison of the Soviet, British, and American experiences ranked these economies in the same order as before in terms of the degree of planning (from most to least centralized). It was also believed that the German economy, hindered by party interests vested in economic slack, and by bureaucratic infighting which prevented effective coordination, remained relatively unmobilized until heavy Allied bombing, the invasion of France from the west, and the approach of the avenging Russians from the east, enabled national feeling to overcome these obstacles – but by this time, it was too late.[10]

These generalizations now appear to be inaccurate. As far as distance from the main theatres of combat is concerned, the Italian and Japanese economies remained at a low level of mobilization through 1943, despite the adverse turn of the Pacific War for Japan and the incursion of the front line into the Italian homeland.

As far as the degree of planning is concerned, the Japanese economy became highly centralized, but success in terms of the degree of mobilization was belated, and was swiftly followed by collapse. In both Japan and Italy it was the denial of imports which shackled the mobilization process and ensured, in the case of Japan, that success was self-destructive. The British economy became highly mobilized under centralized administrative controls. But the Soviet economy became even more highly mobilized despite a context of administrative shambles; only after the tide had been turned did centralized administration reassert itself. In the German case, likewise, it now appears that the civilian economy had become relatively highly mobilized by an early stage in the war, notwithstanding the defects of the political and administrative system. If there was slack, it was tied up in wasteful intermediate uses within military industry, not in household consumption.[11]

What was important was not so much to have detailed economic controls as to be able to maintain economic integration under intense stress. This capacity is what Italy and Japan lacked. Their economies were small in global terms, heavily dependent on international trade, far from self-sufficient in fuels and other industrial resources. Their development level was insufficient to compensate. What ensured the failure of their economic mobilization, regardless of the growing threat to vital national or régime interests, and despite intense efforts at economic control, was the disruption of overseas trade, the intensity of Allied blockade, the interruption of supplies of coal, oil, or crucial war materials, and the obstacles to effective sharing of resources among the Axis powers which were never overcome.

The USSR, another low-income, newly industrializing economy, was able to avoid this fate. Offsetting its poverty were advantages of size, access to Allied resources, and, above all, an effective system of economic integration; these gave it resilience under the kind of pressure which destroyed the old Russian empire in World War I, and the contemporary Japanese and Italian empires in World War II. The Soviet economy was held together by coercion, by leadership, by national feeling, by centralized planning and rationing, and by a system for food procurement which ensured that farmers could not deny food to the towns.

Quantity and quality

When the authors of this volume examine the wartime mobilization of the great powers' economies, their main aim is to understand what quantity of resources was delivered to the front, by what means, and with what results for economic life. The military qualities of the resources supplied, and what use the generals made of them, would be entirely beyond our scope, were it not for the fact that the relationship between qualities and quantities was interactive.

It would be tempting to conclude from the experience of World War II that, since ultimately the powers of the Axis were overwhelmed by quantity, quality did not really matter. Since the quantity of military resources was limited by overall resources, it was the fact that the Allies' total GDP was greater than the total GDP of the Axis which decided the outcome of the war.

But the question of the military value of resources cannot be avoided. For one thing, the quantities do not explain why German and Japanese leaders deliberately undertook acts of war against economically more powerful adversaries, or how they achieved such success in the early stages. It was the very high quality of their military assets, the fighting power of their armies and navies, which, in the first years of the war, was almost decisive. In 1939–41 Germany and Japan achieved sweeping military gains and conquered huge territories in spite of economic disadvantage, because of the military qualities of their soldiers and the highly effective use made of very limited resources. Indeed the Axis leaders saw the warlike qualities of their military assets as providing a military substitute for productive powers, a means of neutralizing the quantitative advantages of the enemy, and an expansionist solution to their countries' position of economic weakness. Germany and Japan deployed superior combat organizations which, if quantities had been held equal on both sides, would have remained capable of defeating the opposing forces throughout the war.[12] However, the Red Army, too, unexpectedly displayed some elements of superior fighting power, and these qualities increased in the course of the war.

The quick victory which Germany and Japan sought was frustrated by two factors. One was the unanticipated will to resist which became apparent at different stages in London, Moscow, and Washington. The other was the unexpected military capacity of the Allied powers to delay defeat and win time, a precious breathing space within which superior Allied resources could be mobilized and brought to bear.

Once the quick victory which Germany and Japan sought had been frustrated, qualitative factors continued to exercise a major influence over the course of the war. It was the quality, not the quantity, of German and

Japanese military resources which postponed their defeat for so long, forcing their wealthier adversaries to accumulate a vast quantitative advantage in personnel and weapons before the defeat of the Axis could be assured. It is true that, in the closing stages of the war, both Germany and Japan were able to delay defeat by using the advantages of the terrain, for example in Italy where it was hard for the Allies to turn their flank, or on Okinawa in the Pacific.[13] But it was also a qualitative feature of the German and Japanese soldiers that they consistently maximized these advantages, even when hampered by huge material inferiority.

The responses of the two sides to Axis qualitative superiority were illustrated in tables 1.5 and 1.7. In the western front and the Pacific, the British and Americans used 1942 and 1943 to accumulate a three-to-one advantage over the opposing forces, while the Russians fought harder on more finely balanced, fiercely contested terms. With the Anglo-American invasion of France, and the increasing likelihood of an Allied invasion of the Japanese islands, the Japanese mobilized millions of additional soldiers, while the Germans transferred part of their forces from east to west. As a result, in 1944, although the Axis cause was already lost, the contest had become more even again, with Allied burdens more evenly shared between east and west.

The qualitative development of weaponry was very important in the evolution of the war, the development of war production, and the mobilization of industry. But this qualitative development cannot be understood in purely national terms. The technological improvement of weaponry was a global process, in which all the military powers participated. Table 1.9 suggests that each country produced at least some high quality weapons, although probably only Germany was able to do so across the board. They were stimulated to do so by the development of the battlefield, as each country strove to keep at least one step ahead of the adversary. The evolution of the tank in armament, armour, and speed of movement clearly illustrates this process. In Russia in 1941, the Germans encountered superior tanks, and were driven to fresh efforts of innovation. By 1943 the new German tanks were better than existing Soviet models, and Soviet designers now had to run faster to keep up. The same process was visible in the design of fighter aircraft, in the rivalry to match and exceed the enemy's speed, manoeuvrability, armament, and radar.

Strategic choice also played a role. The German and Japanese strategy relied on quality of armies and armament to compensate for their deficiencies in the quantity of overall resources. At sea the Germans tried to compensate for the Allied surface fleet predominance by means of submarine technology. The British and Americans failed to produce good tanks, but compensated with fast-moving, well-supplied infantry supported by excellent means of tactical air power. The Russians did not compete in strategic air or naval power, but they did not need to do so.

Thus, not every country produced high quality weapons, but there was no strong correlation with economic development level. The Soviet Union had an excellent defence industry, despite being poor by European standards. Japan and Italy, the one a relatively poor country, the other nearer to Germany than Russia or Japan in development level, both produced high-quality ships and aircraft, only their number was deficient. Germany produced most weapons better than America, although America was the richest of the great powers. If the Russians made a priority out of tank design, and if it was the design of aircraft and ships that came first for the British, Italians, and Japanese, then the Germans made the quality of weapons in general their priority; Germany, as a medium sized industrial power, could not compete in quantity, but was still well enough developed to be able to compete in quality across the board.

In leaving the subject of quality, it is important to stress that quantity was essential to the Allied strategy. The Allies knew they could not make better soldiers than the Germans or Japanese. They could not make better guns, ships, or airplanes, but they could make more of them. While the British and Americans devoted major resources to the atomic bomb project, there was no guarantee of ultimate success. Until the bomb was available, there was no alternative to a stress on quantity. In the west the Axis powers could only be beaten by an immense numerical advantage. This is what the Allies accumulated in 1942–3, and directed first against Italy, then in 1944–5 against Germany and Japan. On the eastern front the Russians also enjoyed a quantitative advantage over Germany, but the fighting power of the Red Army meant that they could beat Germany with a smaller quantitative edge than the western Allies required.

Winning the war, losing the peace

Postwar convergence

Over the postwar decades the general pattern among the former wartime allies and enemies was one of catching up and convergence. *Catching up* refers to the gap between the productivity leader, the United States, and the followers. *Convergence* is of two kinds. In the literature β-convergence requires an inverse relationship between initial income levels and sub-sequent growth, whereby poorer countries grow faster; σ-convergence takes place when the cross-country inequality of income levels diminishes.[14] Table 1.10 illustrates catching up and both kinds of convergence, but also

Table 1.9. *Weapons systems of the great powers in World War II: military-technical specifications*

(A) Fighter aircraft	Engines, no. × horse power	Max. speed, km per hour	Max. altitude, m	Time required (minutes) for ascent to 3,000m	5,000m	Range, km	Armament, no × cal. (mm) cannon	machine guns
USA								
P-40k Warlike	1×1,215	550	11,700	4.8	7.3	>2,000	—	6×12.7
F-4	1×1,200	530	8,500	3.6	—	1,800	—	6×12.7
P-39q Aerocobra	1×1,325	620	10,500	3.4	5.8	1,200	1×37	4×12.7
P-51b Mustang III	1×1,300	700	9,100	3.0	—	3,600	—	4×12.7
UK								
Hurricane IIb	1×1,435	550	11,150	—	8.4[a]	1,260	—	12×7.69
Spitfire IX	1×1,600	657	13,100	—	6.7[a]	1,365	2×20	4×7.69
Mosquito II	2×1,450	596	10,700	—	7.0[b]	—	4×20	4×7.69
USSR								
La-5	1×1,700	630	10,000	—	5.2	581	2×20	—
Yak-7b	1×1,210	593	10,000	—	5.7	750	1×20	2×12.7
Yak-9	1×1,210	597	10,400	—	5.5	1,400	1×37	1×12.7
Germany								
Me-109g	1×1,555	630	11,400	—	6.0[c]	820	1/3×20	2/4×7.92
Me-110	2×1,150	545	11,500	—	8.4	1,400	1×20	5×7.92
FW-190a3	1×1,760	625	12,000	—	6.8	840	2/4×20	2×7.92
Japan								
I-01 Nakajima	1×1,130	515	10,500	—	6.2	2,000	2×20	2×12.7
I-02 Mitsubishi	1×1,320	605	10,500	—	4.2	1,250	2×20	2×12.7
I-02 Kawasaki	2×1,060	547	10,000	—	7.0	1,500	2×20	1×7.7 2×12.7

Notes:
[a] To 6100m.
[b] To 4600m.

| (B) Bombers | Engines no. × horse power | Max. speed, km per hour | Max. altitude, m | Range, km | Armament, no.×cal. (mm) | | Payload, kg |
					cannon	machine guns	
USA							
B-25J Mitchell	2×1,700	458	7,620	2,900	—	13×12.7	1,450
A-20b Havoc	2×1,600	510	7,000	3,300	—	3×12.7 3×7.62	908
B-17g Flying Fortress	4×1,200	466	10,900	3,870	—	13×12.7	5,800
B-24d Liberator	4×1,200	466	9,500	5,600	—	10×12.7	5,800
UK							
Halifax XV	4×1,280	419	6,400	3,060	—	9×7.69	<5,900
Wellington III	2×1,370	410	5,950	3,530	—	8×7.69	<2,040
Lancaster III	4×1,300	435	5,800	<3,800	—	10×7.69	<6,360
USSR							
Pe-2	2×1,050	540	8,800	1,315	—	4×7.62	600–1,000
Tu-2	2×1,850	550	9,500	2,250	2×20	3×12.7	1,000–3,000
Il-4 (Db-3f)	2×1,100	425	10,050	3,300	2×20	3×7.62	1,000–2,500
Pe-8	4×1,700	405	9,000	5,800	2×20	3×7.62	<6,000
Germany							
Ju-87	1×1,200	395	8,100	850	1×15	2/4×7.92	700
Ju-88	2×1,200	465	8,500	2,000	1×20	5/7×7.92	1,200
He-111	2×1,500	408	7,350	1,760	1×20	5/7×7.92	2,800
He-177	2×2,700	480	6,900	3,000	2×20	3/5×7.92	4,000
Japan							
Sb-97 Mitsubishi	2×1,490	475	9,500	2,250	1×20	4×7.7 1×12.7	<2,000
Sb-99 Kawasaki	2×1,105	367	9,700	2,250	—	3×7.7 1×12.7	750

Table 1.9 (cont)

(C) Tanks	Muzzle velocity of shell, m/sec	Armament, no.× cal. (mm) cannon	machine guns	Shells in magazine	Max. depth of armour, mm	Combat weight, tons	Speed km/hr	Range of travel, km
USA								
M5 A1	880[a]	1×37	3×7.62	147	<38	16.9	<60	270
M3 A4 Grant	880[a]	1×37	4×7.62	179	57	29.0	40	140
	620[a]	1×75		50				
M4 A2 Sherman	620[a]	1×75	2×7.62 / 1×12.7	97	100	34.2	46	180
UK								
Valentine Mk III	810[a]	1×40	1×7.69 / 1×7.92	—	60	16.5	25	225
Churchill Mk IV	815[a]	1×57	1×7.69 / 2×7.92	81	150	45.0	25	245
USSR								
T-70	760[a]	1×45	1×7.62	70	45	10.0	45	250
T-34	750[a]	1×76	2×7.62	100	52	30.9	55	300
KV-1s	750[a]	1×76	3×7.62	114	82	42.5	43	250
Germany								
T-III (modernized)	823[a] / 1,198[b]	1×50	2×7.92	78	50	22.3	40	175
T-IV (modernized)	925[a] / 1,120[b]	1×75	2×7.92	87	<50	24.0	40	200
T-V Panther	925[a] / 1,120[b]	1×75	3×7.92	79	100	45.0	46	177
T-VI Tiger	810[a]	1×88	2×7.92	92	100	55.0	38	100
Japan								
Model 95 Kani	—	1×47	1×7.7	160	16	7.7	50	400–200
Model 97	—	1×57	2×7.7	80	47	15.4	40	160
Model 99	—	2×37	2×7.7	—	40	30.0	—	150

Notes:
[a] Armour-piercing shell.
[b] Sub-calibre shell.

(D) Self-propelled guns	Based on tank type	Calibre of weapon, mm	Weight, tons	Max. depth of armour, mm	Armament penetration (mm) at range 500 m	1 km	Shells in magazine	Range travel, km
USA								
USA								
M7 Priest (1942)[a]	M3	105	<24	57	—	—	69	265
USSR								
SU-76 (1942)[b]	T-70	76	10.5	35	<70/90[c]	<60	60	320
SU-122 (1942)[a]	T-34	122	<40.0	45	<140[c]	<140[c]	40	400–600
SU-152 (1942)[d]	KV-1	152	45.5	60	<132	<125	20	165–300
Germany								
Assault cannon (April 1942)[b]	T-III	75	24	80	<90	<80	99	105
Assault howitzer (March 1943)[a]	T-III	105	30.4	100	—	—	—	200
Naschorn anti-tank cannon (Feb. 1943)[b]	T-IV	88	24	30	<180	<160	40	200

Notes:
[a] Howitzer.
[b] Cannon.
[c] Hollow-charge projectile.
[d] Howitzer-cannon.

Table 1.9 (*cont*)

(E) Artillery systems	Weight in combat position kg	Weight of shell, kg	Muzzle velocity, m/sec	Range of fire, km	Armour penetration at range 500m	1,000m	Rapidity of fire, per minute	Speed of travel, km/h
USA								
57mm M1a	1,220	2.84	823	6.5	<66	<58	<30	—
76.2mm M5[a]	2,210	7.0	792	—	<81	<72	<12	—
105mm M2A1[b]	1,920	15.0	473	11.2	—	—	<4	—
114.3mm M1[a]	5,600	25.1	693	18.3	—	—	<3	—
155mm M1[b]	5,430	43.1	564	15.1	—	—	<3	—
106.7mm M1A1[d]	134	10.4	175	2.2	—	—	<20	—
UK								
57mm[a]	1,130	2.85	702	—	—	<65	10–15	20–25
87.6mm[a]	1,800	11.3	520	12.0	36	30	4	15–18
114.3mm[a]	5,370	24.9	685	18.7	—	—	—	—
182.9mm[b]	10,000	91.6	518	15.45	—	—	—	—
106.7mm[d]	120	9	175	3.74	—	—	—	—
USSR								
45mm M-42 (1942)[a]	570	0.85–2.1	<1,070	5	<80	<50	<20	25–60
57mm (1941/43)[c]	1,150	1.79–3.75	<1,270	6.6	<147	<101	<25	25–60
76mm ZIS-3 (1942)[a]	1,116	3.02–6.21	<950	13.2	<90	<75	<25	10–50
122mm M-30 (1938)[b]	2,400	13.3–21.8	<515	11.8	<140	<140	5–7	35–50
122mm A-19 (1931/37)[a]	7,250	25	810	19.8	<155	<145	3–6	20
152mm ML-20 (1937)[c]	7,270	43.6–56.0	655	17.2	—	—	3–5	20
152mm D-1 (1943)[b]	3,650	40.0	<508	12.4	!	—	2–5	20–40
152mm Br-2 (1935)[a]	18,200	48.5	880	<25.1	—	—	1–2	8–15
120mm (1938)[d]	280	15.9	272	5.7	—	—	12–5	15–60
(1943)[d]	256							

Germany								
50mm (1938)[a]	986	2.06	823	9.4	<58	<50	15	—
75mm (1942)[a]	1,425	6.8	<933	—	<95	<84	12–14	—
105mm Model 18/40[b]	1,800	14.8	<540	12.3	—	—	<6	—
105mm Model 18/40(42)[a]	5,620	15.1	910	21	—	—	<6	<15–20
150mm Model 18[b]	5,510	43.5	<520	13.3	—	—	<4	15–20
150mm (1939)[a]	12,200	43	<865	24.8	—	—	<2	<15
105mm (1940)[d]	785	8.65	130–310	6.2	—	—	—	—
Japan								
37mm Model 94[a]	324	0.7–0.8	800	4.5	30[e]	—	10–12	—
47mm Model 01[a]	800	1.54	820	3.7	—	<40	15–20	—
75mm Model 95[a]	1,497	6.4	500	11	—	—	10–12	—
105mm Model 92[a]	3,730	15.8	760	18.2	—	—	6–8	—
105mm Model 91[b]	2,000	16.0	544	10.5	—	—	6–8	—
105mm Model 96[b]	4,100	31.1	540	12	—	—	3–4	—

Notes:
[a] Cannon
[b] Howitzer
[c] Howitzer-cannon
[d] Mortar
[e] at 300m

Source: IVMV, vol. VI (1976), 354–62.

Table 1.10. *GDP per head of the great powers, 1938–1987 (selected years)*

	1938	1950	1973	1987
GDP per head, dollars and 1990 prices				
USA	6,134	9,573	16,607	20,880
UK	5,983	6,847	11,992	15,265
Germany	5,126	4,281	13,152	17,032
France	4,424	5,221	12,940	16,366
Italy	3,244	3,425	10,409	14,659
Japan	2,356	1,873	11,017	16,101
USSR	2,150	2,834	6,058	6,943
Catching up with the United States: GDP per head, per cent of US GDP per head:				
UK	98	72	72	73
Germany	84	45	79	82
France	72	55	78	78
Italy	53	36	63	70
Japan	38	20	66	77
USSR	35	30	36	33
β-convergence: Spearman rank correlation coefficient of income growth over the previous period with income level in the previous period				
Seven countries	—	0.29	−0.75	−0.11
exc. USSR	—	0.71	−0.94	−0.77
σ-convergence: coefficients of variation of income level (per cent):				
Seven countries	36	50	25	25
exc. USSR	30	37	16	13
exc. USA, USSR	31	39	9	5

Source: Taken or calculated from Maddison (1995), appendix D.

suggests their limits. The results are already well known, and are reported here to illustrate the particular outcomes for the major powers.

According to table 1.10, there was no catching up over the transwar period (1938–50); in this period every other major power fell back relative to the United States. This was partly because the US economy had a much higher stock of unutilized capacity in 1938 than the others; this was mobilized in wartime, and contributed to the very high US growth rate up to 1950. There was no catching up in the case of Japan and Germany also because of the war's negative impact which was still strongly felt. Over the next quarter of a century, however, the continental west Europeans and Japan restored the lost ground and closed some of the gap. By the late 1980s, all were within 70–80 per cent of the US benchmark; this was also the British case but for Britain it did not mark an improvement over the past. In the Soviet case the gap remained a yawning chasm.

Under the heading of β-convergence we see that between 1938 and 1950 the growth of the wartime powers was *positively* associated with initial income level, as shown by its positive Spearman coefficient (0.29). This mainly reflected the great expansion of the richest economy (the United States) and the collapse of the poorest (Japan). But once the war was over a strong, negative, β-convergent association of growth with initial income set in (-0.75 for 1950–73, but a much weaker -0.11 for 1973–87). Significantly, however, the USSR did not participate in β-convergence, the evidence for which becomes much stronger when the Soviet economy is omitted. This is particularly so after 1973, when Soviet incomes, already lowest among the major powers, were falling further behind.

As for σ-convergence, the dispersion of income levels among the major powers was greater in 1950 than in 1938 (the coefficient of variation rising from 36 per cent to 50 per cent), but much less by 1973 (a coefficient of variation of 25 per cent). Much of the remaining income inequality is provided by the Soviet Union's failure to converge, so when the Soviet case is excluded a sharp increase in the rate of convergence is shown. Finally, the process is shown to have been regionally rather than globally convergent (the regional focus being western Europe and Japan) when the USA is omitted as well, which leaves us with the well-known uniformity of incomes achieved by Britain, France, Germany, Italy, and Japan by the late 1980s.

Thus slow postwar economic growth was common to the United States, Britain, and the Soviet Union, while the growth of Germany, Italy, and Japan was more rapid, in inverse ratio to their initial GDP per head. In other words, the former Allies, although victorious in wartime, were now on the 'losing' side in postwar growth terms. The cliché that 'those who won the war lost the peace' therefore contains a grain of truth.[15] At the same time (like all clichés) its validity is strictly limited. Britain and America grew more slowly after the war mainly because they were already immensely rich and had suffered relatively little. The losers grew more rapidly, mainly because they had been relatively poor to begin with and also had to make up substantial wartime losses. Only the Soviet economy began poor, lost significantly, and remained poor in relative terms despite reasonable postwar growth (hence the 'defeated victor' of chapter 7).

The influence of the war

In what ways did wartime experience influence these long-run trends and the postwar institutions which presided over them? Every country tried to draw something positive from the ordeal of the war, but what this was differed according to national circumstances. Most widespread were conclusions regarding an integrated world economy, capital accumulation, and mass production.

Global economic integration

First, the cause of an integrated world economy received a decisive boost from the outcome of the war. American thinking found one of the causes of World War II in the interwar disintegration of the world economy, and the spread of great-power protectionism within trading blocs based on colonial lines. Italian and Japanese wartime experience (and German experience too, if to a lesser extent) showed the impossibility of autarkic mobilization, and convinced the postwar leaders of these countries that each must find its place in a new worldwide division of labour. Thus the Americans and their former enemies plunged eagerly back into the world market. Italian and Japanese participation, although heavily regulated at first, was nonetheless genuine. All these countries became active participants in the multinational institutional framework of the postwar global economy – the IMF, IBRD (later the World Bank), and GATT. There was no turning back to the economics of the German *Grossraumwirtschaft* or the Japanese Greater East Asia Co-prosperity Sphere.

Only the British and Soviet empires survived the war. The Soviet empire was soon greatly augmented by the adherence of the east European satellites, whereas the British would preside over the dissolution of theirs, in some cases willingly, too often grudgingly. Both would eventually pay the price for clinging to empire trade, the British first.

Capital accumulation

Second, the war imposed great losses of both human and physical capital upon the great powers. Precise comparisons are still difficult, but available measures are summarized in table 1.11. They show direct war losses in proportion to prewar stocks. Wartime disinvestment and birth deficits (the demographic equivalent of disinvestment) are not taken into account; nor is wartime investment, which in the case of industrial fixed capital sometimes exceeded war damage and depreciation combined. The two poorest countries, the USSR and Japan, suffered the greatest losses. The losses of physical capital typically outweighed those of human capital, at least in percentage terms (except in the case of the United States, where both were negligible). Thus, the direct effect of warfare was to bring about a relative shortfall of physical assets.

The war itself saw significant industrial investment, certainly in the less industrialized powers, each of which became more industrialized in conse-

Table 1.11. *War losses attributable to physical destruction (per cent of assets)*

	Human assets 1	Physical assets	
		national wealth 2	industry fixed assets 3
Allied powers			
USA	1	0	—
UK	1	5	—
USSR	18–19	25	—
Axis powers			
Germany	9	—	17
Italy	1	—	10
Japan	6	25	34

Note:
Figures are war damage to fixed assets and war deaths amongst the working population; they take no account of wartime replacement of either fixed or human capital.
Sources:
Human assets
USA, Germany: total war deaths divided by prewar population from Urlanis (1971), 295.
UK: chapter 2 (p. 71).
USSR: table 7.13.
Italy: chapter 5 (p. 213).
Japan: excess deaths, 1941–5, compared with 1940 population, from table 6.8.
Physical assets
UK (physical destruction, per cent of 1938): table 2.20.
USSR: table 7.13.
Germany (war destruction in the postwar Anglo-American occupation zone, per cent of 1936): table 4.20.
Italy: chapter 5 (p. 211).
Japan (war damage, per cent of the sum of 1945 assets plus war damage): table 6.14 (col. 5).

quence. For the German economy, industrial fixed investment was an effective countermeasure to Allied bombing of the German war economy. In Germany, Italy, and Japan, the postwar stock of industrial fixed assets was not less than the prewar stock. Each of our six countries, and France as well, finished the war with a larger stock of machine tools than before.[16] Losses in residential structures, household durables, vehicles, and ships were more likely to have persisted. After the war, each country embarked on a further drive of physical accumulation to restore the war losses, and the general pattern was for domestic investment ratios to be substantially higher after World War II than in the interwar period.

Investment was stimulated everywhere by what Barry Eichengreen has termed the 'postwar settlement' between firms, workers, and the state.[17] Under this settlement firms pursued high investment policies in exchange for workers' high effort and wage moderation on one hand, and on the other, government activism to stabilize aggregate demand and the international trading environment. The same settlement was enforced under state socialism in the USSR and eastern Europe as was pursued more by consensus under capitalist arrangements in the west.[18]

Equally widespread were conclusions regarding the importance of human capital accumulation, and the network of social and political relationships which sustains it. But, as Stephen Broadberry has shown, precise perceptions differed.[19] German and Japanese industry emerged from the war with enhanced emphasis on job rights, craft training, and worker participation. There, human capital investment was directed towards skilled labour and apprenticeships. In Britain, wartime experience had also promoted the concept of human assets, and this was expressed in schemes for universal health care, secondary education, and social insurance which were implemented after 1945. These were advances, to be sure, but they still left British concepts of human capital half a century behind postwar continental practices. As the postwar period wore on, British practice increasingly emulated the American emphasis on unskilled labour for standardized mass production, at the same time lagging behind in adoption of the associated stress on management education.[20]

In the same way investment in R&D ('knowledge capital') was boosted everywhere, but in the United States, Britain, and the Soviet Union the process was more centralized, with more emphasis on national goals, particularly in defence fields with the additional implication of secrecy. In Germany, on the other hand, R&D spending was more oriented to diffusing innovation capabilities throughout industry by means of investment in supportive processes.

On average the defeated had lost more heavily than the victors, but from the point of view of the immediate setback to growth the Soviet Union had more in common with the losers. The German, Japanese, and Soviet economies were all traumatized. Tests for trend breaks in GDP per head applied by Nick Crafts and Terry Mills suggest that, for most countries of the present-day OECD there was no negative wartime shock to growth – but that there was such a shock in the cases of defeated Austria, Finland, France, Germany, and Japan. All these display marked declines in trend GNP growth over 1940–50 compared with 1920–39. In contrast, for neutral Switzerland, and victorious Australia, Canada, and the United States, 1940 initiated an acceleration phase.[21]

As for the long-run impact of the war on growth, for all the market economies but one in the Crafts/Mills sample, victors and vanquished alike, trend growth was more rapid after 1950 than before 1940. This was not just a matter of recovery to a prewar trend since, with minor exceptions (Finland, Sweden, and Switzerland) postwar OECD trend growth rates remained more rapid than before 1940 until 1989, long after any recovery effect had faded. Germany was technically also an exception, with trend growth in GDP per head at 3.12 per cent (1956–89) compared with 3.30 per cent (1920–39), 0.71 per cent (1940–50), and 13.89 per cent (1951–5); thus German growth after 1956 was slower than before 1939, but on the other hand by 1956 the level of German GDP per head was already roughly 30 per cent *above* the extrapolated prewar trend. Thus, despite the scale of wartime destruction, the losers did not suffer a lasting penalty. In contrast, on the evidence presented in chapter 7, by 1950 Soviet economic growth had either resumed its prewar trend at a lower level of GNP per head than before the war, or was undergoing temporary acceleration on a path of recovery to the prewar trend but with little evidence of permanent acceleration.

Mass production/flexible production
Third, one of the factors which differentiated losers from winners was the shared commitment of postwar American, British, and Soviet industry to an American model of technological leadership based on centralized, large-scale mass production. This model owed much to wartime experience. The Allied countries were each enormously impressed by the victory of American standardized mass production. The peacetime merits of the craft system more favoured by German and Japanese industrial tradition had evaporated in the heat of war mobilization. The Soviets, having moved towards an American mass production model in the interwar period, now intensified it uncritically. Postwar attitudes in British industry also shifted towards an Americanized way of thinking. The Americans themselves appeared poised to dominate the world supply of industrial products for decades to come.

In wartime as the Germans, Italians, and Japanese discovered, craft production did not work. The quantitative superiority of the Allies in weaponry was based on standardized products in a limited assortment, interchangeable parts, specialized factories and industrial equipment, an inexorable conveyor belt system of serial manufacture, and deskilled workers who had neither the qualifications nor the discretion to alter designs or specifications. As long as the German system emphasized the small firm, the artisan, and the continual improvement of the product,

German industry was condemned to low utilization, high costs, and small quantities.[22] Only in 1942–3 did the Germans begin to break with their own tradition and convert to a mass production technology, making substantial production gains in the process. The Japanese, too, found huge advantage in converting to mass production of weapons.[23] The failure of Italian war production was in part a failure of the Italian corporate structure based on the craft system (see also chapters 4, 5, and 6).

German, Italian, and Japanese industry did not forget about craft production, however, and reaped the benefits later. Whatever the merits of mass production for turning out huge numbers of identical weapons, they were overtaken increasingly by the advantages of the craft system for civilian production in the postwar period. These advantages were accentuated by the advances in information technology which made possible the emergence of 'flexible manufacturing'.[24] In the postwar decades it was flexible manufacturing which eventually brought global technological leadership to Germany and Japan. Thus the wartime losers 'won' the peace in the sense that they came to dominate the postwar global industrial economy and world trade in manufactures.

Notes

1 In considering these issues, the authors are happy to acknowledge the pioneering contributions of Alan Milward (1977) and Gyorgy Ránki (1993). Our ability to go beyond them has been made possible only by the passage of time, the opening of archives, and the advantages of international collaboration.
2 Overy (1995b), 15.
3 Goldsmith (1946), 69.
4 Compare the picture of relative under-capitalization of the Axis forces advanced by Harrison (1988), 175.
5 For discussion of this topic in a comparison with World War I, see Gatrell, Harrison (1993).
6 Liberman (1996), 112.
7 Milward (1977), 132–68.
8 Liberman (1996), 36–68.
9 Hancock, Gowing (1949), 368.
10 For examples see Kaldor (1946), Klein (1959), Milward (1965), Harrison (1988).
11 Overy (1994), esp. 343–75.
12 Van Creveld (1985), 5–6.
13 I thank Hugh Rockoff for making this point to me.
14 On catching up, see Maddison (1995), and on convergence Crafts, Toniolo (1995). On the two types of convergence see Barro, Sala-i-Martin (1991).
15 Thus Richard Overy (1995b), xi, writes: 'When people heard that the title of my next book was to be "Why the Allies Won", it often provoked the retort: "Did they?".'

16 For the USA, UK, Germany, France, and Italy, see Milward (1977), 334, and for Japan, table 6.14. In the USSR, according to TsSU (1972), 61, the stock of metal-cutting machine tools more than doubled between November 1940 and March 1951, but there are no figures for intervening dates.
17 Eichengreen (1993).
18 Crafts, Toniolo (1995).
19 Broadberry (1994, 1995).
20 Broadberry (1995), 85–7.
21 Crafts, Mills (1996), 425.
22 For a comparative summary see Overy (1995b), 180–207.
23 Sasaki (1994).
24 Broadberry (1995).

References

Barro, R., and Sala-i-Martin, X. (1991), 'Convergence across states and regions', *Brookings Papers on Economic Activity*, 107–82.
Broadberry, S. N. (1994), 'Technological leadership and productivity leadership in manufacturing since the industrial revolution: implications for the convergence debate', *Economic Journal*, vol. 104, 291–302.
    (1995), 'Comparative productivity levels in manufacturing since the Industrial Revolution: lessons from Britain, America, Germany and Japan', *Structural Change and Economic Dynamics*, vol. 6, 71–95.
Crafts, N. F. R. and Mills, T. C. (1996), 'Europe's golden age: an econometric investigation of changing trend rates of growth', in van Ark, B., and Crafts, N. F. R., eds., *Quantitative aspects of Europe's postwar growth*, Cambridge, 415–31.
Crafts, N. F. R., and Toniolo, G. (1995), 'Post-war growth: an overview', in Crafts, N. F. R., and Toniolo, G., eds., *Economic growth in Europe since 1945*, Cambridge, 1–37.
Eichengreen, B. (1993), *Reconstructing Europe's trade and payments*, Manchester.
Förster, J., Messenger, C., and Petter, W. (1995), 'Germany', in Dear, I. C. B., ed., *The Oxford companion to the Second World War*, Oxford, 455–81.
Gatrell, P., and Harrison, M. (1993), 'The Russian and Soviet economy in two World Wars', *Economic History Review*, 2nd ser., vol. 46(3), 425–52.
Goldsmith, R. (1946), 'The power of victory: munitions output in World War II', *Military Affairs*, vol. 10, 69–80.
Hancock, W. K., and Gowing, M. M. (1949), *The British war economy*, London.
Harrison, M. (1988), 'Resource mobilization for World War II: the USA, UK, USSR and Germany, 1938–1945', *Economic History Review*, 2nd ser., vol. 41(2), 171–92.
    (1994), 'The Second World War', in Davies, R. W., Harrison, M., and Wheatcroft, S. G., eds., *The economic transformation of the Soviet Union, 1913–1945*, Cambridge, 238–67.
IVMV (1973–82), *Istoriia Vtoroi Mirovoi voiny 1939–1945 gg.*, vols. 1–12, Moscow.
Kaldor, N. (1946), 'The German war economy', *Review of Economic Studies*, vol. 13, 33–52.

Kedward, R. (1995), 'France', in Dear, I. C. B., ed., *The Oxford companion to the Second World War*, Oxford, 391–408.

Klein, B. H. (1959), *Germany's economic preparations for war*, Cambridge, MA.

League of Nations (1940), *Statistical yearbook of the League of Nations, 1939/40*, Geneva.

Liberman, P. (1996), *Does conquest pay? The exploitation of occupied industrial societies*, Princeton, NJ.

Maddison, A. (1995), *Monitoring the world economy, 1820–1992*, Paris.

Milward, A. S. (1965), *The German economy at war*, London.

(1977), *War, economy and society, 1939–1945*, London.

Overy, R. J. (1994), *War and economy in the Third Reich*, Oxford.

(1995a), 'Statistics', in Dear, I. C. B., ed., *The Oxford companion to the Second World War*, Oxford, 1059–63.

(1995b), *Why the Allies won*, London.

Ránki, G. (1993), *The economics of the Second World War*, Vienna.

Sasaki, S. (1994), 'The rationalization of production management systems in Japan during World War II', in Sakudo, J., and Shiba, T., eds., *World War II and the transformation of business systems*, Tokyo, 30–54.

TsSU SSSR (1972), *Narodnoe khoziaistvo SSSR. 1922–1972 gg. Iubileinyi statisticheskii sbornik*, Moscow.

Urlanis, B. (1971), *Wars and population*, Moscow.

van Creveld, M. (1985), *Fighting power: German and U.S. Army performance, 1939–1945*, London.

2 The United Kingdom: 'Victory at all costs'

Stephen Broadberry and *Peter Howlett*

Introduction

In this chapter we aim to provide an overview of the mobilization of resources for World War II in the United Kingdom, using a framework to facilitate international comparisons.[1] The next section examines the process of mobilization for war, which can be seen as an essentially short-run matter, best tackled using flow data from the national accounts.[2] We then complement the macroeconomic approach of this section with an examination of the experience of industry. After that we turn to the impact of the war on economic development, an essentially long-run matter. This issue needs a national balance sheet approach to assess the impact of the war on the stock of wealth, broadly defined to include human as well as physical capital and intangible as well as tangible capital.

Mobilization for war

The scale of mobilization

We begin our analysis of the British war economy with an outline of developments in national income and the mobilization of resources. Table 2.1, using Feinstein's figures, reminds us of the considerable range of uncertainty over the path of real GDP during the war.[3] Estimates based on expenditure and income are available for all years, while the output figures are only available for 1938 and 1946. Although the expenditure and income series are in broad agreement for the trend growth of GDP between 1938 and 1946, the expenditure series shows a substantially higher peak in 1943. More disturbing, however, is the fact that the output series shows a much smaller increase between 1938 and 1946 than either the expenditure or income series. Since the compromise estimate is obtained as the average of the available series, it is likely that this index overstates the growth in GDP

Table 2.1. *Real GDP of the UK at constant factor cost, 1939–1946 (per cent of 1938)*

	Output 1	Expenditure 2	Income 3	Compromise 4
1939	—	102.1	99.7	101.1
1940	—	118.8	103.7	111.1
1941	—	126.3	116.2	121.2
1942	—	127.7	120.5	124.2
1943	—	130.1	123.6	127.0
1944	—	123.7	119.9	121.9
1945	—	115.0	117.8	116.6
1946	105.1	114.1	115.4	111.5

Source: Feinstein (1972), table 6.

to 1945 (when only the rapidly growing expenditure and income estimates are available) and then exaggerates the fall in GDP between 1945 and 1946, when the output index is averaged in. Despite its limitations, however, the compromise estimate is probably the best series available to indicate the broad path of overall economic activity during the war period.

Table 2.2 presents indices of population and employment to put alongside the output series from table 2.1. Although there was only a very small population increase, employment rose much more dramatically, peaking with output in 1943. This reflects the elimination of the mass unemployment of the 1930s and an increase in labour force participation. The huge increase in the armed forces was accompanied by only a small decrease in civil employment, as the sharp fall in male civil employment was offset by a large increase in female civil employment.

Combining the compromise estimate of GDP from table 2.1 with the population and total employment data from table 2.2, we obtain in table 2.3 indices of GDP per head and per employee (see also figure 2–1). The latter can be regarded as an indicator of labour productivity and shows, by peacetime standards at least, a less than impressive rise over the war period, particularly when the increase in hours worked per person is taken into account.[4]

In evaluating the contribution of the above increase in output and productivity to the Allied victory, we need to take account of the level of development of the British economy on the eve of World War II. For, as Harrison notes, a large proportionate increase in output from a low productivity economy may still add up to less than a small proportionate increase in output from a high productivity economy.[5] Here it is worth

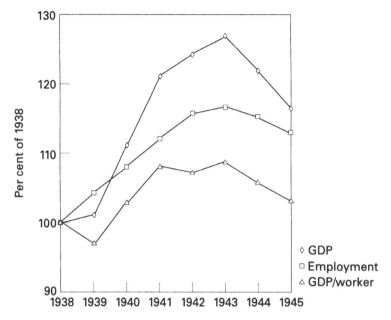

Figure 2.1 GDP, employment, and output per worker in the UK, 1938–1945
Source: tables 2.1, 2.3

noting that although the standard data on international comparisons of labour productivity from Maddison indicate substantially higher total GDP per worker in Britain than in Germany on the eve of World War II, in manufacturing German labour productivity was broadly equal to the British level.[6] In table 2.4 we see that Britain's labour productivity advantage over Germany was in agriculture and services. This suggests that we should not expect any great advantage from higher overall labour productivity to have accrued to Britain in terms of the production of munitions. Rather, the greater level of development and, in particular, the absence of a low productivity agricultural sector may be seen as allowing a greater degree of flexibility.[7] For the US/UK comparison, we see that the US productivity lead was much larger in manufacturing, suggesting a tremendous advantage to the allies in terms of the supply of munitions, as the United States became the 'arsenal of democracy'.

The next step is to evaluate the proportion of GDP and employment devoted to war work, since it is clearly possible for a country with a smaller level of GDP to mobilize more intensively. Table 2.5 presents Feinstein's data on the components of expenditure on GDP at constant market prices, and shows a sharp rise to a peak in 1943 in public authorities' current expenditure on goods and services at the expense of consumers'

Table 2.2. *UK population and employment, 1939–1946 (per cent of 1938)*

	Population 1	Employment, inc. armed forces 2	Female civil employment 3	Armed forces 4
1939	100.6	104.1	104.9	111.1
1940	101.1	107.9	115.0	525.5
1941	101.0	112.1	128.1	782.4
1942	101.4	115.8	142.7	946.8
1943	102.2	116.7	146.8	1,106.5
1944	102.7	115.3	143.5	1,155.1
1945	103.1	113.0	136.2	1,187.5
1946	103.1	107.4	—	631.9

Source: Feinstein (1972), tables 55, 57; Central Statistical Office (1951), table 9.

Table 2.3. *UK GDP per head and per employee,*
1939–1946 (per cent of 1938)

	GDP per head 1	GDP per employee 2
1939	100.4	97.0
1940	109.9	103.0
1941	120.0	108.1
1942	122.5	107.3
1943	124.3	108.8
1944	118.7	105.7
1945	113.1	103.2
1946	108.1	103.8

Source: Tables 2.1, 2.2, using compromise GDP.

Table 2.4. *Output per person employed in the*
USA and Germany, 1937 (per cent of UK)

	USA 1	Germany 2
Whole economy	150.0	76.0
Manufacturing	208.3	99.9
Agriculture	103.0	57.0

Source: Broadberry (1994).

Table 2.5. *Components of UK expenditure on GDP at constant market prices, 1938–1946 (per cent of total)*

	Consumption 1	Government 2	Investment 3	Net exports 4
1938	78.8	13.5	12.1	−4.4
1939	76.2	19.6	10.9	−6.7
1940	60.4	39.9	9.2	−9.5
1941	54.6	47.2	6.1	−7.9
1942	53.5	49.0	3.8	−6.3
1943	51.9	49.7	3.9	−5.5
1944	56.0	48.8	0.7	−5.5
1945	63.5	42.2	1.1	−6.8
1946	70.5	23.3	8.5	−2.3

Note:
Investment includes stockbuilding as well as fixed capital formation.
Source: Feinstein (1972), table 5.

Table 2.6. *The distribution of UK net national expenditure, 1938–1944 (per cent of total)*

	Consumption 1	War 2	Non-war investment 3
1938	87.2	7.4	5.4
1939	82.6	15.3	2.1
1940	71.1	43.8	−14.9
1941	62.4	52.7	−10.8
1943	55.5	55.3	−10.8
1944	56.5	53.4	−9.9

Source: Combined Committee on Non-Food Consumption (1945), 144.

expenditure and gross investment in fixed capital and stockbuilding.[8] Table 2.6 presents a similar picture, but this time working in terms of net national expenditure and distinguishing more carefully between war and non-war items. The importance of net disinvestment, as well as the reduction of consumption, is apparent in the build-up of the war effort to the 1943 peak.

Achieving mobilization

We now turn from the scale of mobilization to the issue of how the mobilization of resources was achieved. This involves a consideration of both financial and real aspects of the resource allocation process. It should be noted that the traditional literature is very heavily imbued with a Keynesian view of the world and a strong belief in the superiority of controls over market forces. Although some questioning of these assumptions has occurred in the literature on the American war economy, the traditional analysis of the British war economy has received few challenges.[9]

Fiscal policy

The traditional account usually places Keynes's contribution to the conduct of fiscal and monetary policy close to the centre of the story.[10] Keynes developed the idea of an 'inflationary gap' to analyse the problem of war finance. He argued that the traditional 'Treasury View' of calculating how much tax revenue would be available on the principle of how much people would be willing to pay was a recipe for inflation.[11] Rather, he argued that the government needed first to calculate national income, so as to assess the war potential of the economy, and then set taxes at the level required to bring about the necessary transfers from taxpayers to the government. The extra wartime taxes could be treated as forced savings or deferred pay to be repaid after the war. This had the additional advantage of building up potential purchasing power that could be released in the event of a postwar slump, as well as financing the war effort. To the extent that the government failed to achieve the required levels of taxation or forced savings, there would be an inflationary gap, since the excess of aggregate demand over aggregate supply would bid up prices.

Keynes's proposals initially met opposition from the Treasury and the Labour Party. The Treasury feared that forced savings would undermine the voluntary savings movement and increase pressures for wage increases.[12] There were also doubts about the accuracy of the national income estimates.[13] The Labour Party were worried about the need to tax working-class incomes for the first time, despite the proposal to treat wartime taxes as deferred pay.[14]

This opposition was gradually overcome during 1940–1 as inflationary pressures built up and the military situation called for more desperate measures. Keynes was co-opted into the Treasury in June 1940, and fed into the budgetary process the improved national income statistics of Meade and Stone and the detailed survey work of Madge which showed rapidly rising working-class incomes (especially in munitions towns) and a disappointing response to the National Savings movement.[15]

The 1941 Budget is usually seen as one of the turning points in the Keynesian revolution, making explicit use of the national accounts and the idea of the inflationary gap. The basic statistics that took shape in the last weeks before the budget are set out by Sayers and are reproduced here in

Table 2.7. *The UK inflationary gap, 1941 (£ millions)*

	£m
Domestic expenditure	3,700
Revenue on current basis	1,636
Impersonal savings, inc. depreciation accruals, etc.	900
Personal savings	700
Total 'finance'	3,236

Source: Sayers (1956), 72.

Table 2.7.[16] A shortfall in revenue below expenditure of the order of £500 million became generally accepted, and it was this inflationary gap that the Chancellor Sir Kingsley Wood sought to close. It was believed that personal savings could be raised by £200 million to £300 million, partly through making attractive offers to savers, but more generally through reducing spending opportunities. To close the rest of the inflationary gap, the Chancellor aimed to raise about £250 million through taxation. The biggest changes were in income tax, with allowances reduced and marginal rates raised; the standard rate of income tax increased from 42.5 to 50 per cent.[17] However, a movement towards Keynes's forced savings or deferred pay proposal was made, since payment of the extra taxes was to result in the accumulation of postwar credits. In fact, the scale of the deferred pay was never as large as envisaged by Keynes, and the credits were only repaid to pensioners and other special cases, and then only in much depreciated money.[18] The principle of postwar credits was also applied in the 1941 Budget to the Excess Profits Tax, which had been raised from 60 to 100 per cent in the panic of May 1940, and was feared to be adversely affecting incentives.

The 1941 Budget dealt not only with measures to limit demand-pull inflation, but also with measures to tackle cost-push inflation through cost-of-living subsidies.[19] To this end, subsidies on foodstuffs, already running at an annual rate of £100 million, were extended to all essential goods and services.[20] However, it should be noted that the Keynesian approach to fiscal policy largely ignores the incentive effects of taxation, a theme to which we shall return when considering the long-run impact of the war.

Monetary policy

The traditional Keynesian view assigns only a subsidiary role to monetary policy. Although Bank Rate was raised from 2 per cent to 4 per cent on 24 August 1939, it was quickly lowered again to 3 per cent on 28 September, when it was felt that controls rendered the rate of interest redundant for regulating either domestic demand or the exchange rate. Interest rates then remained low for the duration of the war, which cheapened the cost of financing the large budget deficit and led to the memorable phrase of 'A three per cent war', as *The Economist* put it in an article of 20 January 1940.[21] The government chose to finance the large budget deficit through borrowing to avoid inflationary money finance. The aim was to persuade private sector agents to hold government debt, preferably long-dated to keep them as illiquid as possible. This was achieved through restricting alternative investment opportunities as well as through expanding the range of government financial instruments.

Alternative investment opportunities were tightly controlled through a Capital Issues Committee and restrictions on bank advances.[22] This left the government free to act as a discriminating monopolist, offering different terms to different classes of investor, at the lowest rates necessary to attract each class of funds.[23] This involved Defence Bonds and National Savings Certificates for small investors as well as War Bonds and Exchequer Bonds for institutional investors.[24] In addition, from 1941, Tax Reserve Certificates were offered to firms setting aside funds to meet future tax liabilities.

As Pollard notes, any funds not invested in these instruments normally ended up in banks, so it was important that the government developed ways of utilizing banks' liquid reserves.[25] This was done through the introduction of the Treasury Deposit Receipt in addition to the Treasury Bill. The upshot of these changes was a transformation in the balance sheet position of the London clearing banks. On the asset side, commercial advances declined even in nominal terms, while holdings of government paper grew explosively. On the liabilities side there was a dramatic rise in average net deposits, much of it in the form of business deposits.[26]

The monetary consequences of the central government deficit are summarized in table 2.8. As Sayers notes, about two-thirds of the deficit was financed by long-term domestic borrowing, with only one-third financed by short-term floating debt, principally in the form of Treasury Bills and Treasury Deposit Receipts.[27] Only a small fraction of the deficit was financed through the expansion of the monetary base. Furthermore, the inflationary consequences of even this were muted by the extensive controls exercised over the banking sector, thus limiting the money multiplier effects.

The relationship between money and prices is considered in table 2.9. Although broad money (M3) approximately doubled over the war, the price level rose by only about 50 per cent, as reflected in Feinstein's GDP deflator at factor cost and retail price index.[28] It should be noted that the substantially smaller rise in the official Ministry of Labour cost-of-living index

Table 2.8. *Financing the UK central government deficit, 1938–1945*
(£ millions)

| | Total revenue 1 | Total expenditure 2 | Current deficit 3 | Increase in | | |
				long debt 4	short debt 5	monetary base 6
1938	673	781	108	77	−179	18
1939	771	1,261	490	72	280	18
1940	1,158	3,273	2,115	983	517	70
1941	1,905	4,727	2,822	1,650	903	109
1942	2,314	5,223	2,909	2,100	476	191
1943	2,759	5,585	2,826	1,955	1,017	200
1944	2,897	5,569	2,672	1,711	1,081	190
1945	2,806	4,937	2,131	1,885	557	184

Sources: Central Statistical Office (1951), tables 184–185; Capie and Webber (1985), table 1.1.

Table 2.9. *Money and prices in the UK, 1939–1945 (per cent of 1938)*

	M3 1	GDP deflator (Feinstein) 2	Retail price index (Feinstein) 3	Cost of living (Ministry of Labour) 4
1939	99.3	104.4	103.3	101.0
1940	109.2	113.4	117.0	117.8
1941	125.9	123.6	128.8	126.7
1942	142.0	132.5	137.3	127.7
1943	162.4	138.6	141.8	126.7
1944	184.4	146.9	145.1	128.7
1945	208.5	151.3	147.7	129.7

Sources: Capie and Webber (1985), table 1.3; Feinstein (1972), tables 61, 65; Central Statistical Office (1951), table 190.

reflects the unrepresentativeness of the 1904 working-class expenditure weights. This excess of monetary growth over inflation would suggest quite a significant role for controls in containing inflation. However, as Capie and Wood note, the role of controls is dwarfed by the role of bond finance; a counterfactual calculation indicates that if the war had been financed completely by printing money, the price level would have risen from 100 in 1939 to 1,023,824.3 by 1945.[29]

Table 2.10. *The UK balance of payments, September 1939 to 1945*
(£ billion)

	Current account			Net grants from US	Sale of investments	Rise in liabilities
	deficit 1	credits 2	deficit 3	4	5	6
1939.IX–XII	0.3	0.1	0.2	0.0	0.0	0.1
1940	1.5	0.7	0.8	0.0	0.2	0.2
1941	1.9	0.8	1.1	0.3	0.3	0.6
1942	2.6	0.9	1.7	0.9	0.2	0.5
1943	3.6	1.5	2.1	1.6	0.2	0.7
1944	4.2	1.7	2.5	1.9	0.1	0.7
1945	2.8	1.2	1.6	0.7	0.1	0.7
Total	16.9	6.9	10.0	5.4	1.1	3.5

Source: Sayers (1956), 499.

Financing the external deficit

A central issue in most accounts of the mobilization of resources for war in Britain is the external deficit. Although the Treasury initially hoped to meet the import requirements from gold reserves and exports, and to this end instituted an export drive, by March 1941 it was clear that this was not feasible.[30] The introduction of lend-lease considerably relaxed the external constraint and allowed a much greater degree of specialization by Britain on war work than would otherwise have been possible.[31]

Despite the massive current account imbalance, the exchange rate was maintained at a fixed rate of £1 = $4.03, about 20 per cent below the old gold standard parity, protected by a system of import controls and foreign exchange controls.[32] As with so many other aspects of the war economy, the price became artificial and attention switched to quantities.

The evolution of the British balance of payments is tracked in table 2.10. The largest debit item on the current account was imports, accounting for £12.2 billion of the £16.9 billion, with government overseas expenditure (excluding munitions) accounting for the bulk of the rest. With export volumes falling to less than one-third of their prewar level by 1943, current account credits lagged seriously behind debits, creating an accumulated current account deficit of £10 billion over the war as a whole. The single most important method of finance was grants from the United States under lend-lease, although there was also a substantial accumulation of liabilities and sale of investments.

The evaluation of lend-lease has been a major source of controversy. The

Table 2.11. *UK overseas debts in mid-1945 (£ million)*

	£m
Sterling Area, total	2,723
Australia, New Zealand, S. Africa, Eire	384
India, Burma, Middle East	1,732
Colonies and other Sterling Area	607
North and South America	303
Europe and overseas dependencies	267
Rest of world	62
World total (inc. Sterling Area)	3,355

Source: Sayers (1956), 439.

prime minister described it as 'the most unsordid act in the history of any nation'.[33] Others, however, (including Keynes) have been less charitable, seeing American self-interest behind the aid.[34] First, lend-lease was offered 'for the defense of the United Sates', and deliveries were liable to sudden cancellation or amendment at the whim of the American services in the period before the US entered the war.[35] Second, the Americans were careful to see that the British were as near as possible bankrupt before assistance was given. Third, British exports using lend-lease supplies, which might compete with American exports, were prohibited. Fourth, Britain was forced by Article VII of the Mutual Aid Agreement of 1942 to subscribe to a pronouncement against discrimination in international trade, widely seen as an attack on the system of Imperial Preference. Fifth, lend-lease was ended abruptly one minute into the first day of official peace. However, whatever the long-term consequences of the way lend-lease was administered for the postwar bargaining strengths of Britain and the United States, there can be no doubt about its short-term benefits for the British economy.

The accumulation of liabilities, the other major source of finance for the current account deficit, resulted in the pattern of overseas debts shown in table 2.11. By mid-1945, Britain had overseas debts of £3.4 billion, the bulk of which was held in the form of (blocked) sterling balances by countries within the Sterling Area. This represented a large financial burden, which was to plague monetary policy throughout the early postwar period.[36]

Rationing and 'manpower' budgeting

Even if the inflationary gap could be closed at the macroeconomic level, there was no guarantee that the consumption of specific key goods, such as petrol and sugar, would be brought smoothly into line with supply.[37] Hence the government also relied on rationing. A number of items were rationed from the outbreak of war and rationing gradually spread to more consumer goods and services. By the spring of 1945, rationing covered about one half of consumer spending on goods at prewar values and about one third of consumer spending on goods and services.[38] Initially, rationing operated on a coupon basis, with consumers entitled to fixed amounts of rationed items.[39] From 1941, however, a more flexible points system was introduced, whereby coupon points could be spent on a limited number of goods, thus allowing consumers some scope for substitution in line with preferences.[40] It has been argued that the rationing system operated more effectively in Britain than in other countries. Although some writers see this as reflecting a greater spirit of voluntary compliance in Britain, Mills and Rockoff attribute it mainly to the greater scale of resources devoted to the issue, with a fuller array of controls, backed up by both financial and legal resources, ensuring a strict supervision of both production and distribution.[41]

We have already seen in table 2.2 the increased utilization of labour at the aggregate level. Table 2.12 offers a rather more detailed look at the problem of labour mobilization. In addition to bringing about the overall increase in labour supply by securing increased female participation to replace males recruited into the armed forces, it was necessary to reorient civilian labour supply away from group III industries producing inessential civilian items and into the essential group I industries producing war supplies, while maintaining employment and output in essential non-war industries such as fuel and power.

Although during the early stages of the war labour problems appeared mainly in the form of bottlenecks with skilled labour, as time went on the general supply of labour was seen as a constraint. From December 1942, with the first Manpower Budget, the problem of the allocation of labour between the production programmes of the different government departments was tackled directly.[42] 'Manpower' was the term coined in that bygone age, less gender-conscious than our own, but in wartime the most rapidly growing element (as table 2.12 reveals) was womanpower. The government had wide powers of labour compulsion which it used to control the supply of labour to both the armed forces and industry, although where possible it relied on voluntarism and cooperation.[43]

An alternative 'classical' view

The analysis so far has reflected the strong Keynesian bias of the literature, with an emphasis on quantities and a belief in the efficacy of government intervention and controls. Although an alternative classical model of the war economy is available, its empirical implementation in the British case

Table 2.12. *Distribution of the UK working population, 1939–45 (mid-June)*

	1939	1940	1941	1942	1943	1944	1945
(A) Thousands							
Total	19,750	20,676	21,332	22,056	22,285	22,008	21,649
male	14,656	15,104	15,222	15,141	15,032	14,901	14,881
female	5,094	5,572	6,110	6,915	7,253	7,107	6,768
(B) Per cent of total							
Unemployed	6	3	1	—	—	—	1
Armed forces	2	11	16	19	21	23	24
Civil defence	—	2	2	2	1	1	1
Group I	16	17	20	23	23	23	20
Group II	27	25	26	25	25	25	26
Group III	49	41	36	32	28	28	29

Notes:
Group I industries: metals, engineering, vehicles, and shipbuilding; chemicals, explosives, paints, oils etc.
    Group II industries: agriculture and fishing; mining and quarrying; national and local government; gas, water, and electricity supply; transport and shipping.
    Group III industries: food, drink, and tobacco; textiles; clothing, boots, and shoes; cement, bricks, pottery, glass etc.; leather, wood, paper etc.; other manufactures; building and civil engineering; distributive trades; commerce, banking, insurance, and finance; miscellaneous services.
Source: Central Statistical Office (1951), table 9.

has been limited to a general analysis of the twentieth century, rather than a detailed analysis of World War II. Nevertheless, from a classical perspective this may be a strength rather than a weakness, with the stark differences between a war economy and a peacetime economy being overdrawn in the traditional analysis. After all, it is unlikely that the declaration of war suddenly makes a government all-knowing and all-powerful or leads to the suspension of all pursuit of selfish interests. There may be some virtue, then, in analysing how we would expect a perfectly competitive economy to react to war. This can then be used as a benchmark against which to assess the impact of the special measures and controls, rather than simply attributing all change to such measures. This is important because Britain's postwar problems are sometimes seen as having stemmed from too ready an acceptance of the beneficial effects of government intervention and controls.[44]

    Ahmed adapts Barro's New Classical model of government spending in a closed economy to the open-economy case and provides an econometric application to the United Kingdom in the twentieth century.[45] An increase in government spending to fight a war is viewed as temporary, and Ricardian equivalence between taxation and bond finance is assumed (i.e. private spending decisions are unaffected by the form of finance of government spending, since bond finance represents a future tax liability the present value of which is the same as the taxes which would otherwise have to be raised now). A temporary increase in government spending by one unit ($\Delta G = 1$) directly raises aggregate demand (AD) by one unit, but since it substitutes for a fraction q of private spending, consumption goes down by q units (this is known as direct crowding-out). Hence the total effect on aggregate demand is a rise of $(1-q)$ units. Since government spending is assumed to have a positive marginal product (MPG), aggregate supply (AS) rises by MPG units. There is thus excess demand ($AD-AS$) of $(1-q-MPG)$, which is met by a deterioration in the balance of trade deficit.

The model seems to capture the crude features of the British war economy. Activity rises, consumption falls less than in proportion, and excess demand spills over into the balance of payments. Furthermore, the issue of taxes versus bonds in a Ricardian framework becomes simply one of intergenerational transfers and tax smoothing, with a greater reliance on bond financing spreading the burden onto future generations of taxpayers. Doubtless many of the strong assumptions of the model do not hold, particularly with regard to the competitive structure of the economy. Nevertheless, it suggests that we should not be too quick to attribute all changes during wartime to the efficacy of regulations and controls.

For the time being, however, the classical view can only be seen as a qualification to the majority Keynesian analysis. As yet, there has been no detailed historical study of the British mobilization during World War II from a classical perspective.

Industry

Output and employment by industry

'Manpower' was seen as the ultimate constraint on the British war economy. Austin Robinson, one of the key wartime planners, said that manpower 'was the only unit in which one could add the use of resources by the armed forces to that for munitions production and civil consumption'.[46] Thus, given the problems of wartime prices and the lack of adequate monetary estimates of the output of different sectors and industries, the easiest way to gauge relative shifts within the economy is to consider changes in the distribution of labour. This is shown in table 2.13, which uses

Table 2.13. *Total persons in UK employment by branch, 1939–1945*
(thousands)

	1939	1940	1941	1942	1943	1944	1945
Agriculture	950	925	981	1,002	1,047	1,048	1,041
Total industry	7,930	8,227	8,431	8,791	8,764	8,439	7,815
munitions	3,106	3,559	4,240	4,990	5,233	5,011	4,346
other industry	4,824	4,668	4,191	3,801	3,531	3,428	3,469
Construction	1,310	1,064	1,043	893	726	623	722
Transport	1,233	1,146	1,194	1,217	1,176	1,237	1,252
Distribution	2,887	2,639	2,332	2,173	2,009	1,927	1,958
Civilian services	3,690	3,757	3,770	3,802	3,722	3,693	3,628
Military services	480	2,273	3,383	4,091	4,761	4,967	5,090
Total employment	18,480	20,031	21,134	21,969	22,205	21,934	21,506

Notes:
An attempt has been made to follow the categories used for the Soviet Union (table 7.8 below).
   Agriculture includes fishing; munitions is equivalent to Group I (see notes to table 2.12).
   'Other industry' is composed of mining and quarrying; gas, water, and electricity supply; food, drink, and tobacco; textiles, clothing, boots, and shoes; cement, bricks, pottery, glass etc.; leather, wood, paper etc.; and other manufactures.
   Civilian services comprise national and local government, civil defence, fire service, and police; commerce, banking, insurance, and finance; and miscellaneous services.
Source: Central Statistical Office (1951), table 9.

a branch-of-employment categorization broadly similar to that used for the Soviet economy in chapter 7 (table 7.8).

Although the total number of people in employment increased from 17.8 million in 1938 to a peak of 22.2 million in 1943, all sectors except munitions and military services saw their shares decline until 1943–4 (or, in the case of agriculture 1941–2) before making a modest recovery which still left them with shares below prewar levels. The munitions and related industries had already overtaken the distributive trades to become the third largest sector in 1939. Munitions and related industries was the largest sector by 1941, peaking in 1943 with 23.6 per cent of the employed labour force. In 1942 military services became the second largest sector, and indeed in 1945 eventually overtook even munitions and related industries with a 23.7 per cent share. Thus, from 1942 onwards more than 40 per cent of the employed workforce was in either the munitions and related industries or military services.

These shifts in the composition of civil employment reflected the strategic priorities of the war that called for the transfer of resources (labour, capital, raw materials, shipping capacity, and factory space) from civilian industries to war production. The state used a barrage of measures to ensure that this transfer occurred, including production quotas placed on civilian industries (normally as a reduced percentage of prewar production), the central allocation of scarce resources (such as steel and capital) by the state, and the use of rationing and other measures to curtail consumer demand.[47] The state also implemented a temporary wartime concentration of production drive in many consumer industries, which released 250,000 workers and 70 million square feet of capacity for the munitions and related industries.[48] In terms of output, the net result of these measures was a contraction of the production of consumer industries and a dramatic increase in the production of munitions, which can be seen in table 2.14.

Munitions

Tables 2.13 and 2.14 show clearly the expansion of the munitions and related industries during the war, with employment rising from 3.1 million in 1939 to 5.2 million in 1943. To take one important example of the increased output, whereas in 1938 a mere 2,828 aircraft were produced at an average structure weight of 3,472 lb, by 1941 more than 20,000 aircraft were produced at an average weight of 4,342 lb, and by 1944 output had risen to 26,461 aircraft with average weight leaping to 7,880 lb, mainly as a result of heavy bomber production coming on line.

In the absence of adequate or meaningful price data, the diversity of munitions production makes it difficult to derive a single consistent measure for output. Fortunately, however, the British wartime planners designed an index of total munitions output for the United Kingdom, which has recently been revised by Harrison.[49] The Harrison index, rebased on the fourth quarter of 1939, is shown in table 2.15. The index has three components, reflecting the production programmes of the Ministry of Supply, the Ministry of Aircraft Production, and the Admiralty. The Ministry of Supply index is based on the finished output of warlike stores, the Ministry of Aircraft Production index is based on the total structure weight of completed aircraft adjusted for man hours to take account of the different labour input requirements of the various aircraft types, while the Admiralty index is based on the displacement tonnage of completed warships.[50] The three components were weighted by the employment shares of the three departments in the first quarter of 1941. The index shows that munitions production peaked in the first quarter of 1944, when production was 552 per cent greater than it had been in the last quarter of 1939. This probably understates the gains made because the index does not take into account the changes in the quality of munitions.[51] As many weapons, but

Table 2.14. *UK output of selected commodities, 1939–1945 (physical units)*

	1939	1940	1941	1942	1943	1944	1945
Grains, thou. tons	4,264	5,231	5,942	7,113	7,737	7,445	7,132
Potatoes, thou. tons	4,354	5,375	6,783	8,162	8,537	8,026	8,702
Meat, thou. tons	1,180	1,072	902	772	754	783	812
Aircraft, units	7,940	15,049	20,094	23,672	26,263	26,461	—
Aircraft, mn lb	29	59	87	133	185	209	—
Warships, thou. tons	76	170	226	234	174	171	—
.303 rifles, thou.	34	81	79	595	910	547	—
Mortars, units	2,822	7,559	21,725	29,162	17,121	19,046	—
Coal, mn tons	231	224	206	205	199	193	183
Electricity, mn kWh	27,733	29,976	33,577	36,903	38,217	39,649	38,611
Iron ore, mn tons	14.5	17.7	19.0	19.9	18.5	15.5	14.2
Steel, mn tons	13.2	13.0	12.3	12.9	13.0	12.1	11.8
Aluminium, thou. tons	25.0	19.0	22.7	46.8	55.7	35.5	31.9
Machine tools, thou.	37.0	62.0	80.9	95.8	76.2	59.1	47.5
Cotton yarn, mn lb	1,092	1,191	821	733	712	665	597
Raw wool, mn lb	69	91	80	72	62	59	58
Footwear, mn pairs	—	—	—	108	103	100	100
Construction, £m	442	425	470	425	350	290	290

Notes:
Grains are the sum of wheat, barley, and oats harvested (59); potatoes (59); meat is home killed meat (68); aircraft (152–3); warships include battleships, aircraft carriers, monitors, cruisers, destroyers, and submarines, and are measured by displacement tonnage (133); .303 rifles (144); mortars (143); coal (Supple (1987), 9); electricity generated (86); iron ore (101); steel (British Iron and Steel Federation (1948), 328–329); aluminium, virgin (110); machine tools (158; Postan (1952), 207); cotton yarn (126); raw wool (Mitchell (1988), 336); footwear (Hargreaves and Gowing (1952), 646); construction is the value of gross output (Kohan (1952), 426, 488).
Source: Central Statistical Office (1951), with page references given in parentheses in notes, except where noted above.

particularly aircraft, became heavier and more complex the average quality almost certainly rose.

These impressive gains in output are not surprising given the rapid expansion of labour, capital, and capacity in the munitions and related industries. It is not clear, however, that the rapid gains in output were matched by gains in productivity, especially in the first eighteen months of the war. There were inevitable time lags as new capacity was built or existing capacity was converted to munitions production, as new labour was absorbed and trained or gained experience, and as the state evolved its policies for the centralized direction of resources and the planning of war production.[52] However, as the war progressed, productivity almost certainly

Table 2.15. *Quarterly index of total munitions output of the UK, 1940–1944 (per cent of 1939.IV)*

Quarter	I	II	III	IV
1940	—	—	233	249
1941	269	292	307	381
1942	418	535	542	567
1943	591	616	586	628
1944	652	633	547	537

Note:
The Harrison index base period is the first quarter of 1941.
Source: Harrison (1990), 665.

rose, particularly when the production run remained relatively stable. Thus, for example, at one aircraft firm the number of operatives employed per aircraft produced fell from 487 in April 1942 to 220 in April 1943.[53] Although we lack reliable or consistent estimates of wartime productivity in industry, existing data suggest that output per employee did increase in many of the industries in the munitions and related sector between the production census years of 1935 and 1948.[54]

Textiles

Table 2.14 illustrates the collapse in the production of consumer industries such as cotton and construction. Within the 'other industry' sector of table 2.13 the two largest industries were textiles and coal. The official wartime historians of civil industry and trade, Hargreaves and Gowing, reported that many textile manufacturers felt that wartime methods such as the introduction of new techniques and bulk buying, and the standardization of demands via the utility scheme, had increased their output per head by between 10 per cent and 75 per cent.[55] However, such claims are no substitute for a rigorous examination of the actual productivity performance of textiles. Given the array of different industries encompassed by the textile sector (including cotton spinning and weaving, woollen and worsted, silk and rayon, textile bleaching, printing, dyeing and finishing, linen, jute and hemp) and the difficulties created by the introduction of physical and price controls at different times in the various industries and by their varied experience of the concentration of production drive, it has not been possible to derive a wartime index of labour productivity for textiles.[56] Even attempting to derive a measure of wartime labour productivity within the cotton industry, which was the largest industry in the textile sector, is not without its difficulties.[57] However, the existing evidence does suggest that, contrary to the optimism of Hargreaves and Gowing, between 1939 and 1947 the cotton industry (with the exception of fine mule spinning) experienced a significant decline in productivity.[58] This, in turn, reflected the increasing pressure under which the textile industry as a whole came during the war to curtail its production, via the official restriction of raw material supplies, labour supply, civilian demand, capital equipment and floorspace.[59]

Coal

There is little doubt that the coal industry performed poorly during the war. Table 2.14 shows that output declined significantly and continuously during the war years, from 231 million tons in 1939 to 183 million tons in 1945. Both output and labour productivity in the industry were adversely affected by several factors, including transportation difficulties caused by bad planning and German bombing, the curtailment in the supply of vital inputs such as timber and steel, and the loss of experienced workers to the armed forces.[60] Another problem that dogged the industry was poor industrial relations, with the number of days lost due to industrial disputes averaging over 894,000 a year during the war, and 2.48 million days lost during 1944 alone.[61] Finally, although the percentage of coal cut mechanically increased from 61 per cent in 1939 to 72 per cent by 1945 and the percentage conveyed mechanically rose from 58 per cent to 71 per cent, the fall in output meant that the absolute tonnage of coal cut and conveyed mechanically declined throughout the war.[62]

The overall impact of these changes was that labour productivity, measured in terms of manshifts actually worked at the coal face, fell, but less drastically than output. Output per manshift at the coal face fell from 3 tons in 1938 to between 2.7 and 2.8 tons in 1945.[63] The official historian of the wartime coal industry argued that this wartime decline in labour productivity reflected underlying problems in the industry which, although aggravated by the war, had their roots in the decades before 1939.[64]

Agriculture

Hancock and Gowing called agriculture an 'outstanding example' of an industry whose efficiency increased during the war.[65] The major task facing British agriculture was the need to replace lost imports, which had accounted for 70 per cent of Britain's prewar food requirements.[66] Between 1939 and 1942, for example, imports of animal feedstuffs fell by 94 per cent, imports of butter by 69 per cent, sugar by two-thirds and wheat by a third.[67] The situation was not helped by the loss of experienced workers to the armed forces. The increased employment in agriculture shown in table 2.13 reflected the absorption of inexperienced workers into the sector from the Women's Land Army, casual and volunteer labour and, later, prisoners-of-war.[68] Furthermore, given the need to produce enough calories to sustain the population, a large portion of the experienced workforce was diverted from the livestock to the arable sector, where they too were relatively inexperienced.[69] The impact of all this can be seen in table 2.14, with grain production increasing by 81 per cent between 1939 and 1943 while meat production fell by 36 per cent.

The improvements that did occur in part reflected the impressive expansion of the use of agricultural machinery during the war. Thus between 1939 and 1945 the production of tractors increased by 48 per cent, of disc harrows by 514 per cent, of potato spinners by 381 per cent, and of threshing machines by 121 per cent, while fuel consumption increased by 159 per cent.[70] Although the war accelerated the trend towards increased mechanization in agriculture it did not start it. Murray notes that the trend towards mechanization went back at least to the mid-1920s, in response to the increasing differential between agricultural wages and prices.[71] The improvements in wartime yields in both meat and crops were also due to greater use of fertilizers, to greater scientific involvement with farming and improved farm management.[72]

The assessment of the wartime performance of the agricultural sector as a whole has been aided greatly by the quantitative work of Williams, endorsed by the official historian of agriculture during the war.[73] Williams provides an index of real net output that takes account of the changing composition of final outputs and intermediate inputs, and an index of employment that adjusts for the changing quality of the labour force as more female and prisoner-of-war labour was used. These figures, given in table 2.16 (cols. 1, 3), would seem to refute the Hancock and Gowing claim that the productivity record of agriculture was outstanding. The labour productivity index calculated using these figures (col. 4) shows no clear upward trend during the war. Furthermore, this does not take into account change in capital inputs. Given the large increase in the use of agricultural machinery it seems likely that total factor productivity in agriculture fell substantially during the war.

The key to this apparent conflict of views lies in calories. The main concern of wartime policy makers was to keep the population as well nourished as possible given the wartime constraints, particularly on shipping. Thus, they were less interested in the volume of wheat or meat produced, and more interested in the calorific content of agricultural output.[74] Thus table 2.16 (col. 2) offers an alternative measure of agricultural output in terms of domestically produced calories. Combined with the Williams employment index, we see that labour productivity on this basis (col. 5) rose substantially.

Table 2.16. *Output, employment, and labour productivity in UK agriculture, 1939/40–1945/6 (per cent of 1937/9)*

	Real value of net output 1	Calorific value of net output 2	Employment 3	Real output per employee 4	Calories per employee 5
1939/40	104	110	99	105	111
1940/1	106	125	101	105	124
1941/2	98	136	103	95	132
1942/3	111	168	107	104	157
1943/4	115	191	108	106	177
1944/5	108	—	109	99	—
1945/6	111	—	107	104	—

Sources and notes:
1. An index of net output of domestic agriculture in 1945–6 prices from Williams (1954), 338, based on 1937/9=100.
2. An index of the calorific content of net output from Murray (1955), 242, based on 1938/9=100.
3. An index of employment based on 1937–9 using a 'labour content' conversion to standardize the labour input using relative earnings in 1945–6 to 1948–9 (thus males over 21 had a weight of 1.0, casual female labour had a weight of 0.5, unbilleted prisoners-of-war had a weight of 0.4, and so on) (Williams, 1954, 333).
4. Col. 1 divided by col. 3.
5. Col. 2 divided by col. 3.

The long-run impact on industry

The question of whether the war had an impact on the long-term structure of British industry is complicated by the changes introduced by the Labour government in the immediate postwar years. Wartime controls, including the concentration of production drive, appear to have had a significant impact on concentration in only a small number of industries.[75]

Despite fears by business that the massive extension of state regulation and controls would result in a backdoor nationalization programme, only three firms were nationalized during the war, all of which were important to the war effort and had resisted state attempts to solve their problems through voluntary methods.[76] Indeed, the wave of postwar nationalization, although by no means the most important factor, would appear to be much more significant than any wartime changes in explaining both increased concentration and Britain's postwar industrial performance. For example, Jeremy uses data on the hundred largest employers at various dates to argue that the increased concentration in British industry between 1935 and 1948 was to a large extent due to nationalization, with six nationalized companies accounting for 10 per cent of the workforce in 1955.[77] Finally, if one accepts the Broadberry and Crafts argument that an important factor in explaining British manufacturing's productivity gap with the USA during the 1930s was the weakened 'competitive environment', then nationalization, which further weakened the incentive of industry to be efficient, was hardly the way forward.[78]

A more significant impact was on the relative share of employment within manufacturing, as a result of the international division of labour amongst the Allies. Howlett has argued that changes in the relative employment shares of industries within manufacturing were much more marked during the war period, 1938–45, than in the interwar period, 1924–38, and that these shifts were not reversed in the postwar period, 1948–55.[79] Furthermore, the wartime declines in the employment shares of food, drink, and tobacco, and textiles and the very large increase in engineering and allied industries were reflected in their shares of net manufacturing output.[80]

Matthews *et al.* suggest that the sectoral reallocations of resources induced by wartime specialization had some adverse consequences for productivity.[81] They note that, over the transwar period 1937–51, the three sectors where inputs of capital and labour grew more rapidly or declined less rapidly than in other periods, namely agriculture, mining, and manufacturing, experienced much slower growth of total factor productivity in the transwar period than in the preceding and following peacetime periods. They see this as evidence that 'the policy of pushing resources into these three sectors in the transwar period may have brought them up against diminishing returns'.[82]

World War II also left its mark on technology in British industry. During the war, many British industrialists were brought face to face with the much higher labour productivity achieved in American industry as the two economies were integrated in the Allied war effort. Wartime visits by British industrialists to the United States were followed up after the war by the Anglo-American Council on Productivity (AACP), which sponsored visits by productivity teams made up of managers and trade unionists in a wide range of industries.[83] However, attempts to adopt American technology in British conditions were not very successful. As well as meeting the inevitable opposition of craft workers who saw the value of their skills being eroded, American technology was often unpopular with managers, who were not used to exercising the degree of shopfloor control required to make it profitable. The antagonistic industrial relations that emerged during this technological upheaval formed an important part of the postwar British industrial culture, and came to be seen as one of the major symptoms of the 'British disease' in the literature on economic decline.[84]

The long-run impact on wealth

An accounting framework

The development of national income accounting during the 1930s and 1940s produced an emphasis on flows of income, expenditure, and output. Much less attention was paid to the behaviour of stock variables, and it was some time before the concept of the national balance sheet was developed. In the United States the work of Goldsmith *et al.* was important in developing a national balance sheet framework, while in the United Kingdom a similar framework was developed by Revell.[85] In this approach, national wealth is equal to domestic physical capital, *plus* net overseas assets. The long-run impact of the war can then be assessed through changes in national wealth.

Recent work in growth theory suggests that the level of development can be explained by capital, so long as a broad concept of capital is used.[86] This prompts us to amend the conventional national balance sheet to include human as well as physical capital, and intangible as well as tangible capital. This taxonomy is taken from a study of the US economy by Kendrick.[87] Tangible non-human capital is the conventional form of capital, consisting of land, structures, equipment, and inventories. Intangible non-human capital is cumulated expenditure on R&D, which is seen as improving the quality of the tangible non-human capital. Tangible human capital is the spending required to produce an uneducated, untrained worker, i.e. basic rearing costs. Intangible human capital is mainly spending on education and training to improve the quality of the human capital, although there are a couple of other minor items such as spending on health and safety, and mobility costs.

A number of the categories of capital suggested by Kendrick are particularly appropriate for gauging the impact of war. It is clearly inappropriate to ignore the loss of life when examining the effects of war, yet, as Milward notes, postwar birth rates typically rise, so that it is not clear that there are permanent demographic effects.[88] Nevertheless, those who are killed by warfare do have human capital embodied in them and this investment is wasted, irrespective of future demographic trends. This must be seen, then, as having a negative impact on the national balance sheet, just as much as damage to the physical capital stock. Postwar catching-up is necessary precisely to make good wartime losses. However, war can also be seen as stimulating intangible investments, which must be taken into account in the national balance sheet. The benefits of technological change noted by Bowley can be captured in the national balance sheet approach by the public subsidization of R&D.[89] Equally, the effects of war in stimulating social spending, noted by Titmuss, can be seen as having a positive impact on the national balance sheet to the extent that they contribute to intangible human capital.[90]

Studies based on World War I

The confusion over stock and flow concepts can be conveniently illustrated from the literature on World War I. The Carnegie Endowment for International Peace sponsored a large number of war-economy studies, one of the most interesting of which is the attempt by Bogart to quantify the costs of the war.[91] Bogart's conclusions can be summarized in two tables, reproduced here as tables 2.17 and 2.18. Table 2.17 presents what are described as direct costs. These costs are calculated as the flows of spending by governments on the prosecution of the war, i.e. spending over and above prewar normal levels. It is clear that this is related to the issue studied by Harrison of the extent of mobilization.[92] A couple of problems with the way the data are presented by Bogart should be obvious. First, it is inappropriate simply to add up nominal sums spent at different times, given the wartime inflation. Second, this problem, as well as the related problem of the conversion of all values to dollars can be avoided if the war expenditure data are presented as a proportion of national income in each year. Third, the presentation of the data on an annual basis as by Harrison is highly informative about the time profile of the war effort, which is worthy of study in its own right.[93]

Turning to table 2.18, Bogart introduces a number of indirect costs. At first sight, it might appear that Bogart had in mind a national balance sheet approach, adding up losses to human and physical capital. Note, however, that there are a number of indefensible accounting procedures. Perhaps the most obvious problem is that Bogart simply adds the direct and indirect costs together, a serious confusion of stock and flow concepts. This crime is compounded by the inclusion of lost production (a flow concept) as an indirect cost (a stock concept). Although the losses to physical capital are correctly accounted for (remembering that cargoes can be seen as stocks), the treatment of human capital is not consistent with the national balance sheet approach. The problem is that the capitalized value of human life overstates the social loss, since people consume as well as produce. In a national balance sheet framework, all that we require is the cost of rearing and training a worker, since this is what is lost to society by premature death. Finally, note that some of the government spending on the war effort, included negatively in direct costs, should actually enter positively in the national balance sheet, contributing to intangible non-human capital in the form of cumulated R&D spending and to intangible human capital in the form of spending on health and mobility.

Table 2.17. *Bogart's 'direct costs' of World War I ($ million)*

	Gross cost 1	Advances to allies 2	Net cost 3
United States	32,080	9,455	22,625
Great Britain	44,029	8,695	35,334
Rest of British Empire	4,494		4,494
France	25,813	1,547	24,266
Russia	22,594		22,594
Italy	12,314		12,314
Other Entente allies	3,964		3,964
Entente powers total	145,288	19,697	125,591
Germany	40,150	2,375	37,775
Austria-Hungary	20,623		20,623
Turkey, Bulgaria	2,245		2,245
Central powers total	63,018	2,375	60,643
Grand total	208,306	22,072	186,234

Source: Bogart (1920), 267.

Table 2.18. *Bogart's 'direct and indirect costs' of World War I ($ million)*

	$m
Indirect costs	
Capitalized value of human life	
soldiers	33,551
civilians	33,551
Property losses:	
on land	29,960
shipping and cargo	6,800
Loss of production	45,000
War relief	1,000
Loss to neutrals	1,750
Total indirect costs	151,612
Total direct costs, net	186,234
Grand total	337,846

Source: Bogart (1920), 299.

Table 2.19. *An official balance sheet evaluation of the effects of World War II on the UK economy (£ billion)*

	£bn
Physical destruction	
on land	1.5
shipping (including cargoes)	0.7
Internal disinvestment	0.9
External disinvestment	4.2
Total	7.3
Prewar national wealth	30.0

Source: Cmd 6707, table 12.

British data covering World War II

Some of the data needed for an evaluation of the effects of World War II on the national balance sheet of the United Kingdom are contained in Cmd 6707, a report presented by the Chancellor of the Exchequer to parliament in 1945 on the statistical material presented during the Washington negotiations. Table 2.19 sets out the summary data. The physical destruction represents the direct loss of physical capital due to enemy action both on land and at sea. As noted earlier, the loss of cargoes can be seen as a loss of stocks. Internal disinvestment captures the extent to which the deferment of all but essential maintenance and repairs adversely affected postwar production capacity. Although the report goes on to point out that wartime government capital spending should be set against this, it argues that the peacetime value of these assets is unlikely to be large.[94] The external disinvestment includes the realization of external capital assets, the increase in external liabilities and the decrease in gold and US dollar reserves. This represents the loss of overseas wealth which Britain suffered to finance the war effort. The total deterioration in the national balance sheet of £7.3 billion is compared with prewar national wealth estimated at £30 billion. The loss of national wealth across the war is thus put at about 25 per cent.

For a study published at the end of 1945, Cmd 6707 is a considerable achievement. Nevertheless there are a number of ways in which this study can be improved upon to arrive at a fuller balance sheet evaluation of the impact of World War II on the British economy. To begin with, some of the items in table 2.19 have been calculated in current prices, while others have been calculated in constant 1945 prices. Thus in table 2.20 we rework the figures in constant 1938 prices, using information on the time profile of the

Table 2.20. *Revised UK national balance sheet calculation on a conventional basis (£ million in constant 1938 prices)*

	£m
Physical destruction:	
on land	860
shipping (including cargoes)	380
Internal disinvestment	612
External disinvestment	3,256
Total losses	5,108
less government financed investment	513
Net losses	4,595
Prewar stock of physical capital	19,520
plus prewar net overseas assets	5,160
Prewar national wealth	24,680

Source: See text.

losses contained in the report. The price deflators are taken from the work of Feinstein and we use the capital goods deflator for physical destruction and internal disinvestment and the GDP deflator for external disinvestment.[95] Although the report suggested that government-financed investment was of little postwar value, subsequent work on the postwar capital stock by Dean suggests that this was not the case.[96] Hence we need to make an allowance for government-financed investment to arrive at net losses. It is now possible to arrive at a more accurate estimate of the value of physical capital and net overseas wealth in 1938. Table 2.20 gives the figures for 1938 national wealth on the conventional basis, consisting of physical capital *plus* net overseas assets. Prewar physical capital is the 1938 gross reproducible capital stock at current replacement cost from Feinstein.[97] Net overseas assets in 1938 are taken from Feinstein.[98] On this basis, UK national wealth in 1938 was £24.68 billion, which means that wartime net losses amounted to 18.6 per cent of prewar wealth.

The conventional national balance sheet approach can be augmented to allow for human capital. In table 2.21 we present some tentative calculations for the United Kingdom. Tangible human capital per head is the cost of rearing a child to working age in the period up to 1938, expressed in prices of 1938 for comparison with the figures in table 2.20. The figure is based on Rowntree's estimate of the cost of maintaining a child above the primary poverty line in York in 1936.[99] A weekly cost of 6s 2d translates

Table 2.21. *UK human capital losses during World War II (1938 prices)*

Tangible human capital per head (£)	239
plus intangible human capital per head (£)	160
Human capital per head (£)	399
Total human capital losses (£mn)	143.64

Source: See text.

into an annual cost of £16.03. Using Feinstein's deflator for retail prices yields a cost of £17.04 in 1938 prices.[100] Up to the school-leaving age of 14, then, rearing costs total £238.56 per child.

Intangible human capital per head is based on education spending to improve the quality of the labour force. Data on education spending in England and Wales in 1938 from Vaizey and Sheehan are combined with data on the number of pupils from Mitchell to obtain a figure for educational spending per head.[101] In 1938 prices, educational expenditure was £8.88 per pupil in primary schools and £29.78 in secondary schools. On the assumption that the typical pupil received primary education for seven years and secondary education for three years, this results in total educational spending per child of £159.84 in 1938 prices.

It is worth considering the implications of the above figures for the stock of human capital in 1938. For an adult population of about 35 million, total tangible human capital works out at £8,365 million, while total intangible human capital is £5,600 million.[102] These figures suggest a ratio of human to physical capital of 71.5 per cent, somewhat lower than in Kendrick's study for the United States.[103] However, it should be noted that we have not allowed for a number of items of intangible human capital, notably further education and training. Spending on items such as health and safety, included in Kendrick's study, are difficult to allow for. Although Titmuss argued for a strong effect of the war on social spending, Peacock and Wiseman's study shows a faster rate of growth of social spending between the wars than across World War II.[104] Furthermore, Lindert's comparative study of the rise of social spending finds no evidence of a discontinuity across World War I, when similar pressures may be presumed to have operated.[105]

These figures suggest a figure for tangible and intangible human capital per head of £399 in 1945 prices. Hancock and Gowing report war-related deaths amounting to 360,000 during 1939–45, so this translates into a total human capital loss of £143.64 million, to set beside the physical capital loss of £1,240 million reported in table 2.20 above.[106] Clearly, then, British losses of human capital were not great during World War II, a conclusion which follows inevitably from the small casualty figures, representing just 0.75 per cent of the 1938 population. However, it seems likely that the human capital losses were of much greater significance for other countries which suffered much heavier casualties, especially Germany, Japan, and the USSR.

Turning to consider intangible non-human capital, it is possible to see government spending on R&D as a beneficial effect of the war. Although figures on government-financed R&D during the war are not available, we do have data for the immediate postwar period. Edgerton argues that government R&D expenditure probably did not fall after the war, so these postwar figures can be taken as representative of the wartime research effort.[107] If attention is restricted to civil R&D, then the effects are tiny. Figures in Cmnd 3007, a Report on Science Policy by the Council for Scientific Policy, give total government expenditure on civil research and development in 1945–6 as £6.58 million.[108] Using Feinstein's GDP deflator this becomes £4.35 million in 1938 prices.[109] Assuming six years of spending at this level gives a total boost of £26.1 million. Although this is a relatively large sum when set against the Federation of British Industries estimate of £5.4 million spending on R&D by private firms in 1938, it is a small sum when compared with the figures for capital losses in table 2.20.[110] It would require truly enormous spin-offs from defence R&D to alter this conclusion.

The catch-up perspective

It has been argued by Olson that there are benefits to defeat in war, since it results in the destruction of interest groups that act to block change.[111] However, recent work on catching-up by backward countries suggests that to a large extent this is a confusion between growth rate and levels effects.[112] Amongst the major industrialized countries, there is a negative correlation between initial level of productivity and subsequent productivity growth.[113] This means that a setback to the national balance sheet such as that caused by wartime destruction is likely to be followed by relatively rapid reconstruction growth as a devastated country reinvests. However, this does not mean that the devastated country has benefited from defeat. Rather, it has been necessary to devote extra resources simply to get back to previously attained levels of productivity. Recent work by Dumke suggests that the effects of the wartime fall in output continued to exert an influence on postwar growth in Europe and Japan into the 1960s.[114]

One interesting issue that arises from a comparison of the effects of World Wars I and II is the extent of postwar catching up, which was far more muted after 1918 than after 1945. Williamson argues that over the last century and a half convergence of living standards has occurred only during periods characterized by high levels of global factor and product market integration.[115] The widespread use of protection, capital controls and migration restrictions in the interwar period, then, can be seen as prolonging the detrimental effects of the wartime destruction. By the same token, the emergence of a liberal world order after 1945 can be seen as important in limiting the damage.

Government and endogenous growth

It is sometimes argued that the war led to a permanent increase in the role of government, and that this had detrimental effects on Britain's long-run economic performance.[116] Usually, the economic mechanisms providing a link to the growth rate are not set out clearly. However, a recent study by Cooley and Ohanian has clarified these links between the wartime extension of government and postwar growth in an endogenous-growth framework.[117] They note that, compared with earlier wars and policies used in the United States, Britain relied very heavily during World War II on the taxation of factor incomes. In an endogenous-growth model, this can be seen as having adverse consequences for growth by reducing incentives to accumulation. Simulations by the authors on a calibrated model suggest that these policies had substantial welfare costs, although it should be remembered that in such exercises the model is imposed rather than tested.

Conclusion

This chapter has reached a number of conclusions concerning the British economy during World War II.
1. The scale of mobilization for war is best measured by the proportion of GDP devoted to the war effort, which rose to a peak of 55.3 per cent in 1943.
2. The literature on mobilization for war in Britain is dominated by a government-oriented Keynesian perspective, with a strong emphasis on quantities and a belief in the superiority of controls over market forces. The time is now long overdue for a more sceptical interpretation of the powers of government and a more balanced treatment of the role of incentives.
3. The long-run impact of the war can be assessed through its impact on the national balance sheet. Using conventional balance sheet analysis, based on physical capital, war losses amounted to 18.6 per cent of prewar national wealth. Taking account of tangible and intangible human as

well as physical capital does not greatly affect this picture, largely because loss of life was relatively limited in the British case.

Notes

1 Hansard, 13 May 1940, col. 1502 reports Prime Minister Winston Churchill as saying: 'You ask, what is our aim? I can answer in one word: Victory, victory at all costs, victory in spite of terror, victory, however long and hard the road may be; for without victory, there is no survival.'
2 Following Harrison (1988).
3 Feinstein (1972).
4 Department of Employment (1971), table 43.
5 Harrison (1992).
6 Maddison (1991); Broadberry (1993).
7 Olson (1963); Offer (1989).
8 Feinstein (1972).
9 Higgs (1992); Mills and Rockoff (1987); Ahmed (1986).
10 Sayers (1956); Pollard (1983); Feinstein (1983).
11 Keynes (1939).
12 Booth (1989), 63.
13 Ibid., 67.
14 Peden (1985), 132–3; Sabine (1970), 171–2.
15 Meade, Stone (1941); Madge (1940a, 1940b, 1941); Booth (1989), 65.
16 Sayers (1956), 72.
17 Sabine (1970), 186.
18 Peden (1985), 133.
19 Sayers (1956), 90.
20 Sabine (1970), 186.
21 Sayers (1956), 159.
22 Ibid., 163–87.
23 Pollard (1983), 215.
24 Sayers (1956), 188–218.
25 Pollard (1983), 215.
26 Ibid., 216.
27 Sayers (1956), 223.
28 Feinstein (1972).
29 Capie and Wood (1993), 33.
30 Pollard (1983), 217.
31 Allen (1946), 524.
32 Pollard (1983), 217.
33 Churchill (1949), 503.
34 Pollard (1983), 221–2; Vatter (1985), 30–1.
35 Sayers (1956), 318.
36 But see Schenk (1994) for a sceptical view of the constraints imposed by the sterling balances during the postwar period.

37 Reddaway (1951), 182.
38 Mills and Rockoff (1987), 209.
39 Hancock, Gowing (1949), 175–6.
40 Ibid., 329–32; Reddaway (1951).
41 Mills and Rockoff (1987).
42 Hancock, Gowing (1949), 446.
43 Robinson (1951), 50.
44 Barnett (1986).
45 Ahmed (1986); Barro (1974, 1981).
46 Robinson (1992), 376.
47 Wiles (1952); Booth (1985).
48 Howlett (1994), 142–6.
49 Harrison (1990).
50 Ibid, 662–4.
51 Ibid., 664.
52 Howlett (1993); Postan (1952), 166–7, 208–11.
53 Inman (1957), 204.
54 Brown (1954).
55 Hargreaves and Gowing (1952), 477–9.
56 Ibid., 570; Howlett (1994), 143–5.
57 Shaw (1950).
58 Ibid., 23.
59 Lacey (1947); Hancock and Gowing (1949), 321–3.
60 Supple (1987), 500–10.
61 Department of Employment (1971), 396.
62 Supple (1987), 548.
63 Ibid., 539.
64 Court (1951), 25.
65 Hancock and Gowing (1949), 550.
66 Murray (1955), 242.
67 Central Statistical Office (1951), 167.
68 Murray (1955), 188–9.
69 Williams (1954), 335.
70 Central Statistical Office (1951), 158; Williams (1954), 336.
71 Murray (1955), 274.
72 Ibid., 243; Clark et al. (1954), 349.
73 Williams (1954); Murray (1955), 243, 273.
74 Murray (1955), 241–2.
75 Evely and Little (1960); Howlett (1995), 249–51.
76 Edgerton (1984); Howlett (1995), 237–47.
77 Jeremy (1991), 94.
78 Broadberry and Crafts (1992), 554; Dunkerley and Hare (1991), 404–9, 415.
79 Howlett (1995), 251–3.
80 Howlett (1994), 23.
81 Matthews *et al.* (1982).

82 Ibid., 235.
83 Hutton (1953).
84 Broadberry and Wagner (1996).
85 Goldsmith *et al.* (1963); Revell (1967).
86 Romer (1986, 1990).
87 Kendrick (1976).
88 Milward (1984), 14.
89 Bowley (1930).
90 Titmuss (1950).
91 Bogart (1920).
92 Harrison (1988).
93 Ibid., table 3.
94 Cmd. 6707 (1945), 13.
95 Feinstein (1972), table 61.
96 Dean (1964).
97 Feinstein (1972), table 46.
98 Ibid., table 50.
99 Rowntree (1941), 102.
100 Feinstein (1972), table 61.
101 Vaizey and Sheehan (1968), 153–4; Mitchell (1988), 800–5.
102 Adult population from Mitchell (1988), 15–17.
103 Kendrick (1976).
104 Titmuss (1950); Peacock and Wiseman (1967), 92.
105 Lindert (1994).
106 Hancock and Gowing (1949), 549.
107 Edgerton (1992), 103.
108 Council for Scientific Policy (1966).
109 Feinstein (1972), table 61.
110 Federation of British Industries (1943).
111 Olson (1982).
112 Abramovitz (1986).
113 Baumol (1986); Maddison (1991). On so-called β-convergence see chapter 1 above.
114 Dumke (1990).
115 Williamson (1995).
116 Barnett (1986); Gamble (1985); Middlemas (1986).
117 Cooley and Ohanian (1995).

References

Command papers and official reports

Cmd 6707, Chancellor of the Exchequer (1945), *Statistical material presented during the Washington Negotiations*, London.
Cmnd 3007, Council for Scientific Policy (1966), *Report on science policy*, London.
Combined Committee on Non-Food Consumption (1945), *The impact of the war*

on civilian consumption in the United Kingdom, the United States and Canada, London.
Hansard.

Books, articles and discussion papers

Abramovitz, M. (1986), 'Catching up, forging ahead and falling behind', *Journal of Economic History*, vol. 46, 385–406.

Ahmed, S. (1986), 'Temporary and permanent government spending in an open economy: some evidence for the United Kingdom', *Journal of Monetary Economics*, vol. 17, 197–224.

Allen, G. C. (1946), 'Mutual aid between the US and the British Empire, 1941–45', *Journal of the Royal Statistical Society*, reprinted as Appendix III of Sayers, R. S. (1956), *Financial policy, 1939–45*, London, 518–56.

Barnett, C. (1986), *The audit of war: the illusion and reality of Britain as a great nation*, London.

Barro, R. J. (1974), 'Are government bonds net wealth?', *Journal of Political Economy*, vol. 82, 1095–117.

(1981), 'Output effects of government purchases', *Journal of Political Economy*, vol. 89, 1086–121.

Baumol, W. J. (1986), 'Productivity growth, convergence and welfare: what the long run data show', *American Economic Review*, vol. 76, 1072–85.

Bogart, E. L. (1920), *Direct and indirect costs of the great World War* (2nd edn.), New York.

Booth, A. (1985), 'Economists and points rationing in the Second World War', *Journal of European Economic History*, vol. 14, 297–317.

(1989), *British economic policy, 1931–49: was there a Keynesian revolution?*, Brighton.

Bowley, A. L. (1930), *Some economic consequences of the Great War*, London.

British Iron and Steel Federation (1948), *Statistical Year Book for 1946*, Part 2: *Overseas Countries*, London.

Broadberry, S. N. (1988), 'The impact of the World Wars on the long run performance of the British economy', *Oxford Review of Economic Policy*, vol. 4(1), 25–37.

(1993), 'Manufacturing and the convergence hypothesis: what the long-run data show', *Journal of Economic History*, vol. 53, 772–95.

(1994), 'Local convergence of European economies during the twentieth century' (unpublished, University of Warwick).

Broadberry, S. N., and Crafts, N. F. R. (1992), 'Britain's productivity gap in the 1930s: some neglected factors', *Journal of Economic History*, vol. 52, 531–58.

Broadberry, S. N., and Wagner, K. (1996), 'Human capital and productivity in manufacturing during the twentieth century: Britain, Germany and the United States', in van Ark, B., and Crafts, N. F. R., eds., *Quantitative aspects of postwar European growth*, Cambridge.

Brown, B. C. (1954), 'Industrial production in 1935 and 1948', *London and Cambridge Economic Bulletin*, December, v–vii.

Capie, F., and Webber, A. (1985), *A monetary history of the United Kingdom, 1870–1982*, vol. I: *Data, sources and methods*, London.

Capie, F., and Wood, G. (1993), 'The anatomy of a wartime inflation: Britain 1939–1945', in Mills, G. T., and Rockoff, H., eds., *The sinews of war: essays on the economic history of World War II*, Ames, IA, 21–42.

Central Statistical Office (1951), *Statistical digest of the war*, London.

Churchill, W. S. (1949), *The Second World War*, vol. II: *Their finest hour*, London: Cassell.

Clark, C., et al. (1954), 'Discussion of Williams', *Journal of the Proceedings of the Agricultural Economics Society*, vol. 10, 347–55.

Cooley, T. F., and Ohanian, L. E. (1995), 'Post-war British economic growth and the legacy of Keynes' (unpublished, University of Rochester and University of Pennsylvania).

Court, W. H. B. (1951), *Coal*, London.

Dean, G. A. (1964), 'The stock of fixed capital in the United Kingdom in 1961', *Journal of the Royal Statistical Society*, ser. A, vol. 127, 327–351.

Department of Employment (1971), *British labour statistics: historical abstract, 1886–1968*, London.

Dumke, R. (1990), 'Reassessing the Wirtschaftswunder: reconstruction and postwar growth in West Germany in an international context', *Oxford Bulletin of Economics and Statistics*, vol. 52, 451–91.

Dunkerley, J., and Hare, P. G. (1991), 'Nationalized industries', in Crafts, N. F. R., and Woodward, N. W. C., eds., *The British economy since 1945*, Oxford.

Edgerton, D. (1984), 'Technical innovation, industrial capacity and efficiency: public ownership and the British military aircraft industry, 1935–1948', *Business History*, vol. 26, 247–97.

(1992), 'Whatever happened to the British warfare state? The Ministry of Supply, 1945–51', in Mercer, H., Rollings, N., and Tomlinson, J. D., eds., *Labour governments and private industry: the experience of 1945–51*, Edinburgh, 91–116.

Evely, R., and Little, I. M. D. (1960), *Concentration in British industry*, Cambridge.

Federation of British Industries (1943), *Industry and research*, London.

Feinstein, C. H. (1972), *National income, expenditure and output of the United Kingdom, 1855–1965*, Cambridge.

Feinstein, C. H., ed. (1983), *The managed economy: essays in British economic policy and performance since 1929*, Oxford.

Gamble, A. (1985), *Britain in decline: economic policy, political strategy and the British state* (2nd edn), London.

Goldsmith, R. W., Lipsey, R. E., and Mendelson, M. (1963), *Studies in the national balance sheet of the United States* (2 vols.), Princeton, NJ.

Hancock, W. K., and Gowing, M. M. (1949), *British war economy*, London.

Hargreaves, E. L., and Gowing, M. M. (1952), *Civil industry and trade*, London.

Harrison, M. (1988), 'Resource mobilization for World War II: the USA, UK,

USSR and Germany, 1938–1945', *Economic History Review*, vol. 41, 171–92.

(1990), 'A volume index of the total munitions output of the United Kingdom, 1939–1944', *Economic History Review*, vol. 43, 657–66.

(1992), 'Russian and Soviet GDP on the eve of two World Wars: 1913 and 1940', (University of Birmingham, Centre for Russian and East European Studies, Soviet Industrialisation Project Series no. 33).

Higgs, R. (1992), 'Wartime prosperity? A reassessment of the US economy in the 1940s', *Journal of Economic History*, vol. 52, 41–60.

Howlett, P. (1993), 'New light through old windows: a new perspective on the British war economy in the Second World War', *Journal of Contemporary History*, vol. 28, 361–79.

(1994), 'British business and the state during the Second World War', in Sakudo, J., and Shiba, T., eds., *World War II and the transformation of business systems*, Tokyo, 133–53.

(1995), "The thin end of the wedge'? Nationalization and industrial structure in the war', in Millward, R., and Singleton, J., eds., *The political economy of nationalization, 1920–1950*, Cambridge, 237–56.

Hutton, G. (1953), *We too can prosper*, London.

Inman, P. (1957), *Labour in the munitions industries*, London.

Jeremy, D. J. (1991), 'The hundred largest employers in the United Kingdom, in manufacturing and non-manufacturing industries, in 1907, 1935 and 1955', *Business History*, vol. 33, 93–111.

Kendrick, J. W. (1976), *The formation and stocks of total capital*, New York.

Keynes, J. M. (1939), 'How to pay for the war', *The Times*, reprinted in D. Moggridge, ed., *The collected writings of John Maynard Keynes*, vol. XXII: *Activities 1939–1945, internal war finance*, London, 41–51.

Kohan, C. M. (1952), *Works and buildings*, London.

Lacey, R. W. (1947), 'Cotton's war effort', *Manchester School*, vol. 15, 26–74.

Lindert, P. H. (1994), 'The rise of social spending, 1880–1930', *Explorations in Economic History*, vol. 31, 1–37.

Maddison, A. (1991), *Dynamic forces in capitalist development*, Oxford.

Madge, C. (1940a), 'Wartime saving and spending: a district survey', *Economic Journal*, 50, 327–39.

(1940b), 'The propensity to save in Blackburn and Bristol', *Economic Journal*, vol. 50, 410–48.

(1941), 'Public opinion and paying for the war', *Economic Journal*, vol. 51, 26–46.

Matthews, R. C. O., Feinstein, C. H., and Odling-Smee, J. C. (1982), *British Economic growth, 1856–1973*, Oxford.

Meade, J. E., Stone, R. (1941), 'The construction of tables of national income, expenditure, savings and investment', *Economic Journal*, vol. 51, 216–33.

Middlemas, K. (1986), *Power, competition and the state*, vol. I: *Britain in search of balance, 1940–61*, London.

Mills, G. T., and Rockoff, H. (1987), 'Compliance with price controls in the United

States and the United Kingdom during World War II', *Journal of Economic History*, vol. 47, 197–213.

Milward, A. S. (1977), *War, economy and society, 1939–1945*, London.

(1984), *The economic effects of the two World Wars on Britain* (2nd edn), London.

Mitchell, B. R. (1988), *British historical statistics*, Cambridge.

Murray, K. A. H. (1955), *Agriculture*, London.

Offer, A. (1989), *The First World War: an agrarian interpretation*, Oxford.

Olson, M. (1963), *The economics of the wartime shortage: a history of British food supplies in the Napoleonic wars and in World Wars I and II*, Durham, NC.

(1982), *The rise and decline of nations*, New Haven, CT.

Peacock, A. T., and Wiseman, J. (1967), *The growth of public expenditure in the United Kingdom*, 2nd edn, London.

Peden, G.C. (1985), *British economic and social policy: Lloyd George to Margaret Thatcher*, Dedington.

Pollard, S. (1983), *The development of the British economy, 1914–1980* (3rd edn), London.

Postan, M. M. (1952), *British war production*, London.

Reddaway, W. B. (1951), 'Rationing', in Chester, D. N., ed., *Lessons of the British war economy*, Cambridge, 182–99.

Revell, J. (1967), *The wealth of the nation: the national balance sheet of the United Kingdom, 1957–1961*, Cambridge.

Robinson, E. A. G. (1951), 'The overall allocation of resources', in Chester, D.N., ed., *Lessons of the British war economy*, Cambridge, 34–57.

(1992), 'Munitions output of the United Kingdom, 1939–1944: a comment', *Economic History Review*, vol. 54, 376–7.

Romer, P. M. (1986), 'Increasing returns and long run growth', *Journal of Political Economy*, vol. 94, 1002–37.

(1990), 'Endogenous technological change', *Journal of Political Economy*, S71–S102.

Rowntree, B. S. (1941), *Poverty and progress: a second social survey of York*, London.

Sabine, B. E. V. (1970), *British budgets in peace and war, 1932–1945*, London.

Sayers, R. S. (1956), *Financial policy, 1939–45*, London.

Schenk, C. R. (1994), *Britain and the Sterling Area: from devaluation to convertibility in the 1950s*, London.

Shaw, D. C. (1950), 'Productivity in the cotton spinning industry', *Manchester School*, vol. 18, 14–30.

Supple, B. E. (1987), *The history of the British coal industry*, vol. IV, *1913–1946: The political economy of decline*, Oxford.

Titmuss, R. M. (1950), *Problems of social policy*, London.

Vaizey, J., and Sheehan, J. (1968), *Resources for education: an economic study of education in the United Kingdom, 1920–1965*, London.

Vatter, H. G. (1985), *The US economy in World War II*, New York.

Wiles, P. J. D. (1952), 'Pre-war and war-time controls', in Worswick, G. D. N., and Ady, P. H., eds., *The British economy 1945–50*, Oxford, 125–58.

Williams, H. T. (1954), 'Changes in the productivity of labour in British agriculture', *Journal of the Proceedings of the Agricultural Economics Society*, vol. 10, 332–47.

Williamson, J. G. (1991), 'The evolution of global labor markets since 1830: background evidence and hypotheses', *Explorations in Economic History*, vol. 32, 141–96.

3 The United States: from ploughshares to swords

Hugh Rockoff

Introduction

Between 1939 when World War II began and 1944 when US output reached its wartime peak, the US economy grew at a remarkable rate. Contemporaries described it as a 'production miracle'. In many ways it was the obverse of the Great Depression. Between 1929 and 1933 real GNP collapsed, shaking the faith of Americans in their economic system; between 1939 and 1944 real GNP rose by an even larger percentage restoring the faith of Americans in their economic system – provided it was given a strong dose of centralized control. The Great Depression was without doubt the most important macroeconomic event of the twentieth century; the mobilization of the American economy in World War II is a close second. Yet the economic history of the Great Depression has been studied in great depth, while World War II remains comparatively unknown.

This chapter is concerned mainly with three questions about the war economy. First, where did the United States find the resources it needed? Second, how was this effort financed? Third, what were the long-run economic consequences? The chapter argues that the answers traditionally given to these questions need to be modified. To take the first question for example, there is a tendency when explaining the growth of real output to focus on a single factor, usually the high level of unemployment prevailing before the war, or the entry of more women into the labour force. As we will see, however, no single factor can explain the expansion of real output during the war.

Modifications of the traditional picture are needed in part because we tend to think of the war as a single, undifferentiated event rather than as an unfolding historical process. The emphasis on the role of unemployment, to return to the first question, flows from our tendency to forget the substantial changes that took place in the economy between the outbreak of the war in Europe and Pearl Harbor. In December 1941, when all out mobilization began, unemployment had already fallen to about 6 per cent of the labour force – other ways had to be found to increase production.

In the section on finance I argue that our tendency to think of the war as a unified period has led us to neglect the role of monetary expansion. And in the section on long-run consequences I argue that attempts to link postwar prosperity in the United States to changes on the real side – to the new initiatives in education, to the capital constructed during the war, or to the favourable position in world trade in which the US found itself – are likely to prove disappointing. Instead, the key factor appears to have been the new macroeconomic régime.

The chapter also provides a discussion of the meaning and limitations of the basic time series, to facilitate comparisons between the United States and other countries.

The production miracle

Guns and butter

In this section I discuss the composition of output in the war economy. There are, of course, numerous measurement problems also discussed below, but the transformation of the economy was so dramatic that measurement problems cannot obscure the broad outlines of what happened.

One measurement problem which does not arise from the data themselves is how to measure growth. Percentage changes in this chapter are measured as the natural logarithm of a variable at the end of a period less the natural logarithm at the beginning, multiplied by 100. A 50 per cent increase measured by differences in natural logarithms corresponds roughly to a 65 per cent increase measured as the absolute difference divided by the initial value. One advantage of using natural logarithms is that when a variable rises to a peak and then returns to its initial position, the percentages are the same in absolute value going up and going down.

The division of real GNP (at 1958 prices) into civilian output and military output is shown in table 3.1. The basic story is clear. Real GNP rose sharply, about 55 per cent, between 1939 and the peak in 1944 (for the United States during these years the difference between GNP and GDP was, for our purposes, negligible). The share of military spending in GNP rose from 1.4 per cent in 1939 to 45 per cent in 1944 (at 1958 prices; the figure was 42 per cent at current prices). The United States squeezed the civilian sector in 1942 (severe limits on consumer durable production were

Table 3.1. *United States GNP and military outlays, 1938–1948 ($ billion and per cent of GNP)*

	At current prices			At 1958 prices		
	nominal GNP	nominal military outlays	per cent of GNP	real GNP	real military outlays	per cent of GNP
	1	2	3	4	5	6
1938	84.7	1.0	1.2	192.9	2.5	1.3
1939	90.5	1.2	1.3	209.4	2.9	1.4
1940	99.7	2.2	2.2	227.2	5.5	2.4
1941	124.5	13.8	11.1	263.7	29.6	11.2
1942	157.9	49.4	31.3	297.8	94.1	31.6
1943	191.6	79.7	41.6	337.1	145.2	43.1
1944	210.1	87.4	41.6	361.3	162.4	45.0
1945	211.9	73.5	34.7	355.2	138.4	39.0
1946	208.5	14.7	7.1	312.6	25.7	8.2
1947	231.3	9.1	3.9	309.9	13.9	4.5
1948	257.1	10.7	4.2	323.7	15.4	4.7

Sources:
1. Bureau of the Census (1975), series F1.
2. Bureau of the Census (1975), series F68.
3. Col. 2, divided by col. 1.
4. Bureau of the Census (1975), series F3.
5. Bureau of the Census (1975), series F67 (adjusted by the ratio of nominal military expenditures to nominal government purchases).
6. Col. 5 divided by col. 4.

the most important) and then put the civilian sector 'on hold' for the remainder of the war, turning the increase in GNP over to the military.

As a result real civilian GNP in 1944 was only a bit below the level achieved in 1939. Most of the increase in war production came from the increase in output. Below I will examine how this result was achieved. First, however, I need to consider the conceptual problems that underlie wartime estimates of real GNP and related variables.

Measurement problems

The difficulties inherent in measuring national income were magnified by the war. They can be considered under three headings: first, the decision whether or not to include war output in GNP; second, errors in the measurement of prices and quantities in the war sector; and third, errors in the measurement of prices and quantities in the civilian sector.

The inclusion of war output in GNP

Recently, Robert Higgs argued that most war output, perhaps all, should be excluded from GNP because war output does not contribute directly to the current or future flow of goods and services that create utility. War output should be treated, in his view, as an intermediate product. Thus, his estimate of real GNP declines between 1941 and 1944.[1]

Earlier, Simon Kuznets, the father of national income accounting in the United States, had considered the same question, reaching a somewhat different conclusion. Kuznets argued that in peacetime only the formation of durable war goods should be included in GNP; the rest should be excluded on grounds similar to those invoked by Higgs.[2] Kuznets, however, concluded that in a major war there were really two final purposes of economic activity, production of goods for the civilian sector and production of goods for the military sector, and that both should be included in aggregate output.

The point is debatable. Many expenditures ordinarily included in GNP would have to be excluded if the Higgs or Kuznets criterion was applied consistently. Medical care, for example, would have to be excluded because it does not contribute directly to current or future flows of goods and services that create utility. Or perhaps, following Kuznets, one would exclude ordinary check-ups from GNP (peacetime expenditures), and include radiation therapy for cancer (wartime – two final purposes!). Indeed, the frequency with which the discussion of illness is carried out with military metaphors reveals an underlying psychological analogy. Cancer 'invades the body', the Nixon Administration launches a 'War on Cancer', and Paul Ehrlich discovers a treatment for syphilis, a 'magic bullet'.[3] Munitions production, in other words – like medical expenditures or like expenditures for police and fire protection – is important because it protects future flows of consumption.

I do not raise this point to argue that munitions production must always be included. Different measures of aggregate production are useful for different purposes. The Higgs measure is useful for making the point that Americans were better off once the war was over and production could be redirected toward civilian goods, whether for aggregate consumption (in Higgs's account) or for the sum of aggregate consumption and net investment. But for other purposes, such as determining the pace of the mobilization, or comparing the performance of the United States with that of other belligerents, both central concerns of our present volume, an output measure that includes munitions is the only one that makes sense.

But it is also important to keep in mind that there is a variety of aggregate measures; it is not necessary to use GNP to answer every question. If one is concerned with how civilians fared during the war, an index of consumption is best; to measure the speed of mobilization, an index of war output is best.

Prices and quantities in the war sector[4]

The prices for tanks or planes specified in government contracts represented only a small part of the funds flowing from the government to munitions makers: a wide array of subsidies was also used to stimulate production. Thus deflating total spending on war goods by a price index based on contract prices probably overestimates the increase in war output. Kuznets made an attempt to solve this problem in his *National product in wartime*. He began by noting that resources provide a common denominator between the civilian and military sectors. Guns and butter both require labour to produce them. War output can be estimated in terms of prewar resource costs if spending on war goods is deflated by an index of resource costs.

But how does one go from resource costs to war output at final product prices? Kuznets then estimated efficiency in the war sector relative to efficiency in the non-war sector, basing his estimates on scattered bits of qualitative and quantitative data. He concluded that the level of efficiency in the war industries during the war was substantially below that of similar (i.e. metal fabricating) civilian industries in 1939 because the civilian industries had matured slowly under peacetime conditions. Despite significant increases in efficiency between 1939 and 1943, the war industries, in Kuznets's view, still suffered from labour and raw material hoarding, and other wasteful practices. By deflating war output at resource cost by his efficiency index, Kuznets produced estimates of war output at final product prices that showed substantially less expansion of war output than the figures published by the Commerce Department.

Subsequently, Milton Friedman and Anna J. Schwartz developed an alternative approach: they used current nominal income to interpolate the NNP deflator during the war because changes in current income were probably less vulnerable to measurement error. Table 3.2 shows their estimates, together with an alternative developed by Geofrey Mills and myself which tries to improve on the Friedman and Schwartz estimates by using wages paid as an additional interpolator, and several related series.[5] Evidently, measurement errors in the price indexes make it impossible to make precise statements about the size of the expansion. Nevertheless, even allowing for substantial errors in the deflators leaves us with a remarkable increase in output.

Rapid technological progress in arms production, changes in the scale of munitions production, and possibly changes in the institutional structure of munitions production, moreover, make comparison of arms prices at

Table 3.2. *United States price trends, 1939–1948 (per cent of 1938)*

	GNP deflator		NNP deflator				Wholesale prices	
			adjusted by Friedman and Schwartz (1929)	adjusted by Mills and Rockoff (1929)	unadjusted (1929)	Consumer prices (1982–4)	industrial commodities (1967)	all commodities (1967)
	(1958)	(1987)						
	1	2	3	4	5	6	7	8
1939	98.4	99.1	99.3	99.3	99.3	98.6	99.8	98.3
1940	100.0	100.9	100.4	100.4	100.4	99.3	101.4	100.0
1941	107.5	107.3	108.3	108.3	108.3	104.3	109.0	111.4
1942	120.7	112.8	122.5	122.5	122.5	115.6	116.8	125.7
1943	129.4	114.7	138.6	136.6	133.5	122.7	118.7	131.6
1944	132.6	115.6	148.9	144.5	137.5	124.8	120.5	132.3
1945	136.0	122.0	155.5	148.6	141.6	127.7	122.1	134.8
1946	151.9	153.2	156.8	154.1	151.6	138.3	133.6	153.8
1947	169.9	171.6	169.5	169.5	169.5	158.2	163.1	188.9
1948	181.3	183.5	180.6	180.6	180.6	170.9	177.2	204.4

Note:
Original base period in parentheses.

Sources:
1. US Bureau of the Census (1975), series F5.
2. US Department of Commerce, Bureau of Economic Analysis (1993), table 7.13.
3. Friedman and Schwartz (1982), table 4.8, col. 3.
4. Mills and Rockoff (1987), 203.
5. Friedman and Schwartz (1982), table 4.2, col. 10.
6. US Department of Labor, Bureau of Labor Statistics (1989), table 113.
7. US Bureau of the Census (1975), series E24.
8. US Bureau of the Census (1975), series E23.

distant points in time problematic. In the postwar years munitions prices have risen relative to prices in other sectors. This means that the bulge in wartime production looks larger, the later the date we use for measuring relative prices. Measured at 1958 prices (table 3.1), the increase was 55 per cent, but 69 per cent when measured at 1987 prices (the most recent estimates considered here). The solution I adopt is to use, when possible, a base year relatively close to the war, so that we see the war from the perspective of the generation that experienced it.

Prices and quantities in the civilian sector
Price controls and rationing produced the usual problems in the civilian sector. Quality deteriorated – cheap fillers were added to candy bars, clothing was made from coarser weaves, maintenance expenditures on rental properties were reduced, and so on. So called 'forced uptrading', the elimination of lower priced lines of merchandise, was a major problem. And classic black markets developed: one could buy off-ration meat, gasoline, or tyres for the right price if one knew the right people.

The Bureau of Labor Statistics tried valiantly to cope with these problems. When a lower-priced line disappeared, for example, the Bureau counted part of the difference between the lower-priced and the higher-priced lines as a price increase. But inevitably, adjustments were incomplete. Rationing created a related problem. A consumer prevented from buying good X because of some form of rationing was in much the same position as a consumer prevented from buying X by an increase in price. But the price index was not adjusted upward to reflect the scope of rationing and hence deflated spending did not reveal this loss in consumer welfare.

Not all of the measurement problems worked in the direction of over-stating the size of the civilian sector. There was a sizable black market, especially in the last years of the war, and production in the black market was not reflected fully in the statistics on aggregate spending.

In short, the penumbra of uncertainty that always surrounds economic measurements expanded during the war. But for what it is worth, my judgement is that the aggregate statistics are nonetheless useful for painting a broad-brush picture of the mobilization.

The composition of output

Let us take a closer look at what happened in the civilian sector by making use of the traditional decomposition of GNP into consumption, investment, net private exports, and government spending (table 3.3).

Government spending increased rapidly in 1942 and 1943 and peaked in 1944. Most of this increase, as noted above, came out of the increase in total

Table 3.3. *United States GNP by final use, 1938–1948 ($ billion and 1958 prices)*

	Personal consumption 1	Gross private domestic investment 2	Government purchases of goods and services 3	Net exports of goods and services 4	GNP 5
1938	140.2	17.0	33.9	1.9	192.9
1939	148.2	24.7	35.2	1.3	209.4
1940	155.7	33.0	36.4	2.1	227.2
1941	165.4	41.6	56.3	0.4	263.7
1942	161.4	21.4	117.1	−2.1	297.8
1943	165.8	12.7	164.4	−5.9	337.1
1944	171.4	14.0	181.7	−5.8	361.3
1945	183.0	19.6	156.4	−3.8	355.2
1946	203.5	52.3	48.4	8.4	312.6
1947	206.3	51.5	39.9	12.3	309.9
1948	210.8	60.4	46.3	6.1	323.7

Note:
Outlays on lend-lease are counted under government purchases, not net exports.
Source: US Bureau of the Census (1975).

GNP. At the same time, private investment was squeezed quite a lot. Private consumption was squeezed a bit in 1942, and then rose a bit in 1943 and 1944. The decline in consumption would probably be greater if we adjusted for the problems in the deflator and total spending. But my guess is that the general impression created by the table would not be changed: the United States put consumption 'on hold' during the war while generating the means to defeat the Axis by squeezing private investment and expanding total output.

To some extent the long-term effects of the squeeze on private investment were offset by government spending on industrial plant and equipment (aluminium and synthetic rubber factories, for example) sold to the private sector after the war. *Private* net exports were also squeezed, actually turning negative during the war (see below for a discussion of exports that includes lend-lease and other government transfers).

Government outlays on goods and services, the total shown in table 3.3, are not precisely the same as military spending, but in fact come close. Table 3.4 shows three measures of war spending, each as percentages of GNP (all figures in current dollars). The lowest estimate (col. 1) is simply the sum of army (which included the air force) and navy spending as shown in the

Table 3.4. *United States government outlays on war, 1938–1947: alternative measures (per cent of GNP at current prices)*

	Outlays on the army and navy 1	Government purchases of goods above the 1938 level of government non-defence outlays 2	Outlays on 'National Security' 3
1938	1.54	1.46	1.57
1939	1.75	1.70	1.39
1940	4.04	2.25	2.23
1941	11.71	10.47	11.08
1942	27.33	30.30	31.39
1943	36.38	40.10	41.95
1944	37.25	40.33	42.18
1945	29.19	33.29	35.83
1946	13.89	7.31	10.16
1947	5.78	5.77	5.77

Note:
The budget figures (cols. 1, 3) are for a fiscal year that ends on 30 June. To make them comparable to calendar year figures, I averaged the estimate for one fiscal year estimate with the estimate for the succeeding fiscal year.
Sources:
1. US Bureau of the Census (1975), series Y458, Y459.
2. US Bureau of the Census (1975), series F66, adjusted to calendar year basis.
3. Kendrick (1961), 291–2.

Federal Budget. The middle estimate (col. 2) is government purchases of goods and services less civilian purchases in 1938 (total government less army and navy). The highest (col. 3) is the Commerce Department's estimates of 'National Security' expenditures. In the peak year, 1944, army and navy spending was 37 per cent of GNP, government purchases of goods and services above the level of civilian purchases in 1938 were 40 per cent of GNP, and the official Commerce Department estimate of national security spending was 42 per cent of GNP. Even the Commerce Department estimate can be considered only a first approximation: many government expenditures (investments in new plant and equipment, for example) served civilian as well as military purposes; and many civilian expenditures (for example, the costs incurred in moving to war production centres) served military as well as civilian purposes. Nevertheless, the Commerce Department estimate of a maximum 'effort' of 42 per cent seems reasonable.

Table 3.5. *Commerce Department estimates of United States personal consumption expenditures, 1939–1948*

	Total personal consumption ($ billion and current prices)		real consumption per head		real consumption per resident
	$ and 1939 prices				
	(1970)	(1987)	(1970)	(1987)	(1987)
	1	2	3	4	5
1939	66.8	67.2	510	511.3	512.7
1940	70.8	71.2	531	530.8	532.7
1941	80.6	81.0	559	556.0	563.7
1942	88.5	88.9	539	549.0	565.4
1943	99.3	99.7	547	558.2	598.7
1944	108.3	108.5	558	567.4	624.2
1945	119.7	119.9	589	601.9	660.2
1946	143.4	144.3	649	649.3	663.4
1947	160.7	162.3	645	648.8	655.9
1948	173.6	175.4	648	653.3	659.9

Note:
Year of estimate in parentheses.
Sources:
1. US Bureau of the Census (1975), series F48.
2. US Department of Commerce, Bureau of Economic Analysis (1993), table 1.1.
3. Col. 1 deflated by total population (US Bureau of the Census (1975), series A6) and prices (derived from the lower half of F48).
4. Col. 2 deflated by total population (US Bureau of the Census (1975), series A6) and prices (US Department of Commerce, Bureau of Economic Analysis (1993), tables 1.1 and 1.2).
5. As col. 4, but deflated by resident civilian population (US Bureau of the Census (1975), series A8).

The level of consumption

Many historians have maintained that real consumption was high during the war – 'Americans never had it so good'; Americans on the home front engaged in a 'carnival of consumption'.[6] But scepticism is justified, as Higgs has recently stressed, because of measurement errors in the price indices, and changes in the composition of civilian consumption induced by wartime constraints. The standard estimates of consumption produced by the Commerce Department go some way toward justifying the 'never-had-it-so-good' view (table 3.5). Real consumption per head rises sharply in 1940 and 1941, drops slightly in 1942, but then rises in 1943 and 1944, so

Table 3.6. *United States real personal consumption: estimates based on alternative deflators, 1939–1948 ($ and 1939 prices)*

	Commerce Department 1	Friedman, Schwartz 2	Mills, Rockoff 3	Rockoff 4	Vatter 5
1939	511	511	511	511	511
1940	530	531	531	530	533
1941	555	555	555	555	560
1942	546	533	533	546	549
1943	551	521	529	538	548
1944	561	521	537	536	530
1945	591	546	571	550	522
1946	646	644	656	602	560
1947	645	658	658	645	—
1948	648	655	655	648	—

Sources and methods:
1. As table 3.5 (col. 4).
The other columns were derived by replacing the Commerce Department's deflator for personal consumption expenditures with another as follows:
2. Friedman and Schwartz (1982), table 4.8 (col. 4).
2. Mills and Rockoff (1987), 203.
3. Rockoff (1978), 417.
4. Vatter (1993), 222.

that the level in 1944 is an all-time high. If one divides total consumption by the resident civilian population, rather than total population, the results are even more dramatic: the decline in 1942 disappears, and average consumption in 1943 is already well above past achievements.

A number of years ago I constructed a consumer price index that incorporated adjustments for rationing, the decline in the maintenance of rental property, and similar problems. And Harold Vatter constructed an upper-bound estimate of the consumer price index by assuming that the price level reached in 1947 (after controls were removed) had effectively been reached by 1945 although the inflation was hidden by controls.[7] Table 3.6 shows real consumption per head calculated using these deflators, and perhaps somewhat inappropriately in this case, the alternative NNP deflators discussed above. It now appears that consumption per head may have been depressed in the years of total war (1942–44) compared with the years of neutrality (1939–41).

Higgs's emphasis on the fall in real consumption per head from the level reached in 1941 thus partly justifies his challenge to the claim that Americans 'never had it so good'. But while Higgs's basis of comparison,

1941 or 1946, makes sense to us now, these are probably not the years that most Americans, or most historians, had in mind when they dwelt on how good Americans had it during the war. The war years look pretty good compared with the Great Depression. Note that in table 3.6 none of the estimates of real per capita consumption fall below the level of 1939. Real consumption per head in 1939, moreover, was the highest of the decade, exceeding the level even of the boom year 1929. Legally and militarily 1941 was the last year of peace for the United States, so it is technically correct to compare consumption during the war with 1941 levels. But it probably comes closer to what people were actually talking about, when they said 'we never had it so good', if we compare 1941 and the years that followed with the Depression.

It is also likely that when historians write about the prosperity of the war years they are focussing to some extent on the lower part of the distribution of income. Poor people from the south and from pockets of rural poverty in the midwest, 'hoosiers', were drawn to war production centres in the midwest, the south, and the Pacific coast by high real wages. It is true that these workers often had to endure crowded living conditions and to work long hours at a pace to which they were not accustomed, so that the improvement in their economic welfare was not as great as the increase in their measured consumption. But such costs must have been offset at least in part by the hope that these conditions were temporary, and that at long last they had escaped from a life of grinding rural poverty.

Additional insight can be gained by looking at the major components of consumption. Production of new consumer durables, particularly those containing metal, was curtailed drastically during the war; automobile production, for example, was halted. The impact on consumers, however, was cushioned by running down firms' inventories and by postponing normal replacements until after the war. Construction of new housing, and repair and maintenance expenditures on existing housing, declined during the war, but again the effect on consumers was cushioned to some extent because current consumption could be maintained while repair and maintenance could be postponed until after the war. The expansion of the armed forces also reduced pressures on the civilian housing stock: the number of civilians per occupied dwelling declined from 3.63 in 1940 to 3.30 in 1944.[8]

Housing shortages were severe, however, in war production centres such as the aircraft and shipbuilding centres on the Pacific Coast. It would have been difficult in any case for new construction in those areas to keep pace with the influx of workers seeking jobs in defence plants. But uncertainties about postwar viability of defence plants, rent controls, and shortages of construction materials hampered construction.

Civilian food consumption (table 3.7) held up well. Total civilian

Table 3.7. *United States civilian food consumption, 1938–1948*

	Calories per day) 1	Protein (grams per day) 2	Vitamin C (mg per day) 3	Meat (lb per year) 4	Edible fat (lb per year) 5
1938	3,260	90	114	127.1	45.3
1939	3,340	92	116	133.6	46.4
1940	3,350	93	115	142.2	46.4
1941	3,410	94	115	143.7	47.6
1942	3,320	97	117	140.3	44.9
1943	3,360	100	115	146.8	41.5
1944	3,350	99	125	154.2	40.9
1945	3,300	102	125	145.2	39.1
1946	3,320	102	123	154.1	40.0
1947	3,290	97	119	155.3	42.0
1948	3,200	94	112	145.5	42.6

Sources:
1. US Bureau of the Census (1975), series G851.
2. Ibid., series G856.
3. Ibid., series G855.
4. Ibid., series G881.
5. Ibid., series G886.

consumption of calories fell slightly from the high level recorded for 1941, but the average during the war (when many heavy consumers of calories were in the armed forces) was comparable to the late Depression and early prewar years. Protein consumption, with an abundance of meat, fowls, and eggs, reached an all time high.

Table 3.7 (col. 3) shows consumption of vitamin C which rose to a new high, partly as a result of a government supplementation programme. Col. 4 shows annual meat (beef, pork, and lamb) consumption. Today, reaching a higher level of meat consumption would be considered a sign of moral and intellectual bankruptcy; but at the time it was considered a sign of prosperity. Col. 4, moreover, is a good example of a category probably understated because of the black market. Towards the end of the war beef sometimes moved from ranches to black market slaughterhouses to restaurants or households, completely bypassing legal channels. It is doubtful that these supplies were counted by the Department of Agriculture. Wartime meat shortages, clearly, were the result of large increases in demand combined with price controls, rather than decreases in supply.

Consumption of edible fats, particularly butter, was down somewhat during the war. Thus in a strict sense the United States did not have guns and butter. The reasons are not clear, but the long-term decline in butter consumption probably played a role. Ice cream consumption, which had been rising for a long time, continued to rise. Thus, the United States did have guns and ice cream. The decline in edible fat consumption was a major concern, and the meat rationing system was designed to provide each family with an adequate fat ration. The concern about fats aside, food production held up well.

Clothing, on the other hand, suffered from quality deterioration. Only shoes were rationed, however, because of the shortage of high-quality leather and rubber. And, although shoe inventories were run down, overall sales of shoes stabilized during 1942–4 at 5 per cent above their 1941 level.[9]

Other areas of consumption also suffered somewhat owing to wartime strains. The buildup of the army and navy medical services undoubtedly hurt civilian medical care, and the rapid pace of internal migration exposed large numbers of people to new disease environments. Vatter summed it up as follows: 'Except for malaria, typhoid, and smallpox, the incidence of most diseases among the civilian population increased as compared with 1940.'[10] Long hours in hastily constructed industrial plants increased the rate of industrial accidents. Shipbuilding, a dangerous business in the best of times, was especially dangerous when undertaken by inexperienced workers in yards crowded with supplies.

Overall, Vatter's judicious conclusion concerning consumption levels appears correct. 'Although there were specific pockets of civilian deprivation and harsh regional differences, particularly with respect to durable commodities, the overall flow of per capita consumer goods and services was maintained at a surprisingly high level.'[11]

The foreign sector

In the spring of 1940 Britain began placing large-scale orders with American factories. Initially, Britain paid for weapons by running down its dollar balances by $235 million, by selling $335 million worth of US securities requisitioned from British holders, and by transferring over $2 billion in gold. The policy was known as 'Cash and Carry'.[12] US neutrality laws required foreign governments to pay cash for weapons and carry them away in non-US shipping, which limited the scale of British procurement, but still favoured Britain above Germany, since Germany lacked dollar reserves and had little or no freedom of movement for surface shipping in the Atlantic.

In March 1941, however, the United States began paying for British weapons under lend-lease. This euphemistic name was intended to suggest that weapons would only be lent or leased temporarily to our future allies, and that the weapons would be returned after the war was over. Various forms of compensation, such as the right to British military bases, were exchanged for lend-leased weapons. But the main purpose of the title and the compensation provisions was to defuse potential criticism from the still potent, although diminished, anti-war forces in Congress.

Lend-lease lasted from March 1941 until June 1945. Altogether some $50 billion was spent under the Act. Table 3.8 (cols. 1, 2) shows the effects of lend-lease. Both the relatively small increase in exports relative to GNP in 1940–1 under cash and carry, and the unprecedented increase in 1942–5 under lend-lease are evident. (The increase in imports during the war was partly the result of military purchases in foreign countries, although other imports increased as well.) Thus, even though the increase in exports in 1940 and 1941 threatened to exhaust Britain's ability to pay, these amounts were small compared with what followed.

It is sometimes claimed that lend-lease 'boosted' the economy. The intended picture is Keynesian. The government, in this view, increased spending on arms for its future allies, and this produced a multiple increase in real GNP. Lend-leased weapons, on this view, more than paid for themselves. True, unemployment was still high in March 1941 when lend-lease was inaugurated; but the economy was then expanding smartly under monetary and fiscal stimuli already in place. During the winter of 1942 the US reached full employment. In 1942, 1943, and 1944, when huge lend-lease transfers had to be made, they had to be made the old fashioned way – at the expense of other goods.

The production possibilities curve

The production possibilities curve provides a way of describing the increase in war production that clarifies the economic and technological possibilities open to the United States at each point in time. In figure 3.1 real civilian output is plotted on the horizontal axis and real military spending (both at 1958 prices) on the vertical axis.

The resulting picture shows that the war years can be divided into four phases.

1. Between 1939 and 1941 the United States made gains in both civilian production and war production by reemploying unemployed resources. This involved moving in a northeasterly (outward) direction toward the outer envelope of the production possibilities curve.
2. Between 1941 and 1942, however, some civilian output had to be sacrificed to achieve more war production. There was a northwesterly (lateral) movement along the production possibilities curve.
3. The curve itself then shifted upward, so that in 1944 the economy was

Table 3.8. *The balance of payments of the United States, 1938–1948 ($ millions)*

	Exports 1	Imports 2	Balance of goods and services 3	Private transfers 4	Government transfers 5	Net capital flows 6	Transactions in official reserves 7	Errors and omissions 8
1938	4,336	3,045	1,291	−153	−29	441	−1,799	249
1939	4,432	3,366	1,066	−151	−27	1,498	−3,174	788
1940	5,355	3,636	1,719	−178	−32	1,457	−4,243	1,277
1941	6,896	4,486	2,410	−179	−957	−1,031	−719	476
1942	11,769	5,356	6,413	−123	−6,213	−92	23	−8
1943	19,134	8,096	11,038	−249	−12,658	1,078	757	34
1944	21,438	8,986	12,452	−357	−13,785	377	1,350	−37
1945	16,273	10,232	6,041	−473	−6,640	516	548	8
1946	14,792	6,985	7,807	−673	−2,249	−4,417	−623	155
1947	19,819	8,202	11,617	−682	−1,943	−6,538	−3,315	861
1948	16,861	10,343	6,518	−697	−3,828	−1,372	−1,736	1,115

Sources:

1. US Bureau of the Census (1975), series U1.
2. Ibid., series U8.
3. Ibid., series U15.
4. Ibid., series U16.
5. Ibid., series U17.
6. Ibid., the sum of U18 through U23.
7. Ibid., series U24.
8. Ibid., series U25.

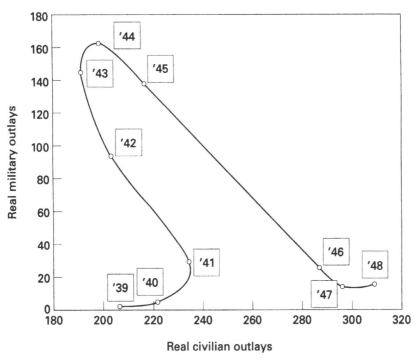

Figure 3.1 The US production possibilities curve, 1939–1948 ($ billion and 1958 prices)
Source: table 3.1

producing considerably more munitions without further reductions in the size of the civilian sector. The exact position of the curve in 1943–5 is unknown because of the measurement problems described above. It seems likely that if the price deflators and spending measures were adjusted for measurement problems, the high points on the graph (1943–5) would migrate toward the southwest. But in any case, it is clear that the shift in the curve permitted the United States to produce a vast supply of munitions in 1943–5 with a surprisingly small reduction in civilian output.

4. With peace came a second lateral movement in a southeasterly direction along the production possibilities curve, this time away from guns and towards butter, leaving the economy in 1946–7 producing war goods at a rate only slightly below that of 1941, but with a much higher level of real civilian output.

The factors of production

In this section I use John Kendrick's estimates of inputs and total factor productivity to explain the shifts in and movements along the production possibilities curve.[13] My major aim, of course, is to explain the upward shift in the production possibilities curve.

The labour force

Before turning to the workforce, let us look briefly at vital statistics. In wartime the crude death rate for the domestic population (table 3.9, col. 4) remained around the level reached in the late 1930s, providing additional evidence that the civilian sector remained 'on hold' – civilians experienced neither downward pressure on health and nutrition levels, nor rapid improvement. The crude birthrate (col. 6), increased slightly during the war, then dramatically in 1946.

The 1946 increase in the crude birth rate was the result, partly, of the reuniting of couples separated during the war. But there was more to the 'baby boom' (which lasted well into the 1950s) than romantic reunions. The baby boom was a response to the rise in rise in real income per head, and perhaps even more important, to the rise in economic security that came with the return of full employment.

The crude death rate, when the deaths of military personnel stationed overseas are included (table 3.9, col. 3), rose substantially in 1944 and 1945 with the intensification of the fighting. Nevertheless, neither to the home front, nor to the fighting fronts, was the supply of labour seriously compromised by the losses sustained in 1944 and 1945. The United States could have fought much longer and harder had it proved necessary.

Table 3.9 (col. 5) shows the crude death rate for military personnel stationed overseas. If it appears somewhat low by comparison with losses sustained by the other belligerents, it is because of the large number of support personnel in the US military. The death rates for men headed for the killing lines, for riflemen and bomber crews, for example, were extremely high. Indeed, losses in rifle companies in the European theatre were so heavy that American commanders had to contend with a severe shortage of riflemen despite their superiority in men and material in almost every other category.

To achieve the 'production miracle' the United States first of all increased the supply of labour. The increase in Kendrick's estimate of total labour inputs can be divided into the contributions of the increased number of workers, the rising average number of hours worked, and the residual, which I have labelled 'reallocation'. These are shown in table 3.10. The increase in the number of workers was the most important factor and will

Table 3.9. *Vital statistics of the United States population, 1938–1948*

	Population (thou.)		Crude death rate (per thou.)			Crude birth rate (per thou.)
	including armed forces overseas	armed forces overseas	total population	excluding armed forces overseas	armed forces overseas	
	1	2	3	4	5	6
1938	129,825	—	—	10.6	—	19.2
1939	130,879	—	—	10.6	—	18.8
1940	131,820	151	—	10.8	—	19.4
1941	133,402	281	10.5	10.5	10.9	20.3
1942	134,860	940	10.5	10.3	27.6	22.2
1943	136,739	2,494	11.0	10.9	16.4	22.7
1944	138,397	5,512	11.4	10.6	29.2	21.2
1945	139,928	7,447	10.8	10.6	15.1	20.4
1946	141,389	1,335	9.9	10.0	5.6	24.1
1947	144,126	680	10.0.	10.1	2.7	26.6
1948	146,631	538	9.9	9.9	2.4	24.9

Sources:
1–5. US Department of Health, Education and Welfare, National Office of Vital Statistics (1950), 145–6.
6.   US Bureau of the Census (1975), series B5.

Table 3.10. *The composition of increases in the United States supply of labour, 1939–1948 (per cent change over 1938)*

	The increase in the number of workers 1	The increase in average hours 2	Reallocation effect 3
1939	3.0	1.5	1.0
1940	6.7	1.8	2.1
1941	15.4	2.6	5.7
1942	24.2	4.6	8.9
1943	33.5	7.4	12.7
1944	35.3	8.0	13.4
1945	32.8	4.1	12.9
1946	23.9	−0.3	10.2
1947	24.5	−1.8	10.3
1948	26.1	−2.8	10.7

Sources:
1. Kendrick (1961), table A-VI.
2. Ibid., table A-X.
3. Ibid., table A-XIX.

be considered in more detail below. Average hours worked per week increased, but only about 7 per cent between 1940 and 1944, from 43.9 hours to 47 hours, and the work week remained below the level of 1929 (48.7 hours).[14] Hours increased greatly, however, in factories producing munitions. The term 'reallocation' is given to the residual because the main component of the residual is the effect of moving a worker from a low-paid, low-productivity job involving low hours, for example in southern agriculture, to a high-paid, high-productivity job involving longer hours, for example building tanks in Detroit.

All three factors were making substantial contributions to the increase in labour inputs at the peak in 1944. After the war, annual hours per worker fell back to their prewar level, and by 1948 had fallen noticeably below the level of 1938. But the increase in total employment and the gains from the reallocation of labour persisted, providing part of the explanation for the permanent upward shift in the production possibilities curve. The southern agricultural worker who moved to Detroit to build tanks stayed to build automobiles.

In table 3.11 the increase in the size of the paid labour force, the major factor in table 3.10, is attributed to three sources: the reduced unemploy-

Table 3.11. *The working population of the United States (thousands, annual average of monthly series)*

	Total	By employment status				By gender	
		civilian employees	armed forces	employed population total	unemployed population total	male	female
	1	2	3	4	5	6	7
Numbers, thousand							
1938	54,872	44,142	340	44,482	10,390	—	—
1939	55,588	45,738	370	46,108	9,480	—	—
1940	56,180	47,520	540	48,060	8,120	41,940	14,160
1941	57,530	50,350	1,620	51,970	5,560	43,070	14,650
1942	60,380	53,750	3,970	57,720	2,660	44,200	16,120
1943	64,560	54,470	9,020	63,490	1,070	45,950	18,830
1944	66,040	53,960	11,410	65,370	670	46,930	19,390
1945	65,290	52,820	11,430	64,250	1,040	46,910	19,304
1946	60,970	55,250	3,450	58,700	2,270	43,690	16,840
1947	61,758	57,812	1,590	59,402	2,356	44,258	16,683
Sources of the increase in employment over 1940, thousands							
1941	—	—	—	3,910	2,560	1,130	490
1942	—	—	—	9,660	5,460	2,260	1,960
1943	—	—	—	15,430	7,050	4,010	4,670
1944	—	—	—	17,310	7,450	4,990	5,230
1945	—	—	—	16,190	7,080	4,970	5,144
1946	—	—	—	10,640	5,850	1,750	2,680
1947	—	—	—	11,342	5,764	2,318	2,523

Note:
Col. 4 is calculated as cols. 2+3; col. 1 is calculated as cols. 4+5. Col. 1 should also equal cols. 6+7 but there are minor discrepancies. In the second part of the table, the role of the reduction in unemployment (col. 5) is calculated as the increase in unemployment but with opposite sign.
Source: US Bureau of the Census (1975), D5, D8, D30, D36.

ment of both men and women, and the increased participation of women and of men separately. The labour force increased by at least 17.3 million workers between 1940 and 1944 (as explained in the table there are some discrepancies among the figures). The reduction in the number of unemployed workers (7.5 million) contributed about 40 per cent of the increase, and the increased participation by women (5.2 million) and men (5 million) about 30 per cent each.

It is clear that there are grey areas in the estimates. On the one hand, many of the workers counted as not participating in the labour force in 1940 were discouraged workers who could, with some justice, have been counted as unemployed. On the other hand, a substantial part of the labour force designated as unemployed in 1940 actually had jobs in emergency relief agencies such as the Civilian Conservation Corps and the Works Progress Administration; these agencies were shut down as wartime jobs were created. These workers were being reallocated to more productive jobs rather than moving from unemployment to employment.[15] Something similar could be said of many of the women who entered the labour force; they began producing for the market rather than for the home, a reallocation which adds to GNP partly because home production is not adequately valued in the national accounts. Many of the workers reemployed in 1940 and 1941, moreover, were set to work producing civilian goods and then reallocated to war goods: starting in a later base year would change the picture.

When all is said and done, however, it is clear that the war produced a remarkable increase in total employment. The reasons are not completely clear. The most likely candidates among the possible explanations are the increase in real wages, the expectation that high real wages would be temporary because the Depression would return after the war (a desire to 'make hay while the sun shines'), and patriotism. In some cases compulsion may have been a factor; working in a war plant could (sometimes) persuade a draft board to grant an exemption, but compulsion was probably not a major factor in the increase in the supply of labour.

Who were the women who entered the labour force after 1940? A breakdown by marital status (available only for selected years) is shown in table 3.12. There the increase in the number of women in the labour force is divided into four categories: married women with husband present (which includes husbands absent in the military), married women without husband present, single women, and widowed and divorced women. Married women with husband present accounted for over 40 per cent of the increase up to 1944. Many of these women had husbands in the military. The image of American women building the weapons of war while their husbands served in the armed forces has a foundation in fact, although as table 3.12 shows, there were substantial increases in all four categories.

The shifts in labour force participation by women between 1944 and 1948 are surprising. The number of women with husbands present in the paid labour force increased by another 1.3 million between 1944, the peak of the mobilization, and 1948. Decreases were recorded, but these were confined to single women and to married women with the husband not present. A full analysis is beyond the scope of this chapter. Undoubtedly, part of the story is a change in attitudes. Women who worked during the war developed a taste for work, and some employers realized that they were good

Table 3.12. *The increase in female employment in the United States compared with 1940, by marital status, 1944 and 1948 (March figures, thousands)*

	1944	1948
Married with husband present	2,026	3,353
Married with husband not present	1,367	−112
Single	832	−767
Widowed, divorced	384	841
Total	4,609	3,315

Source: Taken or calculated from US Bureau of the Census (1975), series D49–D53.

workers. But another part of the story must be improved economic conditions combined with the long-term trend towards increased labour force participation of women. Increased family incomes, on the other hand, permitted young single women and married women with husbands not present to return to school.[16]

Together, the additional sources of labour made it possible for the United States to increase substantially the amount of labour devoted to producing munitions, without significantly reducing the amount of labour in other sectors. Between 1939 and 1943 workers in manufacturing durable goods increased by a factor of 2.4, from 4.7 million to 11 million. At the same time employment in most other sectors was held roughly constant. Perhaps the major exceptions were agricultural and household workers (not accurately counted in the data underlying this breakdown of the labor force because it is based on surveys of businesses).

An alternative view of how the increase in the labour force was allocated, which may be useful when comparing the United States with other belligerents, is provided in table 3.13. It is based very roughly on the British wartime sector-of-origin breakdown of the labour force: Group I consists of workers in durable goods manufacturing, which in wartime provided the foundations of the munitions industry; Group II consists of workers in agriculture, mining, government, transportation, and public utilities, the 'essential' sectors; and Group III consists of workers in non-durable manufacturing, construction, finance, and services – the 'inessential' trades. In Britain the idea was that effective war mobilization would reallocate as many workers as possible from Group III to Group I.[17]

This breakdown provides still another illustration of the decision by the

Table 3.13. *Composition of the United States labour force by industry group, 1938–1948 (thousands)*

	Group I 1	Group II 2	Group III 3
1938	—	16,586	—
1939	4,715	16,515	18,119
1940	5,363	16,619	18,849
1941	6,968	17,106	20,695
1942	8,823	18,023	21,368
1943	11,084	18,695	20,717
1944	10,856	18,633	20,263
1945	9,074	18,386	20,634
1946	7,742	18,445	23,415
1947	8,385	18,589	24,900
1948	8,326	18,813	25,732

Sources:
1. US Bureau of the Census (1975), series D131.
2. US Bureau of the Census (1975), the sum of series D128, D133, D139, and Kendrick (1961), table A-VI (col. 7).
3. US Bureau of the Census (1975), the sum of series D129, D132, D134, D137, and D138.

United States to put the civilian sector, particularly consumption, on hold. Group I employment rose remarkably, while Group II remained about constant. Group III fell, but only slightly, and only in the peak years 1943 and 1944.

The stock of capital

Existing factories were converted to war production and new factories, specially designed to mass produce arms, were constructed. Ford halted automobile production, and began turning out tanks; Ford also built a huge plant at Willow Run for mass producing B17 bombers. The decision to invest heavily in new plants at the start was controversial: it slowed down the conversion, perhaps so that firms could maintain profitable lines of production for the civilian market. But the decision paid off in the long run by assuring that the United States could outproduce Germany and Japan.

A good deal of the plant and equipment built during the war was afterwards converted to the production of civilian goods. Much of this capital, which had been financed by the Defense Plant Corporation and other federal agencies, was sold to private firms at bargain prices after the war, and so was undercounted in the official estimates of the capital stock. In a famous article published in 1969, Robert J. Gordon put a price tag on the understatement: '45 Billion [1958 dollars] of US Private Investment Has Been Mislaid'. The $45 billion was mislaid, of course, by economists not by businessmen.[18]

Although the wartime expansion of industrial capital was striking to contemporaries, it is easy to exaggerate its importance during the war and, especially, for the postwar years. Between 1939 and 1946 the increase in the net private capital stock, including Gordon's estimate of the missing capital, was only 14 per cent. It is not surprising, therefore, that in a total factor productivity framework the increase in the capital stock accounts for only a small part of the increase in output.

Total factor productivity

The estimates of labour and capital discussed above can now be used to divide the increase in output into the amounts contributed by the increase in labour, the increase in capital, and the increase in total productivity. The increase in labour is additionally subdivided into lower unemployment, more workers, longer hours, and labour reallocation. Kendrick's estimates are used throughout except that I have adjusted his estimates of the capital input upward to reflect Gordon's findings, but the adjustment has a relatively small effect on the overall results, which appear in table 3.14.

Increased inputs, especially labour, provided the bulk of the increase in output. Comparing 1944 with 1940, we find that increased supplies of labour contributed 73 per cent of the increase in output, increased supplies of capital contributed about 3 per cent, and increased total factor productivity contributed about 24 per cent. In addition, the share attributed to total factor productivity may be exaggerated. Greater intensity of work effort (for example, speed up on production lines), faster depreciation of existing capital, and overstatement of output because of underestimate of price increases, all get thrown into the residual labelled total factor productivity.

The most important lesson to be drawn from the table is that no single factor accounts for the rise in output. Americans who were unemployed went back to work, many who were not part of the paid labour force decided to go to work, they worked longer hours, and they moved from the South and other low-wage areas to industrial production centres. Capital was converted to war production, and new plant and equipment was built, and considerable gains were made in total factor productivity. Success, in other words, was the result of an across-the-board effort to mobilize resources.

Table 3.14. *Output, inputs, and total factor productivity in the United States economy, 1939–1949 (per cent of 1938)*

| | Output | Labour inputs | | | | |
	1	total 2	reduced unemploy- ment 3	increased partici- pation 4	longer average hours 5	reallo- cation effect 6
1939	108.8	105.7	101.5	100.9	102.1	101.0
1940	116.4	111.2	101.8	101.6	105.3	102.1
1941	142.5	126.7	102.6	104.2	112.0	105.9
1942	161.3	145.7	104.7	105.4	120.8	109.3
1943	181.3	171.0	107.7	111.1	125.9	113.5
1944	193.6	176.2	108.3	112.2	126.8	114.3
1945	191.3	164.4	104.2	109.9	126.3	113.8
1946	172.6	140.4	99.7	101.9	124.7	110.8
1947	169.3	139.2	98.3	102.6	124.5	110.9
1948	172.9	140.5	97.2	104.2	124.6	111.3
1949	170.2	135.2	96.2	103.4	122.4	111.0

| | Capital inputs | | Total factor input | | Total factor productivity | |
	7	adjusted for GOPO 8	9	adjusted for GOPO 10	11	adjusted for GOPO 12
1939	99.9	99.9	104.2	104.2	104.4	104.4
1940	101.4	101.4	108.7	108.7	107.1	107.1
1941	104.8	105.1	121.3	121.4	117.5	117.4
1942	107.6	108.7	136.2	136.5	118.5	118.2
1943	107.7	109.9	155.1	155.8	116.8	116.4
1944	106.5	109.2	158.8	159.6	121.9	121.3
1945	104.8	107.9	149.5	150.4	127.9	127.2
1946	107.0	110.1	132.0	132.8	130.7	129.9
1947	113.6	116.5	132.8	133.6	127.5	126.8
1948	120.5	123.6	135.5	136.3	127.7	126.9
1949	125.7	128.8	132.6	133.3	128.3	127.7

Sources:
1, 2, 7, 9. Kendrick (1961), table A-XIX.
3. Ibid., table A-X (col. 1).
4. Ibid., table A-VI.
5. US Bureau of the Census (1975), series D8 and D18. This series has been weighted so that the percentage changes in cols. 4 and 5 sum to the percentage change in Kendrick (1961), table A-VI ('total persons engaged').
6. Computed as a residual.
8, 10. GOPO stands for government owned, privately operated capital. I multiplied Kendrick's estimate of capital inputs by one plus the ratio of Gordon's estimates of government owned, privately operated capital, Gordon (1969), table 4, to Kendrick's estimates of total domestic capital.

Financing the war

The effort described above was produced by a great flood of money that poured out of Washington and affected, ultimately, every town and hamlet in the country. In this section I will focus first on how the government raised the financial resources it needed, and then on the inflationary consequences of its financial policies.

Taxes, bonds, and money

It is a commonplace that there are three ways of financing government spending: raising taxes, borrowing, and printing money. This is, to be sure, a simplification that ignores other sources of finance that may be important during wartime, including the liquidation of existing assets, the commandeering of resources both domestically and from conquered nations, voluntary contributions both domestically and from abroad, and even financial transactions such as the refinancing of government debt.

In the United States during World War II the most important form of commandeering was the drafting of men into the armed services. The difference between the pay draftees would have required to serve voluntarily and what they were actually paid was a tax that went unreported in the standard financial accounts. Similarly, the difference between what true volunteers could have earned in the civilian sector and what they earned in government service could be considered a gift to the government. In addition to true volunteers (not induced to volunteer by the threat of the draft) in the armed services one could also consider the 'Dollar a year men'. These were executives who worked for the War Production Board and other agencies for the nominal sum of a dollar per year. Their civilian employers, who continued to pay their salaries, could be considered as gifting these salaries to the federal government. It has been argued, however, that these companies often received various long-term benefits from having their employees in Washington. Despite these and similar qualifications, the traditional tripartite division is useful for understanding how the war was financed.

In a world in which money consisted solely of paper issued by the government the calculation of the tripartite division would be straightforward. Taxes would be measured by tax receipts, borrowing by the interest-bearing debt issued, and money creation by the amount of paper money issued. The existence of the banking system, however, creates an additional complication. When the government prints paper money or creates deposits for itself on the books of the central bank, the banking system receives additional reserves which it uses to expand its asset holdings while creating additional deposit money. Or as it is sometimes put, the government shares the

Table 3.15. *Sources of the increase in United States government spending, 1942–1945 (per cent of the increase in total spending over the previous year)*

	Taxes raised 1	Money creation 2	Bond sales 3
1942	24.0	41.3	34.7
1943	53.7	27.9	18.5
1944	132.4	−42.3	10.0
1945	12.4	61.5	26.1

Sources:
All series are expressed as percentages of the change in total Federal government expenditure (from US Bureau of the Census (1975), series Y457); all series were first adjusted to a calendar year basis.
1. US Bureau of the Census (1975), series Y343.
2. Ibid., series Y491 and X594.
3. Ibid., series Y457, less the sum of cols. 1 and 2.

seignorage with the banking system. Thus, that part of the interest-bearing debt issued by the government, which is held by banks or by individuals who have financed their acquisition of debt with bank loans, must be considered as financed indirectly by money creation.

If one assumes that all government debt acquired by commercial banks was financed by money creation and that none of the debt held by the public was so financed then we get the following results. On average during the years of large wartime deficits (1942–5) taxes accounted for 47 per cent of total spending, money creation 26 per cent, and borrowing from the public 27 per cent.[19] The monetary share can be further divided into spending financed directly by government-created money (6 per cent) and spending financed indirectly by money created by the banking system (20 per cent).

Table 3.15 shows how wartime government spending was financed. Taxes could finance only about one quarter of the additional spending in 1942 compared with 1941; it takes time to legislate, levy, and collect new taxes. The extra taxes raised in 1943 paid for more than half of the continuing rise in government spending in that year. And in 1944 the increase in taxes was sufficient to permit a reduction in reliance on the printing press, while borrowing was stabilized. But the further increase in spending in 1945, partly the result of the unexpectedly strong resistance put up by the Germans and Japanese, required increased reliance on money creation, so that with respect to reliance on the printing press 1945 appears to be something of a reprise of 1942.

In recent years professional economic opinion has swung towards the view that it was permissible to use deficit finance to smooth taxes. But orthodox thinking at the time held that wars should be financed by taxes, or, as it was usually put, on a 'pay-as-you-go' basis. This view was shared across the political spectrum. Printing money was frowned upon because it was thought to be inflationary. Debt finance was frowned upon because it was thought to burden future generations, which included, most importantly, the young men and women who were now fighting the war, and would later be called upon to repay the debt. But the reality of war finance, as we have seen, was somewhat different. The basic problem was that even in wartime, and even when there was a strong philosophical consensus in favour of tax finance, it was hard to raise taxes. First, there were real technical problems in raising taxes quickly. Second, politicians were not hobbled by the need for philosophical consistency. When faced with a vote on a tax increase, a politician could easily forget the burden on future generations and remember the disincentive effects of higher taxes.

Money and inflation

Between June 1939 and June 1945 the stock of money (M2) increased by a factor of more than 2.5, from $48.4 billion to $125.3 billion (table 3.16). Most of the increase can be accounted for by changes in the monetary base by a factor of 2.4, from $17.3 billion to $41.6 billion.

The increase in the monetary base for the war period as a whole can be explained in turn by the decision to finance part of the war by printing money. But during the national defence period the dominant force behind the increase in high-powered money was the stock of monetary gold, which increased from $13 billion to $22.7 billion between 1938 and 1941, before levelling off for the remainder of the war. Cash and Carry, and the arrival of private capital seeking a safe haven, explain the rapid increase in the stock of monetary gold before Pearl Harbor. Both factors were brought to a halt by American entry into the war. Indeed, because of the halt in the expansion of the stock of monetary gold, the increase in high-powered money was actually less in 1942 than it had been in the years immediately preceding.

The increase in the stock of money in turn produced intense inflationary pressures. To some extent these pressures were contained by price controls and rationing, particularly during 1943–5.[20] When controls were released in 1946 there was a considerable jump in prices. Part of this jump, however, was a mirage. During the war the official price indexes understated the true inflation because they did not fully adjust for quality deterioration, black markets, rationing constraints, and so on. Immediately after the war the

Table 3.16. *Monetary statistics of the United States, 1938–1948*

	High-powered money ($ bn) 1	Deposit–currency ratio 2	Deposit–reserve ratio 3	M1 ($ bn) 4	M2 ($ bn) 5	M3 ($ bn) 6	Monetary gold ($ bn) 7
1938	14.6	4.21	7.12	29.7	44.8	55.5	13.007
1939	17.3	3.68	7.02	33.3	48.4	59.3	16.195
1940	21.8	3.14	7.22	39.7	55.3	66.2	20.049
1941	23.0	3.59	6.50	46.3	62.3	73.2	22.713
1942	25.2	4.09	5.23	54.1	69.8	80.7	22.759
1943	29.5	5.48	4.68	73.5	91.1	103.1	22.399
1944	35.6	5.72	3.98	83.9	105.1	119.0	21.194
1945	41.6	6.10	3.93	98.1	125.3	141.7	20.294
1946	44.3	6.40	4.22	107.5	140.1	158.7	20.341
1947	44.5	6.67	4.48	112.1	146.0	166.8	21.417
1948	45.2	6.28	4.65	112.0	147.8	169.3	23.74

Notes:
Cols. 1–3 generate an estimate of M2 according to the formula:

$$M2 = H \cdot [dr \cdot ((1+dc)/(dr+dc))]$$

where H is high-powered money, dr is the deposit–reserve ratio, and dc is the deposit–currency ratio. This estimate differs slightly from col. 5 which incorporates certain refinements developed between the publishing of the two volumes.
Definitions:
1. The sum of bank reserves and currency held by the public.
2. The ratio of bank deposits to bank reserves.
3. The ratio of bank deposits to currency held by the public.
4. Currency held by the public plus demand deposits in commercial banks.
5. Col. 4 plus time deposits in commercial banks.
6. Col. 5 plus deposits in mutual savings banks and the postal savings system.
7. All gold coin and monetary bullion within the United States (except earmarked gold).
Sources:
1–3. Friedman and Schwartz (1963), table B-3 (cols. 1–3), June figures.
4–6. Friedman and Schwartz (1970), table 1 (cols. 8, 9, and 11), June figures
7. Cagan (1965), table F-7 (col. 1).

indexes overstated inflation because they did not adjust for the return to normal quality levels, the disappearance of black markets, and the elimination of rationing. This is why the indexes that make an allowance for these factors (table 3.2 above, cols. 3, 4) show a smaller increase between 1945 and 1946 than the other indexes.

Full equilibrium was not reached in 1946. Between 1938 and 1947 (the first full postwar year for which we can rule out any distortion in the price indices produced by controls) most of the price indices in table 3.2 above show an increase of around 50 per cent. Over the same period M2 grew by about 117 per cent and real NNP by about 43 per cent. The increase in money per unit of output, 74 per cent, therefore considerably outdistanced the increase in prices. The resulting monetary 'overhang' probably reflected an understandable decision to delay the final dispersal of wartime accumulations: the overhang was gradually run down during the early postwar years.

The long-run consequences of the war

Measuring the costs (and benefits) of World War II is, as John Maurice Clark wrote with respect to World War I, 'either a relatively simple matter of tabulation and fiscal allocation; or else it is an economic problem of insoluble difficulty'.[21] Like Clark, all I can offer are a few calculations that may shed some additional light on a complex issue. First, through an 'adding up' approach, based on the work of Kendrick and Denison, I look at the direct impact of the war on the stocks of human and physical capital. Second, I provide an alternative estimate of the cost of the war by comparing the actual path of consumption in the war and postwar years with a counterfactual path based on the assumption that the war was avoided. Third, I consider the relationship between the war and the change in macroeconomic régimes, which I believe was the most enduring legacy of the war.

Adding up the costs of the war

Human capital losses were undoubtedly the most important direct losses. Damage to the physical capital stock was relatively small, the most important losses being ocean shipping. The most straightforward way of calculating the loss of human capital is to compute the present discounted value of the future earnings of the men and women killed in the war and the loss in earnings of those who were partially or totally disabled.

To get a crude measure I assume that the typical soldier or sailor entered the military at age 18 in 1941, and that, barring injury or death, this individual would have earned the average real earnings in the economy in each year of his or her working life, and then would have retired at age 65. I then adjusted those earnings for the expected death rate for civilians, and discounted the result at an interest rate of 5 per cent. Multiplying the expected lifetime real earnings by the number of people killed (364,111) yielded a total cost for men and women killed of $12.9 billion at 1940 prices. The total number of men and women suffering non-mortal wounds was 281,881. I assumed that the earnings capacity of each wounded man or women was reduced, on average, by 25 per cent, yielding a total of $2.5

billion at 1940 prices in diminished work capacity resulting from wounds. The total loss from war-related deaths and injuries at prewar prices thus came to about $15.4 billion.

A number of technical questions could be raised about this calculation, as well as the philosophical question of whether it makes sense to put a dollar value on a human life. For one thing, the calculation assumes that veterans earned the average income of all employees. In fact, veterans typically earned more on the job and suffered less unemployment than non-veterans, partly because women and African-Americans were under-represented in the veteran population.[22] The postwar ability of the United States to replenish losses of labour through immigration (including highly skilled labour, for this was the era of the 'brain drain') raises a further problem. US losses were spread throughout the world economy in the postwar period to the extent that the places that would have been filled by men killed or injured were filled instead by additional immigrants. The distribution of income within the United States was undoubtedly different from what it would have been had there been no war. The extent to which total output of the economy was altered, however, is debatable.[23]

Leaving these doubts and qualifications to one side, the estimate of $15.4 billion appears reasonable. It amounted to about one quarter of consumption in 1940; and to about 10 per cent of the Goldin–Lewis type estimate of total losses discussed below.

To the extent that American economists think about the long-term effects of the war on the labour force, it is probably more in terms of increased investment in human capital than of the lives lost. Wartime increases in educational attainment were relatively small, but they are, nonetheless, surprising given the war effort, and they ushered in a period of rapid improvement. Perhaps, the best way of seeing this is by considering Edward F. Denison's index of the amount of education, measured by its ability to produce output. Denison constructed his index by weighting years of schooling by the relative earnings of each level of schooling. This index rose from 100 in 1941 to 103.3 in 1947, to 107.1 in 1953, and to 111.2 in 1959. In 1948, according to Denison, 8.8 per cent of the male labour force had 4 years of schooling or less; by 1959, this group had fallen to 5.8 per cent.[24] Even more dramatic were the changes at the other end of the education distribution. In 1948, 12.3 per cent of the male labour force had one or more years of college; by 1959, this group had risen to 18.3 per cent. By 1976, the last year in Denison's table, the percentage of males with one or more years of college had risen to 32.5 per cent.

The education revolution cannot be attributed primarily to the war. The growing faith in education, and particularly higher education, as a way of bringing everyone into the mainstream of American life had produced important developments, such as the high-school movement and the land grant college acts, long before World War II. But the GI Bill of Rights (officially, the Servicemen's Readjustment Act of 1944) undoubtedly accelerated the expansion of higher education. The bill provided help to veterans in a number of ways: medical care, low-interest home mortgages, vocational rehabilitation, job placement, unemployment benefits, and stipends covering tuition and living expenses for veterans attending trade schools or colleges. The educational benefits were viewed as a double-edged sword. They would help veterans upgrade their skills, and at the same time keep down the number of job seekers in what was expected to be a weak postwar job market. Overall some 10 million veterans received educational benefits between 1944 and 1956, when the programme ended.

While the GI Bill did contribute to the postwar boom in higher education, this can at most explain only a small share of the postwar prosperity in the United States.

A similar conclusion could be drawn concerning other changes on the real side of the economy. While wartime construction of plant and equipment did partially offset the decline in private investment spending during the war, it is likely that, had a similar boom taken place in peacetime, the increase in the capital stock would have been much larger.

It is true, as is often pointed out, that the United States gained a temporarily favourable position in world trade compared with some of its chief industrial rivals as a result of the war. But the United States was not export-oriented. In 1929 US exports were 4.4 per cent of GNP; in 1949 they were still only 4.6 per cent. It is doubtful that war-related improvements in the terms of trade affecting such a small part of the economy could be the key to prosperity.

The most likely explanation for the postwar prosperity, in my view, was the change in the macroeconomic régime. A new macroeconomic régime prevented a recurrence of the sort of financial crisis that had undermined prosperity in 1930–3.

A counterfactual approach

Some years ago Claudia Goldin and Frank Lewis measured the economic cost of the American Civil War by discounting the differences between the actual flow of goods and services to consumers and a counterfactual flow based on the assumption that the war was avoided (a technique that, as far as I know, they originated).[25] The idea is that the loss of life, the destruction of physical capital, the disruption of trade relations, and so on that occur during a war are important only to the extent that they reduce the flow of consumer goods in the long run below what it otherwise would have

Table 3.17. *Actual and counterfactual consumption in the United States, 1941–1960 ($ billion and 1940 prices)*

	Actual consumption 1	Counterfactual consumption 2	Weighted counterfactual *less* actual consumption 3
1941	69.2	70.8	1.5
1942	69.2	85.0	14.3
1943	71.2	101.9	26.5
1944	73.8	110.4	30.1
1945	78.6	106.0	21.4
1946	85.7	101.9	12.1
1947	87.3	97.9	7.6
1948	89.4	98.8	6.3
1949	91.5	97.2	3.7
1950	96.2	103.1	4.2
1951	98.4	105.9	4.4
1952	101.6	107.9	3.5
1953	105.9	111.3	2.9
1954	108.6	113.3	2.4
1955	115.2	119.2	1.9
1956	118.7	122.1	1.6
1957	121.5	124.5	1.3
1958	123.4	126.0	1.1
1959	129.7	131.9	0.9
1960	133.2	135.1	0.7

Source: See text.

been. An illustrative estimate is shown in table 3.17, based on the following five assumptions.

1. An aggressive monetary and fiscal policy would have produced a vigorous economic expansion between 1941 and 1946, even if the war had not occurred. Of course it is possible to argue that, in the absence of the war, the Depression would have dragged on indefinitely. In that scenario attributing *any* cost to the war via foregone consumption would become problematic.
2. In 1946, if there had been no war, real GNP would have been equal to the level that obtained in 1943. In other words, I assume that the counterfactual real GNP in 1946 resulting from a vigorous peacetime boom would have been higher than actual real GNP in 1946.
3. The gap between the counterfactual GNP and the actual GNP would have gradually narrowed and almost disappeared by 1960. In other

words, I assume that 1960 was an equilibrium year in the sense that the economy had returned to 'desired' levels of capital and labour. As Nick Crafts pointed out in his insightful comments on this chapter at our 1994 meeting, this is a strong and controversial assumption. Some modern growth theories imply that consumption would have remained permanently higher, but the issue has not been resolved.[26] What this controversy shows, however, is that the whole subject of measuring war costs needs to be reevaluated in the light of modern growth theory.

4. In the absence of the war the share of consumption in GNP would have been 60 per cent from 1941 to 1950 (it was 59 per cent in 1941, the last prewar year, and 61 per cent in 1960, the fourth postwar cyclical peak); after 1950 I use the actual ratio of consumption to GNP.

5. I discount differences between the counterfactual consumption path and the actual path with an interest rate of 5 per cent, about twice the rate on corporate and government bonds during and after the war, and hopefully representative of the average rate of interest.

The result of this computation, the sum of the last column in table 3.17, is a cost of the war amounting to about $148 billion at 1940 prices, or about 2.27 years of consumption in 1941. This is actually a slightly higher cost than Goldin and Lewis's estimate for the north in the Civil War (1.8 years), reflecting the greater intensity of mobilization during World War II.

The postwar macroeconomic régime

The war played a major role in converting American macroeconomists to Keynesian economics. When the war began it was widely believed that the 1930s had shown that monetary policy was ineffective. The Federal Reserve had done its best, but – 'you can't push on a string'. While a few diehards rejected this view, it was not until Milton Friedman and Anna J. Schwartz published their *Monetary history of the United States* (1963) that the profession as a whole began to rethink the view that monetary policy was ineffective. Meanwhile, Keynes's *General theory* (1936) had convinced a brilliant generation of young American economists that increased government spending could restore and maintain full employment.

The case for Keynesian policies, however, had remained a theoretical one in the late 1930s, since deficit spending under the New Deal had not cured the Depression. The war provided the missing evidence. As Herbert Stein shows, by the end of the war a large segment of the economics profession and the general public had been convinced that full employment should be a major policy objective of the federal government, and that this objective could be achieved by fiscal policy.[27] The war, of course, had also produced an extraordinary increase in the stock of money, but monetary policy had been discredited by the Depression. Alvin Hansen's stagnation thesis, moreover, had argued that wartime levels of federal spending were not a temporary aberration: if private investment was permanently depressed then high and growing levels of government spending would be needed to fill the gap.

The wartime experience, however, was not sufficient to satisfy all economists that fiscal policy should be used to maintain full employment, because wartime deficits had been created simultaneously with less attractive policies: During the war inflation had been checked to some extent by wage and price controls, and rationing. Direct controls were not part of the Keynesian promise, and in the early postwar years many American economists were concerned that Keynesian economics might, nevertheless, require a permanent set of direct controls. As Paul Samuelson put it in the first edition (1948) of his classic textbook, 'The war years have shown fiscal policy to be a very powerful weapon. Indeed, some would argue that it is like the atomic bomb, too powerful a weapon to let men and government play with; that it would be better if fiscal policy were never used.'[28]

But the early postwar experience seemed to suggest that direct controls could be avoided. An initial surge in inflation was followed for several years by fairly stable prices and relatively full employment. Alvin Hansen made this point explicitly in his influential *A guide to Keynes*.

Keynesian critics, however, have exaggerated the dangers of inflation and wage control in a full-employment society. The price inflation of 1946–7 in the United States was a product of the war, not a test of peacetime full employment. Indeed from January to December 1948, the United States enjoyed full employment without inflation despite the absence of price and wage controls.[29]

The evidence, in retrospect, was slim. But taken together the war and the early postwar years seemed to show that full employment could be maintained without inflation or direct controls. For the next three decades fiscal policy was used, although not consistently, to maintain full employment. The major enemies of economic growth in the United States, disastrous slumps and long periods of lagging demand, were avoided.

For economists who analyse macroeconomic fluctuations from a monetary standpoint the ascendancy of Keynesian economics may seem to make the postwar prosperity more rather than less mysterious. But there is a connection between the ascendancy of Keynesian economics and postwar monetary policy. Although Keynesian economics, as it was then understood in the United States, downplayed the role of monetary policy, it did not eliminate it altogether. Monetary policy was assigned the marginal task of fighting recessions by keeping interest rates low. Keynesian economics, in other words, although it did not think monetary policy important, did ensure that monetary policy would be used to fight recessions aggressively. Again the result was to build in a bias towards inflation, while making sure that neither a disastrous slump nor a long period of lagging demand sapped the natural vitality of the economy.

In addition to the revolution in economic thought, three institutional changes reduced the probability of a paralysing financial crisis.

1. Deposit insurance, introduced in 1934, reduced the likelihood that individual failures would spiral into full-blown panics.
2. The accumulation of federal debt by banks during the war greatly strengthened their balance sheets, bringing them a long way towards the once utopian dream of 100 per cent reserves.
3. The accumulation of a good share of the world's stock of monetary gold during the war, particularly during the years of neutrality, and the monetary arrangements established after the war under the Bretton Woods agreement, made the dollar the most important international reserve currency, and effectively freed the Federal Reserve from the real and psychological constraints of the gold standard.

Together these changes made the combination of banking panic and Federal Reserve passivity that had produced the Great Depression a thing of the past. Macroeconomic stability, in turn, had further effects on the economy. Investment spending, for example, must have been encouraged by the new régime. But space does not permit us to explore this effect. The new active approach to monetary and fiscal policy also contained within it an unhealthy bias toward inflation, but that is another story.

Conclusion

While the dramatic collapse between 1929 and 1933 has been studied and re-studied, the equally dramatic expansion between 1939 and 1943 has been neglected. This is unfortunate because the war contributed nearly as much to reshaping the political economy of the United States as did the Great Depression. As a result, while economic historians can usually divide the Great Depression into a long list of phases, they usually tend to think of the war as an undifferentiated lump. At times this leads to a misunderstanding of the wartime experience.

The neglect of the surge in the economy in 1940 and 1941 leads to an exaggeration of the amount of unemployed resources available when conversion moved into high gear in 1942. Instead, the US relied on a variety of means to increase production: the labour force participation of men and women increased, labour was drained from low-wage occupations, hours of work were increased, private domestic investment was reduced, and so on. The focus on the war as an undifferentiated whole has also led economic historians to downplay the role of the printing press in war finance. Beginning with the Civil War, the printing press has been a stopgap method for financing wars that was phased out as tax increases became productive, and so it was in World War II.

It is natural for economic historians to focus on the material legacies of the war – on losses of physical and human capital, on changes in the terms of trade, and so on. A close look, however, shows that the most long-lasting legacy may have been intellectual and institutional: a new macroeconomic régime which reshaped monetary and fiscal policy and profoundly influenced employment and inflation for decades afterwards

Notes

1 Higgs (1992), 45.
2 Kuznets (1945).
3 Sontag (1977), 63–5, and *passim*.
4 I thank Richard Sutch for trying to clarify the issues for me. He cannot be held responsible, however, for the use (or misuse) I have made of his ideas.
5 Friedman and Schwartz (1982), 101–4; Mills and Rockoff (1987).
6 Both phrases are quoted in Higgs (1992), 49, 58. The original quotations are from Melman (1985), 15 and Blum (1977), 90.
7 Rockoff (1978), 407–20; Vatter (1993), 221–2.
8 Vatter (1993), 226.
9 Ibid., 233.
10 Ibid., 236.
11 Ibid., 238.
12 Friedman and Schwartz (1963), 550.
13 Kendrick (1961), table A-XIX.
14 Ibid., 310, 315.
15 Darby (1976).
16 For a fuller discussion of impact of the war on the role of women in the labour force see Goldin (1991).
17 My attempt to match the British sector-of-origin breakdown is only approximate because I have allocated all durable manufacturing workers to Group I, and I have allocated all non-durable manufacturing workers to Group III. A closer look at industry-by-industry data would produce some adjustments in the boundaries among the categories. By way of comparison, consider the previous US estimates of Harrison (1988), 186. In 1940 he estimates 8.4 per cent of the US labour force was in Group I industries; using durable goods manufacturing as a proxy gives 9.5 per cent. In 1943 Harrison estimates 19 per cent of the US labour force was in Group I industries; using durable manufacturing as a proxy gives 17.2 per cent. The durable goods proxy therefore seems close enough for present purposes. The source on which Harrison relied, US War Production Board (1945), gives total labour force figures which differ slightly from those in US Bureau of the Census (1975), so the discrepancy between my proxy and

Harrison's estimates may result from differences in the underlying numbers as well as from conceptual differences.

18 There was some controversy over whether the transfer took place at bargain prices. See Jaszi (1970) for the argument that transfer prices accurately measured the value of the capital.

19 My estimates differ slightly from those reported by Friedman and Schwartz (1963), 571, which I discovered after making my calculations. Their figures are: taxes 48 per cent, money 21 per cent, and borrowing 31 per cent. Friedman and Schwartz evidently used the annual change in M2 to compute the seignorage that went to war finance, assuming (as they note) that none of the seignorage shared with the banking system was diverted to other uses. If one replaces M2 with M4, the largest monetary aggregate that Friedman and Schwartz report, then the results of their calculation are very similar to mine. The similarity in results using different methodologies suggests that the figures in the text are in the right ballpark.

20 I discussed these controls at length in Rockoff (1978), chapters 4 and 5.

21 Clark (1931), xi, quoted in Goldin and Lewis (1975), 300.

22 Taussig (1974), 51–2.

23 Clark (1931) computed the loss to the heirs of the killed and wounded, a calculation most relevant to determining how much the nation needed to spend to create an equitable financial burden among those surviving the war.

24 Denison (1979), 43.

25 Goldin and Lewis (1975).

26 See Mankiw (1995) for a recent survey.

27 Stein (1969), 169–96.

28 Samuelson (1948), 410.

29 Hansen (1953), 229.

References

Government publications

US Bureau of the Census (1975), *Historical statistics of the United States, colonial times to 1970, bicentennial edition*, Washington, DC.

US Department of Commerce, Bureau of Economic Analysis (1993), *National income and product accounts of the United States*, vol. I, *1929–58*, Washington, DC.

US Department of Health, Education and Welfare, National Office of Vital Statistics (1950), *Vital statistics of the United States, 1950*, Washington, DC.

US Department of Labor, Bureau of Labor Statistics (1989), *Handbook of labor statistics*, Washington, DC.

US War Production Board (1945), *American industry in war and transition, 1940–1950*, Part II, *The effect of the war on the industrial economy*, Washington, DC.

Books, articles, and working papers

Alston, L. J., and Ferrie, J. P. (1993), 'The Bracero Program and farm labor legislation in World War II', in Mills, G. T., and Rockoff, H., eds., *The sinews of war: essays on the economic history of World War II*, Ames, IA, 129–49.

Blum, J. M. (1977), *V was for victory: politics and American culture during World War II*, New York.

Cagan, P. (1965), *Determinants and effects of changes in the stock of money 1875–1960*, New York.

Clark, J. M. (1931), *The costs of the war to the American people*, New Haven, CT.

Darby, M. (1976), 'Three and a half million U.S. employees have been mislaid: or an explanation of unemployment, 1934–41', *Journal of Political Economy*, vol. 84, 1–16.

Denison, E. F. (1974), *Accounting for United States economic growth, 1929–1969*, Washington, DC.

(1979), *Accounting for slower economic growth: The United States in the 1970s*, Washington, DC.

Dewhurst, J. F. et al. (1947), *America's needs and resources*, New York.

Friedman, M., and Schwartz, A. J. (1963), *A monetary history of the United States, 1867–1960*, Princeton, NJ.

(1970), *Monetary statistics of the United States: estimates, sources, and methods*, New York.

(1982), *Monetary trends in the United States and the United Kingdom: their relation to income, prices, and interest rates, 1867–1975*. Chicago.

Goldin, C. (1980), 'War', in Porter, G., ed., *Encyclopedia of American economic history: studies of the principal movements and ideas*, New York, 935–57.

(1991), 'The role of World War II in the rise of women's employment', *American Economic Review*, vol. 81, 741–56.

Goldin, C., and Lewis, F. (1975), 'The economic cost of the American Civil War: estimates and implications', *Journal of Economic History*, vol. 35, 299–326.

Gordon, R. J. (1969), '45 billion of U.S. private investment has been mislaid', *American Economic Review*, vol. 59, 221–38.

(1970), '45 billion of U.S. private investment has been mislaid: reply', *American Economic Review*, vol. 60, 940–5.

Hansen, A. (1953), *A guide to Keynes*, New York.

Harrison, M. (1988), 'Resource mobilization for World War II: the U.S.A., U.K., U.S.S.R., and Germany, 1938–1945', *Economic History Review*, 2nd ser., vol. 41(2), 171–92.

Higgs, R. (1992), 'Wartime prosperity? A reassessment of the U.S. economy in the 1940s', *Journal of Economic History*, vol. 52, 41–60.

Howard, F. (1947), *Buna rubber: the birth of an industry*, New York.

Jaszi, G. (1970), '45 billion of U.S. private investment has been mislaid: comment', *American Economic Review*, vol. 60, 934–45.

Kendrick, J. W. (1961), *Productivity trends in the United States*, New York.

Kuznets, S. (1945), *National product in wartime*, New York.

(1952), 'Long-term changes in the national income in the United States of America since 1870', in Kuznets, S., ed., *Income and wealth of the United States: trends and structure*, London, 29–241.

(1961), *Capital in the American economy: its formation and financing*. Princeton, NJ.

Mankiw, N. G. (1995), 'The growth of nations', in Perry, G., Brainard, W., eds., *Brookings papers on economic activity*, vol. I, 275–310, 324–6.

Melman, S. (1985), *The permanent war economy: American capitalism in decline*, rev. edn, New York.

Mills, G., and Rockoff, H. (1987), 'Compliance with price controls in the United States and the United Kingdom during World War II', *Journal of Economic History*, vol. 47, 197–213.

Rockoff, H. (1978), 'Indirect price increases and real wages during World War II', *Explorations in Economic History*, vol. 15, 407–20.

(1984), *Drastic measures: a history of wage and price controls in the United States*, New York.

Samuelson, P. A. (1948), *Economics: an introductory analysis* (1st edn), New York.

Sontag, S. (1977), *Illness as metaphor*, New York.

Stein, H. (1969), *The fiscal revolution in America*, Chicago, IL.

Taussig, M. K. (1974), 'Background paper', in *Those who served: report of the Twentieth Century Fund task force on policies toward veterans*, New York.

Vatter, H. (1993), 'The material status of the U.S. civilian consumer in World War II: the question of guns or butter', in Mills, G. T., and Rockoff, H., eds., *The sinews of war: essays on the economic history of World War II*, Ames, IA.

4 Germany: guns, butter, and economic miracles

Werner Abelshauser

Introduction

Research into German rearmament and the war economy began even before the Third Reich had been completely destroyed. In March 1945, when Anglo-American troops had just begun to occupy the Ruhr, the US Air Force started to take stock. It assembled a group of economic experts to assess the effects of the strategic bombing campaign on the German war economy. The ostensible main purpose was to establish which lessons could be learned from the German experience for the continuing war in the Far East. In fact, already at this stage, the US air force wanted to document its contribution to the Allied victory. Led by John K. Galbraith (later of Harvard University), a team of young experts gathered in Bad Nauheim, whose names read like extracts from 'a roster of the famous of the next economic generation'.[1] Among them were Burton H. Klein (California Institute of Technology), Nicholas Kaldor (King's College, Cambridge), E. F. Schumacher, Paul A. Baran (Stanford University), Edward Denison (Brookings Institute) and Jürgen Kuczynski (Academy of Sciences, East Berlin). The group had access to the transferred records of the Reich Statistics Office, whose 'Prompt statistical reports on war production' documented to the end the efforts of German industry to keep up with the demands of war. A suitable interpreter was found in the head of the Institute for Trade Cycle Research's Industry Department, Rolf Wagenführ, who had prepared these statistics for Albert Speer's planning office.[2] With these favourable conditions the team was able not only to establish the extent of the German war economy's losses in the bombing campaign, but also to take stock of the German economic mobilization for World War II.[3]

In the interim, professional interest in the German war economy has hardly declined – and not merely because no fewer than four members of the USSBS team (Kaldor, Klein, Kuczynski, and Wagenführ) carried on the debate.[4] From the outset, three sets of problems were prominent. First was the character of the economic recovery of the 1930s, the prewar 'economic miracle'. Supporters and opponents of the Keynesian revolution in economic policy made the 1930s a testing ground for their convictions. The question was whether the economic recovery after 1933 was a necessary precondition for the mobilization of resources for the German war economy, or whether it was simply a 'side-effect' of rearmament efforts.

A second area of concern immediately after the end of the war was comparison of the German effort with that of the anti-Hitler coalition. At the heart of this debate lay the attempt to estimate more exactly German military expenditure and to account for the rapid rise in armaments production from 1942.

The third debate was over the question of whether the economy of the Third Reich at the end of the 1930s was best defined as a 'war economy in peacetime' – or whether the war economy of the early 1940s could be characterized as a 'peacetime economy in war', following the supposed dictates of the *Blitzkrieg* ('lightning war') strategy.[5]

All three problem areas in this great and continuing debate are still open; the results of research are controversial. This is also true of a fourth issue, which arises in connection with debate on the origins of the West German 'economic miracle' of the 1950s (thus there were *two* German 'miracles', one prewar and one postwar). What were the long-term consequences of the Third Reich's rearmament and wartime economic efforts, and what was their relation to developments after 1945? These questions are addressed below in order to take stock of the state of research fifty years after the end of the war – even if clear answers are still not possible in every case.

The prewar 'economic miracle'

The role of public spending

Was the German recovery from the Depression a by-product or a precondition of Hitler's rearmament? In March 1933, when the National Socialists seized power, the German economy lay in a coma. It was not far removed from utter destitution, and had been in this state for months. Industrial production had fallen to almost half the pre-crisis (1928) level. Investment in industry covered only one-third of depreciation, not to speak of employment-creating new plant. As in the previous winter, the number of unemployed exceeded the catastrophic figure of 6 million. Every third worker was without work.

The crisis had been close to its lowest possible point already in spring 1932, and it 'stabilized' – with seasonal variations – at this level. The end of

Table 4.1. *The GDP of Germany, total and per head,*
within postwar frontiers of the Federal German Republic,
1929–1945 ($ at 1990 prices and per cent of 1913)

	GDP		GDP per head	
	$ bn	% of 1913	$	% of 1913
	1	2	3	4
1929	176.0	121.3	4,335	113.1
1930	165.2	113.9	4,049	105.6
1931	148.4	102.3	3,618	94.4
1932	134.6	92.8	3,267	85.2
1933	148.7	102.5	3,591	93.7
1934	160.2	110.4	3,846	100.3
1935	174.7	120.4	4,165	108.7
1936	192.9	133.0	4,571	119.3
1937	204.5	141.0	4,809	125.5
1938	220.4	151.9	5,126	133.7
1939	241.1	166.2	5,549	144.8
1940	242.8	167.4	5,545	144.7
1941	258.2	178.0	5,862	152.9
1942	261.7	180.4	5,892	153.7
1943	266.9	184.0	6,046	157.7
1944	273.7	188.7	6,249	163.0
1945	194.7	134.2	4,326	112.9
1946	115.6	79.7	2,503	65.3

Source: Taken or calculated from Maddison (1995), 148–9, 180–1, 194–5.

the decline may be traced to the effects of the first countercyclical programme. Yet there was still no sign of a reversal of the trend, or of an end
to the crisis. On the contrary, at the end of 1932 the situation reached a new
nadir, which for three months was even below that of the previous winter.
The analysis of trade cycle indicators provides no support for the thesis that
the crisis had been essentially overcome at the time of the National Socialist
(NS) seizure of power, and that the recovery would have occurred without
the National Socialists. There is, on the contrary, much to suggest that the
real task of overcoming the crisis was still to be faced.[6]

It is not disputed that this goal was achieved under Nazi rule faster and
more completely than contemporaries in Germany and abroad had envisaged, even in their most optimistic forecasts. By 1937, 6 million unemployed had been reintegrated into the production process. Indeed, a
worrying labour shortage was evident. At the same time, industrial produc-

Table 4.2. *German industrial production within contemporary frontiers, 1935–1944 (per cent of 1928)*

| | Total industry | Consumer goods | Producer goods | |
| | | | total | coal mining |
	1	2	3	4
1935	96	91	99	96
1936	107	98	114	107
1937	117	103	130	124
1938	125	108	144	126
1939	132	108	148	135
1940	128	102	144	165
1941	131	104	149	169
1942	132	93	157	177
1943	149	98	180	185
1944	146	93	178	163

Source: Petzina, Abelshauser and Faust (1978), 61. Over the period 1938–44, producer goods comprised basic industries, armaments, construction goods, and all other investment goods.

tion surpassed its pre-crisis (1928/9) peak. Real GNP per capita was as much as 10 per cent higher, and continued to grow (tables 4.1, 4.2). The output gap gradually dissolved.[7] Idle resources came together with a willing and able workforce. Since the years of hyperinflation, German economic growth had lain far below its potential. Even in the prosperous phase from 1925 to 1929, the growth rate was at the lower end of the normal long-term trend, and real GNP then sank by an annual average of 7.2 per cent between 1929 and 1932. The double-digit average annual growth of 1933–8 is a clear contrast to this.

Unemployment at this time was still around 20 per cent in the USA, and above 10 per cent in Britain. A powerful economic policy performance seemed to lie behind the German development, which foreign observers soon raised to legendary status as an 'economic miracle'.[8] Germany evidently applied to the greatest effect the new range of policy instruments furnished by academic and political outsiders at the beginning of the 1930s as a remedy for the failure of liberal economic policy. In the area of crisis policy, John Maynard Keynes was just one of many to call for the adoption of a 'compensatory financial policy'.[9] According to Keynes, in the extreme case it made sense to use the unemployed to dig holes and fill them in again, provided the resulting incremental income could revive demand and help

Table 4.3. *Cumulative outlays on civilian job creation in Germany, 1933–1934 (RM million)*

		To end 1933	To end 1934
1	Public construction	855.6	1,002.4
2	Housing	723.3	1,280.0
3	Infrastructure	950.8	1,683.9
	of which, motorways	50.0	350.0
4	Agriculture and fisheries	337.4	389.2
5	Promotion of consumption	70.0	70.0
6	Reich Employment Office	164.0	568.0
7	Total	3,101.1	4,994.0
8	For comparison:		
	additional military outlays	100.0	2,780.0

Notes:
1. Roads, maintenance, public buildings, bridges, and tunnels.
2. Maintenance, small settlements, home construction, and urban renewal.
3. Reichsbahn (railways), Reichsautobahnen (motorways), Reichspost (mail), shipping.
4. Land improvement, settlements, fisheries, maintenance.
5. Government campaigns to encourage consumer spending.
6. Basic promotional funds, including funding of labour service (about half of either figure); for funding of the Reich Agency for Homebuilding see under housing (row 2).
7. The sum of rows 1–6.
8. Cumulative military outlays above the 1932 level, including expenditures financed through Mefo-bills. There are varying estimates for 1934. However all document the primacy of civil job creation measures in the early phase of the National Socialist regime. It should also be noted that the bulk of military outlays in calendar 1934 occurred towards the end of the year.
Sources:
1–6. Schiller (1936), 158 ff.
8. As table 4.2 (row 13).

overcome the Depression. The National Socialists applied similar measures to tackle the crisis, and the impression thus arose abroad that Hitler was 'straightening the Crooked Lake, painting the Black Forest white, and putting down linoleum in the Polish Corridor'.[10]

The National Socialists poured up to RM 5 billion into additional outlays on job creation to the end of 1934 – more than three times total industrial investment in the same period (table 4.3). Outlays on the development of public infrastructure, including motorways, and to promote private housing, featured prominently. Considerable military expenditures also featured, although these remained of secondary importance up to the end of 1934 because the Reichswehr did not consider itself able to shorten substantially the timescale of its rearmament plans. On the contrary, the state job creation programmes put forward by the Nazi régime, the first and second Reinhardt plans of 1 June 1933 and 21 September 1933 ('the Reich's battle for employment' and the 'general attack on unemployment' respectively), were not intended to finance rearmament.

Alongside allocations directly for the development of infrastructure, a number of indirect measures also proved extremely effective. This was especially true of the 'marital loan'. 'Certificates of Needs' were allocated to those willing to marry, provided the prospective bride had been in work six months before the marriage and then surrendered her job. These had a maximum value of RM 1,000 and could be used to purchase furniture and domestic fittings. At first glance this measure was astonishingly successful. In 1933 there were 200,000 more marriages than in the previous year; by the beginning of 1935, 378,000 marital loans had been paid out, to a combined value of RM 206 million. These credits were interest-free, and could later be transformed into a child allowance. However, the effect on population was considerably less than on the economy. Most of the extra marriages had been postponed during the Depression, and any rise in the number of marriages was noticeable only in the short term. But the impact of the credits on employment in the consumer goods industry was substantial.

The removal of vehicle tax on 10 April 1933 had a similarly positive effect on car production. This, together with expenditure on motorway construction (beginning with the Frankfurt–Heidelberg route on 23 September 1933), is repeatedly cited as evidence of the latent military character of 'civilian' job creation. This thesis does not survive a confrontation with empirical research. In the view of the armed forces, the strategic value of the motorways was limited; they preferred the railways. Even during the war they saw no necessity for special roads. The routes followed by the new motorways were therefore determined exclusively by technical engineering considerations. There was no 'strategic co-decision' by the armed forces. Where the War Ministry did raise objections to the route of particularly exposed roads, as in 1935 in relation to the Black Forest highway, it was typically overruled, in this case in order to preserve the route's scenic charm.[11] After 1936 the costly motorways were in competition with the munitions industry, a circumstance that Hitler greatly regretted. The military planners would also have preferred 'pure munitions industry' to the expansion of the Volkswagen plant, although in 1933 they had spoken out against the vehicle tax in the interests of an efficient car industry.

More than strategic considerations, it was Hitler's vision (influenced by the American experience) 'that in ten years at the latest the roads will not be sufficient to cope with the traffic', that led him to adopt the plans of the

HAFRABA Society.[12] Beginning with the Hamburg–Frankfurt–Basel route, HAFRABA had wanted to develop a German motorway network in the 1920s. 'The Führer's roads' were not ideal for job creation. It took too long to build up a flow of spending large enough to give a noticeable effect on the trade cycle. At the end of 1934 only RM 350 million had been approved, and less than half of this had been allocated. However, construction was continued until 1941, because of Hitler's personal interest and because the motorways gained the Reich a reputation for technical achievement both at home and abroad.

Breaking the constraints

The job creation programme was mainly financed through the Reichsbank. Even more important than the practice of financing through the sale of bills, which had been introduced earlier, and breached at least the spirit of the Reichsbank law, was the new composition of the Reichsbank leadership. On 16 March 1933, Hjalmar Schacht succeeded the conservative Hans Luther. The Reichsbank was thus led by a man who enjoyed the reputation of a financial genius ever since his involvement in the currency stabilization of 1923, and who was a confidant of Hitler, large-scale industry, and the banking world. Above all, Schacht had the economic policy insight needed to make the necessary sums available for the purpose of job creation – and also for rearmament. In the person of Schacht, Hitler found a figure broadly acceptable both at home and abroad, who could persuade the Reichsbank to agree to his plans and hence render it unnecessary to abrogate the bank's legally established autonomy. This had earlier proved a difficult dilemma in German economic policy, and it was now overcome.

Another limitation on room to manoeuvre had been removed even before the Nazi seizure of power, with the ending of reparations. The financing of large-scale job creation programmes at home no longer cut across the German effort to be considered unable to pay reparations abroad.

Moreover, large-scale industry was now in the process of revising its position. It had earlier sought to block the adoption of generous programmes for direct job creation, believing that there were higher profits in indirect investment incentives. It had become clear to the industrialist camp in the interim that more was at stake with crisis policies than short-term profits or throwing off what they considered to be the burden of the social policies inherited from the Weimar period. If the Depression could not soon be overcome, the very existence of a private sector was threatened. Large-scale industry was then able to accept the allocation of billions of marks to countercyclical policies more easily, when longer-term prospects seemed brightened by the dismantling of trade union opposition and by the planned rearmament.

In addition, agriculture, hitherto a stumbling block to a successful trade cycle policy, was no longer on an opposing course, since the Economics and Agriculture Ministries were combined in the person of Hugenberg. Thus the National Socialists had removed or overcome significant resistance on the part of institutions and interest groups. This resistance had previously stifled the tentative efforts of earlier governments even at their inception.

Thus the Enabling Act of 23 March 1933, which inaugurated the Hitler régime, was merely an outward sign of the extent of dictatorial power which the National Socialists were able to exercise in order to carry through their goal of job creation. After 1933 trade cycle policy changed. External political conditions were more favourable, a larger volume of financing was employed, and the policies of the previous years were implemented more rigorously.

Another difference between the National Socialists and their Weimar predecessors was that the Nazis had a clearer conception of the foundations of an anti-depression policy. It does not contradict this view to note that a range of policy instruments already existed at the start of the Nazi régime, merely waiting to be implemented. Even in early 1932 the NSDAP and its publicists had taken to heart the principles and methods of direct, credit-financed job creation, as developed by the German 'Keynesians before Keynes'.[13] The National Socialists could claim to have been the first major party to incorporate such ideas in their manifesto, in the 1932 *Sofortprogramm*, and to have promoted their adoption even before the seizure of power.[14]

There were also non-NS advocates of an anti-depression demand expansion. For example, the free trade unions of the ADGB had put forward the 'WTB' job creation plan at the end of 1931 and the start of 1932. However, the Social Democrats, and especially their economic policy spokesman Rudolf Hilferding, still supported Brüning's deflation policy. They rejected the trade union job creation plan as 'un-Marxist' and 'inflationary'.[15] It is characteristic of the macroeconomic policy landscape at the nadir of the Depression that the SPD did not even bring the WTB plan to the Reichstag, while the representative of the NSDAP's left wing, Gregor Strasser, there referred to it as a programme 'which one can certainly discuss, and with which we are at all times ready to cooperate, given the right conditions'.[16]

Strasser's own 'Immediate economic programme of the NSDAP' (the *Sofortprogramm*) was circulated widely in pamphlet form by the party's national propaganda unit during the campaign for the July 1932 Reichstag election.[17] In the midst of much propaganda and polemic it contained all the principles and methods which were later proven successful. From autumn 1932, however, in the power struggle over Hitler's candidacy as chancellor, the strongly anti-capitalist thrust of Strasser's programme might have proved a liability. Hitler therefore deemed it politically more advisable to replace the *Sofortprogramm* with the 'NSDAP economic recovery programme'. This latter avoided both appeals to anti-capitalist sentiment among the masses and demands for the 'right to work' directed against industry. Yet the 'recovery programme' retained the decisive elements of direct job creation to the tune of billions of Reichsmarks, and of 'productive credit creation' through the Reichsbank.

It would certainly be an exaggeration to portray the NSDAP as the originator of the new German economic policy. Yet it cannot be overlooked that from the beginning the party leaders had close contacts with the 'German Keynesians'. The party provided a platform for the dissemination of their ideas by repeatedly citing their works in its propaganda, and it rapidly incorporated their demands into its economic programme. Thus, at least in relation to crisis policy, the NSDAP after the seizure of power depended neither on improvization nor – as in so many other areas of domestic policy – on political plagiarism or pure terror.

Already in his Reichstag declaration on 1 February 1933 Hitler had promised the voters concrete successes in job creation: 'The national government will develop the following plan with iron will and stubborn persistence. Within four years the German farmer must be raised from destitution. Within four years unemployment must be completely overcome.'[18] Unemployment did indeed fall drastically after 1933, and as early as two years after his seizure of power Hitler had fulfilled his promise in a manner evident to everyone. In this period unemployment was more than halved, and in the course of 1936 full employment was achieved in Germany, for the first time since the great inflation of the early 1920s.

Public opinion attributed this success to Nazi crisis policies – and justifiably so. The general population did not attach such great importance to any other problem in the 1930s. Then, as now, job creation was the key criterion of a successful policy. Precisely in this area Hitler was now able to demonstrate expert competence and political effectiveness, and to differentiate himself positively from his predecessors. Hitler himself was aware of this from the beginning. Speaking to an NSDAP leadership conference in August 1933, he said as much. According to Hitler, the solution of the unemployment problem, which proved beyond the capabilities of its opponents, would bring the NSDAP a gain in authority achieved by no other régime before National Socialism.[19] Of course, the degree of credibility and trust which Hitler acquired soon after 1933 through management of the economic crisis only partly explains his popularity. However, economic policy contributed more to the growing stability of the régime than sophisticated manipulation techniques and terrorist intimidation.

The material results of the 'economic miracle' of the 1930s created the foundation on which important goals of National Socialism could be implemented, both in foreign and military policy, and in the régime's 'social policy'. It was not the western democracies, but the German dictatorship which first found a practical solution to social catastrophe. This circumstance was enormously significant for the further development of Germany and international politics. Not without some bitterness, the Cambridge economist Joan Robinson concluded, 'Hitler had already found how to cure unemployment before Keynes had finished explaining why it occurred'.[20] Against this background, the National Socialist accomplishment may be evaluated as a 'revolution before the revolution' in a dual sense.[21] The Nazi 'economic miracle' preceded the 'Keynesian revolution' in the capitalist economic system, and it also reinforced the material and (more importantly) psychological basis of the German dictatorship's social revolutionary pretensions. Above all, however, it laid the foundations for the complete mobilization of resources for the coming war.

As much butter as necessary, as many guns as possible

The primacy of rearmament

From 1935, rearmament expenditure considerably exceeded the volume of public investment, and replaced civil job creation programmes as the pacemaker of expansion. Had Hitler's ideas been realizable, this would have been the case from the start. Keynes's intellectually exaggerated conception that the crisis could if necessary be overcome by useless work projects, as long as these were financed through deficit spending, was perversely reflected in Hitler's plans. At a ministerial meeting of 8 February 1933 Hitler demanded the institutional amalgamation of job creation and rearmament: 'Every publicly promoted job creation measure must be judged on the basis of whether it is necessary from the point of view of increasing the military capability of the German people. This thought must be to the forefront always and everywhere.'[22]

In this Hitler met with opposition in the cabinet. At the same meeting the Labour Minister Seldte observed, 'that alongside the purely defence policy tasks there were also other economically useful tasks, which should not be neglected' (Seldte was also leader of the Stahlhelm organization of war veterans). In July the dispute was clearly decided in favour of 'economically useful tasks', i.e. job creation measures, because now Hitler too placed job creation as his priority: 'Each measure is to be so judged: what are its consequences? Does it create more employment or does it create more unemployment?'[23]

In the interim, military projects suitable for the purposes of job creation in the short term were lacking. Yet the aim of rearmament was neither abandoned nor put on the back burner. Job creation was simply recognized as an important precondition. Hitler was convinced that the solution of the unemployment question 'would accord the new system such a position that, thus armed, this government could realise its other tasks step by step'. One of these tasks, as Hitler also made clear, would be to step forward as the 'heirs' of a Russia ruined by Bolshevism.[24]

Rearmament was finally in full swing in 1935; the preceding job creation programmes had already made an impact, and had clearly pulled the German economy out of the depths of the Depression. Figures on unemployment and on capacity utilization in industry showed a correspondingly positive trend. Utilization gradually approached the pre-crisis level, in terms both of workplace employment capacity, and of average hours worked. This reflected the development of industrial production, which returned to the 1928 level in mid-1935 (table 4.2).[25] Unemployment, a 'lagging' indicator of the trade cycle, fell from 5.6 million (1932 annual average) to 4.8 million (1933), 2.7 million (1934) and 1.7 million (mid-1935). In some industries a troublesome shortage of skilled labour was already being felt. In short, the German economy was in the process of recovering from a deep depression. The recovery began from those sectors (e.g. construction, vehicles) directly affected by counter-cyclical programmes, and gradually spread to the consumer goods industries.

The maintenance of deficit spending, now expanded and devoted almost exclusively to rearmament, was not able to speed recovery any further. On the contrary, the resulting excess pressure on supply stood in the way of a transfer of demand into mass consumption. Moreover, it led inevitably to violent imbalances in the economic structure and in the distribution of income. It now became clear that Hitler would not subordinate his military and foreign policy plans to the dictates of economic and currency stability. Rearmament programmes slowly coming on stream at the wrong time were speeded up, and grew to twice or three times the volume of public investment.

This cannot be explained by ignorance of the trade cycle implications. In 1932 in the Reichstag the National Socialists' economic policy spokesman Gregor Strasser had mentioned this danger, and described it as manageable:[26] 'this kind of productive credit creation is not problematic as long as a strong and solvent state is able to turn off the tap at the right time and thus forestall any unwanted developments'. It now transpired that the régime wished not to 'turn off the tap' but to open it further. Its decision in favour of unlimited rearmament was not deterred by anticipation of negative side-effects, but took these for granted. The stage of the trade cycle, now approaching full employment, can only have suggested a restrictive state expenditure policy, but precisely at this point the régime overstepped the limits of macroeconomically appropriate deficit spending. It was thus clear that the Nazi state had not previously held back with rearmament expenditure because of trade cycle considerations, but because teething troubles and the timescales involved in defence spending plans prevented it from pursuing job creation entirely by means of rearmament.

Rearmament expenditure

The exact level of German rearmament expenditure up to the start of World War II is hotly debated (table 4.4). As can be seen, the cumulative totals for the period 1934/5 to 1938/9 vary from RM 34.3 billion (Schacht) to RM 74 billion (Kuczynski). There are many reasons for the wide variations in estimates. The first problem is to determine which expenditures should be classified as rearmament related. Rearmament expenditure includes outlays on military pay and rations, the procurement of weapons, fuels, and soldiers' kit, military construction, the maintenance of buildings and weapons systems, and the promotion of military R&D. However, the military budget includes by no means all of the state's military-related spending. One major reason for the divergent estimates found in the table is differences over whether or not to include indirect outlays such as investment in military industry, and investment in the industrial materials promoted by the (second) Four-Year Plan, especially steel from low-grade German ores, synthetic oil, and synthetic rubber.

In the German case, two additional problems accompany this problem of definition. First, the institutional pluralism of the Nazi régime and the mutual rivalry of state apparatuses implies a further institutional fragmentation of military-economic accountancy. Second, official figures on the size of military expenditure exist only up to 1933. Secrecy and disguise then come to the fore. Hitler himself proclaimed a figure of RM 90 billion in the Reichstag on the outbreak of the war, but this served mainly as propaganda; it is at any rate not confirmed by most estimates.[27]

Unfortunately, Timothy Mason's comment of more than thirty years ago is still apposite: 'One of the many elementary facts which has still to be established is the precise expenditure of the régime on rearmament – the problem is chiefly one of unsatisfactory source material.'[28]

Table 4.4. *Alternative estimates of German military expenditure by fiscal year (1 April–31 March), 1932/3–1939/40, and by calendar year, 1932–1939 (RM million)*

(A) By fiscal year	1932/3	1933/4	1934/5	1935/6	1936/7	1937/8	1938/9	1939/40	Total, 1933/4 to 1938/9
1 Schacht	—	—	2,250	5,000	7,000	9,000	11,000	—	34,250
2 Länderrat	—	1,900	1,900	4,000	5,800	8,200	18,400	—	40,200
3 Wagenführ	—	1,900	1,900	4,000	5,800	8,200	18,400	—	40,200
4 Klein	—	1,900	1,900	4,000	5,800	8,200	18,400	32,300	40,200
5 Hillmann	—	1,900	2,800	6,200	10,000	14,600	16,000	—	51,500
6 Schwerin	630	746	4,197	5,487	10,273	10,961	17,247	—	48,911
7 Stuebel	600	746	4,197	5,487	10,273	10,961	17,247	11,906[a]	48,911
8 Fischer	600	700	4,200	5,500	10,300	11,000	17,200	32,300	48,900[b]
9 Carroll	800	1,900	4,100	6,000	10,800	11,700	17,200	30,000	51,700
10 Overy	—	750	4,093	5,492	10,271	10,963	17,247	—	48,816
11 Köllner	600	700	4,100	5,500	10,300	11,000	17,200	—	48,800
12 Kuczynski	1,000	3,000	5,500	10,000	12,500	16,000	27,000	—	74,000

(B) By calendar year	1932	1933	1934	1935	1936	1937	1938	1939[c]	Total, 1933–9[c]
13 Erbe	620	720	3,300	5,150	9,000	10,850	15,500	—	44,520
14 Schweitzer	—	—	4,433	5,934	10,743	14,515	20,325	13,907	69,857[d]
15 Eichholtz	—	1,500[e]	2,800	5,500	11,000	14,100	16,600	16,300	67,800[f]

Notes:

[a] 1 April–31 August.

[b] Up to the outbreak of war (1 September 1939) approximately RM 61 billion was spent according to Fischer (1968), 67; if we add indirect expenditures, this figure rises by RM 3–4 billion (Fischer (1968), 68).

[c] To 31 August 1939.

d 1934–9. By adding 'estimated outlays of civilian authorities' Schweitzer (1964), 618, arrives at a total of RM 70–74 billion.

e 1 February–31 December.

f RM 4 billion may be added to this total for 'military expenditures of civilian agencies'. By further including 'indirect' military outlays Eichholtz (1969), 32, obtains totals as high as RM 78 billion and even RM 90 billion.

Sources:

1. Schacht interrogation, in IMT, Bd. 41, 249.
2. Länderrat des amerikanischen Besatzungsgebietes (1949), 555.
3. Wagenführ (1954), 16.
4. Klein (1959), 254.
5. Hillman (1952), 253.
6. From the Wilhelmstraße trial, cited by Erbe (1958), 39.
7. Stuebel (1951), 4129; see also Köllner (1969), 81; Kroll (1958), 571 (Kroll gives total expenditure of roughly RM 29 billion for 1939).
8. Fischer (1968), 102.
9. Carroll (1968).
10. Overy (1994), 203.
11. Köllner (1969) 82.
12. Kuczynski (1965), 132.
13. Erbe (1958), 25, 100.
14. Schweitzer (1964), 331.
15. Eichholtz (1969), 31.

Schacht

The lowest figure was provided by former Reichsbank president Schacht, who gave a total figure of RM 34,250 million for military expenditure up to the outbreak of the war, the result of summing annual outlays growing steadily from RM 2,250 million (1934/5) to RM 11 billion (1938/9) (row 1). This figure is regarded as incomplete by other experts; Schacht based it mainly on rearmament financed by the Reichsbank through Mefo bills and similar means, and made only rough estimates of budget-financed military expenditure.[29]

'Länderrat' and others

The Council of Minister-Presidents of the American Occupied Zone offered a slightly higher estimate of RM 40.2 billion, which posits especially significant growth of expenditure in 1935/6 (when outlays doubled over the previous year), and in the last prewar fiscal year, from RM 8.2 billion (1937/8) to RM 18.4 billion (1938/9) (rows 2-4).

Though no sources or calculation methods are given, Wagenführ's identical figures are evidently likewise based solely on armed forces expenditures in the Reich budget, and exclude direct and indirect financing of the military by other departments.[30] The same figures were also adopted by Klein. They recur, but with substantial upward amendment for the years up to 1937/8, in the work of Hillmann.

Schwerin von Krosigk et al.

Former Finance Minister Schwerin von Krosigk presented a further fundamental estimate (rows 6–11, 13). He calculated total rearmament expenditure to be RM 48.9 billion in the period 1933–8, with particularly sharp increases from 1935/6 to 1936/7 (when outlays doubled) and from 1937/8 to 1938/9 (a rise of nearly 60 per cent).[31]

Schwerin's figures, originally from the Wilhelmstraße trial, were adopted by Stuebel, who added the RM 630 million shown in the table in respect of 1932 and a further sum of RM 11.9 billion for the period from 1 April to 31 August 1939, giving a total of RM 60 billion up to the outbreak of war. A number of other estimates are based on Schwerin von Krosigk and Stuebel: explicitly, those of Kroll, Carroll, and Overy, and implicitly those of Boelke, Köllner, and Fischer.[32] In addition, Erbe transformed these figures from fiscal years to calendar years by linear interpolation, obtaining a total of RM 44.5 billion for the period up to and including 1938.

Kuczynski et al.

The last group of figures shares the common feature of including an allowance for investment in military industry. Kuczynski offered an estimate which attempts to bear out Hitler's maximum figure (rows 12, 14, 15). According to Kuczynski the total of RM 90 billion was achieved as follows. The starting point is the fiscal-yearly cumulative development of the Reich debt, to which are added annual cumulative tax income and the armaments expenditure of 1932. Thus a constant level of civilian outlays by the Reich is assumed. To these estimates Kuczynski adds one-third of annual investment in the production goods industries, one-fifth of the corresponding figure for consumer goods industries, the totality of the tax income of the states and the municipalities to which this gave rise, and an estimate of the NSDAP's military and paramilitary expenditure, insofar as this was not financed through the Reich. Over the period 1933/4 to 1938/9 this yields a total figure of RM 74 billion; however, for the period up to the outbreak of the war, 'As even the cautious Erbe is prepared to add around RM 12 billion for April to September 1939, we arrive at around RM 90 billion armaments expenditure.'[33]

Schweitzer presented a somewhat lower, but still very large original estimate. He arrived at a figure of RM 69.9 billion for the period from 1934 to 31 August 1939 (in calendar years), which showed especially marked increases in the years 1936, 1937, and 1938. His figure resulted from combining the sum of military expenditure to estimates of investment in the (second) Four-Year Plan. Schweitzer did not consider related expenditures by civilian ministries, which he estimated at around RM 4 billion, or the quasi-military expenditure of some party organizations. He therefore calls his figure the 'minimum outlay', but adds:

If the estimated outlays of civilian agencies are included, then the total is raised from seventy to seventy four billion marks. Thus Hitler's affirmation that a total outlay of ninety billion marks was spent for military purposes prior to the invasion of Poland seems . . . untenable.[34]

Eichholtz also comes close to Schweitzer's total. He estimated armaments expenditure from February 1933 to August 1939 at RM 71.8 billion, by adding RM 4 billion of military outlays by civilian agencies to the total shown in the table, and 'after consideration of the sources and of the work of Hillmann, Stuebel and Schweitzer, as well as a revision from fiscal to calendar years'. Similarly to Kuczynski, he includes RM 6 billion for paramilitary organizations and regional and municipal expenditures, as well as for further 'significant contributions for both indirect and direct armaments expenditure'.[35]

Too much should not be made of the larger estimates of Kuczynski, Schweitzer, and Eichholtz. Indirect military-related outlays such as investment in military industry and under the Four-Year Plan added to Germany's ability to sustain a larger military burden in the future through

Table 4.5. *German government spending and national income, 1928 and 1932–1938 (RM million)*

	1928	1932	1933	1934	1935	1936	1937	1938
Military (Wehrmacht)	827	620	720	3,300	5,150	9,000	10,850	15,500
Public investment	6,413	1,970	2,430	3,460	3,890	4,220	4,620	5,530
of which infrastructure	2,234	850	1,238	1,694	1,867	2,144	2,400	3,376
Public administration	1,830	800	810	1,200	1,400	1,400	1,420	1,200
Welfare agencies	1,023	218	200	289	390	500	600	700
Housing	1,330	150	185	275	220	175	200	250
Military spending, %								
ratio to public investment	12.9	21.5	29.5	96.2	132.4	213.3	234.8	280.3
share of national income	1.1	1.4	1.6	6.3	8.7	13.7	14.7	18.9

Source: Petzina, Abelshauser and Faust (1978), 149. 'National income' is net national product at factor cost.

accumulation of fixed assets and the stock of knowledge, but did not contribute to German military power in the present. This, as well as comparability with the military outlays reported in other countries, directs our attention first and foremost to expenditures on the armed forces themselves, and only secondarily to wider concepts of military-related outlays.[36]

The share of the armed forces in total public spending rose steadily from 4 per cent (1933) to 18 per cent (1934) and 39 per cent (1936), until ultimately no less that half went on the military in 1938, the last complete prewar year.[37] The ratio of military outlays to public investment and their share in national income also showed this trend clearly (table 4.5).

In summary, the military spending total of RM 90 billion declared by Hitler on the eve of World War II seems to be greatly exaggerated and to have been a tool of psychological warfare. But even the more serious estimates of armaments expenditure, which lie between one third and one half of this fantasy figure are impressive enough to illustrate the exaggerated scale of German rearmament. For example, RM 49 billion (the Schwerin total) was roughly the same as Germany's entire GNP at factor cost in 1932.[38] Military expenditure contributed to the fact that in 1938 the share of government spending in national income was far higher in Germany (at 35 per cent) than in any other western industrial state (see table 4.6). In 1929 this share was still just 23 per cent. To finance the government claim on such a high proportion of GNP and to defend it against the claims of private consumption and investment required extraordinary measures.

Table 4.6. *The share of government expenditure in national income, 1938 (per cent)*

	%
Germany	35.0
France	30.0
UK	23.8
USA	10.7

Source: Erbe (1958), 35. Government expenditure excludes social insurance and expenditures by municipalities.
'National income' is net national product at factor cost.

Financing rearmament

Among the instruments for financing rearmament, the so-called Mefo bills have achieved notoriety. These were however just one of many techniques used to finance rearmament while hiding it from critical foreign observers. In the early phase of the Reich, when the scale of rearmament was still small, the purchase of weaponry could be financed from budgetary means, and notably under the cover of the 'immediate programme for job creation' initiated by Von Schleicher. With the drastic increase in military expenditure from the end of 1934, these possibilities were no longer sufficient. The régime therefore increasingly resorted to financing through the sale of bills, which were apparently accorded the status of 'good bills of exchange' through the use of a 'letterbox', and which could be submitted to the Reichsbank for discounting.

This camouflage manoeuvre was the task of the Metallurgische Forschungsgesellschaft mbH (Mefo), established in 1933 as a front company for four important armaments concerns: Krupp, Siemens, Gutehoffnungshütte and Rheinmetall. It had a modest starting capital of RM 1 million. Because the establishing companies were blue chip (*erste Adressen*) in the sense of the Reichsbank Law, the Reichsbank was legally able to refinance bills drawn on Mefo and thereby to bestow on them the character of means of payment. Companies whose armaments contracts could not be financed from the budget or from public borrowing could draw bills on Mefo and cash them at the Reichsbank. Since they were considered bills of exchange, the true extent of state armaments contracts and its credit-financed character was hidden.

Credit manipulation by means of Mefo bills breached, if not the letter, then certainly the spirit of existing financial legislation. This alone did not make them a despicable instrument of state fiscal policy. Civilian job creation was also financed through evasion of the existing Reichsbank Law, without damaging people. However, the latter was done quite openly, at least initially. The Mefo bills by contrast served to disguise rearmament.

Mefo bills circulated from 1934/5 until 1937/8, and ultimately achieved a circulation of RM 12 billion. Reichsbank president Schacht, considered the 'inventor' of Mefo bills, had from the beginning foreseen the ending of their issue at this date; after this point he intended to consolidate the amount in circulation. Yet instead of this, the instrument of Mefo bills was simply replaced by methods which were even more effective from the point of view of the Nazi régime's priorities, being 'quieter' and more discreet. The Reich paid for contracts with its armaments suppliers with treasury bills, i.e. state debt certificates with a six-month term, which were disposed of in the bank system. Tax certificates also played a part once more, as in the first phase of the job creation policy.

The régime became increasingly unrestrained in its choice of means as the coming war came more clearly into focus, shoving the debt problem into the background. This also applied to attempts to create long-term credit directly through savings banks, banks, credit unions, insurance firms (including social insurance), and miscellaneous 'money and capital agencies'. From 1935 the Reich no longer placed its bonds with the saving public, but with such money and capital agencies. Practically all savings and insurance sums were absorbed by these 'noiseless' means, to be replaced by medium and long-term state treasury bonds.

Savers thus became, without their knowledge, immediate creditors of the Reich. During the war the Anglo-Saxon countries also applied this procedure on a large scale. It is however characteristic that it was in use in Germany from 1935. The credit policy Enabling Act of June 1939 merely legalized what had long been practised. This completely removed all institutional controls on state credit and finance policy, crowning a development which had enabled rearmament without significant tax increases and without a loss of public confidence in the value of the Reichsmark.

During 1933 and 1934 the state credit uptake raised rather than lowered the consumption possibilities of the general population, because it stimulated production and helped to generate household incomes. In this phase, and up to the achievement of full employment in 1936, both private and public consumption could expand simultaneously. This was in spite of the fact that the pay freeze decreed in 1933, and rigorously adhered to from the start, reined in the expansion of private demand.

In 1936 this situation changed. Production capacity and labour reserves hitherto idle were now mainly in use. It was now necessary to decide on the future priorities of the German economy's production programme. In principle, this decision had already been made in 1933, but direct intervention in the economic process was now required to secure the growing share of the state at the expense of private consumption. In the area of the external economy this task fell to the 'New Plan' of Economics Minister and Reichsbank president Schacht; in the economy generally, and particularly in relation to armaments production, it fell to the Four-Year Plan run by Hermann Göring. Both packages of measures were aimed at lessening the dependence of the German economy on the foreign sector, especially in view of the coming war, and to correspondingly revise its structure and its regulatory system.

The 'New Plan'

The New Plan was born in 1934, out of the necessity to guarantee the conditions for economic recovery and rearmament. For foreign trade to grow in line with rapid domestic expansion was completely unrealistic, in the light of the contraction and continuing shrinkage of world trade flows. The supply price of imported raw materials was also rising faster than the demand price for German exports. Hence German reserves of gold and foreign exchange had dwindled from RM 2.5 billion (1929) to a pitiful residue of RM 165 million in 1934.

The New Plan must be seen against this background. It heralded the establishment of a virtual state monopoly of foreign trade. It steered import flows towards 'economically important' imports (i.e. armaments and food), promoted exports through subsidies, and concluded bilateral trade treaties with other countries. For the countries concerned, trade with Germany promised advantages, but the Reich believed it could utilize its economic and political strength better in bilateral agreements. In the long-term effort for economic and strategic autarky and the creation of a German large economic space (*Grossraum*) or regional bloc, the redistribution of German foreign trade from western Europe and North America to southeast Europe, the Near East, Latin America, and northern Europe was strategically important. The German Reich acquired an economic hinterland which was less vulnerable than before to blockade in the event of war in the west. At the same time the direction of the future German expansionary thrust was economically prepared.

Hardly any of the New Plan's instruments were novel. Exchange controls and targeted export promotion, through a system of partial devaluation of the Reichsmark, had already been introduced under Brüning. The idea of autarky became widespread during the Depression, because virtually no country could expect favourable effects from foreign trade. On the other hand, developments after 1934 corresponded very closely to the conception of autarky embodied in earlier National Socialist manifestos, entailing the reorganization of German trade within a closed regional bloc. However much the New Plan may appear as a pragmatic German response to the actual problems of the world economy in the 1930s, it also essentially reflects the essence of National Socialist ideas of autarky. Both reality and ideology were in accord in the New Plan. This constellation is typical for the 1930s. It largely explains the resonance which National Socialist economic policy found at the beginning of the Great Depression.

In complete contrast to the bullish rhetoric of the Four-Year Plan, on one side, and on the other side to contemporary foreign criticism of the ostensible German exploitation of the Balkans under the auspices of Schacht's New Plan, the attempt at economic penetration of southeast Europe to the Reich's advantage must today be considered a failure. This applies in the context of Göring's Four-Year Plan, which had to acknowledge that the hopes laid in the southeast had come to nothing at the latest by 1939.[39] It also applies to the development of economic relations generally between Germany and the so-called Reichsmark Bloc (Bulgaria, Greece, Hungary, Romania, Turkey, and Yugoslavia).

It is not necessary to go as far as Alan Milward and suggest that the Balkan states exploited Germany, but the economic facts are clear.[40] Germany was not able to turn its position as sole customer for agricultural surpluses and sole supplier of investment goods and armaments to its economic advantage. The terms of trade in the 1930s actually shifted significantly *in favour* of the Reichsmark Bloc. In order to procure mineral oil, bauxite, and chrome iron ores – products which could all be acquired on world markets – Germany bought up the agricultural surpluses of southeast Europe at prices which lay between 20 and 40 per cent above world market levels.[41] Because Germany paid with inconvertible Sperrmarks or Askimarks (ASKI stood for 'foreigners' special accounts for domestic payments'), it had to spend many times what purchasers offering convertible currencies did for Romanian soya beans or Turkish nuts.

Germany was thus obliged to export ever increasing amounts per unit imported from southeast Europe. In the case of Yugoslavia, Germany's import prices rose by 3.8 per cent between 1935 and 1936, while export prices fell by 2.9 per cent. In total the Reich had to export 5 per cent more goods by volume in order to finance an 8 per cent lower volume of imports.[42] From 1936 to 1937 import prices rose by 10.2 per cent while export prices rose by only 3.6 per cent. Nor was Germany able to push through clearing deficits of the order of tens of millions of Reichsmarks in its favour, as contemporary critics suspected at the time.[43] In reality, German clearings deficits were only accepted by the surplus country when

Table 4.7. *External sources of finance for Germany's military spending,*
1940–1944

(A) Occupation costs paid to Germany, by region (RM billion)	1940 (Jan.– June)	1941	1942	1943	1944 (Jan.– Sept.)	Total
France	1,750	5,550	8,550	11,100	8,300	35,250
Netherlands	800	1,900	2,200	2,200	1,650	8,750
Belgium	350	1,300	1,500	1,600	950	5,700
Denmark	200	200	250	550	800	2,000
Italy (from Sept. 1943)	—	—	—	2,000	8,000	10,000
Other occupied countries	900	1,050	4,500	7,550	8,300	22,300
Total	4,000	10,000	17,000	25,000	28,000	84,000

(B) German clearing debts, cumulative total to end:	RM billion
1940 (Dec.)	1.8
1941 (Dec.)	6.5
1942 (Dec.)	12.8
1943 (Dec.)	23.1
1944 (Sept.)	31.5

Sources:
(A) Federau (1962), 33.
(B) An estimate of the Bank for International Settlements, Basel, from 1944, cited by Lanter (1950), 104–5.

they were linked with comparably high cash receipts of foreign exchange for the respective country.[44]

The outbreak of war did not significantly alter this situation. In the war years Germany acquired the greater part of its external resources from France and the other countries of the later European Community, and not from east and southeast Europe (table 4.7).[45]

The German side certainly drew advantages from the special economic relationship to the Reichsmark Bloc. Against the background of a shrinking world market, between 1932 and 1938 the share of imports from the countries of central and southeast Europe doubled. The share of exports going to these countries trebled. Göring's Four-Year Plan drew raw materials from the area on the basis that 'price is no object'. Without the New Plan, the tempo of rearmament could not have been maintained. Food imports at prices well above those prevailing on the world market were easier to stomach since German agricultural prices also lay well above world levels. With the help of blocked and Aski marks, it was moreover possible in effect to float the Reichsmark, and yet maintain the overvalued Gold Mark rate for the servicing of Germany's foreign debts.

This precisely coincided with the interests of the Reichsmark Bloc countries, who for similar motives had not followed the devaluation of sterling. The New Plan also found that trade policy instruments in the Balkans were compatible with Germany's own foreign economic policy. Most Balkan countries had abandoned free exchange in September 1931. State direction of exports and bilateral clearing agreements were not innovations of their transactions with the Third Reich.[46]

On the whole, the economic advantage clearly lay with the Reichsmark Bloc, which used its special bilateral relations to promote the industrialization of its relatively backward economies. The level of industrialization in the Danube basin did indeed rise slowly but surely. In each country the main thrust in this development was in the textile industry, but the chemical, metallurgical, and engineering industries also benefited.[47] The argument that on the contrary bilateral trade with Germany had limited the Balkan states' room for economic manoeuvre missed the point that, in the 1930s, there was no trade policy alternative to bilateralism.

The Four-Year Plan

The securing of the foreign economic flank alone did not suffice to maintain the planned extent and tempo of Germany's rearmament. Although wages had been frozen at the low Depression level since 1933, the reintegration of 6 million unemployed into production nevertheless brought an unstoppable growth of mass purchasing power. Without decisive intervention in the domestic economy, this expansion of private demand threatened to halt the expansion of the state's demands on GNP. In 1936 supply bottlenecks arose in raw materials for the rearmament sector and in foodstuffs, and a fuel shortage raised questions about the capability of the armed forces. The Four-Year Plan was designed to overcome these acute problems. It was to underpin the 'self-assertion of the nation' with economic means, and to prepare 'the final solution . . . a broadening of both *Lebensraum* and the raw-material and foodstuffs base'. With the Four-Year Plan the Nazi régime built up a 'leading organ of the economy' under the direction of Hermann Göring, to which parts of the private sector as well as government economic administration were subordinated.[48]

The Four-Year Plan utilized both existing and new instruments to manage the economy in the service of the régime's rearmament aims. This entailed wage and price policies, the allocation of labour resources, and the regulation of investment through prohibitions, levies, and direct state investment, alongside exchange controls and demand management. In a fundamental memorandum on economic mobilization, Hitler himself pronounced the goal – in view of the coming war – of establishing 100 per cent autarky wherever this was in any way possible, and thereby rendering the German army ready for battle and the German economy ready for war within four years. To this end he demanded the saving of foreign exchange through import substitution, so that at least imports for which there was no domestic substitute could be paid for. He also demanded other steps. The expansion of the German fuel industry was to be completed within eighteen months; among other initiatives, synthetic rubber was to be mass-produced, and German iron ore resources were to be built up.

The German economy was thus programmed towards the goal of large-scale rearmament 'without consideration of costs'. While the phase of job creation was subsequently referred to as the 'first Four-Year Plan', rearmament was now to be institutionally secured with the 'second Four-Year Plan'. The result of these efforts was by no means a planned economy. But a state 'command economy' (in Petzina's phrase) arose, with the aid of partial plans, new bureaucracies (competing with each other and with the existing bureaucracies of large-scale industry, the defence forces, and the economic administration), and individuals appointed to special executive posts with ever more wide ranging competences. Not without considerable friction, this replaced an earlier steering system for the raw materials industries, which was itself far from being market driven.

For the first time the private sector had to endure extensive interventions which undermined its relative autonomy. This had not happened earlier, in spite of the 'purging' of their associations after 1933. On the other hand, there were close personal and professional interlinkages between particular giant business combines and the Four-Year Plan organization: in some areas this led to a privatization of state economic policy, and an assumption of state authority by private enterprise. Thus, after 1938, IG Farben took virtual control of central areas of management and personal leadership under the Four-Year Plan. Other firms, especially in the consumer goods sector, lost much of their freedom as a result of economic regulation. Even the right to dispose freely of private investments was effectively removed and transferred to the Four-Year Plan.

As Hitler announced in his memorandum on the Four-Year Plan, the motto in the case of conflicts was: 'The Economics Ministry has merely to set national economic tasks, and the private sector has to implement them. If however the private sector believes that it is unable to do this, then the National Socialist state will know how to solve these tasks itself.'[49] This was no idle threat. In 1937 the steel industry in the Ruhr refused to expand the capacity of their mills beyond what had already been achieved. The foundation of the Reichswerke Hermann Göring company in Salzgitter then demonstrated the Nazi régime's determination to subordinate even the interests of large-scale industry to its goals. Reichswerke Hermann Göring was favoured in the allocation of labour, raw materials, and plant. The establishment of the Volkswagen works on a green-field site near Fallersleben (renamed Wolfsburg after the war), can similarly be seen as a response to the refusal of the German car industry to adopt Hitler's ambitious motorization plans with sufficient zeal.

Industry

These and other regulatory measures had wide-ranging consequences for the German economy's structure and production programme. It did not prove possible to increase investment levels generally through investment controls and raw material allocations, but from 1937 the share of plant and equipment in industrial investment rose to more than half. At the same time there was a redistribution from consumer to producer goods industries, as befitted the policy of rearmament.

Paradoxically, the Four-Year Plan thereby created not only the industrial infrastructure for rearmament, but also the foundations for rapid postwar recovery of the West German economy. Despite considerable destruction after 1943, this unprecedented boom in industrial investment meant that in 1945, surviving capital stock in western Germany still exceeded the prewar level by one-fifth. Moreover, the emphasis on the producer goods sector was highly suitable for the demands of reconstruction.[50] In particular a range of new raw-material industries was created under the aegis of the Four-Year Plan to furnish the basis for armaments production, especially with regard to mineral oil, non-ferrous metals, and chemical products. In point of fact no bottlenecks in raw materials arose until the turning point of the war in 1942/3.

On the whole, the planning of the German economy was less comprehensive, and the predominance of the defence economy within the general economy less extensive, than the régime liked to pretend in the late 1930s. This tactic had some success. The Four-Year Plan created the impression abroad of a national economy running at high speed, geared to autarky, and prepared for war. It was also believed outside Germany that there was nothing comparable with which to confront the German machine; this in turn allowed the régime to pursue an exceptionally risk-laden foreign policy.

Agriculture

This course required German agriculture to secure food supplies through autarky. Reduced dependence on foreign supply did not only reflect defence objectives. Agriculture was also to contribute to easing the trade balance through successful 'battles for production', and to freeing foreign exchange for military-related imports. As it happened, exactly the opposite occurred. In autumn 1934 an unfavourable shift in the terms of trade and a poor harvest dramatically worsened the Third Reich's foreign exchange position.

But it was not possible to reduce import dependency in foodstuffs even with rising agricultural production. The recovery brought a strong growth in demand for foodstuffs, which could only be met by extensive imports. In 1935/6 the shortage of foreign exchange reached such an extent that it threatened the whole rearmament policy. In order to prevent the hoarding of important foodstuffs, agricultural policy now effectively became the responsibility of the envoy for the Four-Year Plan, Hermann Göring. Measures of price policy followed, to give farmers an incentive to greater production. These included lower fertiliser prices and higher producer prices for agricultural goods. Where these did not suffice, Nazi agricultural policy also resorted to abrogation of the farmer's right to dispose freely of his property. In addition, no effort was spared to raise the level of mechanization in German agriculture, which was relatively low by international standards. Despite certain successes, the increase in productivity in German agriculture was relatively limited.

Consumption

By contrast, the efforts of Nazi propaganda to redirect the population's consumption met with some success. There was some shift from goods in short supply to those readily available (e.g. from meat to fish), from imported to domestic agricultural produce (e.g. from wheat flour to potatoes), and from more to less expensive goods (e.g. from edible fats to marmalade). Sales of marmalade trebled in 1937/8. Fish consumption also rose considerably, while fat consumption fell by 15 per cent up to 1940.[51] Compared with circumstances abroad, the German diet was remarkably modest. The English tended to eat fish, white bread, sugar, and eggs, while cabbage, rye bread, potatoes and margarine featured in Germany. In the availability of better quality foodstuffs, the Nazi state also compared unfavourably with the Weimar Republic. Annual consumption of meat per head in 1938 (48.6 kg) still lay below the 1929 level (51.7 kg). This situation was accepted with some murmurings of discontent, but without noticeable protests, because so many had an all-too-vivid memory of conditions during the Depression (43.5 kg in 1930).

The blessing of a low starting point in the Depression generally served the goals of the Four-Year Plan. The initial mass unemployment of labour and fixed assets facilitated a curious combination: steady, gradually rising living standards, and rapid, if not planned, rearmament. Alongside terror and manipulation, the application of 'guns *and* butter' was the most solid foundation for the régime's stability. The success of the job creation policy became a precondition for National Socialist policies. The Four-Year Plan had the task of exploiting this economic potential on the principle of 'as much butter as necessary, as many guns as possible'. This balancing between domestic political stability and an assertive foreign policy was largely successful, even if production targets were not quite achieved and the German economy was as dependent on the foreign sector on the eve of World War II as it had been at the beginning of the 1930s.

That ambitious armaments targets were not reached did not only reflect the organizational friction generated by competing administrative command régimes, as typical of the Four-Year Plan as of the Nazi system in general. The German dictatorship developed an almost paranoid sensitivity to popular sentiment; it bolstered the standard of living in the short term at the expense of armaments-related raw materials imports. Import dependence was however held down to the low level of the Great Depression years, even though the German economy after 1933 expanded at an unprecedented rate; in terms of National Socialist policy, this must be considered a success. For the purposes of its creators, the Four-Year Plan was also successful in that it gave the appearance of war preparedness and military-economic self-sufficiency at an early stage.

Social consequences of rearmament

In the Four-Year Plan's division of tasks, it was easy to predict who would be the winners and losers in the Nazi economy. In a system which limited mass consumption for the benefit of rearmament, social groups whose economic prosperity relied on high mass consumption drew the short straw. By definition, all those directly involved in the achievement of rearmament and autarky must be counted among the winners. A consideration of income distribution by source of income shows this tendency in a very general way.

It is particularly noticeable that the self-employed in trade and handicrafts clearly and continually improved their share of total private income, while recipients of wages and salaries were able to increase their share only slightly up to 1936, in spite of an increase in their number. Correspondingly, the interpersonal distribution of income returned to a degree of inequality seen in previous historical periods. Consider the shares of total private income received by the top 10 per cent, the next 40 per cent, and the bottom 50 per cent of income recipients. The following picture emerges.[52] In 1936 the top 10 per cent accounted for almost as large an income share as in 1913. The income share of the lowest 50 per cent group fell sharply between 1928 and 1936, from 25 per cent to 18 per cent. Never before in the twentieth century did those comprising the bulk of the lower 50 per cent of income recipients – workers, clerical staff, civil servants, and self-employed – experience such a loss of economic status.

Yet this is not how the social realities of the 1930s were directly experienced at the time. Among the workforce, wage incomes rose steadily. The 1933 pay freeze could not be fully maintained, notably in production and investment goods industries. The 6 million unemployed who were reintegrated into the process of production up to 1936 certainly did not judge their position in the light of the shortlived phase of prosperity under Weimar. Nor did the experiences of neighbouring countries make this earlier prosperity phase any more relevant. In Germany unemployment fell below 5 per cent in 1936/7, and this was considered tantamount to full employment. Meanwhile unemployment was still over 10 per cent in Britain and as much as 20 per cent in the USA.

To the strategists of the Four-Year Plan, a number of common practices made the labour market resemble an 'unregulated and tendentious unending trench warfare along a long and badly defined front'.[53] Two such practices were open demands for pay rises on the part of the workers and the camouflaging of pay increases through a flourishing system of bonuses and premiums. These included additional health insurance, cheaper canteens, more generous holiday payments, contributions to transport costs, Christmas bonuses, and deposits towards Volkswagen motor cars paid by the employer. Also noticeable were an increase in absenteeism, enticement of workers to change jobs through offers of higher pay and better in-company social benefits, and frequent changes of employment involving breach of contract. From 1936, the realities of the labour market brought the workers considerable gains in this battle.

Despite a lack of leadership, they made remarkable breaches in the front of military-economic planning. The workforce was evidently not prepared to voluntarily tighten its belts in favour of 'higher' political goals. They frustrated the régime by exercising more claims on consumption resources than the régime wished to concede to them. Very few, however, considered themselves involved in any kind of 'war'. Not only had mass unemployment disappeared, but the situation with regard to foodstuffs and supplies had improved, and was visibly approaching the Weimar peak, which itself was more of an exception than a permanent reality. Whether Nazi initiatives like 'beauty through work' or 'strength through joy' only had propaganda effects must also be questioned; the latter in particular seems at least to have had an impact.

There is little to suggest that the rearmament of the 1930s proceeded at the expense either of the general health of the workers or of safety in the workplace. This assumption is generally based on the fact that numbers injured in accidents rose by around 1.2 million between 1932 and 1938, and thus more than doubled. So did the number of illnesses.[54] This argument ignores the fact that numbers insured also rose markedly. If one relates the number of injuries and illnesses to the total number of insured, the result is generally in line with figures from the years of the Weimar boom; in the case of illnesses and fatal accidents, there is even a certain decline.

The unparalleled recovery after 1933 developed a dynamism of its own. It created for the régime an economic potential which could be used to force the pace of rearmament. Simultaneously, however, it forced the National Socialists to adopt extensive regulatory measures, in order to prevent the boom being translated into mass consumption. This aim was not completely achieved. The intention was by means of propaganda to bring the population to a state of 'national intoxication' in which the masses would voluntarily forego consumption in 'appreciation of the necessity of restoring defence capability' or other national goals. This intention was also clearly unfulfilled. Nor did the régime attempt openly to bring the German people to sacrifice 'blood, sweat and tears' willingly in peacetime. This general assertion is confirmed rather than contradicted by the eating of stew on Sunday for the benefit of the Winter Help Organization – six such events took place after 1936, each time during the winter – or by popular educational propaganda campaigns in the style of the 'combat waste' initiative.

General Wilhelm Keitel, in charge of the Wehrmacht within the Ministry of War, described the machinery of the Four-Year Plan from the inside as a 'struggle among all those needing resources for labour, raw materials and money'; the result was that the consumer sector maintained a stronger lobbying power than military-economic planners would have liked. Together with the Labour Front (DAF), and the actions of individual Nazi leaders who feared for their popularity, it was above all the dynamics of the recovery itself which entailed the diffusion of a higher standard of living. Rising wages brought demand pressure, and in 1937 this even caused a temporary halt in the rearmament process (which had already, admittedly, reached a high level). The régime stayed on its cautious course until 1942, well into the war; it obviously considered this advisable in consideration of domestic political stability.

To speak of a 'peacetime economy in war' would be just as misleading as to apply the label of a 'war economy in peacetime'. This latter has been used to describe the macroeconomic regulatory measures and financing methods of the 1930s. A combination of the two is more appropriate for the state of the German economy up to 1942. The National Socialist economic system had elements of both a wartime and a peacetime economy. Tendencies towards the latter were not intentional, but were unavoidable if the system was to be stabilized. A decision for a war economy was taken very early on, but it was not fully implemented until 1942. This explains, for one thing, the 'production miracle' under the auspices of Armaments Minister Albert Speer after 1942, which was made possible by stepping up the war economy. It also makes it clear that, against the background of the Great Depression, the everyday experience of contemporaries after 1933 was characterized more by improvement in living standard in the broadest sense than by the burden of rearmament.

Mobilization for war and the postwar inheritance

The war economy

Rolf Wagenführ's inside view of *German industry at war,* published in 1954, strongly influenced subsequent research. It characterized the military-economic effort of the period 1939–41 as a 'peacetime economy in war'.[55] On one hand, he showed that the régime was not able to guarantee a smooth transition from a peacetime to a war economy. Thus, in 1940 the number of employed persons in industry fell by 10 per cent compared with 1939 (see table 4.17 (A) below). On the other hand, however, in comparing this relatively minor war-induced difficulty with the catastrophic beginning made by the German war economy after August 1914 (the *Kriegsstoß*), Wagenführ spread the belief amongst the first generation of researchers that until 1941 the Nazi régime had followed the complacent slogan of 'business as usual'.

Wagenführ also identified a cyclical pattern of munitions production in the early phase of the war, which, supposedly, followed the deliberate rhythm of the *Blitzkrieg* strategy. According to this interpretation the output of weapons and ammunition was intentionally run down after the victory in France while the production of consumer goods was maintained at peacetime levels (see table 4.8).[56] Moreover, figures for industry group shares in net output (table 4.9) seem to support this position. The share of specialized military industry, still a modest 16 per cent in 1940, stagnated in 1941. The share of consumer goods industries was relatively stable at 30 per cent or so. The main structural shift at work which is visible in the table was in favour of basic goods and armaments to the disadvantage of the construction goods sector.

There is a further argument in favour of the hypothesis that Germany made only a belated start on mobilizing a total war economy. Between the beginning of 1942 and the summer of 1944 German war production trebled (table 4.8 above), but nonetheless there did not appear to be enough time for munitions production to reach full capacity. In Alan Milward's words, 'Theoretically, if not in the real world of warfare, German productive effort had not reached its uttermost limit when it began to falter.'[57]

Table 4.8. *Germany's munitions output, 1929–1944: monthly series (per cent of 1942, January–February)*

	(A) Weapons			(B) Ammunition			(C) Munitions, total			
	1939	1940	1941	1939	1940	1941	1942	1943	1944	1945
January			88	—	74	99	103	182	241	227
February	—	68[a]	120	—	86	112	97	207	231	—
March			114	—	86	105	129	216	270	—
April			117	—	106	108	133	215	274	—
May	—	79[a]	114	—	120	104	135	232	285	—
June			123	—	149	107	144	226	297	—
July			126	—	178	99	153	229	322	—
August	—	83[a]	114	—	127	109	153	224	297	—
September			88	90	112	91	155	234	301	—
October			95	58	103	93	154	242	273	—
November	63[a]	86[a]	91	83	105	100	165	231	268	—
December			83	82	98	92	181	222	263	—

Note:
[a] Quarterly average.
Sources:
1939–41: USSBS (1945), 283.
1942–5: Wagenführ (1954), 178–81.

There are, however, other indicators which are at variance with the traditional explanation put forward by Wagenführ, and alternative explanations of this striking evidence which did not form part of his hypothesis.

Pressure on consumption

First, it is true that the production of consumer goods industries did not fall significantly before 1942. However, by late 1940 most of the consumer branches were already devoting between 40 and 50 per cent of their output to the military, leaving very little for the civilian population.[58] This is clearly visible from the proportions of the workforce of each branch of industry engaged in supplying military orders (table 4.10), which also show that the biggest shift to war work took place in 1939–40. Therefore, the level of output of consumer industries cannot be considered as evidence for the 'peacetime economy in war' hypothesis.

That living standards were no longer protected in 1939 and 1940 is shown clearly by a number of direct indicators. Statistical measures of real consumption per head were falling already in 1939, and by 1941 were at least one-fifth below the prewar benchmark (table 4.11). Within prewar

Table 4.9. *The net output of German industry, by industry group, 1939–1944 (per cent of total)*

	1938	1939	1940	1941	1942	1943	1944
Armaments	7	9	16	16	22	31	40
Basic goods	21	21	22	25	25	24	21
Construction goods	25	23	15	13	9	6	6
Other investment goods	16	18	18	18	19	16	11
Consumer goods	31	29	29	28	25	23	22

Source: Petzina (1968), 187.

Table 4.10. *Numbers employed in Germany on orders for the armed forces, 1939–1943 (31 May, per cent of total workforce and per cent of 1939)*

	1939	1940	1941	1942	1943
Per cent of workforce:					
All industry	21.9	50.2	54.5	56.7	61.0
Raw materials	21.0	58.2	63.2	59.3	67.9
Manufacturing	28.6	62.3	68.8	70.4	72.1
Construction	31.5	57.6	53.8	45.2	46.2
Consumer goods	12.2	26.2	27.8	31.7	38.3
Per cent of 1939:					
All industry	100	229	249	256	278

Source: Overy (1994), 294.

frontiers (the fall was even greater for the Greater German average, as Germany expanded its territory into low-income regions of German settlement). Rationing temporarily deferred increases in consumer prices (table 4.12) and the emergence of a nutritional deficit (table 4.13); however both increases in the cost of living (both food and more especially clothing prices), and cuts in the calorific value of food rations, transpired in 1941.

Rationalization and production mobilization
The indifferent record of industrial production generally at the beginning of the 1940s has also been taken as evidence for a 'peacetime economy in war'; industrial production (table 4.3, above) essentially stagnated between 1939 and 1942. One explanation of this relatively poor record can be seen

Table 4.11. *Consumption and retail sales in Germany, 1938–1944*

	Real consumption per head (per cent of 1938)		Retail sales, Greater Germany, at current prices	
	Germany within 1939 frontiers 1	Greater Germany 2	total sales (RM billion) 3	sales per head (per cent of 1938) 4
1938	100.0	100.0	33.1	100.0
1939	95.0	98.0	37.8	97.3
1940	88.4	80.2	35.7	79.5
1941	81.9	74.4	35.4	77.8
1942	75.3	68.0	33.7	74.2
1943	75.3	67.2	33.0	72.7
1944	70.0	—	31.5	69.5

Source: Overy (1994), 278.

Table 4.12. *The cost of living for a German family, 1939–1944 (per cent of 1938)*

	Food 1	Housing 2	Heating, lighting 3	Clothing 4	Miscellaneous 5	Total 6
1939	101	100	100	102	100	100
1940	105	100	100	107	102	104
1941	105	100	99	121	105	106
1942	108	100	98	132	106	109
1943	110	100	98	137	106	110
1944	113	100	98	141	106	113

Source: Statistisches Jahrbuch (1957), 470–1. These figures are based on the 1934 consumption of a worker's family with five members.

in the fact that in September 1939 the German war economy was being developed at full speed, but the process was not yet complete – German industry was not yet ready for war. Gigantic projects such as the synthetic oil and rubber programmes, chemical facilities for the production of explosives, the Salzgitter and other steelworks being built to make better use of domestic ores, and numerous plants for the flow production of finished weapons, had been begun in and since the mid-1930s, but were still far from a state of completion. They absorbed large quantities of capital and labour

Table 4.13. *Calorific content of food rations for a worker's family member, 1939–1945*

	Period of distribution 1	Calorific content 2
1939/40	2–14	2,435
1940/1	15–27	2,445
1941/2	28–40	1,928
1942/3	41–53	2,078
1943/4	54–66	1,981
1944/5	67–79	1,671
1945/6	80–92	1,412

Source: Riecke (1953), 337; the author was Staatssekretär (undersecretary) in the Ministry for Food and Agriculture.

Table 4.14. *Output per worker in German industry, 1940–1944 (per cent of 1939)*

	1940	1941	1942	1943	1944
Basic industry	104.1	114.6	113.5	108.7	87.6
Munitions production	87.6	75.9	99.6	131.6	160.0[a]
Consumer industry	115.9	133.3	121.1	124.7	132.3
Industry, total	106.6	104.2	109.9	115.5	111.0

Note:
[a] Lower bound.
Source: Eichholtz (1985), 265–6. Eichholtz's calculations are based on Wagenführ (1954), 140, 159, 191, and USSBS (1945), 213 (appendix table 11).

without contributing yet to the current output of munitions. Labour productivity in the munitions sector fell by a quarter between 1939 and 1941 (table 4.14). Temporarily, the supply of weapons was growing much more slowly than the supply of resources to produce them.[59] At the same time, it is true that ambitious civilian projects such as the construction of the autobahn network or the Volkswagen works had not been stopped under the permissive conditions of the *Blitzkrieg* period.

Even more counterproductive than the delay in German readiness for war, was the application of a polycratic model of distribution of power, which meant that competing interest groups within the political régime exercised rivalry within the German war economy too. With the outbreak of war, powerful institutions competed for resources: Walther Funk's Ministry of Economics, the War Economy Office (*Wirtschafts- und Rüstungsamt*) headed by General Georg Thomas at Supreme Headquarters, and Hermann Göring's Four-Year Plan Organization. Below this top level another twenty-seven national offices (*Reichsstellen*) played their part in the prevailing planning anarchy. In responding to demands, priority was given to the armament offices (*Waffenämter*) of the army, navy, and air force. Military leadership of the war economy resulted in the general primacy of military considerations over limitations of cost – and in numerous conflicts between the three competing services.

The Ministry of Armament and Ammunition was established in March 1940 against this background. As a means of limiting military interference in the production process, this was a first step towards better coordination of German military industry. Thus, when Albert Speer took office in February 1942 the reforms initiated by his predecessor, Fritz Todt, had already prepared a new organizational structure for war production dominated by private industry. Step by step Speer took over responsibility for all work on munitions. In the central planning office (*Zentrale Planung/Planungsamt*) he also created the instrument for his purpose. The reorganization of the German war economy was completed in September 1943, by which time all authority was concentrated in Speer's ministry – except responsibility for labour resources and for the armament facilities of the SS.

Thus in 1942 two sources of rationalization of the German war economy came together to expand munitions output dramatically: *organizational rationalization* of the clumsy, counterproductive chain of command in weapons procurement, and *technical rationalization* of the armament facilities now being commissioned at the end of a long gestation period which had begun with the big investment projects launched in the mid-1930s.

New facilities offered the technical preconditions for a mass production system which would make better use of economies of scale. The first rationalization drive led to a concentration of production in the firms most rationally organized and best operated. In 1941 almost all German war factories were still run on a one-shift base. Now manufacturing methods were simplified as well as technical modifications of the weapons programme introduced, which made long production runs economically more feasible. The ministry also encouraged higher levels of shift work and a better use of existing floor space. In 1942 1.8 million men were still engaged in building new factories for which a more rational use of existing floor-space could have been substituted.[60]

Table 4.15. *Labour productivity in German heavy industry, 1938–1944 (per cent of 1939)*

	Ruhr coal-mining (tons per shift per worker)	Machine tool industry			
		tons per worker	tons per hour worked	value per worker	value per hour worked
	1	2	3	4	5
1938	96	—	—	100.5	102.0
1939	100	100.0	100.0	100.0	100.0
1940	97	92.0	94.0	104.0	104.0
1941	95	97.5	95.5	111.0	109.0
1942	89	92.5	90.0	109.0	106.0
1943	78	84.5	82.0	99.5	96.0
1944	75[a]	79.0	76.0	103.0	99.0

Note:
[a] January–June only.
Source:
1. Petzina, Abelshauser and Faust (1978), 62.
2–5. USSBS (1945), 228 (appendix table 31). Figures are based on employment of wage-earners on 31 March of each year.

Both kinds of rationalization combined to boost labour productivity in the armament sector where, by 1944, output per worker was not only at least 60 per cent above the level of 1939, but more than twice the depressed level of 1941 (table 4.14). This stands in sharp contrast to the indifferent productivity performance of other branches of German heavy industry after 1942 (tables 4.14, 4.15).

Rationalization of the resources built up as a result of the efforts of the preceding years played an essential role in wartime mobilization of overall resources. If we consider the changing pattern of final uses of output it becomes apparent that by 1943 Germany was devoting a remarkable 70 per cent of its nominal GNP to war outlays (table 4.16 and figure 4.1). Some of this was made possible by the additional resources being made available in net imports from occupied Europe and other foreign sources (see table 4.7 above). In figure 4.1 the area below the *x*-axis shows the contribution of net imports to total final outlays. If we divide Germany's war outlays by total final outlays (table 4.16) rather than by GNP alone, then the military share drops somewhat but still equals a remarkable 60 per cent. This very high rate of mobilization would have been impossible without the two rationalizations initiated in 1942 on the basis of earlier investment in new facilities.

Table 4.16. *The GNP of Germany, by final use, 1938–1944 (RM billions)*

	1938	1939	1940	1941	1942	1943	1944
At current prices							
Government expenditures	32	45	63	80	98	117	—
war	17	30	53	71	91	112	—
other	15	15	10	9	7	5	—
Consumer expenditures	69	71	68	65	61	61	58
Gross capital formation	14	13	1	−8	−16	−18	—
internal	13	14	10	7	6	6	—
external	1	−1	−9	−15	−22	−24	—
Gross national product	115	129	132	137	143	160	—
Total final outlays	114	130	141	152	165	184	—
At 1939 prices							
Government expenditures	33	45	62	77	93	109	—
Consumer expenditures	70	71	66	62	57	57	53
Gross capital formation	14	13	1	−8	−14	−16	—
internal	13	14	10	7	6	5	—
external	1	−1	−9	−15	−20	−21	—
Gross national product	117	129	129	131	136	150	—
Total final outlays	116	126	138	146	156	171	—

Source: Klein (1959), 257. 'External capital formation' is equivalent to net exports. Total final outlays ('total available product' in the original) equals government expenditures *plus* consumer expenditures *plus* gross internal capital formation (i.e. GNP *plus* net imports).

Rationalization and labour mobilization

One of the main purposes of the new programmes of simplification, standardization, and reorganization of production processes was to allow a more rational use of labour resources. Labour in general, and skilled labour in particular, proved to be a major bottleneck for the war economy from 1942 onward. Until then forced and foreign labour, brought in to fill the gap opened up by the rising demands of mobilization into the Wehrmacht, was mainly used in agriculture where skill did not matter (table 4.17 (B)). It was not until 1943 that rising numbers raised their share of the workforce in industry above that in agriculture.

As table 4.17 (B) shows, by 1945 forced and foreign labour accounted for 25 per cent of industrial employment, and 20 per cent of the total civilian labour force. The rationalization programmes opened the way to this development. It may have been easier to apply rationalization to persons who could not openly resist the deskilling effects of new production methods.

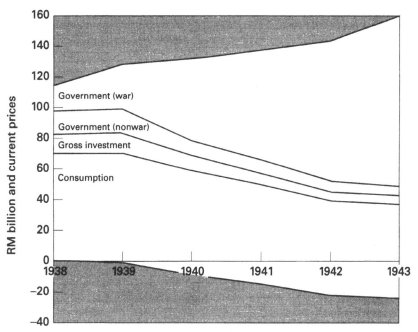

Figure 4.1 Germany's GNP by end use, 1938–1943
Source: table 4.16

Production methods

It is a paradox of the German war economy, that far beyond the mobiliza-
tions of the early 1940s, it created the preconditions for rapid reconstruction of the economy after 1945. Under the pressure of military
requirements and looming defeat, German industry was able to liberate
innovative forces which had not been exploited in the 1920s and early 1930s
because of the restrictive conditions of the Weimar economy. This was especially true of the introduction of new methods of management and production. The German economy was traditionally advanced in this area, but
until well into the 1930s it had not gone beyond theoretical deliberations
and technical experiments. At the outbreak of the war, the German munitions industry lay far behind its American and British counterparts in mass
production. From the autumn of 1941, however, it succeeded in noticeably
reducing the rationalization advantage of the Allies, and it reached a
comparable technical and organizational level by the latest at the end of
1943.[61]

Admittedly the window to top rank status was open only briefly. From
1944 the introduction of new product ranges often failed in the face of

Table 4.17. *The size and composition of Germany's civilian labour force by industry within prewar frontiers, 31 May, 1939–1944 (thousands and per cent)*

(A) Total numbers		1939	1940	1941	1942	1943	1944
Thousands							
1	Agriculture	11,224	10,687	10,721	11,229	11,301	11,185
2	Industry, transport	18,638	16,464	16,873	16,049	16,536	16,723
2.1	industry	10,947	10,012	10,453	10,105	10,645	10,904
2.1a	basic material	2,279	2,201	2,348	2,378	2,544	2,690
2.1b	metalworking	3,761	3,874	4,240	4,411	4,761	5,108
2.1c	construction	1,399	1,054	1,072	801	696	718
2.1d	other industry	3,508	2,883	2,793	2,515	2,644	2,388
2.2	handicrafts	5,336	4,230	4,040	3,504	3,387	3,282
2.3	transport	2,124	2,018	2,170	2,235	2,299	2,334
2.4	electric power	231	204	210	205	205	203
3	Trade, banking	4,603	3,738	3,417	3,219	3,081	2,866
4	Civilian administration	2,677	2,626	2,676	2,421	2,402	2,322
5	Military administration	692	721	844	1,244	1,412	1,457
6	Domestic service	1,582	1,526	1,506	1,466	1,442	1,378
7	Homework	—	—	—	—	—	279
8	Total	39,416	35,762	36,037	35,628	36,174	36,210
Per cent of total							
1	Agriculture	28.5	29.9	29.7	31.5	31.2	30.9
2	Industry, transport	47.3	46.0	46.8	45.0	45.7	46.2
2.1	industry	27.8	28.0	29.0	28.4	29.4	30.1
2.1a	basic material	5.8	6.2	6.5	6.7	7.0	7.4
2.1b	metalworking	9.5	10.8	11.8	12.4	13.1	14.1
2.1c	construction	3.5	2.9	3.0	2.2	1.9	2.0
2.1d	other industry	8.9	8.1	7.8	7.1	7.3	6.6
2.2	handicrafts	13.5	11.8	11.2	9.8	9.4	9.1
2.3	transport	5.4	5.6	6.0	6.3	6.4	6.4
2.4	electric power	0.6	0.6	0.6	0.6	0.6	0.6
3	Trade, banking	11.7	10.5	9.5	9.0	8.5	7.9
4	Civilian administration	6.8	7.3	7.4	6.8	6.6	6.4
5	Military administration	1.8	2.0	2.3	3.5	3.9	4.0
6	Domestic service	4.0	4.3	4.2	4.1	4.0	3.8
7	Homework	—	—	—	—	—	0.8
8	Total	100.0	100.0	100.0	100.0	100.0	100.0

Notes:
1. Agriculture includes forestry and fishing.
2. For 'industry' Wagenführ (1954) provides more accurate and slightly different figures, ignored here for the sake of consistency.

Table 4.17 (*cont.*)

(B) Forced and foreign labour (including German and foreign Jews, and prisoners of war)	1939	1940	1941	1942	1943	1944
Thousands						
1 Agriculture	120	681	1,459	1,978	2,293	2,478
2 Industry, transport	155	402	1,379	1,879	3,566	4,132
2.1 industry	110	256	965	1,401	2,829	3,163
2.2 handicrafts	29	108	310	296	430	537
2.3 transport	16	35	97	171	289	407
2.4 electric power	1	2	17	10	19	26
3 Trade, banking	8	20	58	95	148	188
4 Civilian administration	7	21	51	48	62	94
5 Military administration	2	11	39	60	120	163
6 Domestic service	7	15	33	56	72	72
7 Homework	—	—	—	—	—	1
8 Total	299	1,150	3,019	4,116	6,261	7,128
Per cent of each branch						
1 Agriculture	1.1	6.4	13.6	17.6	20.3	22.2
2 Industry, transport	0.8	2.4	8.2	11.7	21.6	24.7
2.1 industry	1.0	2.6	9.2	13.9	26.6	29.0
2.2 handicrafts	0.5	2.6	7.7	8.4	12.7	16.4
2.3 transport	0.8	1.7	4.5	7.7	12.6	17.4
2.4 electric power	0.4	1.0	3.3	4.9	9.3	12.8
3 Trade, banking	0.2	0.5	1.7	3.0	4.8	6.6
4 Civilian administration	0.3	0.8	1.9	2.0	2.6	4.0
5 Military administration	0.3	1.5	4.6	4.8	8.5	11.2
6 Domestic service	0.4	1.0	2.2	3.8	5.0	5.2
7 Homework	—	—	—	—	—	0.4
8 Total	0.8	3.2	8.4	11.6	17.3	19.7

3. Trade and banking includes insurance.
4. Government administration, excluding police and the Armaments Ministry, plus public and private services, arts, and sports.
5. Armed forces administration includes police and the Armaments Ministry.
6. –.
7. Series for homework not available until 1944.
8. The column totals differ slightly from numbers given in USSBS (1945), appendix table 1.
(B) On forced and foreign labour see also Herbert (1985 and 1986, 143). The column totals given here correspond almost exactly with Herbert's numbers for forced and foreign workers, calculated as follows: 301,000 (1939); 1,151,000 (1940); 3,069,000 (1941); 4,134,000 (1942); 6,460,000 (1943); 7,126,000 (1944). Herbert's figures are not disaggregated by industry branch, however.
Source: USSBS (1945), 202, 204, 206, 210 (appendix tables 1, 3, 5, and 9).

Table 4.17 (*cont.*)

(C) German women		1939	1940	1941	1942	1943	1944
Thousands							
1	Agriculture	6,049	5,689	5,369	5,673	5,665	5,694
2	Industry, transport	3,980	3,887	4,000	3,944	4,242	4,111
2.1	industry	2,765	2,615	2,665	2,579	2,820	2,717
2.2	handicrafts	1,054	1,013	986	931	891	847
2.3	transport	144	237	323	407	502	518
2.4	electric power	17	21	25	27	29	28
3	Trade, banking	2,083	1,946	1,844	1,818	1,818	1,701
4	Civilian administration	849	963	1,036	1,139	1,206	1,200
5	Military administration	105	194	248	332	513	546
6	Domestic service	1,560	1,511	1,473	1,410	1,362	1,301
7	Homework	—	—	—	—	—	256
8	Total	14,626	14,190	13,970	14,316	14,806	14,809
8.1	revised	—	14,386	14,167	14,437	—	—
Per cent of each branch							
1	Agriculture	54.5	56.9	58.0	61.3	62.9	65.4
2	Industry, transport	21.5	24.5	26.3	28.5	31.8	32.9
2.1	industry	25.5	27.4	29.0	30.8	34.5	35.6
2.2	handicrafts	19.9	24.6	26.4	29.0	30.1	30.9
2.3	transport	26.8	12.0	15.6	19.7	25.0	26.9
2.4	electric power	7.4	10.4	12.3	13.8	15.5	15.8
3	Trade, banking	45.3	52.3	54.9	58.2	62.0	63.5
4	Civilian administration	31.8	37.0	39.5	48.0	51.5	53.9
5	Military administration	15.2	27.3	30.8	28.0	39.7	42.2
6	Domestic service	99.0	100.0	100.0	100.0	99.4	99.5
7	Homework	—	—	—	—	—	91.8
8	Total	37.4	41.2	42.7	45.9	48.9	51.1

shortages of skilled labour and of raw materials. At no stage during the war was the German armaments industry able to translate its progress in production methods into superiority, and other bottlenecks preempted the organizational advances. But once this level of technical organization had been achieved, it continued to be available subsequently – admittedly, only after 1945, or, more precisely, after the self-sustaining growth process which followed the Korean crisis.

The car industry is an apposite example. During the Weimar Republic this sector clearly manifested the discrepancy between technical ethos and economic constraints. As in other industries, organizational and technical knowhow was certainly present, as well as a high education level amongst the workforce, and, equally importantly, a keen interest in the new 'Fordist' methods of industrial relations. Yet macroeconomic conditions were unfavourable for the adoption of new concepts. The introduction of assembly lines and continuous production proceeded slowly, even though the first steps were taken as early as 1923. The breakthrough came only with the 'economic miracle' of the 1930s, and then more forcefully with the war economy of the early 1940s. These developments ensured that German industry became capable of mastering technical possibilities not only in theory, but also in practice.[62]

For both the efficiency of the war economy and the success of West German industry after 1945, the reform of the economic regulatory and planning system was at least as important as the rationalization of production methods. This must be understood in the context of the role of industrial associations. The Kaiserreich's system of 'corporate market economy', which gave the late-nineteenth-century German economy its particular dynamism, degenerated in the Weimar Republic to a caricature of a corporate state.[63] It was further damaged by the tendencies to 'state corporatism' and a 'command economy' in the Third Reich. The Todt Organization initiated a significant component of the reform, which was continued by Speer.

Under Todt and Speer, state coercion of and pressure on the economy were restrained in favour of greater industrial self-administration. Speer's system of committees and rings strengthened the role of the entrepreneur and of 'economic leaders' in the armaments industry. It promoted a new type of young, accountable manager ('Speer's kindergarten'), and also had the important advantage of being compatible with the reformist liberal spirit of the 'social market economy'. This latter had become an alternative concept for German macroeconomic management (*Ordnungspolitik*) already in 1932, though not in exactly the same spirit of its later reincarnation. Even during the Third Reich it influenced the economic thinking of entrepreneurs and managers, at universities, in research institutes and in the policy units of major banks and larger industrial concerns. After 1945, all three elements of Speer's reform of the regulatory and planning system influenced the creation of the specific mix of West German *Ordnungspolitik* which allowed the German system of corporate market economy to shine forth in renewed splendour.[64]

The skill composition of the labour force

Although the Nazi régime concentrated on creating economic preconditions of a war for living space and world power status, it simultaneously pursued major economic and social projects. These were at least partially in competition with rearmament efforts, and they first bore fruit in the postwar period. In the economic arena, they included motorway construction and the establishment of the Volkswagen works. An example in social policy was the reform of industrial vocational education, and its long-term effects deserve to be acclaimed.

The trade unions had campaigned for the reform of occupational training in the context of industrial associations' educational programmes since the 1920s, and so had conservative forces associated with heavy industry. The latter included above all the German Institute for Technical Education (DINTA), whose head, Karl Arnhold, had close connections both with heavy industry and with the rising National Socialists. In 1933 DINTA became part of the Labour Front, as the Office for Works Management and Vocational Training (ABB). This implemented the ideas of DINTA piece by piece.[65] In November 1936 all metalworking and construction businesses with more than ten employees were obliged to create apprenticeships, varying in number according to their size, and to organize appropriate training programmes. Control of vocational education lay with the Chambers of Industry and Commerce. The task was later centralized in the Reich Employment Insurance Agency. The new Reich Schools Law of July 1938 finally established the comprehensive introduction of vocational training. Some form of institutionalized vocational training was prescribed for every school leaver, although occasional bottlenecks arose in apprenticeships. As early as 1936 the number of apprenticeships had multiplied; in the course of a few months even smaller businesses arranged apprenticeships and training facilities. Between 1937 and the end of the war almost all males and a rising number of females who left elementary schools completed a three-year apprenticeship.

Internally, the stated reason for this development was the needs of the armaments industry. Yet the vocational training system soon came in conflict with the goals of the armaments economy. More skilled workers were trained than was strictly necessary for actual production requirements. This was not only true in war-related sectors, although the régime attempted to direct workers' choice of trade away from so-called 'fashionable trades' into strategically important branches. Above all, the training offensive gave rise to a remarkable shortage of untrained and unskilled workers, increasingly needed in order to implement the transition to mass production in the munitions industry.

The régime, having made training an important propaganda issue in the early 1930s, now became the prisoner of its own 'skilled-worker ideology'. Curiously, at the start of the war it was the metalworking industries which were stigmatized as the 'current fashion', in order to reduce apprenticeships to a number which better reflected the sector's needs. Yet all efforts to reduce substantially the number of apprenticeships in 1942 and 1943 failed. The number of trainees fell at first, but only from 130,000 to 105,000 annually. In 1943 a further 149,000 started an apprenticeship in metalworking, and up to 1945 this rate fell by only 10 per cent. Shortly before the end of the war there were still between 450,000 and 480,000 traineeships in this branch.[66]

The attempt significantly to cut apprenticeships in sectors unrelated to armaments was also relatively unsuccessful. In 1945, 19,000 youths still planned a training as butchers, bakers, or pastrycooks, while 59,000 were being trained as secretaries. The number of trainee hairdressers rose from 4,000 in 1939 to 5,200 in 1941, and in 1945 the number admitted to traineeships was still 3,600. Another goal of National Socialist policy on apprenticeships also failed, that of encouraging school leavers to enter the mining sector. In this area the failure of so-called steering of trainees was complete.[67]

Industrial vocational training and certification became a mass movement during the Third Reich. Retraining measures complemented efforts in vocational education. At the beginning of the war there were 1,143,000 trainees in Germany. To suspend this for even a year would have increased labour reserves by 5 per cent, but this option was not politically feasible. Instead the gap had to be filled from two sources of labour force recruitment: women and foreign labour (table 4.17 (B), (C)). Both sources were drawn upon principally for unskilled and untrained work.

For a large part of the German male workforce the war entailed an effective 'upgrading' of competences, beyond their professional training. The impact of this 'learning by doing' on the skill structure of the German workforce can hardly be overestimated. The same was true for the effects of the programme of industrial vocational training, although they generally came too late to be of use to the war economy. During the war negative effects, including the loss of unskilled workers to apprenticeships, far outweighed positive effects. The National Socialists came to criticize the 'overtraining' of the labour force, and wanted again to abandon three-year apprenticeships in favour of a one-year basic training.[68] The reform of the vocational education system was however an important precondition for the reconstruction of the years after 1945.

Capital stock

One foundation of the early technical supremacy of German armaments lay in the efforts made to overcome the huge shortfall which the defence forces and the armaments industry faced in 1933 *vis-à-vis* potential enemies east and west. Before 1933, military expenditure in Germany was well below the levels of the western powers. Apart from a few 'shadow' armament factories, the 'secret rearmament' of the Weimar Republic had not gone beyond the embryonic stage of military research. The consequences of subsequent rapid catching-up were reflected in both the age profile and the quality of industrial plant. This was true of industrial development generally, but it applied especially to the armaments industry broadly defined, which enjoyed clear priority over civilian industries after 1935.

In 1935 only 9 per cent of gross industrial fixed assets was less than five years old. This proportion had risen to 34 per cent by 1945. The proportion of plant aged between five and ten years also rose slightly, so that in 1945 an impressive 55 per cent of gross fixed assets was less than ten years old (table 4.18). Analysis by branch shows that the most marked rejuvenation of capital stock took place in the raw materials and producer goods industries. In this area nearly two-thirds of gross fixed assets was less than ten years old – all the more remarkable in that this heading also included mining, not counted as one of the winners in the Nazi rearmament boom; the renewal was therefore even stronger among other sectors in this category.

Hence the corresponding relationship of gross and net values. Increasing values of the *Gütegrad*, a well-known index in German industrial statistics, reflected the rapid renovation of plant and equipment. It rose from 49.7 per cent in 1935 to 61.3 per cent in 1945. This far exceeded the hitherto best values of the 1920s (table 4.19). The positive trend is even more evident when we consider investment goods or the raw materials and mining industries. The improvement in the *Gütegrad* from the mid-1930s corresponds to the fact that available gross fixed assets rose by no less than 75 per cent (table 4.20). These investments incorporated the latest technological standard; depending on the branch, this generally stood comparison with world standards.[69]

Measured by German industry's real gross output, the investment boom favoured the construction and investment goods sectors, as well as the raw materials sector. Consumer goods industries clearly counted among the losers, showing declining value of gross output (table 4.21). The favoured industrial branches included machinery, vehicles, iron and steel, metal goods, light engineering, optics, chemicals, fuels, iron ore, and non-ferrous metals. It is hardly surprising that the textiles industry and the construction industry brought up the rear. As the growth pattern of the German war economy clearly shows, those industries which profited most from rearmament later comprised the foundation of West German economic reconstruction. This state of affairs was not decisively changed, quantatively and qualitatively, either by wartime devastation or by the dismantling of assets in the years 1945–8 (table 4.20).

Table 4.18. *Age structure of gross fixed capital of West German industry, 1935, 1945, and 1948 (1 January and per cent of total)*

	1935	1945	1948
Mining, raw materials, and intermediate goods			
0–5 years	9	40	18
5–10 years	21	24	40
Over 10 years	70	36	42
10–15 years	—	5	12
over 15 years	—	31	30
Investment goods			
0–5 years	7	37	19
5–10 years	15	20	32
Over 10 years	78	43	49
10–15 years	—	5	12
over 15 years	—	38	37
Consumer goods			
0–5 years	10	18	10
5–10 years	22	16	21
Over 10 years	68	66	69
10–15 years	—	8	12
over 15 years	—	58	57
Food and foodstuffs			
0–5 years	12	21	13
5–10 years	23	18	22
Over 10 years	65	61	65
10–15 years	—	10	14
over 15 years	—	51	51
Small industry			
0–5 years	9	15	9
5–10 years	15	14	17
Over 10 years	76	71	74
10–15 years	—	9	12
over 15 years	—	62	62
All industry[a]			
0–5 years	9	34	16
5–10 years	20	21	34
Over 10 years	71	45	50
10–15 years	—	6	12
over 15 years	—	39	38

Note:
[a] Excluding electricity supply and the construction industry.
Source: Krengel (1958), 52 ff.

Table 4.19. *The Gütegrad: net fixed assets of West German industry, 1936, 1945, and 1949 (1 January, per cent of gross fixed assets)*

	1936	1945	1949
Mining, raw materials, and intermediate goods	49.0	63.7	56.3
Investment goods	47.6	62.8	57.4
Consumer goods	54.1	54.9	53.7
Food and foodstuffs	52.5	55.1	53.3
Small industry	50.7	50.9	49.1
All industry	49.9	61.3	55.7

Note:
The *Gütegrad* measures the ratio of the depreciated (net) value of the stock of fixed assets to its undepreciated (gross) value. In a steady state, when annual gross investment equals the depreciation flow, the *Gütegrad* tends to equal 50 per cent. When gross investment is more than sufficient to cover depreciation, the *Gütegrad* rises above this critical value. It also provides a steady-state measure of the proportion of the expected lifetime of the stock of fixed assets which remains unexpended.
Source: Krengel (1958), 79.

Table 4.20. *Gross industrial fixed assets in the British–American occupation area, 1936–1948 (per cent of 1936 and prices of 1936)*

	%
Gross fixed assets, 1936	100.0
Change in assets, 1936–45	
gross industrial investment	+75.3
depreciation	−37.2
destruction by war	−17.4
Gross fixed assets 1945	120.6
Change in assets, 1945–8	
gross industrial investment	+8.7
depreciation	−11.5
restitution of stolen assets	−2.4
dismantling in reparations	−4.4
Gross fixed assets, 1948	111.1

Source: Abelshauser (1989), 20.

Table 4.21. *The growth of real gross output of German industry, by branch and sector, 1936–1944 (per cent of 1936)*

	Growth (+) or decline (−) %
By group	
Construction and investment goods	+65.0
Mining and raw materials	+37.5
All industry[a]	+29.1
Consumer goods	−8.2
By sector	
Machinery, steel, vehicles[b]	+143.1
Iron, steel, metal goods	+116.9
Light engineering, optics	+91.4
Chemicals, fuels	+72.9
Electricity supply	+71.3
Iron ore, nonferrous metals, foundries	+58.7
Timber, woodworking	+28.5
Mining	+19.0
Food, foodstuffs	+4.0
Quarrying, glass, ceramics	−15.6
Paper, printing	−17.6
Leather, clothing	−22.6
Textiles	−25.6
Construction	−71.7

Notes:
[a] Excluding energy.
[b] Including shipbuilding and aircraft.
Source: Calculated from Gleitze (1956), 169.

Conclusion

1. In order to understand the specific advantages and deficiencies of German economic mobilization for World War II properly it is necessary to include the late Weimar Republic in the analysis. The economic crisis of the early thirties left large capacities of capital stock and human capital idle, a fact which made its direction towards war production easier. Overcoming the crisis earlier than all other World War II powers, therefore, was a precondition for a successful economic mobilization for war. This was achieved by a 'Keynesian' approach to economic recovery and employment policy which started with credit financed civilian outlays and ended up with 'Military Keynesianism' on a large scale.

Starting from an extremely low level of private consumption also allowed the regime to give priority to rearmament and, nevertheless, to improve at the same time continuously the standard of living of most German families. Therefore, the sacrifices the forced mobilization process demanded from the consumer were not fully realized by the public. This helped to minimize conflicts over the distribution of resources between rearmament and private consumption and hence contributed much to the stability of the political régime.

2. The Weimar heritage was, however, a burden, too. Even before the crisis of the early thirties, Weimar's economy could not make full use of the rich rationalization potential which had accumulated since the twenties. This rationalization lag continued during the first years of the Third Reich, because emphasis had to be laid on job creation and not on the use of labour saving technologies. When, after the mid-thirties, the way for organizational as well as technical rationalization was largely open, German war industry, under the aegis of Todt and Speer, enjoyed a 'miraculous boom' which, however, came too late to influence the outcome of the war decisively.

3. German war industry was to a large degree dependent on foreign resources. Although one of the main aims of the régime's war strategy was to get hold of the potentially rich reserves of resources (*Lebensraum*) in eastern Europe and, in particular, in Russia this was by no means the main source of foreign support to the German war effort. This is also true of the countries of south-east Europe, which, under the auspices of the 'New Plan' of Hjalmar Schacht, enjoyed a special relationship to Germany. The most important foreign basis of the German war economy lay rather in western Europe. The economic relations with and the inflow of resources from western Europe after the *Blitzkrieg* period were far more relevant for keeping the German war machinery going.

4. Analysis of the German war economy is also essential to understanding the economic dynamism of West Germany after 1945. West Germany had clearly gained the material preconditions for economic success in the postwar period. The military defeat and economic collapse of 1945 left Germany temporarily impoverished, with ruined urban housing, farms run to seed, and consumer shortages of every kind. But the development potential of the industrial economy had been substantially enhanced, as the dynamism of the following years would demonstrate.

Notes

1 Galbraith (1981), 199.
2 Die Deutsche Industrie (1939); Länderrat des amerikanischen Besatzungsgebiets (1949); Wagenführ (1954).

3 USSBS (1945).
4 Kaldor (1946); Wagenführ (1954); Klein (1959); Kuczynski (1965).
5 See especially the controversy between Overy (1994) and Milward (1965), among many others.
6 Henning (1975), 172 ff.; Kroll (1958), 417.
7 Abelshauser and Petzina (1981).
8 Thus for example *Das deutsche Wirtschaftswunder*, the title of Priester (1936).
9 Bombach, Ramser, Timmermann and Wittmann (1976).
10 Robinson (1974), 7.
11 Ludwig (1975), 52 ff.
12 Hitler on Volkswagen, the motorways and the future of motorization (5 September 1938), in von Kotze (1974), 35 ff.
13 'Keynesianer vor Keynes', the title of Garvey (1976).
14 Jacobsen, Jochmann (1961).
15 Gates (1974), 219.
16 Strasser (1932), 2512.
17 Jacobsen and Jochmann (1961).
18 Appeal of the Reich government to the German people, in Die Reden (1934), 7.
19 Cited by Schulthess (1933), 89 ff.
20 Robinson (1972), 8.
21 Abelshauser and Faust (1983), 13–60.
22 Ministerial meeting of 8 February 1933, minutes in Die Regierung Hitler (1983), 50 ff.
23 Reichsstatthalter Conference of 6 July 1933, minutes in Die Regierung Hitler (1983), 632.
24 Die Regierung Hitler (1983), 633.
25 Wagemann (1935), 52.
26 Strasser (1932), 2514a ff.
27 'I have now worked on the build-up of the German defence force for six years. In this period over RM 90 billion have been used for the build-up of our defence force. It is today the best equipped in the world, and far exceeds any comparison with 1914! My trust in it is unshakeable!' Domarus (1965), 13.
28 Mason (1964), 78.
29 Thus notably Erbe (1958), 39.
30 See also Henning (1975), 126.
31 Schwerin von Krosigk (1953), 316, reaffirmed this figure. However, Schwerin (1962), 228, adopted the American figures given in table 4.2 (row 2), to which he added a further RM 19.8 billion for the fiscal year 1939/40 and arrived at a total of RM 60 billion.
32 Kroll (1958), 571; Carroll (1968), 184, 263; Overy (1994), 203; Boelcke (1978), 28. For Köllner and Fischer, see table 4.2.
33 This figure represents Kuczynski's second estimate of armaments expenditure. He published an earlier one as early as 1937 in the periodical *The Banker*, which diverged only slightly from the final estimate. Kuczynski's earlier estimate was also used by Sternberg (1939), 233 ff., and by Bettelheim (1974), 221.
34 Schweitzer (1964), 323.

35 Eichholtz (1969), 31 ff.
36 See also Carroll (1968), 267.
37 Petzina (1977), 117.
38 Klein (1959), 251: 'national income at factor cost', plus 'depreciation allowances'.
39 Thomas (1966), 145–52.
40 Milward (1981), 401; similarly Neal (1979), 391–404, Marguerat (1977), and Abelshauser (1994a), 263–86.
41 Guillebaud (1958), 157 ff.
42 League of Nations (1937), 41.
43 Basch (1944), 174.
44 Ritschl (1993), 298 ff.
45 See the balance of payments estimates in Ritschl (1993), 309 ff.
46 Schönfeld (1975), 205 ff.
47 Teichova (1988), 138 ff.
48 Petzina (1968), 114.
49 Jacobsen and Jochmann (1961).
50 Abelshauser (1975), 118.
51 Petzina (1968), 176.
52 Petzina, Abelshauser and Faust (1978), 103.
53 Mason (1981), 310.
54 Kuczynski (1964), 183–9.
55 Wagenführ (1954), 25.
56 Ibid., 26.
57 Milward (1977), 82.
58 Overy (1988), 626–9.
59 Overy (1994), 346.
60 Ibid., 358.
61 Ludwig (1979), 462.
62 Abelshauser (1995).
63 Abelshauser (1994b).
64 Shonfield (1965), chapters 11, 12; Abelshauser (1993).
65 Guillebaud (1941), 58–65.
66 BA, R 121/301 (1941/2), 413; Statistisches Jahrbuch (1960), 413. Also Gillingham (1986).
67 Wolsing (1977), 194 ff.
68 Arbeitswissenschaftliches Institut der deutschen Arbeitsfront (1942), 311–57.
69 Gimbel (1990); Glatt (1994).

References

Archives

BA (Bundesarchiv)
IMT (International Military Tribunal)

Books, articles, and working papers

Abelshauser, W. (1975), *Wirtschaft in Westdeutschland 1945–1948*, Stuttgart.
(1993), *Wirtschaftsgeschichte der Bundesrepublik Deutschland (1945–1980)*, Frankfurt (7th edn, 5th edn 1989).
(1994a), 'Mitteleuropa und die deutsche Außenwirtschaftspolitik', in Buchheim, C. et al., eds., *Zerissene Zwischenkriegszeit. Wirtschafts-historische Beiträge, Knut Borchardt zum 65. Geburtstag*, Baden Baden, 263–86.
(1994b), 'Wirtschaftliche Wechsellagen, Wirtschaftsordnung und Staat: die deutsche Erfahrungen', in Grimm, D., ed., *Staatsaufgaben*, Baden Baden, 199–232.
(1995), 'Two kinds of Fordism: on the differing roles of the automobile industry in the development of the two German states', in Shiomi, H., and Wada, K., eds., *Fordism transformed. comparative perspectives in the implementation and modification of the Ford system*, Oxford, 269–96.
Abelshauser, W., and Faust, A. (1983), 'Wirtschafts- und Sozialpolitik: eine nationalsozialistische Revolution?', in DIFF, ed., *Nationalsozialismus im Unterricht*, 4, Tubingen, 13–60.
Abelshauser, W., and Petzina, D. (1981), 'Krise und Rekonstruktion. Zur Interpretation der gesamtwirtschaftlichen Entwicklung Deutschlands im 20. Jahrhundert', in Abelshauser, W., and Petzina, D., eds., *Deutsche Wirtschaftsgeschichte im Industriezeitalter*, Königstein/Ts, 47–93.
Arbeitswissenschaftliches Institut der deutschen Arbeitsfront (1942), *Das Problem der Ungelernten*, Berlin.
Basch, A. (1944), *The Danube basin and the German economic sphere*, London.
Bettelheim, C. (1974), *Deutsche Wirtschaft unter dem Nationalsozialismus*, Munich.
Boelcke, W. A. (1978), *Die Kosten von Hitlers Krieg*, Paderborn.
Bombach, G., Ramser, H. J., Timmermann, M., and Wittmann, W. eds. (1976), *Der Keynesianismus*, vol. II, Berlin.
Carroll, B. A. (1968), *Design for total war*, The Hague and Paris.
Die Reden Hitlers (1934), *Die Reden Hitlers als Kanzler. Das junge Deutschland will Arbeit und Frieden*, Munich.
Domarus, N. (1965), *Hitler. Reden und Proklamationen 1932–1945. Kommentiert von einem deutschen Zeitgenossen*, vol. II, *Untergang*, Munich.
Eichholtz, D. (1969), *Geschichte der deutschen Kriegswirtschaft 1939–1945*, vol. I, *1939–1941*, Berlin; (1985), vol. II, *1941–1943*, Berlin; (1996), vol. III, *1943–1945*.
Erbe, R. (1958), *Die nationalsozialistische Wirtschaftspolitik 1933–1939 im Lichte der modernen Theorie*, Zurich.
Federau, F. (1962), *Der Zweite Weltkrieg. Seine Finanzierung in Deutschland*, Tübingen.
Fischer, W. (1968), *Deutsche Wirtschaftspolitik 1918–1945*, Opladen.
Galbraith, J. K. (1981), *A life in our time: memoirs*, Boston, MA.
Garvey, G. (1976), 'Keynesianer vor Keynes', in Bombach, G., Ramser, H. J., Timmermann, M., and Wittmann, W., eds., *Der Keynesianismus*, vol. II, Berlin, 21–34.

Gates, R. A. (1974), 'Von der Sozialpolitik zur Wirtschaftspolitik? Das Dilemma der deutschen Sozialdemokratie in der Krise 1929–1933', in Mommsen, H., et al., eds., *Industrielles System und politische Entwicklung in der Weimarer Republik*, Düsseldorf, 206–25.

Gillingham, J. (1986), 'The "deproletarianization" of German society: vocational training in the Third Reich', *Journal for Social History*, vol. 19(3), 423–32.

Gimbel, J. (1990), *Science, technology, and reparations. exploitation and plunder in postwar Germany*, Stanford, CA.

Glatt, C. (1994), 'Reparations and transfer of scientific and industrial technology from Germany: a case study of the roots of British industrial policy and of aspects of British occupation policy in Germany between post-World War II reconstruction and the Korean war, 1943–1951', unpub. Ph.D. dissertation, European University Institute, Florence.

Gleitze, B. (1956), *Ostdeutsche Wirtschaft*, Berlin.

Goebbels, J. (1934), *Die Reden Hitlers als Kanzler. Das junge Deutschland will Arbeit und Frieden*, Munich.

Guillebaud, C. W. (1941), *The social policy of Nazi Germany*, Cambridge.

(1958), *The economic recovery of Germany*, London.

Henning, F. W. (1975), 'Die zeitliche Einordnung der Überwindung der Weltwirtschaftskrise in Deutschland', in Winkel, H., ed., *Finanz- und wirtschaftspolitische Fragen der Zwischenkriegszeit*, Berlin, 135–73.

Herbert, U. (1985), *Fremdarbeiter. Politik und Praxis des "Ausländer-Einsatzes" in der Kriegswirtschaft des Dritten Reiches*, Berlin.

(1986), *Geschichte der Ausländerbeschäftigung in Deutschland 1880 bis 1980. Saisonarbeiter, Zwangsarbeiter, Gastarbeiter*, Berlin and Bonn.

Hillmann, H. C. (1952), 'Comparative strength of the great powers', in Toynbee, A., and Ashton-Gwatkin, F. T., eds., *Survey of international affairs, 1939–1946: the world in March 1939*, London.

Jacobsen, H. A., and Jochmann, W., eds. (1961), *Ausgewählte Dokumente zur Geschichte des Nationalsozialismus 1933–1945*, Bielefeld, E, 1–16.

Kaldor, N. (1946), 'The German war economy', *Review of Economic Studies*, vol. 13, 33–52.

Klein, B. H. (1948), 'Germany's economic preparations for war: a reexamination', *American Economic Review*, vol. 38, 56–77.

(1959), *Germany's economic preparations for war*, Cambridge, MA; 2nd edn (1969).

Köllner, L. (1969), *Rüstungsfinanzierung*, Frankfurt.

Krengel, R. (1958), *Anlagevermögen, Produktion und Beschäftigung im Gebiet der Bundesrepublik von 1924 bis 1956* (Sonderhefte des DIW, 42), Berlin.

Kroll, G. (1958), *Von der Weltwirtschaftskrise zur Staatskonjunktur*, Berlin.

Kuczynski, J. (1964), *Die Geschichte der Lage der Arbeiter unter dem Kapitalismus*, vol. VI, Berlin.

(1965), *Studien zur Geschichte des staatsmonopolistischen Kapitalismus in Deutschland 1918–1945*, Berlin.

Länderrat des amerikanischen Besatzungsgebiets, ed. (1949), *Statistisches Handbuch von Deutschland 1928–1944*, Munich.

Lanter, M. (1950), *Die Finanzierung des Krieges. Quellen, Methoden und Lösungen bis Ende des Zweiten Weltkrieges von 1939 bis 1945*, Lucerne.

League of Nations (1937), *Revue de la situation économique mondiale 1936/37*, Geneva.

Ludwig, K.-H. (1975), 'Strukturmerkmale nationalsozialistischer Aufrüstung bis 1935', in Forstmeier, F., and Volkmann, H.-E., eds., *Wirtschaft und Rüstung am Vorabend des Zweiten Weltkriegs*, Dusseldorf, 39–64.

——— (1979), *Technik und Ingenieure im Dritten Reich*, Dusseldorf.

Maddison, A. (1995), *Monitoring the world economy, 1820–1992*, Paris.

Marguerat, P. (1977), *Le IIIe Reich et le pétrole roumain 1938–1940*, Leiden.

Mason, T. W. (1964), 'Some origins of the Second World War', *Past and Present*, no. 29, 67–87.

——— (1981), 'Arbeiteropposition im nationalsozialistischen Deutschland', in Peukert, D., and Reulecke, J., eds., *Die Reihen fast geschlossen. Beiträge zur Geschichte des Alltags im Nationalsozialismus*, Wuppertal.

Milward, A. S. (1965), *The German economy at war*, London.

——— (1966), *Die Deutsche Kriegswirtschaft 1939–1945* (Schriftenreihe der Vierteljahrshefte für Zeitgeschichte, 12), Stuttgart.

——— (1977), *War, economy and society, 1939–45*, London.

——— (1981), 'The Reichsmark Bloc and the international economy', in Hirschfeld, G., and Kettenacker, L., eds., *Der 'Führerstaat': Mythos und Realität. Studien zur Struktur und Politik des Dritten Reiches*, Stuttgart, 377–413.

Minuth, K.-H. (1983), *Die Regierung Hitler*, vol. I, Part I: *1933/34*, in Bloms, K.-H., ed., *Akten der Reichskanzlei, Regierung Hitler 1933–38*, Boppard am Rhein.

Neal, L. (1979), 'The economics and finance of bilateral clearing agreements: Germany 1934–1938', *Economic History Review*, vol. 32, 391–404.

Overy, R. J. (1988), 'Mobilization for total war in Germany, 1939–1941', *English Historical Review*, vol. 103, 613–39.

——— (1994), *War and economy in the Third Reich*, Oxford.

Petzina, D. (1968), *Autarkiepolitik im Dritten Reich. Der national-sozialistische Vierjahresplan* (Schriftenreihe der Vierteljahrshefte für Zeitgeschichte, 16), Stuttgart.

——— (1977), *Die deutsche Wirtschaft in der Zwischenkriegszeit*, Wiesbaden.

Petzina, D., Abelshauser, W., and Faust, A. (1978), *Sozialgeschichtliches Arbeitsbuch, vol. 3, Materialien zur Statistik des Deutschen Reiches 1914–1945*, Munich.

Priester, H. (1936), *Das deutsche Wirtschaftswunder*, Amsterdam.

Reichsamt für wehrwirtschaftliche Planung (1939), *Die Deutsche Industrie. Gesamtergebnisse der amlichen Produktionsstatistik* (Schriftenreihe des Reichsamts für wehrwirtschaftliche Planung, 1), Berlin.

Riecke, H.-J. (1953), 'Ernährung und Landwirtschaft im Kriege', in *Bilanz des Zweiten Weltkriegs. Kentnisse und Verpflichtungen für die Zukunft*, Hamburg, 329–46.

Ritschl, A. (1993), 'NS-Devisenbewirtschaftung und Bilateralismus in Zahlen', in Schremmer, E., ed., *Geld und Währung vom 16. Jahrhundert bis zur Gegenwart*, Stuttgart, 289–314.

Robinson, J. (1972), 'The second crisis of economic theory', *American Economic Review: Papers and Proceedings*, vol. 62, 1–10.

(1974), 'What has become of the Keynesian Revolution?', *Challenge*, vol. 16(6), 6–11.

Schacht, H. (1953), *Sechsundsiebzig Jahre meines Lebens*, Bad Wörrishofen.

Schiller, K. (1936), *Arbeitsbeschaffung und Finanzordnung in Deutschland*, Berlin.

Schönfeld, R. (1975), 'Die Balkanländer in der Weltwirtschaftskrise', *VSWG*, vol. 62, 179–213.

Schulthess (1933), *Schulthess Europäischer Geschichtskalender 1933*.

Schweitzer, A. (1964), *Big business in the Third Reich*, London.

Schwerin von Krosigk, L. (1953), 'How was the Second World War financed?', in *Bilanz des Zweiten Weltkriegs. Kentnisse und Verpflichtungen für die Zukunft*, Hamburg, 311–28.

(1962), *Staatsbankrott: die Geschichte der Finanzpolitik des deutschen Reiches von 1920 bis 1945, geschrieben vom letzten Reichsfinanzminister*, Frankfurt and Zurich.

Shonfield, A. (1965), *Modern capitalism: the changing balance of public and private power*, London.

Statistisches Jahrbuch (1957), *Statistisches Jahrbuch für die Bundesrepublik Deutschland, 1956*, Wiesbaden.

(1960), *Statistisches Jahrbuch für die Bundesrepublik Deutschland, 1959*, Wiesbaden.

Sternberg, F. (1939), *Die deutsche Kriegsstärke. Wie lange kann Hitler Krieg führen?* Paris.

Strasser, G. (1932), in *Verhandlungen des Reichstages*, vol. 446 (Reichstag speech of 10 May 1932).

Stuebel, H. (1951), 'Die Finanzierung der Aufrüstung im Dritten Reich', *Europa Archiv*, vol. 6, 4128–36.

Teichova, A. (1988), *Kleinstaaten im Spannungsfeld der Großmächte, Wirtschaft und Politik im Mittel- und Südosteuropa in der Zwischen-kriegszeit*, Munich.

Thomas, G. (1966), *Geschichte der deutschen Wehr- und Ruestungswirtschaft (1918-1943/45)*, Schriften des Bundesarchivs 14, Boppard am Rhein.

USSBS: United States Strategic Bombing Survey (1945), *The effects of strategic bombing on the German war economy*, Washington, DC.

von Kotze, H. ed. (1974), *Heeresadjutant bei Hitler 1938-1943. Aufzeichnungen des Major Engel* (Schriftenreihe der Vierteljahrshefte für Zeitgeschichte, 29), Stuttgart.

Wagemann, E., ed. (1935), *Konjunkturstatistisches Handbuch 1936*, Berlin.

Wagenführ, R. (1954), *Die deutsche Industrie im Kriege, 1939 bis 1945*, Berlin; 2nd edn (1963).

Wolsing, T. (1977), *Untersuchungen zur Berufsausbildung im Dritten Reich*, Ratingen.

5 Italy: how to lose the war and win the peace

Vera Zamagni

Introduction

Two world wars cut across Italian industrialization in the crucial decades immediately following the country's take-off. During World War I, some Italian industrial firms became large enough to place Italy within the small number of countries having technologically advanced industrial firms. But it was very difficult for such firms to survive in peacetime, during the troubled 1920s and the even more difficult 1930s, so that the Italian state had to engage in substantial bailing-out operations by the end of which many of the country's largest firms had become publicly owned, including some banks. During World War II, the existing firms (plus a few newly created ones) were strengthened and further enlarged through public spending on munitions.

This chapter will try to explain why the level of development reached by Italy before and during the war did not allow the country to fight the war decently, let alone win it, but also how Italy's engaging in the war ended by strengthening Italian industrial technology in such a way as to allow the ensuing 'economic miracle' to take place. I certainly do not want to argue that Italy could only have deepened her industrialization through the war nor that this was the best way of doing so, but rather that, given the political inevitability of war, Italy developed plans of industrialization through the war that were conducive to the subsequent sustained economic development.

The chapter is organized as follows. First, a review of the most important macroeconomic aspects of the war economy (production, with special reference to munitions, consumption, and employment) comes to the main conclusion that output could not have been substantially expanded, mainly because of the disruption of foreign trade, but that there was some diversion of resources to heavy industry. Second follows an analysis of public spending, with the aim of ascertaining the degree of mobilization of the

177

economy for war purposes, which turns out to have been much more limited than in all the other combatant countries. Third, war losses are discussed in the context of reconstruction and the ensuing 'economic miracle'; it is seen that the loss of human capital was quite small, and that of physical capital was of the order of 10 per cent, but, in certain key sectors like engineering, capacity at the end of the war was larger than before the war. Finally, some conclusions are offered.

The war economy

Aggregate production, raw materials, and energy

The available GDP indices (see table 5.1) point to an expansion of production in the last year before the war, between 1938 and 1939, followed by stagnation in the initial war years up to 1942, then by decline. The decline appears less steep in the most recent Rossi–Sorgato–Toniolo (hereafter RST) estimate; the 1945 trough is fixed at 65 per cent of 1938 versus 58 per cent in the earlier Vitali series. By 1948 the prewar level of GDP was regained.[1] The basic view that these aggregate figures convey is, therefore, that any expansionary effort in the field of war production had to be based mainly on diverting resources from peacetime uses to war production. It proved impossible for the Italian economy to expand overall output beyond the 1939 level, for reasons on which I will try to speculate later.

From table 5.1 (cols. 9–11) we can obtain a view of the initial transfer over overall resources (see also figure 5.1). Real private consumption remained virtually constant up to 1941, while public consumption, which includes military outlays, increased by one-third, and investment by 10 per cent. Then private consumption started to decline, eventually falling below the 1938 level by one-quarter (we will see later what this implied on the standard of living of the population), while investment plummeted to one-third of the 1938 level. Public consumption, in contrast, rose to more than double its 1938 value in 1943 but then declined, falling to a level lower than in 1938 by the time the war was over.

It appears from these data that only in 1942–3 was there a serious effort to transfer resources. The share of private consumption, 58 per cent of total resources available in 1938, declined to 49 per cent in 1943; that of public consumption, 16 per cent in 1938, rose to 40 per cent in 1943, while the investment share declined from 14 per cent to 10 per cent, the main changes taking place in 1942–3.

With table 5.2 we move to industrial production. The index numbers of overall output (discussed in detail in the notes to the table) place the peak as early as 1940 – and it is a modest overall increase of about 10 per cent over 1938. For individual industries we have only contemporary indices up

Table 5.1. *Italian GDP and capital stock, 1938–1948*

(A) GDP and the stock of net reproducible capital (billion 1938 lire and % of 1938)

	Gross domestic product				Net capital stock			
	Vitali 1	% of 1938 2	RST 3	% of 1938 4	Vitali 5	% of 1938 6	RST 7	% of 1938 8
1938	165	100.0	199	100.0	432	100.0	480	100.0
1939	177	107.3	213	107.0	444	102.8	495	103.1
1940	175	106.1	208	104.5	454	105.1	508	105.8
1941	174	105.5	204	102.5	462	106.9	518	107.9
1942	170	103.0	205	103.0	460	106.5	524	109.2
1943	151	91.5	194	97.5	446	103.2	523	109.0
1944	121	73.3	166	83.4	425	98.4	514	107.1
1945	96	58.2	130	65.3	409	94.7	503	104.8
1946	126	76.4	163	81.9	413	95.6	507	105.6
1947	149	90.3	187	94.0	423	97.9	519	108.1
1948	163	98.8	199	100.0	431	99.8	528	110.0

(B) Trends in expenditure on GDP (per cent of 1938)

	Consumption				
	private 9	public 10	Investment 11	Exports 12	Imports 13
1939	102	112	112	92	89
1940	102	122	110	77	89
1941	98	135	104	81	67
1942	94	176	91	72	65
1943	82	238	68	72	81
1944	82	179	41	18	49
1945	76	115	34	9	57
1946	86	109	85	45	81
1947	103	82	108	81	179
1948	113	85	105	136	155

Notes:
Gross domestic product
The Vitali revision of the ISTAT (1957a) series, now reprinted in Rey (1991–2), vol. I, consisted in revaluing investments and recalculating deflators; it therefore does not differ basically form the original ISTAT series. The recent work of RST (1993) starts from an original recalculation of GDP in 1911 published in Rey (1991–2), vol. II, and of GDP in 1951 published in Golinelli, Monterastelli (1990). RST take the new absolute values of the major components of GDP for 1911 and 1951 from the above-quoted studies and interpolate and retropolate the remaining years by means of ISTAT's trends. The result is a higher level of GDP in general and also a somewhat different overall trend of GDP, given the different weights of its major components.

Notes to Table 5.1 (*cont.*)

Another reconstruction of Italian GDP based on a similar method, that of Maddison (1991), has not been considered here, because it deals with the problems of deflation in an unnecessarily controversial way for present purposes. Pending a thorough revision of Italian historical statistics following the approach laid out in their work concerning 1911, I consider RST to be the best estimate for the period concerned in the present work.

Stock of net fixed reproducible capital
RST (1993) have published only a net series. Their revision of the Vitali series not only raises the level, in connection with the upgrading of investment for 1911, as explained above, but evidently modifies the trend as well. The result appears frankly unacceptable over the years considered here. The increase in the stock shows a trend similar to Vitali's up to 1942, but scarcely shrinks in the subsequent years, while Vitali's series decreases by about 12 per cent from its 1941 peak to the 1945 trough. In the latter year, Vitali's stock is 5 per cent smaller than in 1938, which might still be considered an understatement of war losses, but at least makes some accommodation for them. For further discussion of war losses see the text.

Exchange rate of the lira in 1938
$1 = 19 lire
£1 = 92.97 lire
FF1 = 0.55 lire
Sources: Cols. 1, 5 from Fuà (1969); cols. 3, 7, 9–13 from RST (1993).

to the first quarter of 1943. With the exception of engineering the index numbers are all based on output figures and are therefore quite reliable; in the case of engineering, lack of output data forced the use of employment to build the index, with the hidden assumption that productivity of the marginal workers was constant and equal to that of those already employed. Since this assumption is unacceptable, we cannot trust the trend depicted in col. 3, which would suggest a 50 per cent overall increase of engineering output, with a continuous upward trend until the first quarter of 1943 . As I have explained in the notes to table 5.2, we could use total availability of steel (from table 5.3) as a good proxy for engineering output, which suggests a peak in 1941, 14 per cent higher compared to 1938. We have only one other case of a peak in 1941, namely public utilities (electricity, gas, water supplies), while in three cases (notably chemicals) the peak is in 1939. Confirmation of the robustness of these conclusions comes from physical output figures in table 5.3. The peak in most series is in 1940; sometimes in 1941, and in 1942 only in two cases.

The picture which emerges from these data is of only a modest shift of resources to heavy industry. If we consider data on consumption of electricity by industrial branch, we are driven to the same conclusion.[2] By 1941 metallurgy, engineering, and chemicals had increased their share of total consumption of electricity from 62 per cent to 66 per cent, but this was mostly due to the adoption of more electricity-intensive processes of production. In the case of metallurgy, domestic production stagnated, but

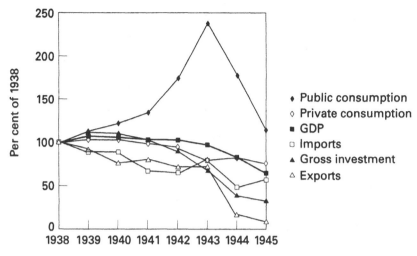

Figure 5.1 Trends in Italy's GDP by end use, 1938–1945
Source: table 5.1

consumption of electricity shot up by 54 per cent, because of the more intensive use of electric furnaces. The share of electric pig iron increased from 9 per cent in 1938 to 25 per cent in 1942; that of electric steel was already 27 per cent in 1938 and reached 40 per cent in 1942.[3]

Italian energy supplies are shown in table 5.4. This table suggests that for energy too the peak was reached in 1940 at a level 10 per cent higher than in 1938. This result was due to exceptionally high imports of coal in 1940. The supply of electricity peaked in 1941, but falling coal imports left total availability 5 per cent down on the previous year. Three factors affect the subsequent restriction of energy supplies. First, in a more recent estimate the 1940 increase in total availability is put at only 7 per cent above 1938, which makes the scope for expanded energy production even more modest.[4] In the second place, there was some effort to support the production of energy in 1941–2, but a sharp downward fall followed in 1943, when imports of coal were severely cut. Third, decline in the availability of oil and petrol had begun already in 1940, pointing to severe hardships for users of liquid fuels.[5] On the whole, the availability of raw materials and energy expanded only very marginally and the burden of rising military require-ments was met by redistribution away from existing users. Whether this lack of expansion was due to supply constraints or to a weak internal demand is something that I hope to clarify. We can start with an enlightening comparison with World War I with the help of table 5.5.

It is evident from the energy series that domestic production was more

Table 5.2. *Indices of industrial production 1939–1948 (per cent of 1938)*

(A) Production by sector, 1939–43

	Textiles 1	Metals 2	Engineering 3	Paper 4	Building 5	Public utilities 6	Mining 7	Chemicals 8
1939	107	101	112	110	134	112	105	125
1940	111	101	129	109	91	119	93	121
1941	95	97	144	100	48	132	87	108
1942	71	89	147	82	40	132	82	93
1943	64	88	150	63	27	123	71	67

(B) Alternative measures of industrial production, 1939–48

	Cols. 1–8 9	Re-weighted 10	Barberi 11	Vitali 12	RST 13
1939	114	111	107	110	110
1940	112	112	109	112	111
1941	98	106	96	106	105
1942	85	97	75	93	92
1943	74	88	65	73	72
1944	—	—	36	45	45
1945	—	—	22	34	34
1946	—	—	38	76	77
1947	—	—	—	95	97
1948	—	—	—	100	100

Sources:

1–9.   *Annuario Statistico Italiano*, 1944. Figures for 1943 only refer to the first quarter. These are the figures generally quoted; see for example Covino, Gallo and Mantovani (1976).

10.   The Ministero delle Corporazioni started calculating indices of industrial production in 1934 (using previous work done since 1928) on the basis of methods set up by ISTAT (see Ministero delle Corporazioni (1937)). Of the series in cols. 1–8, seven are based on physical production, while engineering is based on employment and is therefore particularly weak, requiring the assumption of constant productivity of workers. As there are good reasons to maintain that during the war the productivity of marginal workers was declining, the rise in the engineering series can definitely be considered overstated.

The overall index in col. 9 is unacceptable anyway, however, for two other reasons: (a) branch weights are based on employment rather than on value added; (b) two important branches are missing – building materials, and food and beverages. Adding these two branches (the first represented by production of cement, and the second by availability of foodstuffs) and using value added in 1938 from ISTAT as weights for the ten series, yields the reweighted estimate in col. 10.

The reweighted series shows a slower decline after 1940 compared with cols. 9 and 11. Comparing it with cols. 12 and 13 and disregarding 1943 (which in col. 10 refers only to the first quarter) shows considerable similarity.

sustained in World War II than in World War I. Interestingly, the better performance in World War II was due to the more sustained supply of coal, the availability of which had dropped during World War I. On the other hand, the increase in electricity supply was proportionally larger in World War I than in World War II. It is however the contribution of imports that was startlingly different: imports declined during World War II, though not as dramatically as it was believed, but had expanded considerably during World War I, supported by loans from the USA and UK.

I cannot pursue the comparison further here, but what has been shown is significant in pointing to the absence of external support for the Italian war effort in 1939–43. This is something that cannot certainly be argued for either Germany or the UK. At the beginning of the war, with great effort and not much success, Italy struggled to secure at least the same level of foreign supply of energy and raw materials as in normal years, but was unable to obtain more. The reason is to be ascribed to Italy's choice of alliance. During World War I, Italy could avail herself of the alliance with the UK and the US and was able to expand imports considerably, as can be seen from the increasing share of imports from the USA. Allied with Germany during World War II, Italy's reliance on imports from Germany increased even more dramatically than her reliance on the USA during World War I, but in a context of declining imports.

Germany was unwilling to supply Italy with munitions; at the most, it sent to Italy some of the military material seized in France or elsewhere.[6] Germany did supply Italy with some key raw materials (essentially coal and steel), but only at the cost of lengthy negotiations, and the provision by Italy

Notes to Table 5.2 (*cont.*)

There still remains the problem of overvaluation of the engineering series. If we use availability of steel as a proxy for engineering output, the overall index resulting resembles Barberi's index (col. 11) quite closely. Clearly, more work is needed for firmer results, but any amendment is likely to produce a decline in the overall industrial index steeper than the one depicted in cols. 12–13.

Very little is known of the procedures followed by ISTAT to estimate 1944 and 1945; they must in any case be largely based on available physical indicators to fill the gap between 1943 and 1946. Concerning the postwar years, I have previously argued that the ISTAT estimates are more acceptable than the many alternatives circulated at the time; see Zamagni (1986).

11–13. Col. 11 comes from a document attributed to Barberi (one of the most important collaborators in ISTAT national income calculations in the 1930s to the 1950s), entitled 'Il reddito nazionale dell'Italia', found in ASBI, *Fondo Studi*, cart. 378, 21, presumably written at the beginning of 1947. Sources for cols. 12, 13 are as table 5.1; RST (1993) only give series in current prices, so I have used Vitali's deflators to produce series at constant 1938 prices, which turns out to be exactly the same as Vitali's, as was to be expected from the approach followed by RST.

Table 5.3. *Italian output of selected industrial products and raw materials 1938–1948 (excluding energy)*

	Iron ore thou. tons 1	Lead ore thou. tons 2	Zinc ore thou. tons 3	Copper ore thou. tons 4	Manganese thou. tons 5	Pyrites thou. tons 6	Sugar thou. tons 7	Cotton yarn thou. tons 8
1938	990	68	201	23	48	930	370	178
1939	948	74	229	21	45	978	441	192
1940	1,179	75	212	19	51	1,061	560	178
1941	1,340	67	192	16	60	1,023	420	115
1942	1,085	51	172	24	60	971	388	76
1943	836	31	105	26	45	776	n.a.	49
1944	390	6	48	17	24	229	54	17
1945	134	4	31	8	3	108	18	10
1946	132	24	65	1	8	401	255	139
1947	227	38	117	—	27	643	220	180
1948	549	47	146	—	25	836	410	189

	Cotton cloth thou. tons 9	Artificial fibres thou. tons 10	Pig iron thou. tons 11	Steel thou. tons 12	Aluminium thou. tons 13	Ships launched thou. gross tons 14	Railway carriages, units 15	Road vehicles, units 16
1938	135	125	864	2,323	26	106	1,500	70,777
1939	141	144	1,005	2,283	34	134	2,432	68,834
1940	145	170	1,062	2,258	39	102	1,409	47,856
1941	109	195	1,038	2,063	48	109	3,642	38,798
1942	78	153	887	1,934	44	85	6,325	30,407
1943	54	108	648	1,727	46	69	4,376	21,134
1944	27	32	233	1,026	17	19	2,091	13,781
1945	16	4	65	395	4	21	2,350	10,290

	Ammonia thou. tons 17	Soda thou. tons 18	Hydrochloric acid thou. tons 19	Nitric acid thou. tons 20	Fertilizer thou. tons 21	Paper thou. tons 22	Cement thou. tons 23
1938	113	165	55	304	1,406	479	4,608
1939	147	200	66	385	1,653	531	5,020
1940	165	196	71	437	1,431	535	4,707
1941	167	198	65	467	1,136	498	2,707
1942	149	162	53	414	716	409	2,093
1943	122	113	45	344	67	—	—
1944	50	33	22	167	20	—	—
1945	17	20	10	42	176	—	—
1946	61	81	43	167	645	227	4,327
1947	100	195	59	226	1,041	357	7,938
1948	124	206	50	216	1,225	375	3,353

Sources: Rey (1991); for steel, Barberi (1961).

Table 5.4. *Italian energy supplies, 1938–1948*

	Solid fuels, thou. tons			Liquid fuels, thou. tons			Methane gas, million cu. m	Electricity, million kWh	All energy, petroleum equivalent, per cent of 1938
	coal, domestic 1	coal, imported 2	total, coal equivalent 3	oil 4	petrol 5	total, coal equivalent 6	7	8	9
1938	1,480	11,895	17,421	184	261	2,426	17	15,027	100
1939	2,024	11,021	17,154	187	358	3,084	20	17,707	105
1940	2,282	13,522	20,455	139	264	2,125	28	18,686	110
1941	2,393	11,435	19,994	72	129	699	42	20,151	105
1942	2,521	10,686	20,650	73	136	767	55	19,566	103
1943	1,358	6,166	14,345	50	87	436	55	17,894	92
1944	613	—	4,988	1	1	5	49	13,197	52
1945	758	—	5,059	—	—	2	42	12,375	42
1946	1,167	5,594	11,926	85	175	1,363	64	16,904	72
1947	1,354	8,789	15,371	234	537	4,369	93	19,717	96
1948	973	8,355	13,973	202	530	3,643	117	21,918	96

Notes:
2. 1944 coal imported from Germany amounted to 4 million tons according to Ilardi (1972).
3, 6. These include other items not reported in the table.
Sources: Rey (1991–2), vol. I; Barberi (1961). The original source for col. 9 is Pierantoni, Piacentini and Vestrucci (1980).

Table 5.5. *Total energy available, and exports and imports: Italy in two world wars (per cent of 1914 and 1938)*

World War I

	Total energy available	Exports	Imports	
			total	% from USA
	1	2	3	4
1914	100	100	100	15
1915	92	98	126	37
1916	94	87	157	41
1917	77	46	152	44
1918	85	54	137	42

World War II

	Total energy available	Exports	Imports	
			total	% from Germany
	5	6	7	8
1938	100	100	100	27
1939	105	92	89	29
1940	110	77	89	39
1941	105	81	67	60
1942	103	72	65	60

Sources: Rey (1991–2), vol. I; exports and imports from RST (1993).

Table 5.6. *Italy's estimated need for strategic raw materials during World War II (thousand tons)*

	Annual require- ment in wartime 1	Domestic output, wartime annual average 2	Import require- ment 3	Actual import, wartime annual average 4
Coal	16,500	2,200	14,300	11,600
Liquid fuel	8,500	120	8,380	1,100
Steel	4,800	2,400	2,400	800
Aluminium	65	32	33	5
Copper, tin	160	1	159	30
Rubber	22	—	22	14

Source: Favagrossa (1946), 97.

to Germany of agricultural and industrial workers and of substantial amounts of (mainly agricultural) exports. As a result, in the crucial years, Italy's bilateral trade with Germany was always in surplus, a factor which favoured the German mobilization of resources at Italy's expense.[7] But other raw materials remained in very short supply, especially liquid fuels, as can be seen from table 5.6, extracted from a work by General Favagrossa, who directed the war production effort. The most dramatic situation was that of liquid fuels, the supply of which reached 3 million tons in 1939 (see table 5.4), falling to 2.1 million the following year, and 0.7 million in 1941, when the only source of imports left was Romania, for the exports of which Germany successfully competed.[8] Even revising downward General Favagrossa's estimate of liquid fuel requirements in time of war, the actual trend of supplies was dismaying.

Favagrossa and the military personnel leading the Italian armed forces certainly overstated the role of raw material shortages in Italian military defeat. They made them the scapegoat for their strategic mistakes and for the shortcomings in the Italian munitions industry reviewed below, both of which were very substantial. However, I think the revisionist view recently put forward by Minniti, Curami, Ceva, and Raspin goes too far in playing down the constraints coming from the supply side.[9] There is no doubt that such constraints were binding, and much ingenuity and resources went into negotiations to secure even the modest supply achieved. Indeed, hardship was so severe that a lesson was learned; one of the basic postwar guidelines of Italian foreign policy was for Italy to be open to trade and international cooperation, to avoid crippling Italian industry which had many problems

Table 5.7. *Italian employment in Confindustria firms,*
1936–1943

	December 1936	December 1941	April 1943
Foodstuffs	255,978	347,247	316,191
Mining	99,200	158,148	149,000
Building	475,388	619,237	437,300
Cement	38,856	39,930	36,880
Metals	—	167,060	165,950
Engineering	567,246	803,355	886,200
Chemicals	116,500	182,601	195,360
Cotton	186,607	225,319	210,200
Other	957,056	1,307,931	1,240,980
Total	2,696,831	3,850,828	3,638,061

Source: ACS, Fondo IRI, num. nera, busta 81, Appunti e relazioni
varie, 'Addetti a ditte "rappresentate" presso la Confindustria'. The
document was kindly supplied to the author by Rolf Petri. 'Other'
industry is calculated from the source.

to worry about other than struggling to get raw materials in sufficient quantity and of the right assortment.

The mobilization of labour

About 5 million men were mobilized into the armed forces. The army comprised about 3 million soldiers at the peak in 1943, the navy 260,000, the air force 130,000; the rest was made up of soldiers wounded or killed, prisoners, and fascist squads.[10]

Concerning the labour force, few data are available and a thorough investigation is still in the future. The best picture of the trend is given by a document of Confindustria reporting data from its bimonthly survey of employment, hours worked, and wages in associated firms (see table 5.7). This survey had been carried out since 1928, but its publication was discontinued in the second half of 1939.[11]

Before commenting on the table, we should note two things. First, artisans are not included in the figures since they were not associated with Confindustria. Second, 1936 is not appropriate as a prewar reference year, but at the moment nothing better is available. The table shows a 43 per cent increase in overall employment between 1936 and 1941. Compared with this there is an increase of 71 per cent in metals and engineering, of 57 per cent in chemicals, and of 59 per cent in mining; on the other hand, cotton increased only by 21 per cent, foodstuffs by 36 per cent, and building by 30 per cent. There is evidence, therefore, of mobilization for war and a shift of 'manpower' from light to heavy industry. In 1943, against a general decline of employment, employment in engineering and chemicals was still somewhat higher than in 1941.

Particularly worth noting is the vast training of new engineering workers during the war. Some came straight from the countryside; others were drawn from the building trades or from artisan shops. When they were laid off after the war, many set up their own firms and became successful entrepreneurs. Recent research traces such cases; for example, Solinas tells the story of the Magneti Marelli plant set up in the province of Modena to produce for the war.[12] There were 1,200 newly trained workers, most of whom were laid off after the war. Solinas is able to trace a number of redundant workers who created an industrial district of small- and medium-sized firms producing machine tools for international markets, and biomedical material.

One final remark must be devoted to workers in Germany. From a volume by Mantelli we learn that there was a remarkable seasonal emigration of agricultural labour to Germany of the order of 30,000–50,000 per year, but many more than this were required by German industry.[13] By the end of 1940 there were 62,000 Italian industrial workers in Germany, increasing to 240,000 by the end of 1941 and to 290,000 by the end of 1942.[14] After the beginning of the German occupation, labour was drafted from Italy, but comprehensive statistics are missing.[15] An interesting document found in the archives of the Bank of Italy contains estimates produced by employees of the Banca Nazionale del Lavoro, responsible for Italian emigrant remittances, for the Bank of Italy in early 1944 (the actual date is missing). The unknown author of the report confirms that in September 1943 the emigration was registered officially at about 300,000, a figure in agreement with documents found by Mantelli and quoted above. But the author adds to this figure 200,000 unofficial workers, and 200,000 Italians arriving in Germany from occupied territories. He states that precise information is lacking for the months after September 1943. But he ends by quoting a letter of 30 January 1944 from the German authorities applying for 1,122,200 bank cards (which allowed remittances to be paid). From this letter the author of the document concludes that 'the number of drafted labourers to Germany would stand at 1,800,000 units', a figure which cannot be checked on present knowledge.[16]

Private consumption

The issue of consumption can help us understand the extent of economic mobilization for war. I approach it with the help of table 5.8. Comparing

Table 5.8. *Italian agricultural production and consumption, 1938–1948*

Agricultural production (% of 1938)	Personal consumption (% of 1938)			Calories per head per day	
	total	foodstuffs	non-foodstuffs	total	rationed
1	2	3	4	5	6
1938 100	100	100	100	2,734	—
1939 105	102	100	103	2,657	—
1940 99	102	101	104	2,631	—
1941 95	98	94	101	2,514	1,010
1942 85	94	88	99	2,362	950
1943 74	82	79	85	2,112	990
1944 71	82	74	89	1,865	1,065
1945 67	76	68	81	1,747	—
1946 82	86	72	96	1,760	—
1947 87	103	84	118	2,114	—
1948 90	113	95	127	2,368	—

Sources:
Agricultural production is calculated from current-price figures in RST (1993), using Vitali's implicit deflator. The result is in agreement with original data in ISTAT (1950).
Personal consumption is from RST (1993).
Calories are from ISTAT (1968). The latter figures differ only marginally from reconstructions by RST (1993) with regard to consumption of foodstuffs; the main difference in the RST series is due to the higher level of consumption of non-foodstuffs. Rationed calories come from a League of Nations publication cited by Milward (1977), 288.

the trend in consumption with the trend in GDP in table 5.1, it is possible to see that in 1941–3 consumption fell more sharply than GDP, corresponding to the transfer of resources into wartime uses. In 1944–5, however, consumption fell less than income, underlining the effects of disengagement from the war and American support. The consumption of foodstuffs fell more severely than aggregate consumption, falling to a low point two-thirds the level of 1938, which matches the decline in calories per head in 1945 compared with 1938.

It must be noted that the ration (first introduced in 1941) represented a calorific entitlement much smaller than the actual intake, which could only be secured by resort to the free and black markets. Such markets became more and more widespread, pushing foodstuff prices up and causing severe hardship to waged employees, whose wages did not grow in line with free-market prices.[17] There was, therefore, a powerful redistribution of income away from dependent workers and in favour of wholesale traders, middlemen, the self-employed, some farmers, and some industrialists.

Munitions

The final objective of economic mobilization in time of war is the production of munitions. Research on this subject is well established and has reached two clear conclusions: munitions output could not be increased substantially and the quality of what was produced was less than satisfactory.

The navy

There is agreement on the fact that, of the three armed forces, the navy came first in the competition for resources.[18] This view is confirmed both by the size of the navy at the start of the war (see table 5.9) and by its claim on output (see table 5.10). It must be noted that Italy did not have aircraft carriers, which were planned but not built, even during the war. If the results were less than brilliant and if so much of the Italian navy was lost, these facts are to be attributed to lack of an appropriate overall strategy, lack of adequate cooperation with the air force, some technical inadequacies, and the incredible story of radar.[19] It appears that Italy not only knew about radar in the 1930s and was able to produce radar equipment, but a non-negligible number of units were actually produced and installed, yet not used before the Armistice, with the consequence that the Italian navy suffered innumerable avoidable losses, and was no longer in a position to face the enemy by August 1942.[20]

The air force

A large body of research has been attracted by the air force. The well-known ability of Italian industry to produce record-breaking aeroplanes and to produce for export has created particular interest in ascertaining the quality of Italian military aircraft.[21] Table 5.11 gives planned and actual output for the period 1933–43. It can be seen that the Ethiopian and Spanish wars enhanced the production of aircraft in the middle of the 1930s: output increased fivefold in 1934–6, then remained steady up to the outbreak of war, when it doubled again in 1940–1, before starting to fall back already in 1942. The gap between plans and results remained small (unlike for tanks and artillery) up to 1941, but then widened; efforts to reduce the number of models and to improve engine quality hindered production without achieving the desired results.

Minniti has made clear that one of the basic shortcomings of the Italian aircraft industry was short production runs associated with an excessive number of models, itself the result of the excessive number of small firms involved.[22] It was already May 1942 when it was proposed to form groups of firms organized by a leader in charge of coordinating production of a few

Table 5.9. *Size of the navies of three combatants in the Mediterranean, June 1940*

	Italy 1	Great Britain 2	France 3
Battleships	4	5	5
Aircraft carriers	—	2	—
Heavy cruisers	7	—	7
Light cruisers	12	10	7
Torpedo-boat destroyers	53	35	41
Torpedo boats	71	—	16
Submarines	115	12	42
Total	262	64	118

Source: Santoni (1991).

established models. But only at the beginning of 1943 were 12 groups formed, with 115,000 workers, and a vertical organization put in place which could also be used to negotiate with the Germans. This was too late and only paved the way to subordination of the Italian aircraft industry to the Germans in the troubled years of German occupation of the north.[23] Alegi confirms Minniti's analysis, insisting on the fact that directions from the Air Ministry to industry were often contradictory.[24]

More recent contributions point to the technical inferiority of Italian military aircraft, especially in relation to the engine and cabin instruments, and to the effects of both this and the excessive model range already noted on operational performance.[25] At the outbreak of war in June 1940 Italy had roughly 4,000 military aircraft, but only half were operative, with no more than 1,101 classified as 'modern' aircraft.[26] The situation did not improve during the war. According to Faldella, the number of effective aircraft (excluding reconnaissance planes) was as follows: 10 June 1940 – 1,780, 31 December 1941 – 1,493, end-November 1942 – 860, end-July 1943 – 890.[27] Lack of adequate infrastructure further limited the operational performance of Italian aircraft.[28]

The army
The army comes last in spite of its size, which was greatly overstated by the fascist regime. All munitions programmes concerning the army were late, contradictory, and not very effective.[29] It is not easy even to ascertain the output achieved, because only fragmentary data are available. I give a few totals in table 5.12.

Table 5.10. *Italian warship construction, 1935–1943 (units and total gross tonnage)*

	Battleships 1	Cruisers 2	Torpedo destroyers 3	Escort torpedo boats 4	Torpedo boats 5	Corvettes 6	Submarines 7	Midget submarines 8	Other torpedo vessels 9
Units									
1935	—	2	—	—	2	—	4	—	—
1936	—	2	—	—	10	—	14	—	—
1937	2	2	4	—	4	—	10	2	—
1938	—	—	5	—	20	—	21	—	—
1939	—	—	7	—	—	—	7	—	—
1940	4	—	—	—	—	—	8	6	—
1941	—	—	—	—	—	—	8	—	—
1942	1	1	5	10	—	5	11	—	18
1943	—	2	—	5	1	23	8	8	17
1935–43	7	9	21	15	37	28	91	16	35
Thou. tons									
1935–43	241.0	63.3	33.9	13.9	24.3	19.0	89.0	0.5	2.2

	Anti-submarine vessels 10	Anti-submarine motor boats 11	Mine-sweepers, etc. 12	Total 13
Units				
1935	—	—	—	8
1936	—	—	—	26
1937	—	26	1	49
1938	—	—	1	48
1939	—	25	1	40
1940	—	—	—	12
1941	—	26	1	41
1942	35	—	—	86
1943	16	1	67	148
1935–43	51	78	70	458
Thou. tons				
1935–43	3.8	2.0	16.0	508.9

Source: Minniti (1978), 49, table XIII.

Table 5.11. *Italian output of military aircraft, 1933–1943 (units)*

	Produced 1	Planned 2
1933	386	424
1934	328	455
1935	895	1,236
1936	1,768	2,031
1937	1,749	1,900
1938	1,610	1,700
1939	1,750	1,930
1940	3,257	3,785
1941	3,503	4,200
1942	2,821	4,800
1943	2,024	3,822

Source: Ministero della Difesa, Direzione delle Costruzioni Aeronautiche (no date).

Table 5.12. *Munitions output for the Italian army, June 1940–June 1943 (units)*

	Minniti et al. 1	Favagrossa 2
Motorcars	83,000	120,000
Motorcycles	33,000	35,000
Guns	—	9,800
Machineguns	—	125,000
Artillery	7,780	12,500
Mortars	—	16,800
Medium tanks	1,862	3,000
Self-propelled guns	645	—
Armoured cars	532	—

Sources: Minniti (1978), Sadkovich (1987), Comitato per la Storia dell'Artiglieria italiana (1953), Favagrossa (1946), 74–5.

After a glance at the table there is no need to dwell on the inadequate quantities produced.[30] The quality left much to be desired as well. Alegi produces a long list of defects of Italian tanks.[31] The fact is that the tanks produced before the war were far too light and hastily designed; the mistakes brought to light were never fully eliminated. There was even an inquiry into the poor quality of armoured plating of Italian tanks.[32] Artillery was of better quality, but completely insufficient in number and difficult to transport, deploy, and redeploy. This meant that the army never had munitions in sufficient quantity to be mobilized fully as a modern armed force. Minniti concludes that 'the Army remained an infantry, without enough means of transport . . . so that we can really talk of a lack of preparation of the Army [for a modern war]'.[33] The defeat would have come much earlier, had it not been for the delay in the attack on Italian territory. Even the supply of soldiers' food and clothing was inadequate, as well as inferior to World War I. Roatta reports that training was often cut back so as not to wear out precious shoes.[34]

Some blame for this situation has been laid at the door of Italian industry. Firms were too few and too small; this caused at the same time lack of competition in many lines of production, fragmentation in other lines, hasty plans to enlarge capacity, and too many prototypes, none adequately tested and none produced in sufficient quantity. It is beyond doubt that Italian industry was utterly inadequate for a modern war in which both quantity and quality mattered.[35] Engineering capacity was certainly enlarged, as we shall see in the next section, but this was not enough to relieve shortages of munitions, given the lack of a mass engineering industry producing in peacetime. However, the most scarce resource was organization, both in the armed forces and in industry.

The cost of the war

In Italy the level of public expenditure was already quite high in the 1930s before the Ethiopian war (17–19 per cent of GDP), and in deficit as can be seen from table 5.13 (cols. 11, 13). Reported military spending (col. 2), however, was low, at around 20 per cent of total budget expenditure. Military spending almost trebled during the Ethiopian War, remaining at that level thereafter, but the GDP share of total budget expenditure increased only marginally, while its coverage by taxation fluctuated between 60 and 70 per cent (col. 8).

In the three war years from June 1940 to July 1943 (which incidentally coincide almost exactly with the fiscal years used in the table) military and other public spending shot up. Public spending increased to 36 per cent of GDP in 1940/1, 38 per cent the following year and 41 per cent in 1942/3,

Table 5.13. *Italian public expenditure, revenues and deficit, 1933–1947 (billions of current lire)*

(A) Expenditures

	Ragioneria		AM-lire	CSVI	Ammassi	Expenditures, total	Revenues	
	total	of which, military					total	% of expenditures
	1	2	3	4	5	6	7	8 (%)
1932/3	22.6	5.0	0.0	0.0	0.0	22.6	18.5	81.9
1933/4	24.4	4.6	0.0	0.0	0.0	24.4	18.3	75.0
1934/5	22.5	5.3	0.0	0.0	0.0	22.5	19.3	85.8
1935/6	35.2	12.1	0.0	0.2	0.0	35.4	21.1	59.6
1936/7	39.2	13.1	0.0	0.2	0.0	39.4	26.7	67.8
1937/8	39.6	12.3	0.0	0.2	0.0	39.8	28.9	72.6
1938/9	40.9	13.4	0.0	-0.1	0.0	40.8	29.0	71.1
1939/40	54.4	24.7	0.0	0.3	0.0	54.7	33.4	61.1
1940/1	98.4	63.2	0.0	-0.1	0.4	98.7	35.6	36.1
1941/2	117.3	66.1	0.0	7.5	0.7	125.5	42.9	34.2
1942/3	148.5	84.9	0.0	25.4	0.8	174.7	49.9	28.6
1943/4	123.4	68.7	42.7	8.2	1.5	175.8	44.9	25.5
1944/5	355.6	74.5	41.5	-0.9	3.3	399.5	62.9	15.7
1945/6	415.0	111.5	40.9	-15.0	5.3	446.2	159.2	35.7
1946/7	800.0	141.1	20.1	-25.6	45.2	839.7	444.9	53.0

(B) GDP and public finance

| | Nominal GDP | Budget balance | | | Overall spending, % of nominal GDP |
| | | Ragioneria | all-inclusive | % of GDP | |
	9	10	11	12	13
1932/3	130.3	−4.1	−4.1	−3	17.3
1933/4	127.6	−6.1	−6.1	−5	19.1
1934/5	136.2	−3.2	−3.2	−2	16.5
1935/6	150.8	−14.1	−14.3	−9	23.5
1936/7	170.9	−12.5	−12.7	−7	23.1
1937/8	191.6	−10.7	−10.9	−6	20.8
1938/9	210.3	−11.9	−11.8	−6	19.4
1939/0	239.8	−21.0	−21.3	−9	22.8
1940/1	277.6	−62.8	−63.1	−23	35.6
1941/2	332.1	−74.4	−82.6	−25	37.8
1942/3	426.5	−98.6	−124.8	−29	41.0
1943/4	660.0	−78.5	−130.9	−20	26.6
1944/5	1,174.5	−292.7	−336.6	−29	34.0
1945/6	2,564.0	−255.8	−287.0	−11	17.4
1946/7	5,464.0	−355.1	−394.8	−7	15.4

Notes:
All figures refer to actual flows; they differed from planned flows sometimes by a considerable amount, especially in troubled years like those under consideration here. All figures are reported for the financial year ending in June; figures for nominal GDP in the calendar year have been correspondingly adjusted

Sources:
1, 2, 7, 10. Ministero del Tesoro, Ragioneria generale dello Stato (1969). The expenditure total computed by Ragioneria for 1944/5 includes a war indemnity paid to Germany amounting to 180 billion current lire (see text for details).

3–6. Cols. 3–5 are from Servizio Ragioneria della Banca d'Italia (1993). These items were not included in the official budget and were all charged directly on to the Central Bank, as explained in the text. Col. 6 is the sums of cols. 1, 3, 4, 5.

9. GDP figures from RST (1993), converted to financial year.

10–11. Col. 10 is col. 7, *less* col. 1. Col. 11 is col. 7, *less* col. 6.

but then began to fall, its GDP share declining by the end of the war to below the level of the early 1930s. Public spending was also less and less covered by taxation, the deficit reaching nearly 30 per cent of GDP at the 1942/3 peak. There was a close association between the magnitudes of the deficit and of reported military spending which was sometimes smaller but more usually a little larger than the deficit. As a result of the deficit, public debt and inflation both increased rapidly.

The fascist regime tried to bring inflation under control, and it must be admitted that, given the difficult situation, there was some achievement in this field up to the Armistice. The cost of living went up by 17 per cent in 1940, by 16 per cent in 1941, by 16 per cent again in 1942, and then by 68 per cent in 1943, but most of the latter rise came after the political turmoil of that year. Subsequently inflation soared as the free and black markets spread their influence.

As I have explained in the notes to table 5.13, I have reported the most reliable series available for the government budget, using actual rather than planned expenditures.[36] However, the military component of the series does not include colonial outlays, so another table is presented below (table 5.14) with more detail on military spending, colonies included. But before we consider this table it must be noted that there are three other items, left out of the official budget but charged to the central bank, which I have reported both in table 5.13 (cols. 3–5) to obtain total public expenditure, and in table 5.14 to derive a more reliable military subtotal. Some historical details of these three items follow.

CSVI

In order of time, the CSVI (Consorzio Sovvenzioni su Valori Industriali) comes first. This institution was created in 1914 by the Bank of Italy to administer financial interventions in support of industry.[37] The large-scale bailing out of banks and industrial firms by the CSVI at the beginning of the 1920s had made the CSVI a candidate for inclusion in the reconstruction of Italian public debt figures which I have carried out recently together with G. Salvemini.[38] Salvemini, an expert in Italian public finance, was against inclusion of the CSVI as a financial institution granting credits to private banking and industrial firms, in spite of this credit enjoying state endorsement, and we left it out from our series ending in 1939. But new legislation was enacted at the end of the 1930s allowing CSVI to carry out 'special operations' according to the following mechanism.[39]

The state issued certificates to cover a given sum of public expenditure, engaging itself to pay the sum off in instalments over a number of years (usually ten). The individual, institution, or company to which the certificate was issued could go to the CSVI, deposit the certificate and

Table 5.14. Italian military expenditure, 1933–1947 (billion lire at current and constant 1938 prices and per cent)

	War Ministry			Navy			Air Ministry		
	ordinary	extra-ordinary	total	ordinary	extra-ordinary	total	ordinary	extra-ordinary	total
	1	2	3	4	5	6	7	8	9
1933	2.620	0.548	3.168	1.153	0.343	1.496	0.770	0.079	0.849
1934	2.355	0.564	2.919	1.088	0.288	1.376	0.669	0.084	0.753
1935	2.539	0.801	3.340	1.241	0.256	1.497	0.619	0.122	0.741
1936	2.368	4.852	7.220	1.554	1.298	2.852	0.937	1.525	2.462
1937	2.513	4.711	7.224	1.705	1.566	3.271	0.952	2.058	3.010
1938	2.995	3.315	6.310	2.037	0.793	2.830	1.146	2.514	3.660
1939	3.769	3.614	7.383	2.131	0.894	3.025	1.546	2.081	3.627
1940	3.954	11.597	15.551	2.207	1.248	3.455	2.171	2.974	5.145
1941	4.631	36.869	41.500	2.950	4.883	7.833	2.732	7.150	9.882
1942	5.582	40.627	46.209	2.882	7.716	10.598	2.746	5.279	8.025
1943	5.739	51.433	57.172	3.540	11.200	14.740	3.344	7.861	11.205
1944	5.120	35.655	40.775	1.850	14.322	16.172	2.221	7.549	9.770
1945	4.879	44.213	49.092	4.367	10.922	15.289	4.135	4.151	8.286
1946	24.531	55.923	80.454	12.619	13.441	26.060	7.204	2.367	9.571
1947	65.004	34.387	99.391	27.135	15.341	42.476	14.447	3.295	17.742

Table 5.14 (*cont.*)

	Colonies			Four ministries			CSVI military	AM-lire plus German indemnity	Nominal military spending total
	ordinary	extra-ordinary	total	ordinary	extra-ordinary	total			
	10	11	12	13	14	15	16	17	18
1933	0.007	0.456	0.463	4.550	1.426	5.976	0.000	0.000	5.976
1934	0.008	0.440	0.448	4.120	1.376	5.496	0.000	0.000	5.496
1935	0.007	0.852	0.859	4.406	2.031	6.437	0.000	0.000	6.437
1936	0.008	4.133	4.141	4.867	11.808	16.675	0.000	0.000	16.675
1937	0.011	5.933	5.944	5.181	14.268	19.449	0.000	0.000	19.449
1938	0.021	6.306	6.327	6.199	12.928	19.127	0.000	0.000	19.127
1939	0.022	4.262	4.284	7.468	10.851	18.319	0.000	0.000	18.319
1940	0.022	5.628	5.650	8.354	21.447	29.801	0.000	0.000	29.801
1941	0.026	5.983	6.009	10.339	54.885	65.224	0.000	0.000	65.224
1942	0.026	1.506	1.532	11.236	55.128	66.364	8.469	0.000	74.833
1943	0.028	1.649	1.677	12.651	72.143	84.794	9.594	0.000	94.388
1944	0.026	1.152	1.178	9.217	58.678	67.895	8.765	42.700	119.360
1945	0.180	0.684	0.864	13.561	59.970	73.531	0.000	220.500	294.031
1946	0.301	1.524	1.825	44.655	73.255	117.910	0.000	40.900	158.810
1947	0.712	3.040	3.752	107.298	56.063	163.361	0.000	20.100	183.461

	Real GDP 19	GDP implicit deflator 20	Real military spending total 21	Military spending, per cent of GDP 22
1933	165.7	82	7.300	4
1934	166.8	79	6.933	4
1935	175.4	80	8.015	5
1936	185.3	84	19.744	11
1937	192.5	92	21.207	11
1938	198.0	100	19.127	10
1939	205.8	106	17.331	8
1940	210.2	118	25.226	12
1941	206.1	140	46.623	23
1942	204.9	168	44.439	22
1943	199.9	223	42.365	21
1944	180.0	390	30.593	17
1945	147.7	864	34.042	23
1946	146.6	1,752	9.063	6
1947	175.3	3,176	5.777	3

Notes:
Figures again refer to actual, not planned outlays. The total of expenditures from the four ministries is larger than aggregate military expenditure calculated by the Ragioneria and reported in table 5.13 (col. 2) by the inclusion here of the internal police apparatus (in the War Ministry), civil aviation (in the Air Ministry, a very small sum) and Colonies

Figures under CSVI show only that part devoted to military outlays, are are therefore smaller than the overall CSVI figures in table 5.13 (col. 4). Figures for AM-lire and the indemnity paid to Germany are included so as to show an upper-bound estimate of expenditure on equipment and operations due to the war.

Sources: Atti Parlamentari (1935–52); AM-lire from table 5.13 (col. 3); GDP and GDP implicit deflator from RST (1993); military CSVI from ASBI, *Fondo CSVI, Verbali delle adunanze del Comitato Centrale Amministrativo e della Giunta,* various years.

receive the total sum immediately. The CSVI was in turn allowed to obtain the money directly from the central bank, which it repaid in due course from the subsequent flow of budget-financed instalments.[40] Over a number of years, therefore, all the public spending financed in this way ought to have appeared in the official budget as the instalments were paid off, and there would be no need for a special treatment of this item. Indeed, if the sums spent through this mechanism remained level, a compensating flow would eventually be set in motion, as can be seen in table 5.13 (col. 4) for the years 1938/9–40/1. But when the value of certificates issued by the state becomes very substantial within a short period, and repayments are discontinued, then it becomes important to take this source of public spending into account. This is exactly what happened in the years 1941/2–43/4, when a total of 41 billion lire was advanced by CSVI, in reality by the Bank of Italy, only 27 billion of which was for munitions production.

This is not the place to reconstruct the very interesting story of CSVI.[41] However, it is worth mentioning that the view that the CSVI funds for special operations were truly to be seen as advances by the Bank of Italy to the government was first put forward by Einaudi, when as governor in 1945 he wrote the missing report of the Bank of Italy for 1943. Of the CSVI he wrote: 'In substance, the intervention by the CSVI has the effect of hiding some of the Bank of Italy advances to the Treasury . . . given that the CSVI would never have granted those billions of lire without the state guarantee, the real debtor is to be considered the Treasury.'[42] The very way in which a solution was found to the indebtedness of the CSVI in the postwar years is revealing. The CSVI special operations were paid off in 1946 through a slice of the newly issued public debt, so that this item effectively disappeared from our public debt reconstruction (see table 5.16 below), because it was subsumed under long-term bonds.

Ammassi

The 'Ammassi' was the financial administration of the compulsory pooling of basic foodstuffs mentioned above. Again, normally, in the long run there would be offsetting flows which would cancel each other out. But in the final war years and especially during the first two years of postwar reconstruction, the administration of the fund was very unbalanced and the Bank of Italy had to finance a heavy deficit until the abolition of the 'political price' of bread.

AM-lire

This item does not qualify as advances to the Treasury, but as a straightforward addition to cash in circulation, being the paper money issued to the Allied military forces for use on their behalf. Here it should be mentioned that this item is recorded in the accounts of the Bank of Italy only from 1946, when this component was included in the official total of cash in circulation. However, in my tables I have reported the sums currently issued, as they appear in the yearly reports of the Bank of Italy. For a thorough account of the story of the AM-lire, it should also be noted that the Americans credited the Italian government with a counterpart fund after negotiations following the conclusion of the war.

Mention must also be made of the indemnity paid by the northern Italian government (RSI) to the Germans during their occupation. There are interesting details of the indemnity in the archives of the Bank of Italy, which throw light on the difficult relations between the late fascist government of the RSI and the Germans. However, this item appears to have already been included in the official reconstruction of the government budget because it was correctly registered as a Treasury outlay for which extraordinary advances were supplied by the Bank of Italy.

These items together make total government expenditure and the budget deficit substantially higher than in the official records for the years 1941/2–46/7. It is worth underlining the fact that, in June 1945, when the German indemnity of 180 billion lire was registered, the combined sum of the indemnity, the AM-lire, and the Ammassi made up fully half of total public expenditure.

Now for military expenditure. In table 5.14, reconstructed from the original budgets, we have military spending broken down by the four ministries concerned (cols. 1–15). To these the military element in CSVI funds, AM-lire, and the German indemnity must be added to obtain the total sum spent on war (cols. 16–18).[43] Translating the series into constant 1938 lire (cols. 20, 21), it can be seen that real war expenditures increased considerably in the first year of the war, but failed to grow further and even declined slightly in the following two years. In terms of the GDP share of military outlays we see again that the peak was reached in 1941 at roughly 23 per cent, falling slightly in the following two years; 1945 shows a higher percentage (but of a much smaller GDP) as a result of the German indemnity.

How much of this represented outlays on industrial goods for military use? Military spending on industrial goods covers much more than the procurement of weapons as such. It is not possible to find out exactly what was spent specifically on weapons from the budget side, because even the original documents are not sufficiently detailed. In table 5.15 I have tried to exclude the ordinary expenditure on employees of the ministries, transfers, pensions, foodstuffs, and garments. What is left should comprise the cost of combat munitions and the means of military operations and construction (transport vehicles and ships, fuel, other transport services, building materials for fortifications, and so on), although it may still include some

Table 5.15. *Estimated Italian expenditure on military equipment, operations, and construction, 1940–1943 (million current lire)*

	1940	1941	1942	1943
War Ministry				
Repairs	1,017	1,237	1,457	1,599
Extraordinary allocation	8,764	35,345	40,297	51,335
Colonies	1,983	734	252	—
Albania	620	679	16	—
Navy				
Repairs	846	1,439	1,230	1,288
New construction	325	835	889	617
Extraordinary allocation	540	3,399	6,734	10,361
Colonies	142	80	14	—
Albania	53	30	1	—
Air Ministry				
Repairs	692	817	919	1,003
New construction	612	796	112	106
Extraordinary allocation	472	5,417	4,850	7,344
Colonies	1,659	187	60	71
Albania	50	31	4	1
Colonial ministry	3,682	4,660	1,123	840
CSVI military outlays	—	—	8,469	9,594
Equipment and operations, total	21,457	55,686	66,427	84,159
Military spending, total	29,801	65,224	74,833	94,388
of which, % on equipment and operations	72	85	89	89
Nominal GDP	239,595	277,565	332,030	426,500
of which, % on equipment and operations	9	20	20	20

Notes:
Of ordinary expenditures only repairs are included, on the grounds that these were connected with maintaining the efficiency of war materials. Of extraordinary expenditures only those explicitly designated for war purposes are included. CSVI military expenditure is included because it was an additional means of financing for outlays on equipment and operations
Sources: As table 5.14.

extraordinary expenditures on foodstuffs and clothing. Table 5.15 therefore shows an upper-bound estimate of expenditure on industrial goods for military use, which remained apparently stable at 20 per cent of GDP for the three war years.

A comparison with other combatants makes it clear beyond doubt that in Italy military spending was far lower than elsewhere in proportion to overall resources, even at the peak in 1941. The same comparison also yields the conclusion that the Italian war effort was limited in 1941–3 not so much by a failure to squeeze private consumption, as by a high level of public spending not devoted to war, combined with a relatively high investment share, all within a context of the failure of overall output to expand.

Finally I return to Italy's public debt. Table 5.16 reconstructs this aggregate using the same methods and definitions as in my essay with Salvemini (previously cited), with some marginal differences explained in the notes to the table. Figures refer not to the fiscal, but to the end of the calendar year, for consistency with my previous work. They show that the burden of public debt increased from 75 per cent of GDP at the end of 1938 to 113 per cent at the end of 1943. Then inflation cut the burden considerably, especially in 1946 when it was halved in the course of a single year.

War losses

There is only one official estimate of war material losses, based on a special ISTAT survey carried out in September 1944 in eighteen Italian provinces comprising all of the south, Latium (including Rome), and Umbria; thus the Marches and Tuscany were missing as well as the whole of the north, still occupied by the Germans and under the fascist regime.[44] After such a good beginning, nothing followed in terms of official estimates. Although the ISTAT study is very detailed and highly interesting, its results are not a good indicator for the Italian situation as a whole, not only because the war continued in the rest of Italy for several more months, but also because most of Italy's industrial capacity was located exactly in the provinces missing from the ISTAT survey, and because the centre and the south suffered much greater losses than the north.

From this survey, we learn that war losses to industrial plants in the area covered were equal to 35 per cent of their 1939 book value, including inventories. Indeed inventories, as was to be expected given the dislocation of transport and trade, made up 41 per cent of total losses, while the evidence is that in normal times inventories accounted for no more than 20 per cent of total capital invested in industry.[45]

Estimates produced immediately after the end of the war arrived at an estimate of 20 per cent of industrial capacity lost.[46] A SVIMEZ study

Table 5.16. Italian public debt, 1938–1946, 31 December (billion current lire)

	Bonds				Bills		
	long and medium term	owned by CDDPP	CDDPP bonds	net total	Treasury	CDDPP	total
	1	2	3	4	5	6	7
1938	102.3	8.0	0.4	94.7	11.0	0.1	11.1
1939	102.2	6.6	0.5	96.1	14.2	0.2	14.4
1940	131.8	19.7	0.5	112.6	24.8	0.2	24.9
1941	162.9	18.4	0.5	145.0	38.6	0.2	38.7
1942	208.6	20.4	0.5	188.8	48.6	0.2	48.8
1943	230.0	22.3	0.5	208.3	57.8	0.2	58.0
1944	244.1	22.2	0.5	222.4	109.8	0.2	109.9
1945	295.4	23.4	0.5	272.5	198.4	0.2	198.5
1946	406.7	40.0	0.5	367.2	259.3	0.2	259.5

	Postal funds				Advances by central bank			
	saving accounts	current accounts	total	notes and coin undelivered	advances	other assets	Treasury current account	other liabilities
	8	9	10	11	12	13	14	15
1938	29.2	1.1	30.4	0.5	3.0	1.7	0.9	0.5
1939	32.0	1.5	33.6	0.8	9.0	1.9	0.5	0.4
1940	37.3	2.2	39.5	1.0	16.0	2.4	-11.0	0.5
1941	46.9	3.1	50.0	1.0	30.0	4.5	1.3	0.6
1942	59.5	3.4	62.9	0.4	50.0	5.1	5.4	2.7
1943	61.3	4.7	66.1	2.7	80.0	6.5	-47.3	7.5

Postal funds / Advances by central bank

	saving accounts 8	current accounts 9	total 10	notes and coin undelivered 11	advances 12	other assets 13	Treasury current account 14	other liabilities 15
1944	65.0	6.3	71.3	2.6	203.6	8.9	−98.4	4.2
1945	91.9	12.8	104.7	18.2	343.7	13.5	20.5	27.8
1946	139.9	25.4	165.3	1.0	343.7	17.2	10.1	9.7

Advances by central bank (cont.) / Cash

	special operations with CSVI 16	Ammassi 17	total 18	cash certificates 19	notes 20	coin 21	notes and coin undelivered 22	AM-lire 23	total 24
1938	0.6	1.1	5.6	0.0	1.9	1.7	0.5	0.0	3.1
1939	0.5	1.5	12.9	0.0	2.4	1.7	0.8	0.0	3.3
1940	0.8	1.4	22.2	0.3	2.6	1.2	1.0	0.0	3.1
1941	3.0	1.4	38.0	0.6	3.5	1.2	1.0	0.0	4.4
1942	17.8	2.7	68.0	0.8	4.7	0.4	0.4	0.0	5.4
1943	40.3	3.1	172.4	0.8	5.5	0.4	2.7	19.9	24.0
1944	41.7	3.1	354.2	0.8	5.5	0.4	2.6	65.4	69.6
1945	40.8	6.9	374.8	1.1	6.3	0.4	18.2	87.2	76.7
1946	0.5	33.2	375.8	1.1	6.3	0.3	1.0	137.0	143.6

Table 5.16 (*cont.*)

| | Other advances | | | Overall public debt | Nominal GDP | Debt/GDP ratio, % |
| | Social security institutes | Banco di Napoli | total | | | |
	25	26	27	28	29	30
1938	2.1	2.3	4.4	149.3	199.0	75
1939	2.4	2.5	5.0	165.1	221.5	75
1940	2.7	5.6	8.3	210.6	258.1	82
1941	3.1	6.8	9.9	286.0	297.1	96
1942	3.4	9.4	12.8	386.6	367.0	105
1943	3.7	16.5	20.2	548.9	486.0	113
1944	2.5	34.3	36.8	864.2	834.0	104
1945	1.5	49.5	51.0	1,078.2	1,515.0	71
1946	2.0	43.3	45.2	1,356.6	3,613.0	38

Sources:

As Salvemini, Zamagni (1992), except that:

I have added items already included in table 5.13, namely AM-lire, special operations with the CSVI, and the deficit from the organization of *ammassi*. No information has been found on one item previously included in the data, namely 'other advances', which has therefore been omitted, probably without great overall loss (it amounted to 1.7 billion lire in 1939, and there is no evidence of any increase during the war years).

Data on long-term bonds, treasury bills, social security institutes and Bank of Naples advances were available only at the end of the fiscal year and have been adjusted recursively to the end of the calendar year.

AM-lire were officially reported in the balance sheets of the Bank of Italy only from 1946, but are reported here from tables in the Bank of Italy annual reports as they were issued.

Figures for State bonds owned by CDDPP (Cassa Depositi e Prestiti), CDDPP bonds, and CDDPP bills in 1946 have been interpolated in the absence of a CDDPP balance sheet for 1946.

GDP comes as usual from RST (1993).

reported by Jacoboni provides geographical detail: the proportion of industrial capacity lost was given as 12.5 per cent in the north, 38.5 per cent in
the centre, 35 per cent in the south, and 12.1 per cent in the islands, with a
weighted average of 19.4 per cent.[47] However, it is unclear whether these
were percentages of the prewar level, or of the peak of capacity reached in
1941–2; the peak was certainly 10–15 per cent higher than in 1938.
Moreover, the estimate included inventories and other damage which could
easily be repaired.

There are also estimates in absolute figures. Most widely credited was a
figure of 450 billion lire at 1946 prices, produced by the Ministry of
Industry.[48] Deflating this figure by a factor of 29, we obtain 15.5 billion lire
of 1938, which is about 12 per cent of the capital stock (including inventories) in industry in 1939 according to the study of Saibante cited previously.
Indeed, a later estimate produced in about 1949 by the Centro di Studi e
Piani Tecnico-economici, jointly run by the CNR and IRI, reduced the previous estimate to 12–15 per cent of the prewar value of plant and inventories, on the grounds that much damage was of little importance and could
be promptly repaired, and some plant concealed to avoid its shipment to
Germany was easily recovered and reinstalled.[49] I have also found a document of the Treasury Ministry, according to which the value of applications
for state contributions to the repair of war damage in industry, received as
of mid-1947, was equal to 314 billion lire at 1946 prices, 70 per cent of the
sum of 450 billion lire cited above.[50] The figure of 314 billion lire corresponds to roughly 10.8 billion 1938 lire or 10 per cent of the prewar value
of industrial fixed capital (excluding inventories). Although this figure may
err on the low side, I still consider it the best estimate of war losses in industry.

Thus, after the initial shock, the view emerged that war losses in industry were relatively limited. This view is confirmed by a survey of the situation of individual industrial branches produced in 1947.[51] There are very
few branches in which the 1946 capacity was inferior to that in 1938. One
was shipyards, where the loss was about 20 per cent; aeronautics was
another, where damage was estimated at 25 per cent; nitrogen, about 50 per
cent; oil cracking, about two-thirds. In many other cases, capacity losses
were only relative to the wartime peak (reached in 1941 or 1942), as in
electricity, where the loss was 11 per cent of the 1941 peak, so that 1945
capacity was higher than in 1938 and equal to that of 1939 (the loss was
also easily made good by 1947); or in steel, where the 1938 capacity of 3
million tons increased to as much as 4.6 million tons in 1942 and was only
cut to 3.4 million tons in 1945; or in pig iron, where capacity of 0.9 million
tons in 1938 had been doubled by 1942 and was then returned to the 1938
level in 1946. Concerning the industrial branch that led Italian reconstruc-

tion, that of engineering, careful study has shown unequivocally a net increase in capacity by about one-third between 1938 and 1947.[52] Indeed the total increase in the war years had been by 50 per cent, and was reduced to one-third only by war damage. The machine-tool industry, among other engineering branches, ended the war greatly enlarged.

Losses in other sectors were somewhat larger, especially in transport. Railways lost one-quarter of their capital; the merchant navy as much as 85 per cent; the stock of road vehicles was cut to 50 per cent. In spite of the heavy bombing, damages to private buildings amounted only to about 6 per cent of the 1941 stock, which was at least 4 per cent higher than in 1938, making the difference between 1945 and 1938 negligible.[53]

In the two series for the stock of net fixed reproducible capital reported in table 5.1, war losses receive an even more profound downward revision. Vitali's traditional estimate suggested an overall increase to 7 per cent above the 1938 level by 1941, and a subsequent decline of 11 per cent below the peak, ending with a 1945 stock 5 per cent below the 1938 level; RST, on the other hand, have proposed a 9 per cent increase between the first two dates and only a 4 per cent decrease between 1942 and 1945, ending in 1945 with a stock of fixed net reproducible capital 5 per cent *higher* than in 1938. This seems implausible and clearly deserves further research. It is, however, quite clear that the tendency of more recent research is to continue to reduce earlier estimates of material war losses.

In the light of what has been argued above, it came as no surprise to me to read, in the Archives of the Bank of Italy, the following exchange of views between Caffè and Baffi in 1945.[54] Caffè had suggested to Baffi on the phone the disturbing hypothesis that war losses after World War I could have been higher than after World War II. On 18 July 1945, Baffi wrote to Caffè that this could not be true; according to the former's calculations, material war losses could be estimated at as much as one-third of national wealth after the second war compared with one-tenth after the first. Baffi's own figure for total material losses in World War II was 3,000 billion 1945 lire, or about 200 billion 1938 lire – a very large sum indeed. Caffè himself, in his letter of thanks to Baffi of 23 July, advanced doubts about such a high estimate, proposing 2,000 billion lire (133 billion 1938 lire) – still far too much! – and suggesting that the Bank of Italy should sponsor an official survey, which was not however carried out.[55] In the light of what has been argued here, it might very well be the case that material losses associated with World War I were higher than those caused by World War II, or at least not much different in proportion to the size of the economy.

If we bring human capital losses into the picture, it is beyond doubt that World War II cost Italy less than World War I, and far less than many other combatants. Military casualties amounted to a total of 291,376 men and

Table 5.17. *Italian military and civil casualties (killed and missing in action) by year and theatre of combat, 1940–1945*

	National territory 1	Germany 2	Greece, Albania 3	Yugoslavia 4	USSR 5	Africa 6	Total 7
1940	2,418	55	5,802	164	110	2,063	13,187
1941	8,647	183	12,748	1,316	1,457	8,786	41,848
1942	12,533	222	1,520	3,626	31,494	6,265	65,785
1943	64,253	2,156	10,060	7,626	44,697	4,075	144,678
1944	83,725	16,392	2,387	2,313	735	623	110,603
1945	45,865	10,401	197	1,189	949	375	60,580
Total	218,389	30,256	33,303	16,677	82,166	22,718	444,523

Source: ISTAT (1957). The share of missing persons (not shown) in the total is as high as 31 per cent, half of them lost in the USSR.

civilian casualties to 180,088 people, plus 1,059 of unknown status, for an overall figure of 444,523 – less than half a million (for details see table 5.17), and equal to 1.3 per cent of the population of more than 10 years of age. Military casualties alone in World War I exceeded 700,000 men.

We can now try to calculate the loss of human capital, both tangible and intangible. Assuming the adult population comprises those of more than the school-leaving age, which was ten years, we have 34.2 million people in the 1936 census, augmented to 34.5 million by 1938. From contemporary budget data we can take 1,700 lire per year as the average expenditure on maintenance, which gives 586.5 billion lire as the total value of tangible human capital in 1938.[56] For intangible capital the average period of education was ascertained at 4.5 years in the 1951 census, so for 1938 we can estimate it roughly at 4 years.[57] Taking annual average expenditure per person in elementary education of 253 lire in 1938, we can add 35 billion lire of intangible human capital.[58] The total stock of human capital in 1938 amounted therefore to 621.5 billion lire. Using the same data, the wartime loss of human capital can be calculated at 8 billion lire, or 1.3 per cent of the 1938 stock of human capital.

Conclusion

This chapter arrives at a number of clearcut findings.
1. The Italian economy was unable to engineer any sizable economic expansion during the war. This mainly reflected constraints arising from the

insufficient availability of raw materials caused by restricted imports, and also resulted in only a limited increase in the output of weapons. However, the difficulty of expanding the output of weapons also reflected a lack of adequate industrial organization.

2. Realized military spending by the government was low, both in absolute and in relative terms. As a proportion of GDP, it was the lowest of all combatants.

3. There was no net foreign support to the Italian war economy. On the contrary, Italy financed the German war economy, the more so if we take into consideration the transfer of human capital and the payment of the occupation indemnity to Germany.

4. Italy was able to remain at war as long as the strategy of the Allies did not envisage fighting on her territory. After the first Allied landings the war was clearly lost, and the willingness to fight it diminished drastically until the removal of Mussolini from power and the armistice with the Allies.

5. In this context, investment and the accumulation of capital, both physical and human, in heavy industry were surprisingly substantial, especially in engineering, and war losses comparatively modest. Industrialists showed a strong interest in enlarging their plant with government financial assistance, showing that they were more attracted by the long-run impact of public spending on productive capacity than by its short-term target of increasing the output of weapons. The number of new engineering workers trained during the war was impressive. Moreover, the loss of human as well as of physical capital was very modest.

6. As a result of limited losses, recovery to the prewar level was achieved in Italy as early as 1948; the years of the Marshall Plan could be devoted to a sustained economic expansion. This expansion capitalized on the sizable switch achieved between the late 1930s and the end of the war, from textiles to metallurgy, engineering, and chemicals. The latter transfer enabled the postwar Italian economy to cater for new export markets and the new domestic demand for durables.

Notes

1 RST (1993); for the Vitali series see Fuà (1969).
2 Bardini (1993), pp.1245–6.
3 See Monti (1946), Arbitrio (1946).
4 Petri (1997).
5 General Carlo Favagrossa, who directed the war production office (Fabbriguerra), refers to increasing production stoppages for lack of fuel since June 1941. See Favagrossa (1946), 162–7.

6 The clearest statements in this regard can be found in Raspin (1986). See for example p. 184: 'Exports of armaments to Italy by Germany were fairly small.' This was the result both of German policy and of an Italian attempt 'to carry on the war from her own resources' (p. 185). The issue of supplies to Italy from France is documented by a senior army general, Roatta (1946), 157–8.

7 In spite of some disagreement between Italian and German sources on the overall clearing account situation, the balance of trade was always positive for Germany, the disagreement arising from the other payments. See Raspin (1986), tables 31–35 of the Appendix.

8 Complaints about lack of fuel appear in all the Italian generals' memoirs. See among many the commander-in-chief of the Italian army Cavallero (1948), 129. On Cavallero's memoirs see Ceva (1975).

9 Minniti (1986); Raspin (1986); Curami (1991); Minniti (1992); Ceva and Curami (1992). Raspin (1986) quotes, among other things, the high level of stocks of raw materials found by the Germans at the start of their occupation. But this may have been due to the disorganization of production which became worse in 1943 during the political turmoil after the Armistice; see Massignani (1993). Curami (1991) concludes with a quotation from Einaudi who says that 'the problem of raw materials does not exist'. Certainly this problem does not exist under normal conditions of free or semi-free international trade, but it can be very relevant under troubled conditions, as not only wartime but other periods also demonstrate. Think, for instance, of the sudden quadrupling of oil prices in the early 1970s, or of the years of the Marshall Plan, which was mostly devised to meet the very problem of imports of raw materials by European countries the normal trade of which had been disturbed by the consequences of war.

10 Ferrari (1992). More details can be found in Favagrossa (1946), Roatta (1946), Raspin (1986).

11 The archives of Confindustria (the Federation of Italian Industrialists) have been opened recently. An investigation of the results of their bimonthly survey for the years up to the middle of 1943, when it was discontinued, would certainly be worthwhile.

12 Solinas (1993).

13 Mantelli (1992).

14 Raspin (1986), 298 writes: 'Italy was for Germany the first major source of imported industrial labour.' The figures which she quotes concerning Italian labour emigration to Germany are, however, implausible.

15 Not even in Klinkhammer (1993) does one find adequate data. See however Mantelli (1996).

16 ASBI, *Fondo Introna*, cart. 87, 'Servizio rimesse lavoratori italiani in Germania (Banca Nazionale del Lavoro)'. The passage cited above reads as follows: 'Si dovrebbe, quindi, da un calcolo molto approssimativo, desumere che il numero dei civili italiani trattenuti in Germania al lavoro forzato superi 1.800.000 unità' (p. 3). I wonder whether this does not include prisoners-of-war who numbered more than 500,000 in 1944. See Schreiber (1990), or the Italian version of this book, Schreiber (1992).

17 On rationing see Colarizzi (1991), who supports the view that the introduction of such strict rationing contributed to the alienation of the masses from fascism. See also Trova (1993), who reports that it was well known at the time that the ration could not guarantee survival. On the growth of the black market, see Klinkhammer (1993), chapter 6, who concludes that 'perfino il governo fascista tollerava i traffici del mercato nero che si svolgevano sotto i suoi occhi' (even the fascist government tolerated the black market which unfolded under its eyes) (p. 248). The compulsory pooling (*ammassi*) of basic foodstuffs, introduced in the 1930s and intensified during the war, was far from effective, as can be seen from the interesting table 13 of Cavazzoli (1989), 77. No more than 50 per cent of wheat was pooled at official prices, 20–30 per cent of maize, 28 per cent of beef, and more than 90 per cent of rice. On wages see the interesting work of Vicard (1946), 24, who finds that wages in industry in 1943 had reached 142 per cent of the 1940 level, and 784 per cent in 1945, while the comparable cost of living index numbers were 224 and 1,965 per cent, suggesting an overall loss of purchasing power of wages of about 60 per cent. According to Zamagni (1976), 378, the comparable index numbers of nominal industrial wages were 158 and 886 per cent. The growth of salaries lagged behind that of wages by even more. See in this connection Banca d'Italia (1947).
18 Giorgerini (1991). The author writes (p. 261) that: 'in realtà e per un periodo abbastanza lungo, la *Royal Navy* rimase nel Mediterraneo inferiore alla Marina italiana' (in reality and for a fairly long period the Royal Navy remained inferior to the Italian Navy in the Mediterranean).
19 On strategy see Santoni (1991).
20 Istituto Storico della Marina Militare (1960). On the question of radar, see Carillo Castioni (1987). The latter author supports the view that radar was not used, not because it could not be produced, but because of resistance on the part of the navy.
21 On Italian exports of aircraft up to 1938, see Mantegazza (1993).
22 Minniti (1981).
23 On this subordination, accepted to avoid further deportations and the destruction of industrial plant, see Klinkhammer (1993).
24 Alegi (1987).
25 Ceva and Curami (1992); Curami (1992).
26 De Lorenzo (1991), 88; Faldella (1970), 109.
27 Faldella (1970), 592.
28 Botti (1991).
29 See Minniti (1973, 1975).
30 Roatta (1946), 64 underlines the fact that the gap between needs and realized output increased during the war.
31 Alegi (1987).
32 Ceva (1991) reports on the results of such enquiries, which underlined the use of defective steel and faults in assembly. The same author comes back to this point in Ceva (1992); in this second essay he discusses also motor vehicles, in terms not of defective quality, but of an excessive assortment of different models in use.

This was a feature of Italian munitions production generally, which made repairs and training particularly difficult.

33 Minniti (1978), 28: 'l'esercito rimase esercito di fanterie, prive per di più del necessario numero di quei mezzi di trasporto e di appoggio che in quegli anni ne rivalutarono il ruolo. Non è esagerato, perciò, e non è semplice eco di un luogo comune, parlare di mancata preparazione dell'esercito.'

34 Roatta (1946), 85.

35 See Ferrari (1993) for a survey of literature on the Italian military industry.

36 My use of actual rather than planned outlays is the main source of discrepancy between my figures and those used in other works. For the best of the latter see Repaci (1952, 1953). In his major book Repaci (1962) builds a comprehensive estimate of the cost of the war, which is however unacceptable for many reasons, including the addition of nominal costs or losses incurred in different periods in current lire of highly variable real purchasing power.

37 More details can be found in Zamagni (1993a), chapters 4, 7, 9.

38 Salvemini and Zamagni (1992).

39 The first of a long list of bills was the RDL 14.11.1935, no.1934, for munitions; then other bills followed up to January 1943 covering drainage, extraordinary public works, and grants to soldiers' families, but mostly munitions again.

40 This mechanism was labelled 'deferred state payments' and was also used for public works. Estimates of deferred payments from the 1930s are mentioned in Salvemini and Zamagni (1992). See also Borgatta (1946), 516 ff.

41 The CSVI archives are deposited with the Bank of Italy. Some of the documents in the Archives of the Bank of Italy concerning the CSVI have been published in Caracciolo (1992).

42 Banca d'Italia (1945), 48–9: 'In sostanza, l'intervento del Consorzio ha esclusivamente per effetto di far apparire minore del reale il ricorso alle anticipazioni da parte del tesoro . . . ma poichè il tesoro non avrebbe fornito mai quei miliardi senza la garanzia dello stato, in verità debitore di essi è sempre il tesoro.' Einaudi adds a few paragraphs later: 'il fatto che all'attivo del bilancio della Banca i 40.292,2 milioni sono scritturati con il titolo di "portafoglio speciale" invece che con quello, che sarebbe vero, di anticipazioni straordinarie al R. tesoro, non muta nulla alla logica conseguenza che al passivo debba per altrettanta somma crescere la cifra della circolazione ed è questo soltanto che in realtà conta'. On relationships between the Bank of Italy and the Treasury, see Banca d'Italia (1993).

43 The German indemnity must be added here because it was charged to the Treasury directly, and did not appear as expenditure by one of the four ministries considered in table 5.14.

44 A careful study of the industrial part of this survey in the context of the problem of southern industrialization was carried out by Padovani (1980). For more details of the costs of reconstruction surveyed in southern Italy see a note sent by the economist Federico Caffè, working in the Ministry for Reconstruction, to Paolo Baffi, at the time head of the research group of the Bank of Italy, 2 August 1945, in ASBI, *Fondo Studi*, cart. 336, 21. The total estimate amounted to 703 billion (southern) lire of 1945.

45 For a very good work on capital invested in industry before the war, and the estimate of inventories reported in the text, see Saibante (1947).
46 Istituto per gli Studi di Economia (1949), 3; Ricossa and Tuccimei (1992), 190 (letter from Einaudi to Parri, 25 June 1945).
47 Jacoboni (1949), 50–1.
48 Comitato Interministeriale per la Ricostruzione (1946), 120; Confindustria (1945).
49 Jacoboni (1949), 51.
50 ASBI, *Fondo Studi*, cart. 336, 20. See also the data gathered in Covino, Gallo, Mantovani (1976).
51 Ministero per la Costituente (1947), chapter 2 ('Rassegna dei principali rami dell'industria italiana. Condizioni attuali e prospettive').
52 Jacoboni (1949), 27.
53 Comitato Interministeriale per la Ricostruzione (1946), 125; on the railways see Repaci (1949). Shipping losses were the result partly of the disastrous error made when, on the day Italy entered the war, one third of her merchant navy was lost, and partly of the inability to defend against enemy attack arising from the lack of operational radar equipment; see Ferrante (1961).
54 ASBI, *Fondo Studi*, cart. 336, 20.
55 This estimate of material losses was shared by many at the close of the war. See for instance Rossi Ragazzi (1946), 390: 'può stimarsi . . . che l'ammontare delle distruzioni e dei danneggiamenti direttamente subiti dal patrimonio nazionale . . . ammonti a circa 150 miliardi di lire ai prezzi del 1938 e cioè al 20 per cento del patrimonio prebellico' (we can fix war losses to a total of 150 billion 1938 lire, equal to 20 per cent of prewar wealth).
56 Galeotti (1950).
57 See Zamagni (1993b).
58 For educational outlays in 1938 see Luzzatti (1970). Comparing my estimate with Broadberry's for the UK, human capital per head in Italy appears to have been 48.6 per cent of the comparable British figure. The cost of further education is not included in either case.

References

Archives and official papers

ACS (Archivio Centrale dello Stato).
ASBI (Archivio Storico della Banca d'Italia).
Atti Parlamentari (1935–52), *Disegni di legge e relazioni, Rendiconto generale per l'esercizio finanziario 1932/33–1946/47*, 14 vols.

Books, articles, and working papers

Alegi G. (1987), 'Qualità del materiale bellico e dottrina d'impiego italiana nella seconda guerra mondiale: il caso della Regia aereonautica', *Storia contemporanea*, vol. 18(6), 1197–219.

Annuario Statistico Italiano (1944).

Arbitrio, F. (1946), 'L'industria siderurgica italiana', *Critica economica*, vol. 1(4), 30–64.

Banca d'Italia (1945), *Relazione 1943*, Rome.

(1947), *Relazione 1946*, Rome.

(1993), *Ricerche per la storia della Banca d'Italia*, vol. IV, *La Banca d'Italia e la tesoreria dello Stato*, Bari.

Barberi, B. (1961), *I consumi nel primo secolo dell'Unità d'Italia, 1861–1960*, Milan.

Bardini, C. (1993), 'I consumi di energia elettrica in Italia, 1931–1986', in Galasso, G., ed., *Storia dell'industria elettrica in Italia*, vol. III, book 2, *Espansione e oligopolio 1926–1945*, Bari.

Borgatta, G. (1946), *La finanza della guerra e del dopoguerra*, Alessandria.

Botti, F. (1991), 'La guerra aerea. Strategia d'impiego: concezioni contrastanti', in Rainero, R. H., and Biagini, A., eds., *L'Italia in guerra*, vol. I, *Il 1° anno, 1940* Rome, 215–43.

Caracciolo, A., ed. (1992), *La Banca d'Italia tra l'autarchia e la guerra 1936–1945*, Bari.

Carillo Castioni, L., (1987), 'I radar industriali italiani. Ricerche, ricordi, considerazioni per una loro storia', *Storia contemporanea*, vol. 18(6), 1221–65.

Cavallero U. (1948), *Comando supremo. Diario 1940–43 del Capo di S.M.G.*, Rocca San Casciano.

Cavazzoli, L. (1989), *La gente e la guerra. La vita quotidiana del 'fronte interno'. Mantova 1940–1945*, Milan.

Ceva L. (1975), *La condotta italiana della guerra. Cavallero e il Comando supremo 1941/42*, Milan.

(1991), 'Grande industria e guerra', in Rainero, R. H., and Biagini, A., eds., *L'Italia in guerra*, vol. I, *Il 1° anno, 1940*, Rome, 33–53.

(1992), 'Rapporti tra industria bellica ed Esercito', in Rainero, R. H., and Biagini, A., eds., *L'Italia in guerra*, vol. II, *Il 2° anno, 1941*, Rome, 215–47.

Ceva, L., and Curami, A. (1992), 'Air army and aircraft industry in Italy, 1938–1943', in H. Boog, ed., *The conduct of the air war in the Second World War*, Oxford, 85–107.

Colarizzi S. (1991), 'Vita alimentare degli italiani e razionamento', in Rainero, R. H., and Biagini, A., eds., *L'Italia in guerra*, vol. I, *Il 1° anno, 1940*, Rome, 279–89.

Comitato Interministeriale per la Ricostruzione (1946), *L'economia italiana nel 1947. Rapporto presentato dalla Delegazione del Governo Italiano al V Consiglio generale dell'UNRRA, August 1946*, Milan.

Comitato per la Storia dell'Artiglieria italiana (1953), *Storia dell'artiglieria italiana*, Rome.

Confindustria (1945), *Annuario*, Rome.

Covino, R., Gallo, G., and Mantovani, E. (1976), 'L'industria dall'economia di guerra alla ricostruzione', in Ciocca, P., and Toniolo, G., eds., *L'economia italiana nel periodo fascista*, Bologna, 171–270.

Curami, A. (1991), 'Commesse belliche e approvvigionamenti di materie prime', in

Rainero, R. H., and Biagini, A., eds., *L'Italia in guerra*, vol. I, *Il 1° anno, 1940*, Rome, 55–66.

(1992), 'Piani e progetti dell'aereonautica italiana 1939–1943. Stato Maggiore e industrie', *Italia contemporanea*, no. 187, 243–61.

De Lorenzo, G. (1991), 'L'Aereonautica in guerra (primo anno)', in Rainero, R. H., and Biagini, A., eds., *L'Italia in guerra*, vol. I, *Il 1° anno*, Rome, 85–138.

Faldella, E. (1970), *L'Italia nella seconda guerra mondiale. Revisione di giudizi*, Bologna.

Favagrossa, C. (1946), *Perchè perdemmo la guerra*, Milan.

Ferrante E. (1991), 'La Marina Mercantile italiana e la lotta per le comunicazioni marittime nel secondo conflitto mondiale', in Rainero, R. H., and Biagini, A., eds., *L'Italia in guerra*, vol. I, *Il 1° anno, 1940*, Rome, 133–8.

Ferrari, D. (1992), 'La mobilitazione dell'esercito nella seconda guerra mondiale', *Storia contemporanea*, vol. 23(6), 1001–46.

Ferrari, P., ed. (1993), 'L'industria bellica italiana 1861–1945. Appunti sulla recente storiografia', *Italia contemporanea*, no. 190, 129–98.

Fuà, G., ed. (1969), *Lo sviluppo economico in Italia*, vol. III, Milan.

Galeotti, G. (1950), 'Contributo all'impostazione del calcolo degli indici del costo della vita', *Rassegna di Statistiche del Lavoro. Quaderno no. 2*, Rome, 24–65.

Giorgerini G. (1991), 'La preparazione e la mobilitazione della Marina italiana nel giugno 1940', in Rainero, R. H., and Biagini, A., eds., *L'Italia in guerra*, vol. I, *Il 1° anno, 1940*, Rome, 255–62.

Golinelli, R., and Monterastelli, M. (1990), 'Un metodo per la ricostruzione di serie storiche compatibili con la nuova contabilità nazionale (1951–1989)', Bologna, nota di lavoro n. 9001.

Ilardi, M. (1972), 'Nuovi documenti sugli interventi tedeschi nell'industria italiana tra il 1943 e il 1945', *Movimento di liberazione in Italia*, no. 24, 77–92.

ISTAT (1950), *Annuario statistico dell'agricoltura italiana, 1943–46*, Rome.

(1957a), 'Indagine statistica sullo sviluppo del reddito nazionale dell'Italia dal 1861 al 1956', *Annali di Statistica*, vol. 86(9), Rome.

(1957b), *Morti e dispersi per cause belliche negli anni 1940–45*, Rome.

(1968), *Sommario di statistiche storiche dell'Italia 1861–1965*, Rome.

Istituto per gli Studi di Economia (1949), *Annuario della congiuntura economica italiana, 1938–1947*, Florence.

Istituto Storico della Marina Militare (1960), *La Marina Italiana nella seconda guerra mondiale*, vol. II, Rome.

Jacoboni, A. (1949), *L'industria meccanica*, Rome.

Klinkhammer, L. (1993), *L'occupazione tedesca in Italia 1943–1945*, Turin.

Luzzatti, E. (1970), 'Introduzione allo studio delle spese pubbliche per l'istruzione in Italia (1862–1965)', *Annali della Fondazione Einaudi*, vol. 4, Turin, 75–141.

Maddison, A. (1991), 'A revised estimate of Italian economic growth', *Banca Nazionale del Lavoro Quarterly Review*, no. 177, 225–41.

Mantegazza, A. (1993), 'L'industria aereonautica italiana tra tecnologia e politica', in Archivio Storico Fiat (1993), *L'industria italiana nel mercato mondiale dalla fine dell'800 alla metà del '900*, Turin, 117–47.

Mantelli, B. (1992), *'Camerati del lavoro'. I lavoratori italiani emigrati nel Terzo Reich nel periodo dell'Asse 1938–1943*, Florence.

(1996), 'I lavoratori italiani trasferiti in Germania dal 1938 al 1945: una tema dimenticato', *Passato e Presente*, no. 38, 101–11.

Massignani, A. (1993), 'L'industria bellica italiana e la Germania nella seconda guerra mondiale', *Italia contemporanea*, no. 190, 37–55.

Milward, A. S. (1977), *War, economy and society, 1939–1945*, London.

Ministero del Tesoro, Ragioneria generale dello Stato (1969), *Il bilancio dello Stato italiano dal 1862 al 1967*, 4 vols., Rome.

Ministero della Difesa, Direzione delle Costruzioni Aeronautiche (no date), *Produzione degli apparecchi italiani tra il 1936 e il settembre 1943*, Rome.

Ministero delle Corporazioni (1937), 'Numeri indici mensili della produzione industriale in Italia', *Sindacato e Corporazioni*, vol. 5, no. 8, 478–504

Ministero per la Costituente (1946), *Atti della commissione per lo studio dei problemi del lavoro*, part 3, *Memorie su argomenti economici*, Rome.

(1947), *Rapporto della Commissione Economica*, part 2, *Industria. Relazione*, vol. 1, Rome.

Minniti, F. (1973), 'Aspetti della politica fascista degli armamenti dal 1935 al 1943', in De Felice, R., ed., *L'Italia fra tedeschi e alleati. La politica estera fascista e la seconda guerra mondiale*, Bologna, 127–36.

(1975), 'Due anni di attività del "Fabbriguerra" per la produzione bellica (1939–1941)', *Storia contemporanea*, vol. 5(4), 849–79.

(1978), 'Il problema degli armamenti nella preparazione militare italiana dal 1935 al 1943', *Storia contemporanea*, vol. 9(1), 5–61.

(1981), 'La politica industriale del Ministero dell'Aereonautica. Mercato, pianificazione, sviluppo (1935–1943)', *Storia contemporanea*, vol. 12(1), 5–55; (2), 271–312.

(1986), 'Le materie prime nella preparazione bellica dell'Italia (1935–1943)', *Storia contemporanea*, vol. 17(6), 205–13.

(1992), 'Il problema degli approvvigionamenti e l'industria militare', in Rainero, R. H., and Biagini, A., eds., *L'Italia in guerra*, vol. II, *Il 2° anno, 1941*, Rome, 205–13.

Monti, I. (1946), *Inchiesta sulla siderurgia italiana*, Milan.

Padovani, R. (1980), 'Le scelte della ricostruzione nel Sud d'Italia', in Mori, G., ed., *La cultura economica nel periodo della ricostruzione*, Bologna, 169–265.

Petri, R. (1997), 'Stima delle disponibilità energetiche italiane 1938–1942', in Zamagni, V., ed., *Come perdere la guerra e vincere la pace*, Bologna.

Pierantoni, F., Piacentini, F., and Vestrucci, P. (1980), 'Un contributo alla conoscenza del problema dell'energia in Italia dal 1861 al 1978', Rome, CNEN-RT/ING, (80)8, mimeo.

Rainero, R. H., and Biagini, A., eds. (1991-2), *L'Italia in guerra*, vol. I, *Il 1° anno, 1940*, vol. II, *Il 2° anno, 1941*, Rome.

Raspin, A. (1986), *The Italian war economy, 1940–1943, with particular reference to Italian relations with Germany*, New York.

Repaci, F. (1949), 'Le ferrovie dello Stato durante la guerra e nel periodo della ricostruzione', *Congiuntura Economica*, vol. 34, Jan., 111–35.

(1962), *La finanza pubblica italiana nel secolo 1861–1960*, Bologna.

Repaci, F. A. (1952), 'La gestione della tesoreria dello Stato durante e dopo la seconda guerra mondiale', *Giornale degli Economisti*, vol. 90(3), 261–303.

(1953), 'Lo sforzo finanziario italiano per la condotta della seconda guerra mondiale', in *Studi in memoria di Gino Borgatta*, Bologna, 119–36.

Rey, G., ed. (1991–2), *I conti economici dell'Italia*, vol. I, *Una sintesi delle fonti ufficiali 1890–1970*, vol. II, *Una stima del valore aggiunto per il 1911*, Bari.

Ricossa, S., and Tuccimei, E. (1992), *La Banca d'Italia e il risanamento postbellico 1945–1948*, Bari.

Roatta M. (1946), *Otto milioni di baionette. L'esercito italiano in guerra dal 1940 al 1944*, Verona.

Rossi Ragazzi, B. (1946), 'Redditi e consumi della popolazione italiana negli anni '44–46 e confronto col periodo prebellico', in Ministero per la Costituente (1946), *Atti della commissione per lo studio dei problemi del lavoro*, vol. III, *Memorie su argomenti economici*, Rome, 383–408.

RST: Rossi, N., Sorgato, A., and Toniolo, G. (1993), 'I conti economici italiani: una ricostruzione statistica, 1890–1990', *Rivista di Storia Economica*, vol. 10(1), 1–47.

Sadkovich, J. J. (1987), 'Minerali, armamenti e tipo di guerra: la sconfitta italiana nella seconda guerra mondiale', *Storia contemporanea*, vol. 18(6), 1267–308.

Saibante, M. (1947), 'Il capitale investito nell'industria nel quadro della ricchezza nazionale', in Ministero per la Costituente (1947), *Rapporto della Commissione Economica. II. Industria. Relazione*, vol. I, Rome, 88–121.

Salvemini, G., and Zamagni, V. (1992), 'Finanza pubblica e indebitamento tra le due guerre mondiali: il finanziamento del settore statale', in Banca d'Italia, *Ricerche per la storia della Banca d'Italia*, vol. II, *Problemi di finanza pubblica tra le due guerre, 1919–1939*, Bari, 139–235.

Santoni A. (1991), 'Strategia marittima e operazioni navali dell'anno 1940', in Rainero, R. H., and Biagini, A., eds., *L'Italia in guerra*, vol. I, *Il 1° anno, 1940*, Rome, 245–54.

Schreiber, G. (1990), *Die italienischen Militarinternierten im deutschen Machtbereich 1943 bis 1945. Verraten-Verachtet-Vergessen*, Munich.

(1992), *I militari italiani internati nei campi di concentramento del terzo Reich, 1943–1945. Traditi-Disprezzati-Dimenticati*, Rome.

Servizio Ragioneria della Banca d'Italia (1993), *I bilanci degli Istituti di emissione, 1894–1990*, Bari.

Solinas, G. (1993), 'Competenze, grandi imprese e distretti industriali. Il caso Magneti Marelli', *Rivista di Storia Economica*, vol. 10(1), 79–111.

Trova, A. (1993), 'L'approvvigionamento alimentare nella RSI', *Storia in Lombardia*, vol. 12(1–2), 171–89.

Vicard, R. (1946), 'Di alcuni sistemi di retribuzione del lavoro. Calcolo di un indice nazionale delle retribuzioni', in Ministero per la Costituente (1946), *Atti della commissione per lo studio dei problemi del lavoro. III Memorie su argomenti economici*, Rome, 7–45.

Zamagni, V. (1976), 'La dinamica dei salari nel settore industriale 1911–1946', in Ciocca, P., and Toniolo, G., eds., *L'economia italiana nel periodo fascista*, Bologna, 329–78.

(1986), 'Betting on the future: the reconstruction of Italian industry, 1946–1952', in Becker, J., and Knipping, F., eds., *Power in Europe? Great Britain, France, Italy and Germany in a postwar world, 1945–1950*, Berlin, 197–226.

(1993a), *The economic history of Italy 1860–1990*, Oxford.

(1993b), 'L'offerta di istruzione in Italia 1861–1987: un fattore guida dello sviluppo o un ostacolo?', University of Cassino, Dipartimento Economia e Territorio, Working Paper no. 4.

6 Japan: guns before rice

Akira Hara

Introduction: the phases of Japan's war economy

The Japanese invasion of China began with the Manchurian Incident of 1931. However, the Japanese economy at the time of the incident was still recovering from the slump which began in 1929. It is only with the Marco Polo Bridge Incident in 1937 and the outbreak of full-scale hostilities between China and Japan that the Japanese economy shifted to a wartime basis. In political or military history, the fifteen-year period between 1931 and defeat at the hands of the Allies in 1945 was one of continuing warfare, but in economic history this applies only to the period after 1937. The years 1932–6 saw little military influence on the economy, which may thus be considered to be basically a peacetime one. The 1934–6 average, being the peacetime peak before Japan commenced aggressive action in earnest, was taken by the Allies as the prewar standard for Japanese postwar recovery, a practice which I shall follow below as far as possible.

From the inception of the wartime economy in 1937 until the freezing of Japanese foreign assets in 1941, overseas trade remained feasible for Japan, but trade was increasingly controlled by regulatory measures designed to ensure the effective use of scarce foreign currency for wartime objectives. After the freezing of assets and the declaration of war on America, Britain, and the Netherlands in 1941, and during the ensuing period of the Pacific War, there was a shift from the control of foreign currency to the control of shipping. Foreign trade became impossible outside the sphere of Japanese influence, and Japan was reduced to managing her wartime economy by controlling the shipping capacity necessary to make use of the commodities originating in that sphere.

After economic collapse in 1945, direct control based on wartime objectives was abolished. But the economy was in a state of disarray as a result of fierce inflation and the severe decline of industrial production, and controls as such remained in full force until the economy was rebuilt on a

peacetime basis. Inflation was stabilised in 1949 with the establishment of
a uniform exchange rate, and it was in or around 1950 that deregulation
finally took place.

Consequently, administrative control was in force in Japan from 1937
until 1950, and market allocation by means of the price mechanism was to
all intents and purposes at a standstill. The principal object of this chapter
is to analyse Japan's wartime economy from 1937 until 1945, but mention
will be made where necessary of the period up to 1950 or thereabouts. The
first such analysis was that carried out by the United States in order to
assess the results of strategic bombing, and this has led to a tendency to
think of the wartime economy only in terms of the period of the Pacific War
(December 1941–August 1945). But Japan had been at war with China
since 1937 and her economy had been organized entirely on a wartime basis
ever since then. Thus it must not be forgotten that Japan had initiated a
wartime economy earlier than the countries of Europe, which had only
done so at the outbreak of the war in 1939. When the Pacific War began in
1941, Japan had already been at war for four and a half years, and this fact
must be taken into consideration in any discussion of the wartime Japanese
economy after 1942. Even during the Pacific War there was fierce fighting
not only against the Americans and the British, but also on the Chinese
front; for this reason many Japanese historians consider that it should be
spoken of not as the Pacific War but rather as the 'Asia-Pacific War'.

While acknowledging the force of these qualifications, for brevity's sake
I refer below to the years 1937–41 as the period of the 'war with China', and
1941–5 as the period of the 'Pacific War'.

Production and expenditure

National income

Let us begin with estimates of wartime national income. The first rough
national accounts were compiled in 1934, when the Ministry of Finance
drew up a reference plan for legislation with regard to wartime credit
control. Some of the results were published in 1947, but their methodology
was flawed. Shortly after the war the United States Strategic Bombing
Survey (USSBS) produced estimates of national income, and Yamada Yuzo
did the same for the wartime period. The continued efforts of governmental
agencies culminated in publication of the old SNA estimates for the period
up to 1944 in the Economic Planning Agency's white papers on national
income. More recently, systematic estimates of national income over the
past century compiled through a large-scale programme of research by a
team of scholars at Hitotsubashi University led by Ohkawa Kazushi and

published under the title *Long-term economic statistics* (LTES) have come to be regarded as providing the most reliable figures, but unfortunately they provide wartime coverage only up to 1940.

More recently, Mizoguchi Toshiyuki and Nojima Noriyuki have published estimates of GNP for 1940–55, picking up where Ohkawa and his team left off. These are the most reliable figures at present available for the wartime period.[1] By comparison, the USSBS estimates will be seen to be somewhat exaggerated, particularly for 1943 and 1944, and it is no longer feasible to pursue an argument on the basis of these. The Hitotsubashi University estimates were conducted with the greatest regard for procedure, and Mizoguchi and Nojima's estimates for the wartime period preserve conformity with these while also making use of the White Paper estimates. Below we rely therefore on the estimates of Mizoguchi and Nojima.

Mizoguchi and his colleagues also calculated real GDP in 1955 prices. Price rises were rapid during wartime (between 1940 and 1944 the GDP deflator almost doubled) and in the postwar confusion (by 1953 the price level had risen 100–fold compared with 1944); a flourishing black market also existed alongside the market controlled by official prices.[2] For this reason, while the Mizoguchi–Nojima estimates adopted the LTES methodology, they rejected use of problematic wartime price data to deflate nominal expenditures in favour of an output-side estimate using real product data at fixed prices for primary, secondary, and tertiary industries.[3] These estimates show only an implicit price deflator for 1940–55. If this is linked with the deflator for the period up to 1940 as shown in LTES and a deflator which takes the years 1934–6 as its base, it is possible to calculate real gross domestic expenditure (GDP(E)), total and per head, as well as an index of GDP as a percentage of the base year. This is shown in table 6.1 and figure 6.1 below.

It will be seen that Japan's GDP increased by about 30 per cent during the war in China (1937–41), was stagnant during the Pacific War (1942–4), and fell dramatically to around 70 per cent of the prewar benchmark after defeat (1945–6), to as low as 55 per cent in comparison with the 1941 peak; rampant inflation reigned until 1949. Thereafter, rapid recovery followed the boom caused by the war in Korea, and the mid-1950s saw a return roughly to 1941 levels, heading towards the 'era of high-speed growth' after 1955. A similar trend is observed in real GDP per head, although rapid population growth meant that the level of GDP per head did not return to the 1934–6 average until the mid-1950s, directly before the period of high economic growth. Through twenty years of wartime and postwar history, Japan's political economy and the way of life of its people had witnessed cataclysmic changes, but the standard of living had not risen one iota as a result.

Table 6.1. *Japan's GDP (expenditure) and population, 1934–1955*

| | GDP(E) | | | GDP per head, |
| | million yen and 1934/6 prices | % of 1934/6 | Population, thou. | yen and 1934/6 prices |
	1	2	3	4
1934	17,422	96	68,309	255
1935	18,366	101	69,254	265
1936	18,763	103	70,114	268
1937	19,949	110	70,630	282
1938	20,173	111	71,013	284
1939	21,954	121	71,380	308
1940	22,848	126	73,114	312
1941	23,387	129	72,218	324
1942	23,445	129	72,880	322
1943	23,083	127	73,903	312
1944	22,538	124	74,433	303
1945	17,095	94	71,998	237
1946	13,083	72	75,750	173
1947	13,674	75	78,101	175
1948	14,754	81	80,002	184
1949	15,138	83	81,773	185
1950	17,547	97	84,115	209
1951	19,619	108	84,541	232
1952	21,555	119	85,808	251
1953	22,513	124	86,981	259
1954	23,286	128	88,239	264
1955	25,399	140	90,077	282

Source: Compiled by the author (see text).

The above estimates all refer to Japan proper. But the prewar Japanese empire formed an economic bloc with its colonies; we should take into account the resources of the whole Japanese empire, not just of mainland Japan. The estimates published by Mizoguchi and Umemura stop short in 1938 because of a dearth of reliable statistical material. However, these estimates at least help us to understand the economic structure of the Japanese empire at the outbreak of full-scale hostilities in China. The GDP of mainland Japan according to these estimates agrees more or less precisely with Mizoguchi and Nojima's nominal value for 1938. The GDP of Japanese-occupied Korea in the same year was approximately 11.2 per cent of that of mainland Japan, while that of Taiwan (Formosa) was 4.5 per cent, the total for all the colonies amounting to 16.7 per cent of mainland Japanese GDP. The economic activity of the colonies was thus equivalent to about one-sixth of that of Japan proper. Add to this the extent of Japanese economic activ-

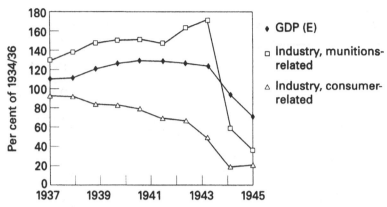

Figure 6.1 Japan's real GDP and industrial production, 1937–1945
Source: tables 6.1, 6.2

ities in the Kwantung Leased Territory, in the puppet state of Manchukuo
(Manchuria), and in those parts of China and south-east Asia which were
under Japanese military occupation, and it becomes clear that the scale of
economic activities in the whole of the economic bloc under Japanese imperial sway was considerably greater than that of mainland Japan alone.[4]

Industrial production

So much for GDP; we now turn our attention to production in mining and
manufacturing, industries which were central to the wartime economy. Six
organizations have compiled production indices for industry in general and
for the mining and manufacturing industries in particular. Table 6.2 compares those which deal with industry in general. In cols. 1–4 the emphasis
is on the aircraft, shipbuilding, and munitions industries, with the result
that an increase is shown up to 1944. The indices in cols. 6 and 7, on the
other hand, are weighted towards the prewar industrial structure centred
on the textile industry, and therefore show a fall immediately after the
commencement of all-out hostilities between Japan and China. Leaving
aside the GHQ index (col. 4) which covers a somewhat shorter period than
the others, I take the average of each of the two groups (cols. 5, 8). Clearly,
munitions-related industries managed to maintain a high level of production until 1944, while consumer-related industries began to decline with the
initiation of administrative control during the war with China (see also
figure 6.1). Once the production of munitions was banned after the end of
the war, the trends in the two sets of figures cease to differ significantly,
although the levels continued to diverge.

Table 6.2. Japan's industrial production: alternative estimates, 1937–1955 (% of 1934/6)

	Munitions-related					Consumer-related		
	MITI	ESB	Kokumin	GHQ	average, cols 1–3	Toyo	Diamond	average, cols 6, 7
	1	2	3	4	5	6	7	8
1937	128	133	124	126	129	125	59	92
1938	133	146	136	129	138	124	59	91
1939	147	152	141	134	147	114	55	84
1940	153	153	143	135	150	113	53	83
1941	159	156	138	136	151	108	51	79
1942	154	151	135	129	147	96	44	70
1943	156	166	166	154	163	93	40	67
1944	159	183	172	172	171	69	32	50
1945	70	66	42	71	59	28	12	20
1946	31	41	40	31	37	30	13	22
1947	39	48	45	38	44	40	17	29
1948	50	64	63	49	59	52	24	38
1949	65	80	77	—	74	66	33	50
1950	79	91	95	—	88	84	31	58
1951	107	124	123	—	118	104	56	80
1952	115	137	130	—	127	113	59	86
1953	139	165	—	—	—	127	68	98
1954	150	—	—	—	—	—	74	—
1955	162	—	—	—	—	—	79	—

Source: Cols. 1–4, 6, 7: KSKS (1990–1), vol. I, 261–3.

Key:
MITI: Ministry of International Trade and Industry
ESB: Economic Stability Bureau
Kokumin: National Economy Research Association (Kokumin Keizai Kenkyu Kyokai)
GHQ: General Headquarters of the Allied Powers
Toyo: Toyo Keizai Shimposha

Table 6.3. *Japanese steel supply, 1934/1936 to 1945 (thousand tons)*

| | Mainland Japan | | | | | |
	total 1	rolled steel 2	forged steel 3	special steel 4	Korea 5	Manchuria 6
1934/36	4,171	3,902	174	95	44	147
1937	5,630	5,163	255	212	66	417
1938	6,150	5,447	372	331	92	490
1939	6,072	5,169	432	471	89	434
1940	5,904	5,040	414	450	82	438
1941	5,565	4,563	489	513	112	333
1942	5,674	4,494	505	675	133	375
1943	6,285	4,786	555	944	107	569
1944	4,652	2,929	517	1,206	88	244
1945	524	289	66	169	12	120

Source: KSKS (1990–1), vol III, 278.

Limits on output

Without going into great detail, it will be evident from tables 6.3 and 6.4 that stagnation in the production of iron, steel, coal and other basic materials throughout the Pacific War (following increases during the conflict in China) fundamentally inhibited the whole Japanese wartime economy. The production of special and forged steels for military needs continued to increase until the final stages of the Pacific War; but that of ordinary iron and steel, which greatly influences the economy as a whole, peaked as early as 1938 and thereafter fell continuously. As we shall see later, the Japanese wartime economy from 1938 until the end of the war was managed around a series of materials mobilization plans. The greatest problem encountered each year in the allocation of materials was fierce rivalry between the army and navy in their demands for increased allocations of ordinary iron and steel. The result was that less and less steel was allocated to civilian industries, which also undermined production for military needs. The allocation of other important materials was implemented in rough proportion to that of ordinary iron and steel. Here also there was strong competition between the army and the navy, and the Cabinet Planning Board, responsible for drafting the plans, found itself forced time and time again to slash allocations to the civilian sector.

It was much the same with coal, the chief source of energy. After peaking in 1940 it proved increasingly difficult to maintain an annual production of

Table 6.4. *Coal supplies to mainland Japan, 1934/1936 to 1945 (million tons)*

	Production 1	Net import 2	Consumption 3	End-year stock 4
1934/6	38.5	3.7	41.7	0.8
1937	45.3	4.5	51.2	1.0
1938	48.7	4.8	55.3	1.1
1939	52.4	6.6	61.3	1.5
1940	57.3	8.6	66.5	1.8
1941	55.6	7.8	63.1	3.3
1942	54.2	7.2	62.0	3.2
1943	55.5	4.9	59.7	3.8
1944	49.3	2.4	50.5	4.0
1945	16.1	0.1	14.6	7.8

Source: KSKS (1990–1), vol. III, 279.

50 million tons, even by the wholesale importing of Korean labour, which by the end of the war accounted for a quarter of all miners. Unsystematic exploitation and lack of materials led to a reduction in coal output per head after 1943, and the lack of coal sufficient to supply munitions factories throughout the country gravely impeded the wartime economy. The coal-producing areas of Japan are situated on the fringes, in Kyushu to the west and Hokkaido to the north, while the munitions factories were concentrated in the more central Tokyo–Yokohama and Osaka–Kobe areas. This necessitated large shipping fleets to transport the coal from where it was produced to where it was used. During the Pacific War, when there was an urgent lack of available ships, the transportation of coal in coastal waters by means of motor-powered sailing vessels became increasingly problematic, as did the marine traffic in coal from northern China and Manchuria to mainland Japan. This proved to be a severe bottleneck in the implementation of the materials mobilization plans, and led to reduced activity in munitions factories. The very fact that the production of such basic materials as coal and steel should have been stagnant throughout the war reveals the fragile nature of the Japanese wartime economy.

The wartime economy was managed by means of materials mobilization plans which began in 1938. Calculations were made each year to fix the availability of more than one hundred important materials. These included ordinary iron and steel, electrolytic copper, aluminium, coal, and cotton. Military and civilian requirements were then adjusted so as not to exceed the supply available. There was a limit to domestic supply, and demands

Table 6.5. *Japan's balance of trade, 1936–1941 (million yen)*

	Yen-bloc trade			Third-country trade		
	exports 1	imports 2	balance 3	exports 4	imports 5	balance 6
1936	631	410	221	2,166	2,515	−349
1937	795	469	326	2,522	3,485	−963
1938	1,234	637	597	1,661	2,198	−537
1939	1,838	728	1,110	2,091	2,398	−307
1940	1,867	756	1,111	1,789	2,697	−908
1941	1,659	855	804	992	2,043	−1,051

Source: Hara (1973), 48.

could be satisfied only by means of imports. The greatest bone of contention between the army, navy, and the civilian sector was always to which commodities scarce foreign currency should be allocated, and to whom the commodities thus acquired should be allocated.[5]

Trade constraints

During the war in China, when overseas trade was still feasible, the materials mobilization plans were already hampered by shortage of foreign exchange. The allocation of materials was cut back as currency stocks dwindled, with the result that ever tighter controls came to be imposed. An important prerequisite for the materials mobilization plans was the drawing up of a trade plan. As the area under Japanese occupation was expanded to form a yen bloc, foreign currency ceased to be needed for imports from countries within this bloc, but at the same time it became impossible to earn foreign currency by exporting to such regions. Japan had always had a trade surplus with the area which corresponded to the yen bloc, whereas it had a large deficit with other countries. Previously it had been possible to use the surplus with the one to cover the deficit with the other, but the formation of the yen bloc at the beginning of the war with China precluded this, and the huge deficit with countries outside the yen bloc placed a great strain on the wartime economy. Table 6.5 shows Japan's current trade balance, and records separate statistics for the two areas. It proves how great the burden of foreign-currency payments to countries outside the yen bloc was for the Japanese economy during the war with China.

Exports to regions within the yen bloc and therefore not capable of earning foreign currency continued to increase as traders sought to profit from advancing inflation there; the government introduced severe restrictions on exports to these regions in order not to import inflation into Japan proper. At the same time imports of materials from the yen bloc, which did not need to be paid for in foreign currency, failed to increase as much as expected, while those of war supplies from countries outside the yen bloc grew rapidly. Of course Japan needed to increase exports outside the yen bloc in order to earn foreign currency to pay for these imports. However, the textile industry, the greatest exporter at the time, depended heavily on the import of raw cotton; when intensifying trade restraints made it necessary to reduce even imports of this sort, it became difficult to contemplate any increase in exports to countries outside the yen bloc.

Under these conditions, drawing up the materials mobilization plans revolved around the issue of dividing the sparse reserves of foreign currency among the army, navy, and civilian sector in order to enable them to import commodities from countries outside the yen bloc, and to which commodities preference should be given.

Economic controls during the war with China

The transition to direct control

Under what circumstances were administered controls first introduced? In the years 1932 and 1933 an increase in military expenditure was approved, paid for by the sale of deficit-financing bonds, in order to stimulate recovery from the recent slump. The policy of the minister of finance, Takahashi Korekiyo, to disregard falling exchange rates and concentrate on increasing exports, paid off, and Japan was among the first to recover from the worldwide depression. However, Takahashi was assassinated on 26 February 1936, having during the previous two years begun to advocate a curbing of military expenditure and a reduction in bond sales for deficit finance. The attempted *coup d'état* failed, but despite this the army's political influence increased.

The minister of finance in the newly appointed cabinet led by Hirota Koki was Baba Eiichi, who enforced a policy of increased deficit finance through bond issues at low interest rates. When the draft budget for 1937 was published later that year, with a huge 3,000 million yen demanded by the military, the anticipated rise in demand and fall in exchange rates sparked off a rapid increase in imports and sudden inflation. By the end of the year the banks were unable to raise sufficient foreign currency, and it became necessary to impose foreign exchange control. In January 1937 Japan's balance of payments was in danger, and the Ministry of Finance held emergency talks with the banks, as a result of which an import exchange control order was exercised and the direct control of trade from the foreign exchange end began. The import surplus for the first half of 1937 was in excess of 600 million yen which represented an increase of 2.3 times on the same period in the previous year and was unprecedented in scale. In the five months up to the end of July, almost all the 340 million yen which the Bank of Japan had laid aside at the time of the Manchurian Incident was shipped.

Of parallel importance to the materials mobilization plans was the productive capacity expansion plan which was passed by the cabinet in January 1939. Whereas the yearly materials mobilization plans enforced short-term economic management, the productive capacity expansion plan was aimed at the medium term. It had originally been conceived in 1936 prior to the outbreak of full-scale war in China as a five-year plan for vital industries centred on the army. The idea took its initial inspiration from the five-year plans of the Soviet Union, and the objective was to build up a proper munitions industry and supporting heavy industries in Japan and Manchuria over a five-year period from 1937 until 1941. The army maintained that to implement the plan Japan must enforce economic control not only in Manchuria but also on the Japanese mainland, and avoid war at all costs for five years.

Political and financial leaders had already agreed on implementing this plan in 1936, and in February 1937 the army was instrumental in bringing the cabinet of Hayashi Senjuro into being. The policies of Baba as minister of finance had been deeply unpopular in financial circles. The new minister of finance was Yuki Toyotaro, the former chairman of the Industrial Bank of Japan, while Ikeda Seihin, a leading figure in the Mitsui financial combine, became governor of the Bank of Japan. An attempt was made to soften the opposition of civilian capital by amending Baba's policies, but the degree of amendment was slight. Contrary to the expectations of the army, Hayashi's cabinet was a weak one. It succeeded in establishing a planning agency and initiating a review of productive capacity expansion policy, but stepped down after a mere four months. The first cabinet of Konoe Fumimaro assumed power in June, resolved to make the expansion of productive capacity a national policy, and proceeded to announce its three principles of finance and economics – expansion of productive capacity, coordination of demand and supply of materials, and maintenance of the balance of international payments.

In fact, before the war with China began in June, there was awareness that any rapid expansion of productive capacity would involve a huge demand for materials, and that to avoid price rises would require stringent control over the supply and demand for each material. It was also realized that to import machinery from overseas without damage to the balance of payments would require foreign exchange controls. Preparations were in place for legislation on various controls including that of finance. It had become necessary to initiate control even before the war with China, and this last event eased their implementation by weakening the opposition of the business world.

The first genuine legislation aimed at administrative control consisted of two acts passed by the Diet in September 1937. The first concerned temporary measures on imports and exports, and gave the government the right to exert direct control over all commodities in this respect. It became the basis for various imperial edicts covering all aspects of control not only of trade but also of commodities and prices. The prewar Japanese economy depended heavily on trade, and it was possible to control commodities in general by placing restrictions on trade.

The second of the two acts concerned the temporary regulation of capital, making it necessary to obtain prior permission when supplying funds for the purchase of equipment. This act sought to promote a shift towards heavy industry first of all from the funding side, by curtailing investment in civilian industry and encouraging the supply of capital to the industries involved in the supply of munitions and investment goods. At the same time it aimed to control equipment funds to prevent the import of machinery for civilian industries and to ensure that the import potential was used for military-related industries.

In addition to these two acts, the Diet resolved to invoke legislation on the mobilization of munitions industries enacted in 1918 as a result of World War I, but in virtual abeyance ever since. It also approved the military budget, and set up a temporary special military account with regard to which the period until the end of the war was to count as one fiscal year; expenditure under this account was to be kept secret.

The two acts became effective in October 1937, and control evolved on the dual fronts of trade and finance. The militarization of the industrial structure was enforced from the side of funding. Industries were classified as military-related, semi-military, or civilian. Provision of equipment funds and foreign currency to military-related industries was permitted, while flows of capital and imports of machinery into civilian industries were severely restricted. Imports of civilian commodities, especially cotton, wool, and timber, were reduced drastically. Control of trade and finance led to direct controls on the prices and allocation of commodities. One after another, every area of the economy was affected by control, and the whole Japanese economy was caught up in an administrative net.

The Planning Board was formed by amalgamating the agency set up to draft the productive capacity expansion plan with another established earlier in connection with the plan for general mobilization. However, the outbreak of full-scale war meant an urgent need to draft concrete proposals for commodity controls. Precedence was given to the drafting of a materials mobilization plan in order to adjust military and civilian demand to currently available supplies; this temporarily pushed the Planning Board's initial responsibility of drafting the medium-term productive capacity expansion plan into the background. The first materials mobilization plan to be drawn up by the Planning Board was in the sum of 3,000 million yen, which was the stock of foreign currency available for use in the calendar year 1938. (However, the draft exchange fund allocation plan drawn up prior to this by a cabinet committee for November–December 1937 was the first materials mobilization plan in the general sense).

The influence of worldwide economic uncertainty in 1937 and the imposition of trade controls sharply reduced imports of cotton and other raw materials for the manufacture of exportables. Therefore, all efforts to expand exports came to nothing in the first half of 1938. The imports anticipated initially in the materials mobilization plan for 1938 ceased to be feasible, and in June the scale of the plan had to be reduced by about 20 per cent. The effect of the 20 per cent reduction was doubled in the second half of the year; civilian demand felt the squeeze particularly severely, and this led to a rapid tightening of economic control measures. This amendment to the materials mobilization plan led to strict limitations on the consumption of domestic civilian commodities; in turn, these were associated with more stringent controls on distribution and a shift towards an official system of price controls, which seriously affected all aspects of civilian industry. The blow dealt to smaller commercial and industrial undertakings was particularly harsh, and controls began to be felt in everyday life. Since any reduction in military demand was fraught with difficulties, civilian demand was repeatedly forced to bear the brunt, while the army and navy continued to argue fiercely about the allocation of foreign currency and the most important basic commodity, ordinary iron and steel.

Until 1938, therefore, there was only temporary legislation for economic control on the basis of which various imperial edicts were issued. The National General Mobilization Act, which gave the government *carte blanche* with regard to all types of controls, was enacted in March 1938 on the assumption that it would be kept in reserve. At first, only a few imperial edicts chiefly concerned with labour were enacted. But after the outbreak of World War II in Europe in September 1939 there were positive moves towards bringing the act into full force. Then controls were reorganized and tightened with the outbreak of the Pacific War and were mostly unified into a scheme of imperial edicts on control based on the General Mobilization Act.

In January 1939 the productive capacity expansion plan was at last adopted by the cabinet as a four-year plan beginning in 1938 and ending in 1941. The target year envisaged in the initial five-year plan was not altered; in fact, the effective period over which a rapid expansion in the capacity of industrial plant was to be attempted was three years. The very fact that they were faced with the need to build up the basic productive capacity of heavy industry from scratch for the sake of the munitions industry, at a time when the costs of war were already taking their toll, proves how low was the level of development of Japan's heavy industry. It was a very different situation from that in the USA, Germany, and the other advanced industrial countries, where it was only necessary to activate facilities which were already in existence but lying idle.

While the decision to implement the productive capacity expansion plan for mainland Japan was delayed, in Manchuria a five-year plan to develop industry was put into operation immediately in 1937. The scale of the plan was enlarged as a result of the war in China. The newly established combine Nissan was transferred to Manchuria as a vehicle for implementing the plan, and reorganized as the Manchuria Heavy Industry Development Company, under which was placed one special subsidiary company for each industry. Similarly in 1938 two large-scale development agencies were established as part of the national policy, the North China Development Company and the Mid-China Development Company in their respective areas, with the object of developing natural resources in the occupied areas of China.

It was decided to base the materials mobilization plan for 1939 on the fiscal year, which begins in April. A plan to cover January–March 1939 was drafted to provide a link with that for 1938 (which had been based on the calendar year). The supply of commodities was already encountering difficulties; restrictions were so tight that the materials mobilization plan could not guarantee the import of high-quality foreign machinery required to implement the nascent productive capacity expansion plan.

January 1939 saw the formation of a new cabinet under Hiranuma Kiichiro. The 1939 materials mobilization plan was decided in May, and from this year the trade plan, transport and electricity mobilization plan, financial control plan, labour mobilization plan and all the other elements of the national general mobilization plan were in place. In April the central committee on prices provided an overall policy on price controls, establishing official and 'fair' wartime prices based on cost-accounting for profits, wages, transport costs, rents, and other structural elements of production costs.

The collapse of trade outside the yen bloc

The denunciation of the Japanese–US treaty on trade and shipping in July 1939, and its lapse in January of the following year, dealt a severe blow to the Japanese wartime economy which relied heavily on America for machine tools, scrap iron, and many other commodities for military use. There was dissension within Hirayama's cabinet over whether or not to conclude a tripartite alliance with Germany and Italy, but the non-aggression pact agreed between Germany and the Soviet Union in August 1939 prompted the cabinet to resign in a body after publicly declaring that the state of affairs in Europe was complex and bizarre. At the end of the month their place was taken by the cabinet of Abe Nobuyuki.

The outbreak of war in Europe resulted in a worldwide rise in prices. The government's response to this was to enforce price controls, pegging wages, salaries, rents for land and accommodation, and prices in general, to the level of 18 September. Higher prices worldwide meant that, though the stock of foreign currency available remained unchanged, the quantity of imports which could be purchased was significantly less, and this added to the difficulties which were being experienced in implementing the materials mobilization plan. July 1939 brought a critical water shortage which, compounded with a shortage of coal, led to restrictions in the supply of electricity. Coal and electricity continued to be in short supply into the autumn, and the worsening situation forced even the munitions factories to reduce operations. At the same time, the drought in western Japan and Korea meant reduced production of rice. Anxious to avert riots, the police became involved in controlling the distribution of rice. The shipping of Korean rice into mainland Japan never returned to its former level, and Japanese agriculture was faced with the task of increasing the production of food supplies despite an insufficient workforce.

In the midst of the confusion caused by the shortages, the Abe cabinet resigned *en masse* in January 1940, to be replaced by one led by Yonai Mitsumasa. In the same month the Japanese–US trade treaty lapsed without hope of renewal, and trade between the two countries ceased to be governed by mutual agreement. In March, Japan recognized the puppet government in China, and relations between Japan and America worsened even further.

In May 1940 German forces began to move on the western front, invading the Netherlands and Belgium and pushing on towards France. In Japan this sparked off debate on southward expansion, and the government expressed keen interest in the Dutch East Indies and French Indochina. In June an emergency materials mobilization plan was drawn up in great secrecy on the assumption that all imports from outside the yen bloc would cease, and Japan was faced for the first time with a decision to go to war on the basis of its own resources in isolation. The conclusion was that, if imports from outside the yen bloc dried up, the supply of most basic commodities would be reduced by half, and stocks of most of them would reach rock bottom at the end of the second year. The 1940 materials mobilization plan was at last passed by the cabinet at the end of June. In the same month special imports were authorized to the tune of 100 million yen by depleting the Bank of Japan's currency reserves; the total value of emergency imports reached 500 million yen by February 1941. Fear that imports would be cut off accelerated the purchase of war materials and reversed the policy of conserving the dwindling reserves of foreign exchange.

As advocacy of expansion to the south strengthened, the movement in favour of a new order gained momentum. In July the Yonai cabinet was overthrown by the army, and the second cabinet of Konoe Fumimaro came into existence. The new cabinet immediately approved the army and navy's draft national policy for southward expansion by military force. The north of French Indochina was occupied, and the tripartite treaty with Germany and Italy concluded, representing an important change of direction in foreign policy. In response to this, America announced in September that it was prohibiting the export of scrap iron to Japan. Pressure for far-reaching amendments to the productive capacity expansion plan was brought to bear from the Japanese iron and steel industry, which had depended on scrap iron for the manufacture of steel, and it became necessary also to make substantial changes in the 1940 materials mobilization plan from the third quarter of the year onwards.

The opportunity was seized upon in October 1940 to strengthen all types of economic control. This included promulgating laws on the control of company management and on fund management in banks and other financial institutions, in addition amending the laws on rents for land and accommodation, price controls, national conscription, registration of availability for work, and wage controls. The coming into existence of the law on fund management meant that not only equipment funds but now also liquid funds were placed under direct control.

A fierce controversy arose concerning a draft for a new economic order which aimed at further tightening of controls. The draft, which had been put forward by reformist bureaucrats at the Planning Board, attacked the liberal capitalist economic framework as the old order, and advocated restricting ownership and the pursuit of profit. It sought to free employers from the limitations of capital and give precedence to the common interest in expansion of output. The document was opposed by the financial world and those on the right, who were in favour of removing bureaucratic controls and respecting the capacity of the people to govern themselves. Compromise was reached in December 1940, the establishment of the new economic order was agreed upon in outline by the cabinet, and the policy for restructuring economic organization was approved with some softening of the wording.

The drafting of the materials mobilization plan for 1941 was greatly delayed, and the portion relating to the first quarter of the year was all that was passed by the cabinet in April. The discussions between Japan and the United States which began in April 1941 reached deadlock, while the continuing negotiations between Japan and the Netherlands were broken off without agreement; in July the Netherlands suspended the oil agreement between the two countries. There was a rapid strengthening of economic sanctions against Japan by the United States, Britain, the Netherlands, and other countries. The outbreak of war between Germany and the Soviet Union in June 1941 closed the Trans-Siberian railway as a route for the import of commodities and that year's materials mobilization plan, already delayed, had to be reworked. Japan engineered special large-scale army manoeuvres and mobilized large numbers of troops on the border between Manchuria and the Soviet Union. In the end, however, they gave up the idea of initiating hostilities against the Soviet Union and resolved on a policy of invading the southern part of French Indochina, not shrinking from the prospect of war with America and Britain.

The freezing of Japanese assets which the United States, Britain, and the Netherlands implemented in response to the decision to invade the southern part of French Indochina resulted in the total stoppage of imports from outside the yen bloc. It was no longer possible for Japan to maintain her wartime economy except by self-sufficiency within her own sphere of influence. The disposal and movement of Japanese external assets was prohibited, and all trade and payments ceased between Japan and countries outside the yen bloc. At the same time there was a total prohibition on the import of oil. The only countries outside the yen bloc with which connections were not severed were French Indochina and Thailand. Thus the Japanese wartime economy was completely isolated from the economy of the world at large.

In this way, every change in the international scene during the period of the war in China played havoc with the import forecasts on which the materials mobilization plans were founded. This brought the need for continuous amendments, and economic controls were tightened in Japan each time this occurred. After the freezing of assets the military became very anxious about the dissipation of national resources, and an imperial conference on 6 September determined that preparations for war against America, Britain, and the Netherlands should be completed by late

October. That month saw the formation of a new cabinet headed by Tojo Hideki, after which the decision was reviewed. The conclusion was that it 'could not be said to be more advantageous to avoid war than to wage it', and on 5 November the imperial conference resolved on military action in early December. Negotiations between Japan and the United States failed, and Japan went to war with the aim of gaining resource-rich territory in the south.

Economic controls during the Pacific War

The yen bloc and the initial victories

After the freezing of foreign assets, Japanese overseas trade came to rely on self-sufficiency within the yen bloc where direct payment in foreign currency was not necessary. This heralds a change in the nature of the wartime economy, which, during the war with China, had evolved a system of controls based on the allocation of foreign currency. During the Pacific War which followed, the most serious shortage facing the Japanese wartime economy was no longer foreign currency but the shipping capacity needed to ferry materials from the various corners of its sphere of influence back to the Japanese mainland. Available shipping space now became the fundamental condition which determined how much of each commodity could be supplied under the materials mobilization plans. Thus the foreign exchange plan of the period of the war with China was replaced with a shipping plan which became the basis for drafting materials mobilization plans during the Pacific War.

According to the assessment of national resources at the time of the decision for war with America, Britain, and the Netherlands, it was judged that economic activity could be maintained at a level similar to that of 1941, provided that 3 million tons of shipping could still be secured for civilian use. This was in addition to vessels requisitioned by the army or navy, although it was assumed that many of these would be released back into civilian service. Once war had been declared, however, this proved unexpectedly problematic, and the average available for civilian use was less than 2 million tons.

During 1942 rather more vessels were released and the figure rose to almost 2.5 million, but with the initiation of the Guadalcanal campaign in August the number of vessels requisitioned rose once more, and the total available for civilian use fell below 1.9 million tons. Thereafter the total usable tonnage decreased rapidly quarter by quarter.[6] The result was a similar decrease both in the steamship tonnage available to carry materials from the occupied territories to mainland Japan, and in the tonnage of motor-powered sailing vessels for shipment of coal in Japanese coastal waters. This naturally reduced the supply of commodities under the materials mobilization plans and made further controls inevitable.

In November 1941 just before the Pacific War was launched, three overriding objectives for military administration of the southern territories to fall under Japanese domination had been determined: the restoration of order, the rapid acquisition of materials necessary for the defence of the country, and the assurance of self-support locally by the fighting forces. In December the whole region was divided into two areas. Area A comprised the Dutch East Indies, British Malaya, Borneo, and the Philippines, which were to be occupied by the Japanese army and ruled directly by a military administration; area B consisted of French Indochina and Thailand, where a continued role for the existing régime was to be permitted and a different method of government applied. In area A emphasis was to be placed on the acquisition of resources, while in area B economic and currency agreements were to be forced on the régime for the purpose of gaining local currency and satisfying the material requirements of the Japanese army without the use of foreign currency.

The development of resources in the south was to be effected without the aid of special companies or investment concerns as was the case in Manchuria and in north and central China. Instead, the state was to nominate a civilian entrepreneur to be responsible for the development of each mine or factory. The idea was to place the development of one site in the hands of one company and thus ensure the effective exploitation of mineral and agricultural resources. Mitsui Bussan, Mitsubishi Shoji, and other trading companies were appointed to procure materials and ship them back to Japan. The policy was not to promote local manufacturing except for shipbuilding, repairs to equipment, and other activities which would alleviate the pressure on shipping.

From the standpoint of trade structure the countries of south-east Asia could be classified into two groups. The first group comprised countries like Malaya, the Dutch East Indies, and the Philippines which lie on or in the ocean. These exported rubber, tin, oil, jute, and other tropical agricultural produce to the colonial powers of Europe and America, and imported foodstuffs. The other group consisted of French Indochina, Thailand, Burma, and the other countries of continental south-east Asia, which produced and exported rice and other foodstuffs for the region. In both groups of countries industrial production had been suppressed, and it was difficult to supply all the needs of everyday life.

Japanese aggression led to the severing of trading relations with the former colonial powers. In the first group this signified the loss of markets for specialised exports; this led to a kind of slump, a rapid accumulation of stocks and fall in prices, with exporters and farmers going out of business, and a rise in unemployment. The supply of imports of essential commodities from Japan to replace that from Europe and America was meagre, the price of industrial products rose dramatically, and ordinary people found themselves trapped between the falling value of the goods they had for sale and the rising price of the commodities they needed to buy. Much of the shipping was enlisted for Japanese military transport requirements and there was a severe shortage of vessels to carry civilian commodities. There was a food crisis in the maritime regions of south-east Asia caused by rice being in short supply; on the continent, a reduction in rice exports caused prices to fall and sparked off a rural crisis. In both regions commodities for the military were being purchased with army notes issued without restriction, and this led to rampant inflation.

As soon as the Pacific War began, various imperial edicts were proclaimed in Japan proper in preparation for wartime. A materials control act replaced the temporary measures on exports which had been in force at the time of the war in China, and this became the legal basis for materials control during the Pacific War. A law governing key industrial organizations was enacted in order to implement the new economic order, and in October 1941 just before the outbreak of war control associations were established for the iron and steel, coal, engineering, and other industries. Trade, railways, and finance were also placed under similar control associations, each headed by the chairman of an important company within the sector concerned.

These control associations were essentially subcontractors to officialdom – an intermediate tier between government and industry. Government devolved part of its authority onto them. The control associations themselves became tinged with bureaucracy, and their efficacy declined. Born out of cartels, the control associations paid great attention to the profits of the industry as a whole and of the large constituent companies. In accordance with an act controlling factories and places of business, the munitions industry was placed under the direct supervision of the army and navy. As the core component of the wartime economy it was not included in any control association. Before their activities had a chance to get under way properly, the control associations became the target of criticism for their bureaucracy and lack of effectiveness, and the companies themselves were shifted to state control under the munitions companies act.

In April 1942 a management committee for privately owned, publicly run shipping was formed. The government requisitioned the vessels and the management committee allocated them, with the owners as operators. The shipping management committee was to play an important role in supporting the wartime economy. In the shipbuilding industry, wartime standard vessel types were decided on in April, and incentives were established for the planned building of ships. In the same month the 1942 materials mobilization plan was ratified, reflecting in optimistic mood the war's initial victories. May saw the successful completion of the initial campaign in the south. June, however, brought defeat in the battle of Midway. This was a turning-point in the war.

The economics of defeat

Huge numbers of vessels were requisitioned for the Guadalcanal campaign, cutting back civilian transportation capacity and the production of basic materials as a result. Emergency measures designed to safeguard the production of iron and steel, aluminium, coal, shipping, and aircraft were passed by the cabinet in October 1942, and at the end of November a temporary committee was set up to find ways of boosting production. All kinds of measures were evolved as a result, including building small-scale smelting furnaces and new facilities for loading and unloading cargoes in the ports. Munitions output was stepped up from spring 1943, and peaked in September 1944 at four times the prewar level. The building of wartime standard vessels was accelerated from November 1942; however, with the loss of naval superiority to the Americans and unremitting submarine attacks, an increase in sinkings of merchant vessels began in the autumn of 1943 and proceeded faster than new vessels could be built. The tonnage of seaworthy shipping decreased sharply, as can be seen in table 6.6, from more than 1.9 million tons in the first half of 1943 to 1.5 million at the end of that year and less than 1 million in November 1944.

The southern occupied territories

Depletion of the number of available vessels caused important changes in the policy of the military administration in the southern occupied territories in May 1943. The policy of suppressing industry was amended in favour of encouraging light industry and the production of everyday essentials; it was hoped that, by promoting regional food self-sufficiency, it would be possible to maintain a minimum lifestyle for the local population and ensure that the army remained self-supporting on a regional basis. At the same time, absolute priority was given to the acquisition of military resources and sending as many commodities as possible back to Japan. In maritime south-east Asia unused agricultural land was compulsorily brought back under cultivation, while on the Asian continent paddy-fields were abandoned and cotton produced under coercion, but all to no avail. The result was simply to turn the farmers even more against Japan.

Insufficient shipping capacity, the most important factor restricting the

Table 6.6. *Japanese shipping available for freight transport, 1941–1945 (thousand tons)*

		Total shipping 1	Civilian shipping 2	Civilian shipping available for use 3
1941	Dec.	5,241	1,715	1,513
1942	I	5,540	1,840	1,612
	II	5,544	2,298	1,957
	III	5,507	2,822	2,370
	IV	5,252	2,619	2,260
1943	I	4,990	2,213	1,846
	II	4,763	2,324	1,971
	III	4,598	2,160	1,789
	IV	4,170	1,939	1,545
1944	I	3,560	1,815	1,454
	II	3,353	1,714	1,275
	III	2,874	1,605	1,167
	IV	1,978	1,311	896
1945	I	1,980	1,279	908
	II	1,857	1,366	892
	Aug.	1,547	1,181	594

Source: Oyi (1953), 292–3.

wartime economy of mainland Japan during the Pacific War, thus had a profound effect on policy towards the occupied territories in the south and forced down the living standards of the population in the whole of southeast Asia. Nor did it prove possible for Japan to replace her former trade with countries outside the yen bloc by materials forced out of the occupied territories.

Occupied China

In the areas of China occupied by the Japanese army there was also a shortage of materials because of restrictions on exports from Japan, and this led to spiralling prices. Both the monetary system and the extent of the price rises differed between Manchuria and the north and south of China; consequently transfers of both money and commodities between these regions were restricted, despite the fact that they were all within the yen bloc. Having created the bloc, Japan was now faced with the need to limit exchange within it. In this sense the yen bloc was not an integrated economic entity.

Manchuria

As the foreign currency crisis in Japan proper worsened, the five-year plans for developing industry in Manchuria also changed significantly after May 1940, from a policy of overall expansion to an out-and-out priority system. The targets for the second five-year plan, agreed upon in September 1941, emphasized increased output of iron and steel, coal, and agricultural produce. The Manchuria Heavy Industry Development Company was unable to respond to the tightening of controls by the government of Manchukuo, and it was resolved to curtail its functions to the provision of funds and management of personnel only, thus negating the policy of granting the exclusive right to develop one industry to one company. The controlled economy of Manchuria was forced to alter its appearance time after time at the request of mainland Japan, a fact which made clear its subordinate nature.

Korea

In Korea the production of gold was curtailed after the beginning of the Pacific War, and the quantity of rice imported into mainland Japan also decreased significantly. The development of raw materials for the textile industry was encouraged, as was that of mineral resources to meet the military demand. An emergency increase in the supply of iron ore from Korea was effected in response to reduced imports of this commodity from China and the south. After the end of 1942 approximately 40 per cent of the planned increase in production of iron and steel using small-scale smelting furnaces was implemented in Korea, and the country also became an important centre for the production of aluminium, which uses large quantities of electricity. Lack of available shipping caused difficulties in the transportation of materials from Manchuria and northern China, and from the end of 1942 a switch was made to transport by land along the Korean railways. By the end of the war approximately 700,000 Koreans had been shipped to Japan to work as forced labour in the mines and elsewhere.

Taiwan

Taiwan also experienced a slump in the production of rice, and exports to Japan were halved. Production levels of sugar also fell, and attempts were made to produce aircraft fuel from sugar. About 15 per cent of Japan's aluminium was produced in Taiwan. From 1944 onwards attention was turned to the fortification of the island, which led to the mobilization of huge quantities of material and labour just before the end of the war.

Mainland Japan

Japanese forces retreated from Guadalcanal at the beginning of February 1943. In March, the iron and steel, coal, shipbuilding, non-ferrous metal, and aircraft industries were designated for special attention, the prime minister's right to issue orders to these five industries was intensified, and they became the focus of a productivity drive. Iron ore, coal, and bauxite (the raw material for aluminium) were given preferential treatment in the allocation of shipping resources. In June of the same year, an outline plan was passed to reorganize industry with a view to increasing its war mobilization. A threefold division was imposed, most factories engaged in peacetime production were closed down, and their equipment and workforces were transferred to the munitions industry. The resources of even the textile industry were diverted more and more into the production of aircraft parts and chemicals, and by August 1944 the reorganization was almost complete. Ever since the freezing of Japanese assets, civilian light industry had been ruthlessly abandoned. The production of cotton yarn, halved during the war with China, was halved again in 1942, and by the end of the war had dropped to less than 4 per cent of the previous peak.

The ministerial system was restructured by a cabinet decision of September 1943. The Ministry for Commerce and Industry and the Planning Board were largely merged with the section of the army and navy's aviation headquarters which supervised civilian factories. The newly formed body was called the Ministry of Munitions. Its Bureau for Aviation and Weapons had sole responsibility for the production of aeroplanes, and the Mobilization Bureau took over the drafting of the materials mobilization plans from the Planning Board. A Ministry of Agriculture and Commerce was established in order to guarantee self-sufficiency in food and the commodities of daily life, while considerations of consolidating transportation capacity led to the amalgamation of the Ministries of Railways and of Communications to form a new Ministry of Transport and Communications.

At the same time as the establishment of the Ministry for Munitions, the government enacted a law on munitions companies. They bestowed this title on certain civilian organizations and then proceeded to exert tight state control over them by becoming directly involved in their internal management. The government reserved the right to issue orders with regard to production, personnel management, procurement of funds, accounting, and all other aspects of management. It also had the right to demand changes in the articles of association. It gave the chairmen of such companies the responsibility for production and enabled them to implement the orders of the minister in charge without the consent of a general meeting of shareholders. Below the chairman was a deputy in charge of production, and the employees, being regarded as having been conscripted at work, were commanded to obey the orders of these two persons. In this way, even civilian

Table 6.7. *Japanese aircraft production, 1934/6 to 1945*

	The aluminium industry			The aircraft industry		employment	
	bauxite output (thou. tons) 1	aluminium output (thou. tons) 2	imported aluminium (thou. tons) 3	airframe output (units) 4	aero-engine output (units) 5	military establishments (thou.) 6	civilian establishments (thou.) 7
1934/6	7.7	19.0	8.8	—	—	2	70
1937	31.5	31.6	13.7	—	—	3	146
1938	48.3	33.1	23.8	—	—	4	170
1939	65.2	43.7	36.7	—	—	5	246
1940	97.5	43.4	—	—	—	6	268
1941	151.9	71.7	—	6,260	11,280	9	433
1942	226.2	103.1	2.0	9,500	16,800	25	749
1943	318.5	141.1	3.0	17,150	26,400	89	1,370
1944	225.2	110.4	4.2	24,000	40,270	82	2,381
1945	16.2	6.6	1.1	5,130	10,280	—	—

Source: KSKS (1990–1), vol. III, 279, 281.

companies were compelled to adopt a militaristic system to enforce increased production.

Special emphasis was placed on the aircraft industry with its direct bearing on war mobilization. Table 6.7 reveals the efforts made to increase aircraft production from the second half of 1943. While all other sectors were showing decreased production, that of airframes continued to rise until the third quarter of 1944.[7] Spring 1944 brought a sudden cut in the import of bauxite, in competition with iron ore and oil, and it ceased altogether in the following February. Aircraft production peaked in November 1944, after which munitions production generally declined rapidly under the increasingly heavy air-raids. The production of engines was already tailing off, having peaked in the second quarter of the same year, and Japan's efforts to increase wartime production crumbled after mid-1944 even in the aircraft sector despite its preferential treatment.

The 1944 materials mobilization plan was decided in outline, but an attempt was made to execute it only for the first quarter of the year. Reductions in shipping capacity led to a 20 per cent fall in production of the most important commodities. Transportation of coal was down to a third, that of most civilian goods was reduced in a similar manner, but the plan itself acknowledged the fact that civilian demand could not be suppressed indefinitely. The year was marked by a succession of makeshift quarterly plans. Even commodities from the occupied territories in the south which could be acquired without foreign currency could not be transported to Japan because of the shipping shortage, and the focus of the materials mobilization plan became the task of securing enough vessels to allocate to each commodity. Naval protection for merchant shipping was completely inadequate, and attempts were made to mobilize motor-powered sailing vessels or switch to transportation by land to offset the large number of steamships requisitioned by the military.

The Japanese economy was constrained during the Pacific War by the difficulties encountered in transporting civilian commodities as a result of the wholesale requisitioning of shipping. As the war proceeded, with the loss of naval superiority more and more cargo ships were lost to submarine attacks. As a result, Japan was forced to abandon shipping routes one by one beginning with the most distant. A surprise attack by a task force on the Truk Islands in February 1944 resulted in the loss of roughly 10 per cent of Japan's available shipping, which now fell below the 4 million ton mark. Additional ships were requisitioned in March, but with the American landing on Saipan in June the shipping route linking Saipan with the Truk Islands was abandoned and there was a sudden increase in losses to submarines.

In July 1944 Saipan fell. Tojo's cabinet was replaced by a coalition cabinet led by Koiso Kuniaki and Yonai Mitsumasa. Vessels were requisitioned for the defence of the Philippines, and the import of rice from Thailand and French Indochina was suspended completely in favour of importing cereals and soyabean cake from Dalian and Pusan. In August the available tonnage dropped to below 3 million tons. The shipping of iron ore from Daye was no longer feasible, and vessels were allocated with extra priority to transporting bauxite from Bintan and iron ore from Hainan. When this also became impossible, Japan had to depend on Korea for supplies of iron ore. An assessment carried out in August 1944 concluded that national resources had peaked early in that year, and had thereafter been following a downward trend. It was anticipated that it would be difficult for them to revive at the end of the year.

In October 1944 Japan lost the mainstay of its combined fleet in the battle of Leyte Gulf. In November and thereafter more requisitions were made for the defence of Taiwan, Okinawa, and the Bonin Islands, but by the end of the year available shipping was down to less than 2 million tons. Transportation priorities were restricted from war supplies in general to certain specific war supplies, and then to oil alone. Finally, in early 1945, with the landing of American troops on Luzon the shipping routes between Manila, Singapore, and Taiwan were abandoned. Routes in the south seas were to be used for shipping oil only, but after February 1945 even imports of this commodity ceased. The transportation of sugar from Taiwan and cereals from Manchuria now became necessary to provide the raw material for manufacturing aviation fuel. It became difficult to ship coal, and before long foodstuffs and weapons were competing with each other for shipping space.

In November 1944 the bombing of munitions factories commenced, Tokyo began to be bombed in February 1945, and on 10 March 100,000 were burnt to death in a huge air raid on the capital. From then until June there were repeated air raids on Nagoya, Osaka, Kobe, and other major cities. With the fall of Iojima in March and the start of the battle for Okinawa in April, communications between Taiwan, Okinawa, and mainland Japan were cut, and in Okinawa 100,000 Japanese troops and 150,000 local inhabitants were killed. In May orders went out to suspend the transportation of arms and give precedence to foodstuffs and salt. The laying of mines in the straits between Shimonoseki and Moji at the end of March, and in the Inland Sea off the ports of Osaka and Kobe in April, made it dangerous to use the shipping routes in the Inland Sea and those between Japan and Manchuria and China. The principal ports were closed and most of the cargo-handling facilities could no longer be used. May saw the laying of mines to close the ports on the Japan Sea, and the north China shipping route ceased to operate in June.

In April a new cabinet was formed under Suzuki Kantaro. In the following month came Germany's unconditional surrender. At an imperial
conference in June, it was announced that production of iron and steel had
fallen to a quarter of the previous year's level; that there was no prospect
for building any new ships, and that factories in key areas had suspended
operations for lack of coal; moreover, it was difficult to secure supplies of
gunpowder and explosives; and there was a serious shortage of transport
and foodstuffs; in short, they were facing the greatest crisis since the beginning of the war. In July the shipping route between Aomori and Hakodate
was completely eliminated, and the supply of coal from Hokkaido ceased.

The Japan's decision to surrender came in August as a result of the dropping
of the atomic bombs on Hiroshima and Nagasaki and the shock effect of
the news that the Soviet Union had joined the war against Japan. However,
lack of available shipping had destroyed the country's wartime economy
long before the air raids began.

During the war Japan suffered approximately 3 million casualties. It lost
all its warships and aeroplanes, some 80 per cent of its shipping, 35 per cent
of its industrial machinery, 25 per cent of its buildings, and in all 25 per cent
of her national wealth. The outstanding government debt grew tenfold,
prices rose approximately threefold, and real wages fell to less than 70 per
cent of their prewar level.

Mobilization of the workforce

Employment and wages

I now look at the effect of the war on the composition of the workforce.
Table 6.8 reports relevant figures for the population and births and deaths.
It is worth bearing in mind that in 1941 mainland Japan accounted for
roughly 70 per cent of the total of demographic resources available: 105
million people, including nearly 25 million in Korea, and 6 million in
Taiwan, the remainder being accounted for by Sakhalin, the South Sea
islands, and the Kwantung Peninsula.[8]

From the standpoint of Japan's demographic trends, two years mark the
significant breaks – 1937 and 1945. Until 1937 the Japanese population followed a pattern of peacetime growth. From 1937 onwards it suffered a
steady annual loss of several hundred thousand excess war deaths and lost
births. The population continued to grow, however, because its natural
increase still exceeded war losses. In 1945, however, there was a huge abnor-
mal loss of population, and an absolute decline in numbers. Over the whole
period of the war economy (1937–45), the demographic loss attributable to
war probably amounted to some 4.6 million.

Table 6.8. *The population of mainland Japan, 1934–1945 (thousands and per thousand)*

		Annual change				
	Total, thou. 1	total change, per thou. 2	natural change, thou.			social change, thou. 6
			total 3	births 4	deaths 5	
1934	68,309	13.0	910	2,144	−1,235	−56
1935	69,254	13.8	1,012	2,182	−1,170	−92
1936	70,114	12.4	1,008	2,246	−1,239	−23
1937	70,630	7.4	980	2,173	−1,194	−442
1938	71,013	5.4	817	2,087	−1,270	−423
1939	71,380	5.2	618	1,897	−1,270	−223
1940	73,114	7.7	886	2,110	−1,224	−273
1941	72,218	4.0	1,108	2,256	−1,148	−817
1942	72,880	9.2	1,147	2,313	−1,166	−479
1943	73,903	14.0	1,012	2,219	−1,207	−17
1944	74,443	7.2	1,016	2,274	−1,258	−492
1945	71,998	−22.9	−245	1,902	−2,147	−1,462

Source: KSKS (1990–1), vol. I, 21.

The foremost influence on the wartime labour market was military mobilization. The statistics for military personnel are not necessarily accurate, and two sets of figures are available. These are given in table 6.9, where it will be seen that the labour market lost large sections of the workforce to mobilization by the army, first in 1937 at the time of the commencement of all-out war with China, then in 1941 when there were large-scale manoeuvres on the Soviet–Manchurian border in response to the German invasion of the Soviet Union. After the start of the Pacific War, 2.4 million men were mobilized up to the beginning of 1944, 1.5 million during 1944, and 1.8 million in 1945 up to the time of defeat. The total figures for those who died on military service are reported to be roughly 2.1 million (as shown in table 6.9), of which a small proportion would have died anyway under normal peacetime circumstances. If we adopt an approximate figure of 4.6 million excess deaths in total, then combat accounted for somewhat less than half of this total.

The national census of October 1940 and the special national census conducted in February 1944 are useful for seeing in detail the structure of the workforce by industry. In addition, Nakamura Takafusa and Arai Kurotake have recently unearthed some surveys of the working population

Table 6.9. *Japanese military personnel, 1930–1945 (thousands)*

			Cumulative totals (Pacific War)		
	Series A	Series B	dead	survived	total
	1	2	3	4	5
1930	250	—	—	—	—
1931	308	321	—	—	—
1932	384	328	—	—	—
1933	439	—	—	—	—
1934	447	—	—	—	—
1935	449	—	—	—	—
1936	507	—	—	—	—
1937	634	1,077	—	—	—
1938	1,159	—	—	—	—
1939	1,620	—	—	—	—
1940	1,723	1,542	—	—	—
1941	2,411	2,431	—	—	—
1942	2,829	2,850	—	—	—
1943	3,808	3,584	—	—	—
1944	5,365	5,396	—	—	—
1945	7,193	8,263	2,121	7,889	10,010

Source: KSKS (1990–1), vol. III, 274–5.

at the end of the war. Table 6.10 links this with the statistics provided by the national census and shows estimates of the working population by sector during the Pacific War. Arai has also published more detailed estimates of the workforce by industry and sex for October of each year up to 1940, and it is now possible to utilize similar figures for 1936, immediately before the outbreak of the war with China.

By comparing October 1936 and October 1940, and coordinating the estimates for October 1940, February 1944, and October 1947 under a consistent classification, it is possible to analyse the changes in the working population between points during the war with China, the Pacific War, and the postwar period of instability. During the war with China the workforce shifted away not only from agriculture but from the textile industry, commerce, services, and domestic work to the rapidly growing engineering and other heavy industries. This trend becomes even more marked after the beginning of the Pacific War, when the decrease in numbers engaged in commerce is particularly noteworthy. Women employed in agriculture increased sharply from the time of the war with China to replace the male workers mobilized into the army and recruited by the munitions industry. In 1945–7, the cessation of munitions output and the delay in reviving civil-

Table 6.10. *Japan's employed population, 1936–1947, selected years (thousands)*

		Primary	Secondary		Tertiary	Whole economy	
			total	of which, manufacturing		total	of which, female
		1	2	3	4	5	6
(A) Census figures							
1936	Oct.	15,116	6,913	5,468	10,030	32,059	11,691
1940	Oct.	14,401	8,604	6,873	9,991	32,996	12,753
(B) Survey figures							
1940	Oct.	14,393	8,620	6,898	9,470	32,483	12,753
1944	Feb.	14,028	10,105	8,089	7,562	31,695	13,250
1947	Oct.	17,812	7,874	5,722	7,643	33,328	12,707

Note:
Primary industry is agriculture, forestry, fisheries, and salt making.
Secondary industry is mining, manufacturing, construction, and gas, electricity, and water supply.
Tertiary industry is commercial and financial services, catering, transport and communications, government administration, and other services.
Source: LTES (1988), vol. II (Umemura et al.), 208–15, 260–1.

ian industry led to a sharp decline of numbers employed in heavy industry. The effects of demobilization from the forces and evacuation from the colonies and occupied territories were witnessed as a huge increase in the number of agricultural workers, as villages became a refuge for the temporarily unemployed.

Each year from 1939 onwards a labour mobilization plan was drafted. The labour demand for the year was calculated and a supply plan formulated. National conscription began in the same year with the enlisting of workers already employed in munitions factories. From 1940 onwards, workers in other industries were conscripted and transferred compulsorily to munitions factories, a practice intensified after September 1943. The number of conscripts at the end of the war had risen to a total of 6.15 million. Korean workers were brought to Japan in ever-increasing numbers after 1942 and forced to work in mines and on building sites. Their numbers rose from 120,000 in 1943 to 280,000 in 1944. Chinese workers brought to Japan and forced to work in the same way totalled 40,000. Nor were the other colonies exempt from this practice.

Towards the end of the war the number of conscript workers ceased to be sufficient, and the wholesale mobilization of schoolchildren commenced.

Children in the third year of middle school and above began to be mobilized for work in June 1943, and in October the first children were sent on active service. From September 1943 female volunteers of school age were mobilized for work in munitions factories. In July 1944 the target of mobilization was expanded to include the lower years of middle school and the senior class of elementary school, and in March of the following year all teaching from this level up to university was suspended. The number of schoolchildren mobilized by the end of the war totalled 3.43 million, and the number of under-age female volunteers had reached 470,000.[9] The growth in number of under-age female workers and workers of retirement age or over heralded a fall in the quality of the workforce, and the proportion of young male workers decreased even in the metallurgical, engineering, and other key industries.

During the war, the implementation of wage control led to the adoption of a system of bonuses and coordinated wage increases throughout the country. At this time the idea of lifetime employment and seniority wages became the norm. With a view to maintaining the stability of the workforce, provisions were also made for health and annuity insurance and other forms of social security. Factory legislation restricting hours of employment was repealed in order that working times might be extended, and special wartime regulations covering employment in factories and mines were enacted.

In the villages which had lost their workforce to the military and to the munitions industry, the number of part-time farmers increased, and women came to account for 60 per cent of all agricultural workers. The quantity of rice produced, the total area under cultivation, and the yield per hectare all declined, and in 1942 legislation on the control of foodstuffs was enacted. To encourage increased production a dual price system for rice was adopted giving preferential treatment to producers over landowners. While this took the form of a price policy, it actually limited the rights of the landowners and extended those of the tenant and independent farmers. In this sense the measure to some degree linked up with postwar agricultural reforms.

Living standards

As the war progressed, the standard of living of the Japanese people fell rapidly. Rice rations were maintained at 2 *go* 3 *shaku* (0.736 pints) from April 1941 until July 1945, but rice itself changed from being 70 per cent husked to being only 50 per cent or 20 per cent husked. Moreover, the share of cereals and other substitute foods grew, the equivalent amount of dry biscuits, soyabeans, sweet potatoes, and so on being subtracted from the rice ration. The supply of vegetables was roughly half of what was needed, and people began to go from the towns into the surrounding countryside to buy provisions. Increased production of pumpkins and sweet potatoes in kitchen gardens was encouraged. The share of cereals in the staple diet rose from 13 per cent in May 1945 to 49 per cent in the following month and 59 per cent in July, and in the same month the amount of the rice ration was reduced to 2 *go* 1 *shaku* (0.672 pints). In 1941 the standard daily requirement had been set at 2,400 calories and 80 grams of protein, but the average quantities in 1945 were 1,800 calories and 60 grams of protein.

Clothing rations were introduced in 1942. Two years later the ration had been reduced by half, and by the end of the war it was down to around one-seventh of peacetime consumption. The establishment of fire-prevention zones as a measure against air-raids led to the demolition of buildings and a consequent worsening of the housing situation. In the spring of 1944 people were encouraged to evacuate the cities if they had relatives elsewhere, and in August the evacuation of young schoolchildren commenced.

One of the characteristics of the Japanese wartime economy is that it lowered the standard of living of the ordinary people excessively. It was only by sacrificing national life that it was possible to sustain a war effort from 1937 right up to 1945.

Mobilization of finance and money

Public finance and the military burden

I now move on to discuss the wartime economy from the standpoint of money. We consider first the effect of the war on public finance. Military expenditure was paid partly from the budget's general account, and partly from its 'special account', under the 'temporary military special account'. Military expenditure from the general account was very low after 1942 because thereafter the majority of military expenditure was made from the special account. Table 6.11 examines the annual expenditure of the central government, and goes on to calculate the share of military expenditure in the net total of government spending from the two accounts after deducting of overlapping items. From this it will be seen that the ratio of military expenditure in 1934–6 was still less than 15 per cent, but that this rose sharply to 30 per cent with the outbreak of full-scale hostilities in China. It then maintained roughly the same level until 1941, but passed the 40 per cent mark once the Pacific War commenced. Lack of basic statistics casts some doubt on the figures, but it apparently reached the astonishing level of 87 per cent in 1944.

Other estimates published by Emi and Shionoya classify the net total of central and local government expenditure by item. According to this the

Table 6.11. *Japanese central government defence outlays, 1934/6 to 1944 (million yen and per cent)*

	Nominal GDP 1	Central government expenditure			
		total 2	of which, defence 3	% of total 4	% of GDP 5
1934/6	—	8,258	1,138	14	—
1937	22,843	11,111	3,441	31	15
1938	26,394	15,017	6,214	41	24
1939	31,230	18,883	6,769	36	22
1940	36,851	23,268	8,247	35	22
1941	47,550	35,851	12,854	36	27
1942	57,729	43,830	19,290	44	33
1943	70,654	63,173	30,328	48	43
1944	97,164	84,785	73,755	87	76

Sources: Money GDP, 1937–40: Mizoguchi (1993); 1941–4: USSBS (1946).
Government expenditures: KSKS (1990–1), vol. II, 223, 247.

ratio of military expenditure is not as large as table 6.11 suggests.[10] Emi and Shionoya have also estimated military and war-related expenditure in the broader sense.[11] Much military expenditure was paid out in the colonies and there was a significant contribution from the occupied territories, so that such statistics alone are insufficient. As an estimate of military expenditure their figures are the most comprehensive available, but differ little in total from those in table 6.11.

These enormous sums were financed mainly by the sale of government debt. Between 1934–6 and 1941 the proportion of the central government's general account financed by borrowing was never less than one-third. In 1940 far-reaching tax reforms were also carried out, and in 1942 a sharp reduction in the growth of the national debt was achieved. After that, however, the proportion of spending financed out of taxation fell steadily, and was less than 50 per cent in 1945.[12] According to the recorded objectives of newly issued inland government bonds, roughly 80 per cent of wartime issues were for military purposes.[13] The military budget expanded at a sharp rate, more bonds were issued, and their purchase was enforced.

Money and inflation

On the money side we now consider trends in the stock of currency issued. Table 6.12, based on estimates by Asakura Kokichi and Nishiyama Chiaki,

Table 6.12. *Money in circulation in mainland Japan,*
1934/1936 to 1947 (billion yen and per cent)

		Cash 1	Cash plus demand deposits 2	Cash plus demand, time, and savings deposits 3
1934/6	average	2.1	6.6	14.0
1937	June	2.2	7.6	16.0
1937	Dec.	3.2	9.0	17.7
1938	June	2.7	9.2	18.7
1938	Dec.	3.5	10.8	21.2
1939	June	3.3	11.7	23.3
1939	Dec.	4.7	15.1	28.0
1940	June	4.7	16.2	30.6
1940	Dec.	6.0	19.2	35.1
1941	June	5.7	20.0	37.5
1941	Dec.	7.8	23.8	42.8
% of 1934/6		370	359	306
1942	June	7.3	25.4	46.5
1942	Dec.	9.3	29.5	52.5
1943	June	9.4	32.4	57.7
1943	Dec.	13.1	36.8	65.1
1944	June	15.7	42.6	76.1
1944	Dec.	22.9	54.7	93.8
1945	June	33.0	72.9	122.9
% of 1934/6		1,558	1,100	878
1945	Dec.	56.7	102.8	166.4
1946	June	44.1	107.6	172.8
1946	Dec.	94.9	196.3	227.9
1947	June	137.9	258.9	284.2
1947	Dec.	220.9	405.1	440.0
% of 1934/6		10,438	6,110	3,144

Source: Asakura, Nishiyama (1974), 36–7.

shows cash in circulation with and without demand, time, and savings
deposits in banks (excluding special banks). By the end of June 1945, cash
in circulation was showing a fifteenfold increase or more against its prewar
base. With the addition of demand deposits the increase was elevenfold,
and with the further addition of time and savings deposits it was somewhat

less than ninefold. This meant that towards the end of the war it had become impossible to avoid the explosive inflation which occurred immediately after defeat. Cash in circulation increased another tenfold by the end of 1947, and was now in excess of a hundred times the prewar stock.

This was the state of affairs in mainland Japan. At the time the colonial Bank of Korea and Bank of Taiwan were also issuing bank notes, as were the Central Bank of Manchuria, and the United Reserve Bank of China and Central Savings Bank in north and central China respectively. In addition to this, army notes were being issued in southern China and all over south-east Asia. It is evident that inflation progressed more rapidly in those areas which were furthest from Japan proper.[14]

While the Japanese army in northern China used United Reserve Bank of China notes, the Chinese national government used the legal currency. In the liberated areas, on the other hand, the Chinese communist army used locally issued notes, and there was a fierce currency war between the three.

In central China the legal currency was strong. The Japanese army used army notes, their basic policy being to maintain the value of these notes. Central Savings Bank notes were issued in January 1941, and thereafter a currency war similar to the one in northern China was waged between them and the legal currency. Inflation proceeded rapidly with the Central Savings Bank notes, and fear of this spreading to occupied northern China resulted in further restrictions on trade with central China and the transfer of money. As the area of northern China under Japanese occupation contracted with the adverse turn in the war, large quantities of United Reserve Bank of China notes were circulated and inflation reached catastrophic proportions.

In each of the countries of the south in what we have called area A, which was under direct military government, army notes in the local currency were in use with the same value as the currency in question. The South Seas Development Bank was established in 1942 and issued its own notes, but in fact these were exactly the same as army notes. A currency linked to the yen was not issued in the south in anticipation of sharp inflation, but the transfer of money between Japan and the occupied territories in the south was prohibited and all imports and exports were handled through the temporary military special account and the Essential Materials Control Corporation.

The indiscriminate issue of army and South Seas Development Bank notes and shortages resulting from lack of shipping capacity kindled rapid inflation in the south also. Despite prohibition of trade and money transfers, rising prices in the occupied territories brought about the growth of deficit-financed spending under the temporary military special account, which accelerated inflation in Japan proper. Temporary military revenue towards the end of the war shows an increased income not only from sale of government bonds but also from the colonies and occupied territories.

Financial regulation

On the money side, the policy of enforced low interest rates meant that these did not reflect supply and demand for funds, necessitating direct control over the allocation of funds. Legislation concerning the Bank of Japan enacted in February 1942 encroached on its neutrality as a central bank and emphasized its nature as a government institution, prescribing its role in industrial finance and as the settlement bank for the Greater East Asia Co-prosperity Sphere. The National Financial Control Association, established in May 1942 with the Bank of Japan at its head, exerted a powerful influence on financial organizations throughout the country. The Industrial Bank of Japan was active in military finance and grew rapidly during the war, forming secret relationships with many large companies.

Huge companies supplying military demands gained wartime profits without worrying about finance and sales, and the efforts of management went only into the procurement of materials. As the control mechanism was put into place, commercial capital was removed gradually, and the mechanism of distribution changed also. Two-tier prices came about as a result of control, and there was a rampant black-market economy. Subsidies were instituted for coal and other commodities in order to maintain production activity. In April the government decided to amend their low prices policy, impose large price increases on essential commodities, and adopt a system of subsidies in order to stimulate increased production.

Among the major banks, Mitsui and Dai-Ichi amalgamated to form the Imperial Bank in April 1943, while Mitsubishi joined forces with Dai-Hyaku, and Yasuda with Nippon Chuya. With its weak financial base the new plutocracy gave way, allowing the spotlight to return to the older plutocracy, which was endowed with all-embracing financial powers. Sumitomo and Mitsubishi, their strengths lying respectively in the metallurgical industry and in shipbuilding and engineering, continued to develop at the core of the munitions industry; while Mitsui and Yasuda, though centred on trade and mining and on finance respectively, attempted to shift their commercial base and enter into munitions. From January 1944 onwards each munitions company had its own designated bank, and the strong relationship built up in this way between bank and company provided the pattern for the postwar financial system.

Table 6.13. *Wholesale and consumer prices in Japan:*
alternative estimates, 1937–1945 (per cent of 1934/6)

	Wholesale prices		Retail prices	
	Bank of Japan 1	Morita 2	Bank of Japan 3	Morita 4
1937	120.6	118.9	109.5	108.5
1938	127.2	125.8	125.4	120.3
1939	145.0	145.4	140.5	134.8
1940	157.6	170.7	163.1	175.0
1941	167.2	184.2	165.1	204.1
1942	179.7	235.9	169.9	265.6
1943	190.6	266.5	180.3	312.3
1944	213.8	325.0	201.9	390.0

Source: Okurasho (1947).

Wartime statistics

This ends our discussion of the development of the wartime economy in Japan from the triple standpoint of materials, labour, and finance. I now add some comments on data which may be of use for purposes of comparison.

Prices

Because wartime prices were controlled, there are numerous problems with the official price indices. During the latter stages of the war and the period of instability which followed, a black market became widespread, and statistics on black-market prices are also doubtful. Morita Yuzo's index contained in the Ministry of Finance's estimates of wartime national income take this point into consideration and provide a practical price index.

Table 6.13 compares these with various other indices. According to official statistics, prices almost doubled between the years 1936 and 1944, but according to Morita's index wholesale prices roughly trebled, while retail prices increased by almost four times. For the LTES series Ohkawa estimated wholesale price indices for mining and manufactured goods on the one hand and for investment goods on the other. As far as mining and manufactured goods are concerned, the figures show an approximately threefold increase, which is of the same order as Morita's index, but investment goods prices are estimated to have risen more than sixfold.[15] Cost-of-living indexes were also prepared by the Asahi newspaper company, the government's Statistics Bureau and Morita. While the other estimates show somewhat less than a twofold increase for the 1944 index of living costs, Morita's is roughly fourfold. A MITI retail price index only goes as far as 1942.[16]

Capital stock and war losses

In the LTES series Ohkawa provided an estimate of gross domestic fixed capital formation (GDFCF), distinguishing between military and non-military uses. It is clear that during the war with China between a quarter and a third of all investment in equipment and construction was for military purposes. Investment in equipment for military use included fixtures, manufacture and repair of machinery and tools, weapons, shipbuilding, and ship repairs; by 1938–40 this alone accounted for at least one quarter of GDFCF. Most military investment in construction was in new buildings for military use.[17]

The only available statistics on national wealth are those of the census of 1935. Buildings accounted for 38 per cent, furniture and household effects for 20 per cent, inventories for 12 per cent; railways, gas and electricity supply facilities, and ships accounted for about 5 per cent each.[18]

Table 6.14 shows the results of a survey carried out in 1948. It is estimated that direct and indirect war losses valued at 105 billion yen destroyed roughly 35 per cent of national wealth by the end of the war. This included one-quarter of the housing stock (22.2 billion yen), nearly one-quarter of household possessions (furniture, household effects, and produce – 17.5 billion yen), one-third of industrial equipment (8 billion yen), and four-fifths of shipping (7.4 billion yen). As a result, Japan's overall national wealth at the end of the war stood at roughly the same level as in 1935. However, between 1935 and 1945 Japan had become significantly more industrialized, and the value of the surviving stock of industrial equipment had almost doubled. In addition, warships and aircraft worth 40.4 billion yen were destroyed.[19]

The balance of payments

It has already been pointed out that Japan's relationship with the foreign sector was quite different during the war with China and during the Pacific War; and that even during the war with China, when foreign trade was of great significance, there was an important distinction between trade within the yen bloc and trade outside it as to whether or not payment was in foreign currency. However, Yamazawa Ippei and Yamamoto Yuzo in their contribution to the LTES series, estimating the balance of payments for Japan proper

Table 6.14. *The loss to Japan's national wealth as a result of the Pacific War (billion yen at prices of August 1945 and per cent of 1935)*

	National wealth		War damage	Cols. 2+3	Rate of loss (%): cols 3/4
	1935	1945			
	1	2	3	4	5
Buildings	76.3	68.2	22.2	90.4	25
Ports, waterways	1.3	1.6	0.1	1.8	8
Bridges	2.3	2.8	0.1	2.9	4
Industrial machinery, tools	8.5	15.4	8.0	23.3	34
Railways	10.9	11.6	0.9	12.5	7
Vehicles	2.5	2.3	0.6	2.9	22
Ships	3.1	1.8	7.4	9.1	81
Gas, electricity facilities	9.0	13.3	1.6	14.9	11
Telegraph, telephone facilities	1.5	1.7	0.3	2.0	15
Water supply facilities	1.7	1.8	0.4	2.2	17
Property	67.1	63.4	17.5	80.9	22
furniture, household effects	39.4	36.9	9.6	46.4	21
produce	23.5	25.1	7.9	33.0	24
coins and precious metal bullion	4.2	1.5	0.1	1.6	5
Miscellaneous	2.6	5.0	1.2	6.2	20
Unclassified	—	—	3.9	3.9	100
Subtotal	186.8	188.9	64.3	253.1	25
Warships, aircraft	—	(6.53)	40.4	40.4	100
Total	—	188.9	104.7	293.5	36

Source: KSKS (1990–1), vol. III, 287.

and for the whole of the Japanese Empire not only up to 1940 but as far as 1944, state that it is not possible to make a distinction between the yen bloc and countries outside it. Throughout the period of the Pacific War Japan ran a current deficit which peaked in 1942 at 1.6 billion yen (but this was still only 3 per cent of GNP).[20] The deficit declined thereafter with the rising interdiction of Japanese trade and erosion of the country's import capacity.

Much of the data necessary for an international comparison of wartime economies may be gleaned from the numerous statistics referred to above, but it can hardly be said to be sufficient for purposes of the present volume. The writer has expended much energy in organizing the statistical material, and only commented in passing on the analysis of the important facts which each of the tables has to tell us. It is difficult to obtain statistical material with respect to wartime, and scholars in Japan have as yet achieved little more than sorting out the materials collected here.

Conclusion: changes due to wartime control

The Japanese economy was subject to administrative control for fourteen years from the outbreak of full-scale hostilities in China to postwar deregulation. During this time it altered its appearance dramatically in many ways, some of which were irreversible.

1. *Heavy industrialization.* Militarization altered the industrial structure in the direction of heavy engineering and chemicals. The production facilities installed during the war remained afterwards, as did the increased number of workers with experience in the heavy engineering and chemical industries.

2. *Labour and employment.* Production techniques had not changed greatly, but there had been important changes in the elements which form the system, and various attempts had been made to control the system itself. Greater turnover made it essential to reorganize controls on the workforce. A system of wages with coordinated pay increases linked to labour control, and a system of bonuses and allowances which had been strengthened and reorganized during the war, had a powerful effect on the postwar system of wages. Health insurance schemes had been expanded during the war in order to guarantee the workforce, and a start had been made on organizing social insurance, which had hitherto been unsatisfactory. The place of the prewar trade unions had been taken by patriotic labour organizations based on the workplace, but, when trade unions were reintroduced after the war, wartime organization influenced the shape of the trade unions which were organized on a company basis.

3. *The corporate structure.* Trade control associations established by the new economic order linked up with postwar trade groups. Even the relationships between large and small firms formed on the basis of the wartime subcontracting system were passed on to the postwar period. The reduction in large shareholdings had lessened the supervision of private management by owners of capital, and the status of professional managers had risen. Companies had borrowed heavily during the war and reduced their ratio of net worth to total capital. The postwar reliance of Japanese companies on banks' overlending was in continuity with this, although it was less aimed at increasing liquid assets than in wartime. The relationship between specific companies and specific banks initiated during the war also became the norm for the postwar investment system. The Industrial Bank of Japan, after growing rapidly in wartime, also became the centre of a group of companies.

4. *The state and industry.* The relationship between the government and companies was quite different from that which obtained prior to the war. In terms of systemic change, the functions of the wartime Planning

Board were inherited by the postwar Economic Stability Headquarters; MITI assumed the prerogative of intervention in civilian companies and business circles previously exercised by the Ministry of Commerce and Industry and the Ministry of Munitions in the somewhat altered form of its administrative guidance. The materials supply and demand plans drawn up under temporary legislation in the period shortly after the war corresponded more or less to the wartime materials mobilization plans. Moreover, the postwar system of foreign currency budgets had regulatory powers like those of wartime foreign currency control. On the funding side, the temporary legislation on procurement of funds remained in place with amendments only to the priority ranking table. Selective loans by the Bank of Japan continued to have a powerful regulatory influence.

5. *Agriculture.* Control of rice under wartime legislation on the control of foodstuffs was not abandoned despite postwar deregulation, and continued to influence this core sector of Japanese agriculture. The two-tier system of rice prices adopted during the war to increase production assumed the shape of postwar price policy and was instrumental in restricting the rights of landowners and expanding those of tenant and independent farmers; this was of importance in connection with the postwar land reform.

Thus the changes which link the prewar and postwar periods do not exhibit a bland continuity. Rather, the prewar structure of the Japanese economy was forced to change under the experience of wartime mobilization and destruction by war, followed by the postwar abolition of the plutocracy by the occupying powers, the emancipation of the labour movement, and other measures such as the land reform. The outcome was to shape the postwar Japanese economy.

Notes

1 The White Paper gross national product and expenditure estimates, GNP(E) according to Hitotsubashi University's LTES and the USSBS estimates, and finally Mizoguchi's estimates amended to conform to the concept of GNP(E), are compared by Mizoguchi et al. (1993), 19.

2 Mizoguchi et al. (1993), 28.

3 Ibid., 18, 20, 25.

4 Mizoguchi and Umemura (1988). For a rough overall computation, see table 1.1 in the present volume.

5 The plans themselves are to be found in Nakamura Takefusa and Hara Akira (1969).

6 Oyi (1953), 292–3.

7 For quarterly series of aircraft production, see KSKS (1990–1), vol. III, 281.

8 KSKS (1990–1), vol. I, 22.
9 KSKS (1990–1), vol. III, 277–8.
10 LTES (1966), vol. VII (Emi and Shionoya), 213.
11 Ibid., 188–9.
12 KSKS (1990–1), vol. II, pp. 224, 254.
13 Ibid., p. 289.
14 Hara (1976).
15 LTES (1967), vol. VIII (Ohkawa et al.), 134, 193.
16 KSKS (1990–1), vol. II, p. 475.
17 LTES (1971), vol. IV (Emi), 228–9.
18 LTES (1966), vol. III (Ohkawa et al.), 5.
19 KSKS (1990–1), vol. III, 287.
20 LTES (1969), vol. XIV (Yamazawa, Yamamoto), 236–7.

References

Japanese names are given in Japanese order, family name first.

Arai Kurotake (1986), 'Taiheiyo Senso ki ni okeru Sangyo betsu Yugyo Jinko no Suii' (Shifts in the working population by industry during the Pacific War), in Hayashi Yuji and Nakamura Takahusa, eds., *Nihon Keizai to Keizai Tokei* (The Japanese economy and economic statistics), Tokyo, 41–52.

Asakura Kokichi and Nishiyama Chiaki (1974), *Nihon Keizai no Kahei teki Bunseki* (A monetary history and analysis of the Japanese economy), *1868–1970*, Sobunsha.

Hara Akira (1973), 'L'économie japonaise pendant la deuxième guerre mondiale', *Revue d'histoire de la deuxième guerre mondiale*, no. 89 (Jan.), 33–78.

— (1976), '"Daitoa Kyoei ken" no Keizai teki Jittai' (The economic structure of the Greater East Asia Coprosperity Sphere, *Tochi-seido Shigaku*, vol. 71 (April), 52–74.

KSKS (1990–1): *Kanketsu Showa Kokusei Soran* (Comprehensive survey of national statistics since the mid-1920s), 4 vols., Toyo Keizai Shimposha.

LTES (1966–88), *Choki Keizai Tokei* (Estimates of long-term economic statistics on Japan since 1868), 14 vols. Toyo Keizai Shimposha. Vol. I, *Kokumin Shotoku* (National income) (Ohkawa Kazushi et al., 1974). Vol. II, *Rodoryoku* (Manpower) (Umemura Mataji et al., 1988). Vol. III, *Shihon Sutokku* (Capital stock) (Ohkawa et al., 1966). Vol. IV, *Shihon Keisei* (Capital formation) (Emi Koichi, 1971). Vol. VI, *Kojin Shohi Shishutsu* (Personal consumption expenditure) (Shinohara Miyohei, 1967). Vol. VII, *Zaisei Shishutsdu* (Government expenditure) (Emi Koichi, Shionoya Yuichi, 1966). Vol. VIII, *Bukka* (Prices) (Ohkawa et al., 1967). Vol. XIV, *Boeki to Kokusai Shushi* (Foreign trade and balance of payments) (Yamazawa Ippei, Yamamoto Yuzo, 1969).

Mizoguchi Toshiyuki et al. (1993), *Dainiji Taisen ka no Nihon Keizai no Tokei teki Bunseki* (Statistical analysis of the Japanese economy in World War II).

Mizoguchi Toshiyuki and Nojima Noriyuki (1992), 'Nihon no Kokumin Keizai Keisan, 1940–55' (Calculations of the Japanese national economy), *Hitotsubashi Ronso*, vol. 107(6) (June), 765–79.

Mizoguchi Toshiyuki and Umemura Mataji, eds. (1988), *Kyu Nihon Shokuminchi Keizai Tokei, Suikei to Bunseki* (Basic economic statistics of the former Japanese colonies, 1895–1938, Estimates and Findings). Toyo Keizai Shimposha.

Nakamura Takafusa and Arai Kurotake (1978), 'Taiheiyo Senso ki ni okeru Yugyo Jinko no Suikei (Estimates of the working population during the Pacific War), 1940–47', *Tokyo Daogaku Kyoyo Gakubu Shakai Kagaku Kiyo* (Bulletin of Social Sciences of the Faculty of General Education of Tokyo University), no. 27 (March),107–29.

Nakamura Takefusa and Hara Akira (1969), *Gendaishi Shiryo – Kokka Sodoin* (1) *Keizai* (Source materials on modern history – the national general mobilisation (1), The economy) (Misuzu Shobo).

Okurasho (Ministry of Finance) (1947), *Showa 15 Nendo yori Showa 19 Nendo ni itaru Kokumin Shotoku Suikei* (Estimate of national income: 1940–1944).

Oyi Atsushi (1953), *Kaijo Goei Sen* (The convoy war at sea), Nihon Shuppan Kyodo.

Somucho Tokeikyoku (Statistics Bureau, Management and Coodination Agency) (1987–8), *Nihon Choki Tokei Soran* (Historical Statistics of Japan), vols. I–V.

USSBS: United States Strategic Bombing Survey, Overall Economic Effects Division (1946), *The effects of strategic bombing on Japan's war economy.*

7 The Soviet Union: the defeated victor

Mark Harrison

Introduction

The Soviet experience of World War II has too often been seen as beyond comparison. Official Soviet historiography tended to present the war on the eastern front as incomparably tragic and heroic, and as the only struggle which really counted. In the west, selective memory dwelt mainly on the war in western Europe and the Pacific, and sometimes neglected the eastern front altogether. The opportunity to address the Soviet experience from a truly comparative viewpoint is therefore welcome.

Another comparison which the scholar may follow profitably is with the Russian experience in World War I. Mobilization to meet the German threat in 1914 and to fight the first campaigns quickly exhausted the Russian armies and military industries. Imperial Russia was able to remain at war after the first winter only because of Allied aid and because Germany, tied down by trench warfare in the west, was unable to launch a serious attack in the east. Despite this limitation, the German pressure eventually brought Russia to the point of economic and social disintegration and political collapse.

In this chapter I ask why the outcome of World War II was so different for Russia's successor state, the USSR, how the resources were mobilized for the Soviet war effort, what price was paid for victory at the time, and what the long-term consequences of this victory may have been.

The economic potential for war

The scale of the Soviet effort in World War II was essentially determined by the country's prewar military-economic potential, combined with the measures taken before and during the war to realize and augment it.[1] The potential for war depended mainly on basic economic factors such as the country's size, and level of economic development; prewar rearmament policy also carried a certain weight.

Size meant population numbers, territory, and GDP, best seen as the ultimate supply constraints on the availability of resources for war. Population numbers limited the potential size of the army; likewise, GDP limited the total of resources potentially available for army equipment, transport, and rations. Size also brought advantages of self-sufficiency: the larger the territory, the more diversified the base of minerals, skills, and industries useful for waging modern wars, without having to rely on foreign supply.

As was shown in chapter 1, the Soviet economy carried many advantages of size into World War II (see also table 1.1). Its large population, which just exceeded the combined population of the Axis powers, made possible the maintenance of a large army, despite heavy losses. The large area of settlement allowed near self-sufficiency of food, fuel, and mineral ores for industry; as a result, prewar industrialization could be accomplished despite economic isolation. The large territory also carried strategic advantages when war broke out – space to retreat, regroup, and manoeuvre for defence in depth. (This large territory also figured in the enemy's plans, however, the European part as living space for German settlers, the Asiatic part as a dumping ground for the Russians to be expelled from the European part.)

The advantages of sheer size, however obvious, have often been overstated. A major penalty which the Soviet economy carried into World War II was its low level of development, measured by GDP per head. First, a high GDP per head, relative to other countries, such as enjoyed by Germany, Britain, or the United States, implied a bigger surplus of resources over basic subsistence which could be diverted from civilian to war uses. It was easier for a rich country than a poor one to commit 50 per cent or more of GDP to military outlays.

A high GDP per head carried two further advantages. One benefit flowed from industrial specialization in the metallurgical and engineering branches essential to the manufacture of modern munitions. The other benefit flowed from the relatively sophisticated infrastructure of technological, commercial, and administrative services; these latter were especially useful for purposes of wartime economic regulation, and fostered the pouring of resources into combat.

In the world wars of this century, the level of development could be construed as more important than sheer scale. For example, on the eve of World War I, Russia, Germany, and Britain had GDPs of roughly equal size. Germany had more territory and population than Britain, and Russia had more of each than either. But the advantage lay with the British economy, which began the war with the highest GDP per head, was able to supply its war effort with resources of superior quantity and quality, and at

Table 7.1. *Agricultural employment and productivity of four great powers, 1938/40*

	Agricultural workers % of working population	Net output per worker, agriculture, % of non-agriculture
USSR	57	33
Germany	26	50
USA	17	40
UK	6	59

Source: Gatrell and Harrison (1993), table 8.

the same time maintained its civilian households in better shape from the point of view of personal health, living standards, and morale.

Conversely, the Soviet economic effort in World War II was constrained by a low development level. Soviet military doctrine called for the mass deployment of mechanized fighting forces, but this was very difficult and costly to achieve for two main reasons. First, machinery was relatively much more expensive in the capital-poor Soviet economy than in Germany, Britain, or the United States. Consequently, the achieved level of mechanization of the Soviet combat forces was much lower. Second, one aspect of the low Soviet development level was a large, low-productivity agricultural sector (table 7.1). This meant that millions of Soviet workers had to be held back from military service and industrial war work; they were retained in agriculture, where their GNP contribution was a decreasing fraction of the contribution of the average industrial worker, in order to supply the army and defence industry with agricultural products.

Even before the war, the Soviet economy had taken significant steps towards overcoming the strategic disadvantages of a low development level through the establishment of a centralized, integrated system for allocation of industrial and agricultural products, directed towards rapid industrialization and large-scale rearmament. All of these would contribute significantly to wartime resource mobilization, and therefore must be counted as part of the Soviet Union's prewar military-economic potential. Rearmament resulted not only in the maintenance of a large army endowed with significant equipment stocks (admittedly of variable quality and uncertain combat value), but also in the establishment of specialized defence industries and the familiarization of wide swathes of civilian industry with the requirements of defence production. In the late 1930s the Soviet Union was probably the biggest defence producer in the world, although by

1940 three great powers (Germany, Britain, and the United States) had caught up.[2] In a broader sense, industrialization built up the educational, scientific, engineering, fuel-energy, and transport infrastructures necessary to support Soviet defence production and military operations. Centralized systems for procuring foodstuffs and rationing industrial products guaranteed defence priorities and ensured the integrity of the allocation system under severe external shocks, offering the best guarantee against the economic dislocations which decisively undermined the Russian war effort in World War I.

These institutions and policies were established at heavy cost. Under the centralized economic system, firms' behaviour was characterized by an inefficient, resource-intensive investment bias. The food procurement system had been established only after a destructive confrontation with the peasantry, and lacked institutional restraints to prevent the state from removing too large a share of the harvest from the countryside. The industrialization process was led by steel, cement, and mechanical engineering, to the detriment of transport, information, and telecommunications; the human elements in Stalin's authoritarian grand design were reduced too often to the status of cogs in the machine of state. Defence plans and the defence industry itself were absurdly vulnerable to disruption by a successful invasion in depth, the possibility of which was systematically denied.[3] Nonetheless, one must suppose that, if the Soviet Union had faced Germany in 1941 in the same condition as the Russian Empire in 1914, the result would have been decisively in Germany's favour.

Still other factors also played a role. Size, development level, and prewar preparations were limiting factors on economic potential for war, but did not determine the extent to which a particular country's potential would be realized in wartime. An important role was played by each country's degree of commitment to the war (including its distance from the front line), the degree of national unity and popular support for the war effort, its leaders' capacity for effective policy improvisation, the degree to which economic integration was successfully maintained under wartime stresses, and the time available to put these other factors into operation.

In summary, Soviet leaders deployed a superior institutional capacity for integration and coordination, which matched or exceeded that of much more highly developed economies, so that, despite having a relatively poor economy, the USSR could commit a very high proportion of national resources to the war effort. This made World War II quite different from World War I. In World War I, the Russian economy disintegrated. Food remained in the countryside, while the war workers and soldiers went hungry. The burdens of war were not distributed fairly amongst the population, and this undermined the Russian war effort both materially and psychologically. In World War II, the systems of planning, procurement, and rationing worked effectively. Sufficient resources were allocated to the soldiers and defence industry to permit a colossal, sustained military effort, under disastrous circumstances, which could match the effort of much more developed economies. In Russia there was not enough food to go round, and millions starved. Yet there was no general collapse of morale of the kind which destroyed the Tsarist monarchy.

Mobilizing the potential

Upon the outbreak of war the Soviet Union faced the problem of how to shift rapidly to a high level of economic mobilization. Within a few months this question, having been roughly solved, was replaced by another, equally difficult and equally critical: how to prevent the mobilization from becoming excessive, precipitating an economic collapse.

The initial turn to mobilization was made possible by three groups of factors. First, the economy was already in 1940 highly militarized by peacetime standards, with almost one-fifth of GNP allocated to defence outlays. Considerable prewar effort had been expended on rearmament, on developing the infrastructure of civilian production and services necessary to support large-scale, specialized defence production, and on contingency planning for the mobilization of civilian industrial capacity for war production, should war break out. Such peacetime preparations were far from optimal. Many things were done in the name of national security which undermined morale and productivity. The quality of war preparations was often sacrificed for the sake of numbers and quick results. The nature and timing of German strategy were misunderstood, and the likely costs of defence against German aggression were also understated. Nonetheless, what was done played a certain part in enabling the rapid Soviet economic response to German attack.

Second, the character of the German war on Soviet territory, aimed at enslavement and extermination of the indigenous population, released huge reserves of national feeling among soldiers and civilians alike, and motivated their resistance to the enemy's plans. The release of reserves of national feeling did not occur all at once, however; this was a process which occupied a period of many months, perhaps even one or two years. To begin with, the message of local nationalism was confused, with more than a few believing that Hitler's framework for the east might offer more scope than Stalin's for the realization of Baltic, Ukrainian, Russian, and Turkic national aspirations. It took time for the reality of German occupation policies to undermine such beliefs. In any case, beyond the ranks of the committed collaborators lay much larger numbers whose first instincts might have been to await the outcome of decisive events before committing themselves; such attitudes were just as threatening to the survival of the Soviet régime as acts of outright collaboration.

The interval between the outbreak of war and the emergence of a powerful wave of national motivation was sufficiently filled by a third group of factors, the decisive actions and initiatives of Soviet leaders, from Stalin downwards. These were the people who organized the initial steps of evacuation of population and industry from the war zones, the conversion of civilian industry and transport in the interior to a war footing, and the rapid buildup of defence production. Again, these actions and initiatives were not always wise, harmonious, or patriotically motivated. At various times Stalin displayed depressive inactivity and Beriia tried to bargain for peace while others pursued economic policies which were contradictory or carried harmful long-term results. Nonetheless, it is an undeniable fact that, despite the mistakes of the leaders and the misgivings of the led, a high degree of economic mobilization was rapidly achieved.

The second question arose naturally in the course of answering the first. Mobilization meant initially that labour was poured into the Red Army to replace the huge initial losses and double and treble its size. The defence industry, its physical and human assets disrupted and dispersed by invasion, was relocated and rebuilt at huge cost in the remote interior. In the process, the civilian economy was stripped of resources – labour, food, power, machinery, building materials. Civilian output plunged, and the output of steel and fuel fell by as much as the output of consumer products. Driven by an unparalleled emergency, in the absence of institutional restraints, the mobilization went far enough to threaten the collapse of the civilian economy.

To mobilize the economy over a period of a few months was not enough. It was also necessary to mobilize the economy in the proportions which could sustain a war effort of several years' duration. Official perceptions of the degree of economic mobilization achieved in 1941, 1942, and 1943 were clouded by statistical interference, which led to a tendency to understate the degree of mobilization actually achieved. This tendency is considered in more detail below; it was partly the result of long-established imperfections in the statistical system, partly the result of violent relative price and productivity effects specific to wartime. I do not suggest that it contributed directly to the excessive mobilization of the economy. In any case, those directly responsible for physical allocation knew perfectly well just how strained the situation had become.

But it is still worth stressing that, from the winter of 1941 through to the spring of 1943, while war production and force levels multiplied, while decisive counterstrokes alternated with staggering reverses, the Soviet economy limped from crisis to crisis, its basic needs not being covered, its population becoming more and more hungry, its fixed assets depreciating and not being replaced.

Already in the winter of 1941 Soviet policy makers had come to understand that to give priority to the army and the defence industry was not enough. The civilian economy, including industry, transport, and agriculture, had also to be revived. Putting this into practice was virtually impossible at first, and was limited to an uncoordinated sequence of crash programmes and emergency measures aimed at heavy industry, agriculture, and the harvest. But in 1942 the situation remained too desperate, and resources too limited, for such policies to acquire coherence. The formation of the 'coherent, rapidly expanding war economy' hailed afterwards by Stalin awaited the more favourable military and economic conjuncture which was formed in the winter of 1942 by the successful Stalingrad counteroffensive, the beginnings of domestic economic recovery, and the widening flow of Allied aid. Thus, if the Soviet economy was perceptibly more 'planned' in 1943 than in 1942, it was more a consequence than a cause of military and economic successes.

The cost of war (I): war finance

How did the Soviet economy meet the costs of war? This question has a short-run and a long-run aspect. From a short-run perspective, what mattered was war finance: the degree of mobilization, or the defence burden, best measured by the share of defence outlays in GNP and the associated share of labour requirements. The defence burden also had a long-run aspect – its permanent impact upon the level and growth rate of GNP, which is considered further below.

In the Soviet case the problem of war finance was 'solved' in the usual way, by allocating resources physically, leaving the financial instruments and indicators to register and control the *ex post* consequences. However, this should not be taken to mean that financial aspects of the war effort were ignored or downplayed. The documentary record of official actions is pervaded by efforts to ensure that the financial costs of the war effort were captured accurately in price formation, cost accounting, and budgetary calculations. For example, the goal of budgetary balance was pursued through the war years. Budget subsidies to industry remained negligible through the worst years of the war, growing only as the war drew to a close. The pricing of weapons was continually adjusted to keep pace with their rapidly changing unit cost. The transfer prices of imported goods were carefully brought up to the domestic price level through levies and taxes. Even the cost of forced labourers to industrial users was regulated to keep

Table 7.2. *USSR state budget outlays and revenues, 1941–1945 (billion rubles)*

	1940	1941	1942	1943	1944	1945
Outlays						
National economy	58.3	51.7	31.6	33.1	53.7	74.4
Sociocultural items	40.9	31.4	30.3	37.7	51.3	62.7
Defence	56.8	83.0	108.4	125.0	137.8	128.2
Administration	6.8	5.1	4.3	5.2	7.4	9.2
Not specified	11.6	20.3	8.2	9.0	13.8	24.1
Outlays, total	174.4	191.4	182.8	210.0	264.0	298.6
Revenues						
Turnover tax	105.9	93.2	66.4	71.0	94.9	123.1
Profit deductions	21.7	23.5	15.3	20.1	21.4	16.9
MTS revenues	2.0	1.4	0.7	0.6	0.7	0.7
Enterprise taxes	3.2	3.1	1.9	2.9	3.4	3.3
Personal taxes	9.4	10.8	21.6	28.6	37.0	39.8
Local taxes, levies	1.9	1.3	2.0	3.4	5.8	6.3
State loans	11.5	11.5	1.5	25.5	32.6	29.0
Not specified	24.6	32.1	55.4	52.4	72.9	82.9
Revenues, total	180.2	177.0	165.0	204.4	268.7	302.0
Official balance	5.8	−14.4	−17.0	−5.6	4.7	3.4
Current balance, net of external finance[a]	−30.2	−58.0	−74.8	−83.5	−100.7	−108.5
NMP produced	385	—	329	415	453	475
NMP utilized	387	—	333	437	489	409

Note:
[a] Lower bound.
Sources:
Budget outlays and revenues, totals and specified subtotals: Plotnikov (1955), 293 (revenues), 324 (outlays). The 'state' budget represents the consolidated union and republican budgets.
   Net material product at currently prevailing prices: GARF, f. 3922/4372, op. 4. d. 115, ll. 10–15. NMP 'utilized' equals NMP 'produced', plus net imports, less insurable asset losses.

it in line with the maintenance costs incurred by the labour camps.[4] There is no doubt, therefore, that the problem of war finance was regarded very seriously at all levels.

As table 7.2 suggests, wartime fiscal policy was driven by defence spending, which rose from 57 billion rubles in 1940 to a wartime peak of 138 billion rubles in 1944. According to published figures at current prices, the peak defence burden was recorded in 1943, when defence outlays reached

Table 7.3. *USSR state budget revenues: the increase officially attributed to wartime financial measures, 1941–1945 (billion rubles)*

	1941	1942	1943	1944	1945
Turnover tax	1.5	17.2	29.2	51.1	65.7
Personal taxes, levies	2.3	15.6	21.8	28.5	34.4
Lotteries	0.4	2.9	3.5	4.9	3.8
Loans	—	5.2	9.8	16.5	14.2
Special deposits	—	1.8	3.1	3.9	3.7
Deposits of service personnel	—	—	3.0	0.3	—
Defence and Red Army funds	1.8	5.3	5.3	3.2	1.0
Mobilization of means of the economy	5.6	5.0	6.7	2.2	1.4
Other:					
lend-lease	—	13.8	18.2	37.0	23.7
special revenues	—	—	—	2.0	21.4
reparations	—	—	—	—	2.3

Source: RGAE, f. 7733, op. 36, d. 1847, l. 53 (dated not later than 1 July 1945).

60 per cent of overall government spending, and 30 per cent of the net material product.

The official accountancy also suggests something of the acute problems associated with financing wartime spending at this level; the budget balance, which had officially been in surplus since 1922, moved into the red in 1941, and the surplus was not restored until 1944. The official balance, however, included revenues from unspecified sources including the increase in savings bank deposits, bond sales, and revenues from foreign trade and tariffs. In wartime large sums were raised not only internally from war loans, but also from counterpart funds created in connection with western economic aid, and tariff revenues levied upon US lend-leased goods. A better measure of domestic fiscal resources than the official balance therefore compares outlays with revenues net of bond sales and unspecified revenues (including revenues from foreign transactions and the increase in savings bank deposits). This suggests an *ex ante* deficit of roughly 20 per cent of the net material product over the whole period from 1942 through to 1945.

Measures to rebalance the budget and finance the *ex ante* deficit were pursued vigorously. As in several other countries, direct taxes, semi-compulsory bond sales, and revenues from foreign transactions took the place of indirect taxes levied on a shrinking domestic consumer market.[5] Table 7.3 shows an official estimate of the effectiveness of such measures, and is noteworthy for incidentally revealing the fiscal aspect of lend-lease operations.

Table 7.4. *The Soviet stock of cash and retail trade, 1940 and 1942–1945 (billion rubles and current prices)*

	1940	1942	1943	1944	1945
Money stock, annual average	23.9	34.8	43.9	58.2	68.0
State and cooperative retail turnover	175.5	77.8	84.0	119.3	160.1
Velocity (ratio of retail turnover to money stock)	7.3	2.2	1.9	2.0	2.4

Source: GARF, f. 4372, op. 4, d. 1585, l. 187. Annual averages for the money stock are obtained by averaging 1 January figures.

Such measures were not sufficient, however, to guarantee monetary stability. Figures in table 7.4 reveal that the money stock trebled during the war years. Its velocity (at least in terms of retail trade within the official sector) slowed abruptly, suggesting the emergence of a much larger monetary overhang. The overhang was held mainly by rural households with food surpluses to trade at inflated prices on the kolkhoz market.[6]

While cash in circulation increased rapidly, supplies available for retail trade collapsed. Table 7.5 shows that by 1943 the real volume of supply to the combined official and unofficial sectors stood at little more than one-third of the prewar level. A rapid inflation corresponded to this imbalance, but the effectiveness of price controls in the official sector ensured that the inflationary thrust was diverted largely into the unofficial sector. Prices in state and cooperative outlets nearly doubled between 1940 and 1945, mainly on account of the rising price of alcohol and tobacco; but in the kolkhoz market they multiplied by leaps and bounds, reaching ten times the prewar level at the 1943 peak of scarcity.

The wartime divergence of prices and wages in different segments of the economy reached astonishing dimensions. The country was flooded by mass-produced weapons produced at much lower unit costs and prices than before the war, while scarcity drove food and consumer prices to astronomical levels. Thus retail prices multiplied; construction and transport costs rose little, and prices of civilian machinery and basic industrial goods also remained stable; weapon prices fell rapidly in line with the decline in unit costs yielded by transition to serial production allowing very long production runs with much more efficient use of materials and labour. In the extreme case, by 1943 the prewar correlation of defence industry product prices and free-market food prices had been changed by a factor of approximately 17 (weapon prices had fallen by 40 per cent, while kolkhoz market prices had risen tenfold).

Public sector wages showed only modest inflation. Table 7.6 shows that,

Table 7.5. *Soviet retail trade and price deflators, 1940 and 1942–1945 (billion rubles and per cent of 1940)*

	1940	1942	1943	1944	1945
(A) Turnover, billion rubles					
Retail trade, total					
at current prices	203.5	160.2	262.9	324.2	294.8
at 1940 prices	203.5	74.5	73.6	92.2	110.5
Kolkhoz trade					
at current prices	28.0	82.4	178.9	204.9	134.7
at 1940 prices	28.0	14.7	17.6	24.9	28.9
State and cooperative trade					
at current prices	175.5	77.8	84.0	119.3	160.1
at 1940 prices	175.5	59.8	56.0	67.3	81.6
(B) Price deflators, % of 1940					
Retail trade, total	100	215	357	352	267
Kolkhoz trade	100	560	1,020	820	470
State and cooperative trade	100	129	148	175	193
exc. alcoholic beverages					
and tobacco products	100	109	114	122	132

Source: GARF, f. 4372, op. 4, d. 1585, l. 213. State plus cooperative trade, and kolkhoz trade (turnover and price indices), are given separately, and aggregate turnover and deflators are calculated from data in the source.

as late as 1945, the real wage in the public sector stood at roughly half its prewar value. This decline would have been offset by increased allocations to households from communal supplies (e.g. catering), but the calculation also makes no allowance for a decline in the availability and variety of consumer goods between the two years.

As a result of the strong relative price effects shown in table 7.6, the ratio of nominal defence outlays to the ruble value of total output changed by much less than the relative change of real volumes, so understating the 'real' defence burden.

Relative productivity and price effects moved in inverse association. The productivity of workers employed in specialized defence production was raised sharply, while the productivity of workers employed elsewhere tended to decline. As a result, the numbers employed in specialized defence industry grew, but by much less than the increase in output of defence products. Here, however, the change in defence industry employment understated the labour requirements of defence, because it left out of account the huge increase in the indirect requirements of war production in other sectors where productivity was falling.

Table 7.6. *Soviet price deflators, 1941–1945 (per cent of 1940)*

	1941	1942	1943	1944	1945
Defence industry	84.5	66.4	60.9	59.2	57.4
Civilian industry					
machinery	—	—	—	103.8	—
basic goods	—	—	—	105.8	—
Construction	—	—	—	126.9	—
Railway freight	—	—	—	125.6	—
Public sector wage	—	—	—	—	132
Retail trade	—	215	357	352	267

Source: Harrison (1996a), as table A.1.

Government documents suggest official awareness of these problems, at least among specialists. A wartime comparison of budgetary defence outlays with the net material product (NMP) revealed the power of wartime relative price effects. At current prices, the defence share in 1942 was shown as 38 per cent (only twice the 19 per cent reported for 1940), yet no less than 57 per cent at constant prewar prices.[7] The reason for this was the violent wartime divergence in relative prices of weapons and foodstuffs. The modest defence burden in current prices was certainly not meaningless, and reflected the very high relative cost of wartime civilian maintenance, which limited the diversion of resources to the war effort; but the much higher defence burden measured at prewar prices more truly reflected the great change in relative magnitudes of real outputs for defence-related and civilian use.

However, we shall also see that, when compensation was made for wartime relative price and productivity effects, official statistics *still* somewhat understated the magnitude of the defence burden in 'real' terms.

Real output and employment

The official statistics

To proceed from discussion of money and prices to a more precise understanding of the allocation of real resources, in a form comparable with the data presented by other countries, presents us with considerable difficulties.

The Soviet statistical agencies were in the forefront of national income accounting in the interwar period.[8] In the 1930s, under the impulse of comprehensive national economic development planning, Soviet statisticians developed ambitious schemes for compiling a 'balance of the national economy', with the national accounts at its core.[9] Soviet statisticians continued to draw up a balance of the national economy each year during the war.

These accounts, however, present us with various conceptual and practical difficulties. The conceptual difficulties are associated with the material product system of accounts (MPS), which differed from the GNP-based western System of National Accounts (SNA) by the exclusion of activity in the services ('non-productive') sector, and by the standard of value (officially fixed prices, including indirect taxes and subsidies); the latter retained only the most tenuous link with the measurement of either factor costs or utilities.

Compounding the conceptual discrepancies were practical problems of statistical distortion, concealment, and fabrication. The outright fabrication of statistics was, however, rare. Statistics were occasionally invented, but sensitive figures were more often concealed. Thus defence spending totals were falsified in the early 1930s because they were embarrassingly large, but embarrassingly poor investment indicators at the end of the 1930s were simply suppressed.[10] Demographic totals enumerated at the end of the 1930s were both suppressed (the 1937 census) and wilfully distorted (the 1939 census). Systematic concealment applied to the products and workforce of the defence industries, non-ferrous metallurgy (including gold, ferroalloys, and uranium), and the labour camps, colonies, and settlements administered by the NKVD, as well as monetary aggregates, foreign currency statistics, and the budgetary contribution of foreign trade. But the evidence does not support the idea that Soviet officials systematically maintained parallel sets of statistics, one set for public consumption and another set for secret official use.[11]

Rather, statistical distortion involved the intervention of various biases which affected figures for official use just as much as those made available for publication, in particular the upward distortion of output figures resulting from their use in management as a success indicator. Output was produced by public-sector firms, and the output figures which they reported were success indicators at every level. A variety of means was available to overstate performance. The level of output could be inflated by inclusion of defective or non-existent output (*pripiski*) in statistical returns denominated in physical units (for example, of relatively homogeneous industrial materials). The apparent growth of real output of more heterogeneous goods could also be exaggerated by hidden inflation of the price/quality ratio. Countervailing forces were often weak, and restrained exaggeration only within wide, variable limits.

Recently Grigorii Khanin has proposed that official data may be classified in two ways: by the *pressure for distortion*, which was essentially a function of the use to which they were put, and by the *ease of distortion*, which depended on the relationship of the data to stocks and flows which are visible and physically homogeneous.[12] The pressure for distortion applied to all series used as success indicators such as the value and volume of output; this also means that data passed upwards into the administrative hierarchy were more likely distorted than data compiled for internal use within the firm. Since aggregation was a necessary aspect of passing data up the hierarchy, more highly aggregated data were also more liable to distortion. Peter Wiles once wrote on the same subject:

The Sovietologist is again and again faced with a synthetic official output index that he must check for mishandling against a large selection of the individual physical series from which it was built up. These latter can only have been misreported, and are therefore a firmer base. As Prof. E. Domar has put it [in conversation]: if you go into a bad restaurant where you mistrust the cooking you do not order hash or fruit salad, you order bacon and eggs or a banana.[13]

Thus, data relating to non-standardized, quality-sensitive engineering products or non-residential construction objects were more easily distorted than figures for basic industrial goods or agricultural commodities. Khanin identified machinery, construction, and road transport as sectors particularly vulnerable to hidden inflation.

The ease of distortion remained greater for value-of-output series than for physical volumes; *pripiski* were directly punishable by law, and more easily exposed by dissatisfied customers. Therefore, independent evaluations of Soviet production have generally been ready to use physical output data as a foundation for alternative estimates, even accepting that some distortion did take place.

Even when the difficulties of statistical distortion are fully recognized and when we have done everything possible to overcome them, there remains a significant index number problem. Long-term structural change involved the relative expansion of the Soviet machinery sector, where relative costs and prices fell rapidly. In early years machinery was relatively scarce and expensive, but abundant and cheap in later years. Consequently, total output measured using early-year prices, such as the 'unchanged prices of 1926/7' favoured by official statistics, rose much more rapidly than the same based on current or late-year prices. Sometimes named after Alexander Gerschenkron, this effect is extremely pronounced for measures of Soviet GNP and industrial production which span the prewar and postwar decades.[14]

Reconstructing Soviet data

Western observers, faced with the deficiencies in official data, soon began to construct their own measures on a western conceptual basis. This work was begun by Colin Clark and Naum Jasny; in America, at least, it soon became a small industry in its own right, with substantial funding and a team of researchers led by Abram Bergson under the sponsorship of the RAND Corporation of the United States Air Force. In later years the work was taken over by the CIA Office of Soviet Analysis. The western researchers found that official growth rates were exaggerated, and presented their own, lower ones; despite the sometimes bitter disputes among them at the time, and, later, their equally acid disagreements with Russian dissidents and *émigrés*, the range of disagreement among them was much less than the gulf which separated them from Soviet official views.[15]

In the context of our perceptions of Soviet official statistics based on peacetime methodologies and practices, it is interesting to examine the Soviet national accounts compiled and analysed in wartime. At the same time, the limited quantity of previously published data can now be compared with the greater detail and more sensitive analysis to be found in hitherto secret official documents.[16] These documents confirmed, first, that the German invasion brought about a substantial fall in Soviet NMP. At 1940 prices the initial estimate for 1942 was a shortfall of 39 per cent (later revised to 44 per cent), or 34 per cent in 1926/7 prices. Moreover, the invader had been expelled from Soviet territory by the end of 1944, but in 1945 output remained well below prewar levels.

The official figures, although indicative, cannot be regarded as fully satisfactory. Peacetime distortions continued to operate, although often in different, unexpected ways. Hidden inflation meant that the wartime trend of real output of the consumer industries was overstated (i.e. its collapse was to some extent concealed). But in defence industry, where prices fell, there was hidden *deflation*. The rapid introduction of improved and modernized weapons at much lower prices than the old product range meant that the trend of real defence industry output was greatly understated. These two biases offset each other in computations of overall industrial production and GNP (although there is no suggestion that the offset was an equivalent one), but pointed together to a significant understatement of the defence burden.

Present estimates are based on thoroughgoing reconstruction of Soviet wartime GNP at prewar prices by sector of origin, and measures of real output, expenditure, and employment.[17] The reconstruction draws upon a number of sources, including copious new documentary evidence from the wartime archives of the former Soviet state. Physical output of industry and agriculture is represented by more than 250 product series, and is accom-

Table 7.7. *Soviet GNP by sector of origin, 1940–1945 (at 1937 factor cost)*

	1940	1941	1942	1943	1944	1945
(A) Billion rubles						
Agriculture	69.9	44.1	27.4	30.5	45.1	47.3
Industry	75.1	73.3	64.8	75.7	84.9	71.9
defence	10.5	16.8	38.7	47.8	52.3	36.7
civilian	64.5	56.5	26.1	27.8	32.6	35.2
Construction	10.6	6.9	3.2	3.4	4.4	4.5
Transport, communications	19.3	17.8	10.2	11.8	13.7	14.9
Trade, catering	11.1	9.3	3.8	3.5	4.1	5.0
Civilian services	46.4	42.3	28.2	30.6	37.7	35.3
Military services	7.9	11.1	17.4	18.2	18.7	18.6
Depreciation	13.6	14.0	11.7	11.8	11.7	11.7
Gross national product	253.9	218.7	166.8	185.4	220.3	209.1
(B) Per cent of 1937						
Agriculture	111	70	44	48	72	75
Industry	115	112	99	116	130	110
defence	246	392	903	1,116	1,221	856
civilian	106	92	43	46	53	58
Construction	101	66	31	32	42	43
Transport, communications	115	106	61	70	82	89
Trade, catering	107	90	36	34	39	48
Civilian services	141	129	86	93	115	107
Military services	200	284	454	474	489	484
Depreciation	145	149	124	126	124	124
Gross national product	120	103	79	87	104	99

Source: Harrison (1996a), tables 5.1, 5.2.

panied by information concerning the trend of prices in different markets. Employment series are also reconstructed, with important new information pertaining to the role of forced labour. The reconstruction of the expenditure side is incomplete, with the best evidence pertaining to the defence budget (at current and prewar prices), its direct and indirect requirements for products and labour inputs, and the role of foreign aid. These are elaborated with the help of an input–output table, the defence sector of which is allowed to evolve in each year of the war.

GNP by sector of origin

The outstanding feature of Soviet wartime GDP, reconstructed by sector of origin in table 7.7, is the huge increase in value added in defence industry and military services, against the contrast of decline and collapse in other sectors. Just between 1940 and 1942 the real output of most civilian branches fell by one half or two-thirds, while that of military services more than doubled, and that of defence industry more than trebled.

This contrast is considerably sharper than that revealed by official index numbers of supply of output at the so-called 'unchanged prices of 1926/7', which concealed both inflation of prices of civilian products and deflation of defence products.[18] Officially, for example, by the 1944 peak, defence industry output had reached 2.5 times the 1940 level, whereas an average of physical product series weighted by prewar prices suggests four times. Similarly, to judge from official figures, the output of most branches of civilian industry had fallen, but by much less than is suggested by product series in physical units.

All the competing estimates agree that by 1945, when all the Soviet Union's prewar territory had been freed from enemy occupation, total output still fell substantially below prewar benchmarks.

Employment and productivity

The pattern of wartime employment by sector of origin can also be reconstructed, although not without difficulty. Table 7.8 shows how available data by branch and employer may be fitted together to tell a story which is at least consistent, if not guaranteed accurate to the nearest hundred thousand. Defence industry employment was not reported directly, but can be gauged roughly from information about defence industry prices and costs; present calculations suggest that employment in specialized defence industry grew by less than half between 1940 and 1944. This can be further checked against official employment totals by supply department, which show a similar trend (however, wartime changes in ministerial specialization and vertical integration preclude the use of these figures directly in calculating defence industry employment).

The other major complication in table 7.8 surrounds the allocation of forced labourers among production branches. Forced labourers in camps, colonies, and labour settlements under the NKVD either worked in NKVD establishments engaged in construction or mineral extraction, or were leased to other ministries. Those leased to other ministries were already counted in official public sector workforce totals, whereas the allocation among production branches of those employed directly by the NKVD must be estimated from indirect evidence.

The gender composition of the workforce changed profoundly. Table 7.9 shows that, with men called up into military service, women's share in public sector employment rose from nearly two-fifths before the war to

Table 7.8. *The Soviet working population, 1940–1945 (millions)*

	1940	1941	1942	1943	1944	1945
(A) By branch of employment						
Agriculture	49.3	36.9	24.3	25.5	31.3	36.1
Industry	13.8	12.6	8.7	9.0	10.2	11.6
defence	1.8	1.9	2.7	2.9	2.9	2.1
civilian	12.0	10.7	5.9	6.1	7.3	9.5
Construction	2.4	2.3	1.5	1.5	1.9	2.2
Transport, communications	4.0	3.5	2.4	2.4	3.0	3.6
Trade, catering	3.3	2.8	1.7	1.7	2.1	2.5
Civilian services	9.1	7.7	4.8	5.1	6.5	7.7
Military services	5.0	7.1	11.3	11.9	12.2	12.1
(B) By type of establishment						
Public sector[a]	31.2	27.3	18.4	19.4	23.6	27.3
Artisan industry	2.1	1.8	0.9	1.0	1.2	1.5
Collective farms	47.0	34.9	22.7	23.8	28.9	33.5
NKVD establishments	1.6	1.8	1.4	1.1	1.1	1.3
Armed forces	5.0	7.1	11.3	11.9	12.2	12.1
Working population	86.8	72.9	54.7	57.1	67.1	75.7

Note:
[a] Included among those counted as employed in public-sector establishments were forced labourers (prisoners and 'special settlers') falling under NKVD jurisdiction but subcontracted by the NKVD to work for civilian agencies. These numbered roughly three quarters of a million in 1940–1, falling to half a million in 1943–5 (for more detail see Harrison (1996a), table I.5).
Source: Harrison (1996a), tables 5.4, 5.5.

nearly three-fifths in 1944. The most dramatic change was on the kolkhoz. The countryside was stripped of men (and not only of men but also of horses and machinery); by the end of the war, four out of five collective farmers were women, who carried out basic agricultural tasks predominantly by hand without the assistance of animals or tractors.

Present estimates imply a very sharp divergence between productivity trends in defence and civilian industry. Table 7.10 suggests that, between 1940 and 1944, value added per defence industry worker trebled, while value added per worker in civilian sectors fell, in some cases substantially. Essentially, much of the gain in defence industry output which followed the German invasion was achieved through more efficient use of existing materials, labour, and fixed capacity.[19] There was no efficiency gain in other sectors, and labour productivity in the rest of the economy declined, increasing the resource requirements of civilian output and making it more difficult to divert resources to military use.

Table 7.9. *Women's share in Soviet employment, 1940–1945 (per cent of total)*

	1940	1941	1942	1943	1944	1945
Public sector	38	—	53	57	57	55
industry	41	—	52	53	53	51
construction	23	—	24	29	—	32
transport	21	—	35	42	45	40
farming	34	—	54	61	—	61
Collective farming	—	52	62	73	78	80

Source: Barber, Harrison (1991), 216.

Table 7.10. *Net value added per worker in Soviet material production, 1940–1945 (rubles and 1937 factor cost)*

	1940	1941	1942	1943	1944	1945
Agriculture	1,417	1,194	1,129	1,193	1,441	1,311
Industry	5,458	5,820	7,484	8,428	8,361	6,215
defence	6,019	8,939	14,108	16,616	18,135	17,788
civilian	5,376	5,273	4,412	4,562	4,483	3,706
Construction	4,503	3,040	2,085	2,256	2,286	2,069
Transport, communications	4,891	5,077	4,361	4,849	4,585	4,160
Trade, catering	3,336	3,286	2,248	2,065	1,976	2,026

Source: Harrison (1996a), table 5.7.

The defence burden and foreign aid

Table 7.11 shows that, when budget outlays on defence (the army, air force, and navy, but not the internal security forces) are deflated to prewar prices and compared with GDP at factor cost, the defence burden rose from 17 per cent in 1940 to 61 per cent in 1942, despite a 34 per cent shortfall in GDP in 1942 compared with 1940 (see also figure 7.1).

The peak defence burden of 61 per cent of GDP was recorded in 1943. The further increase of real defence outlays in 1943 was eased by two developments. One was the beginning of recovery of GDP from the 1942 trough. The other was the increased availability of external resources, which reached 10 per cent of GDP (in figure 7.1 the contribution of net imports to total final outlays in excess of GDP is shown by the area below the *x*-axis). If we assume that all the external resources were utilized for defence purposes, the burden on the Soviet domestic economy in 1942 was not 61

Table 7.11. *Soviet GNP and the defence burden, 1940 and 1942–1944:*
alternative measures (billion rubles at 1937 factor cost and per cent)

	1940	1941	1942	1943	1944
(A) Billion rubles					
Gross national product	253.9	218.7	166.8	185.4	220.3
Defence outlays	43.9	61.8	101.4	113.2	117.2
Net imports	0.0	0.3	7.8	19.0	22.9
Defence outlays,					
less net imports	43.9	61.5	93.7	94.1	94.3
(B) Per cent of GNP					
Defence outlays	17	28	61	61	53
Net imports	0	0	5	10	10
Defence outlays,					
less net imports	17	28	56	51	43

Source: Harrison (1996a), table 5.11.

per cent but 56 per cent, and in 1943 this figure fell to 51 per cent. In terms of all the resources used for defence, regardless of their source, 1943 was the most burdensome year of the war. However, in terms of the strain on domestic supply, 1942 was the worst year, and the military and economic consolidation of 1943 was reflected in a relaxation of domestic strains.[20]

The defining features of the Soviet defence burden are therefore, first, that a fairly high peacetime ratio of defence outlays to GDP (17 per cent) had been achieved by 1940; second, that despite the collapse of domestic output the defence burden on the total of resources available, regardless of source, was boosted to a very high wartime level (61 per cent) by 1943; third, that the pressure of domestic resource mobilization peaked very early, in 1942; and, fourth, that by 1943 the domestic pressure was probably being substantially eased by recovery of domestic output and increased external aid.

By the end of 1942, decisive victories had been won on the Russian front. But the price was an excessive economic mobilization, which stripped out resources from the civilian sector and general economic infrastructure, and left insufficient to maintain the human population and capital stock. It had become immensely urgent to widen the flow of resources for these uses. The first signs of recovery in domestic output in 1943 were insufficient on their own, and the simultaneous rapid buildup of foreign aid was a further necessary condition for developing the Soviet strategic counteroffensive in 1943.

Wartime defence burdens may also be captured in employment terms. At

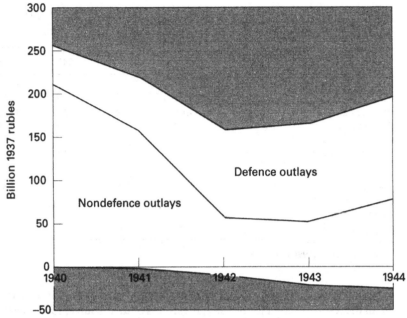

Figure 7.1 Soviet real GDPs and defence outlays, 1940–1944
Source: table 7.11

first sight, numbers of employees present a less ambiguous denominator for defence requirements than rubles, dollars, or marks. The simple part was to count those in uniform. When it came to defining 'war work' behind the front line, however, it was just as difficult to establish the number of workers engaged in supply of the war effort as it was to define the defence burden on national income.

Three possible routes to a definition of war work may be compared. At first sight the most attractive method is to apply the industrial classification developed in the UK Central Statistical Office and used by the British official histories of the world wars, which distinguishes three sectors or 'industry groups': (I) the munitions-related industries, broadly defined, which could be expected to expand in wartime; (II) the essential industries which could be expected to maintain themselves; and (III) the inessential industries which could be expected to shrink. This classification is attractive because its application is no more than a few minutes' work, and because significant comparisons (e.g. of Britain and Germany) already exist in the literature.[21]

In the Soviet case this classification does not work well. Table 7.12, part

Table 7.12. *Soviet defence employment, 1940 and 1942–1944: alternative estimates (millions)*

	1940	1942	1943	1944
(A) British classification				
War workers	11.8	7.8	8.1	9.5
Group I ('munitions')	5.0	3.8	4.0	4.4
Group II ('essential')	6.9	4.0	4.1	5.1
Armed forces	5.0	11.3	11.9	12.2
Defence sector, total	16.8	19.1	20.0	21.7
% of working population	19	35	35	32
(B) Gosplan classification			*prelim.*	*plan*
War workers	8.9	13.9	14.5	16.2
agriculture	4.2	5.7	6.2	7.2
industry	3.5	5.9	5.9	6.1
construction	0.3	0.4	0.3	0.3
transport	0.6	1.4	1.6	2.0
trade	0.2	0.5	0.5	0.6
Army, Navy	4.6	10.8	11.3	11.7
Defence sector total	13.4	24.8	25.9	28.0
% of working population	15	45	45	42
(C) Input/output classification (net of imports)				
War workers	9.8	17.3	12.9	10.9
Army, navy	4.6	10.8	11.3	11.7
Defence sector total	14.3	28.2	24.3	22.6
% of working population	16	52	42	34

Source: Harrison (1996a), table 5.16.

(A), shows that employment in the 'defence sector' (military services, plus group I) increased its share from 19 per cent in 1940 to 35 per cent in 1942 and 1943; however, the rising share was entirely due to the increased numbers of military personnel, the number of war workers alone on the CSO definition (group I) remaining at 14 per cent of the working population in 1940 through 1942. The prewar productivity gap between employees in war production and in the civilian sector, and the growing wartime productivity divergence, would suggest an employment burden lower and less rapidly growing than the GNP burden – but not to this extent.

The main problem with the CSO definition is that it excluded two kinds of war workers: those employed indirectly in supplying the needs of the munitions industries, and those engaged in supply of the armed forces not with specialized military goods but with dual-purpose goods and services (food, fuel, transport, and clothing). Official Gosplan estimates of the

direct requirements plus an incomplete list of first-order indirect requirements of defence outlays allow us to calculate the figures shown in table
7.12, part (B). They confirm a much greater wartime increase in the burden
than was apparent from the CSO definition. The percentage of soldiers and
war workers stood at 15 per cent in 1940, rising to 45 per cent in 1942 and
1943.

Nonetheless, such figures remain incomplete. A full-blown input/output
analysis is required to overcome their defects. The results of such an analysis are shown in table 7.12, part (C). The direct-plus-indirect domestic
requirements of Soviet defence outlays, net of imports (i.e. on a 'domestic
finance' basis) and deflated to prewar prices, are established from their distribution among twenty-seven processing sectors, multiplied by an annually
evolving matrix of Leontief coefficients, and sector series for value added
per worker in each year. From this we find that the employment burden of
defence, already 16 per cent before the outbreak of war, had reached no less
than 52 per cent by 1942. We also find that, when the resource-releasing
effects of the increase in Allied aid in 1943 are taken into account, the
employment burden fell back in that year to 42 per cent, consistent with the
phasing of war burdens suggested above.

Living standards and demography

There remains no satisfactory overview of Soviet living standards during
World War II. A few stylized facts may be presented.[22] For the mass of
people, wartime consumption was limited to the struggle for housing,
heating, basic clothing, and food. Food supplies were the critical factor
determining survival, and during most of the war there was not enough
food to go round. Half the population (mainly soldiers and public sector
employees) was covered by the official rationing system. Food rations were
differentiated by economic role and status. The most important commodity was bread, which supplied 80–90 per cent of rationed calories and proteins. The calories and proteins supplied according to official ration norms
were not guaranteed from central supplies, and in any case were insufficient
to sustain life for more than a privileged minority of essential workers. They
had to be supplemented by access to food supplies from sideline farming
(both organized and individual), and from the unofficial sector. Even when
other aspects of economic life were improving, food supplies per head of
the population tended to deteriorate because of harvest difficulties, and
because the liberation of previously occupied territory increased demand
faster than supply.

Less is known about the living standards of the rural population.
Collective farmers lived off the meagre residual product of the collective

farm and the product of their own sideline activities. The latter was particularly important, given the power of the state to command a prior share of collective farm output, and sideline activities tended to encroach upon the collective sphere during the war years, requiring a sharp postwar campaign of correction. Anecdotal evidence suggests pervasive hardship, and tends to confirm that World War II (in contrast to World War I) saw a loss of social privilege for food producers.[23] The Soviet economy did not disintegrate, food producers did not retain food surpluses, and the burdens of war were forcibly spread across the population, urban and rural alike.

Per capita household consumption in 1940 was already somewhat depressed below the prewar peak by the burdens of rearmament. In 1941 and 1942 it fell sharply, but the fall was cushioned, despite the severe military pressures, by resources released through aggregate net disinvestment. Household consumption per worker, according to the present author's estimate, reached its lowest point in 1943; at this point it was perhaps three-fifths of the 1940 level, rising to four-fifths in 1944.[24]

The demographic consequences of this degree of deprivation are by now clear enough in outline, although not in detail. Succeeding generations of Soviet leaders put the total of war deaths at 7 million (Stalin), 20 million (Khrushchev), and 'more than 20 million' (Brezhnev).[25] More recently, an expert commission of Goskomstat reported the excess mortality of the war years as '26–27 million'; detailed justification of this figure is now available. The mid-1941 population (within contemporary frontiers) is given as 196.7 million, and the population at the end of 1945 as 170.5 million, with a point estimate for war deaths of 26.6 million.[26]

Ellman and Maksudov point out that the figure of 26.6 million does not allow explicitly for wartime and postwar net emigration of 2.7 million, although this number may have already been deducted from the element of the prewar population total representing the western territories absorbed in 1939–40.[27] Of course, 'only' 23.9 million would still be a very large number of premature deaths.

Wartime deaths among military personnel are reported at 8.7 million, but the latter figures includes normal mortality of several hundred thousand.[28] Excess mortality among civilians is represented by the remainder (16 million at the lower limit), although this figure too includes many hundreds of thousands of deaths attributable directly to enemy action rather than to economic conditions.

Malnutrition was widespread and undoubtedly carried off many victims in the interior of the country, not just in famous episodes such as the siege of Leningrad, where hunger and hunger-related causes carried off 1 million people, two-fifths of the city's prewar population. Poor dietary conditions were also conducive to the spread of diseases, and the incidence of typhus, typhoid fever, and tuberculosis rose sharply in 1942. Determined measures checked their further spread.

Death rates for the population as a whole, but presumably excluding those arising from enemy action, are said to have risen from 18 per 1,000 in 1940 to 24 per 1,000 in 1942, falling to 9 per 1,000 in 1945. But even these figures are surely incomplete. Figures for Siberia, remote from the front line, also confirm a mortality peak in 1942, and a particularly sharp increase in mortality amongst the urban population (29 per 1,000 in 1942, compared with 21 per 1,000 in the countryside), despite the rural concentration of younger and older age groups. After 1942 death rates fell, not because conditions were improving, but because the most vulnerable members of society had already been carried off.[29]

The cost of war (II): the long run

Supply shocks and their persistence

The war constituted a profound supply-side shock to the Soviet economy.[30] Both physical and human assets were destroyed on an unprecedented scale. According to present information (table 7.13), the war deprived the Soviet economy of at least 18 per cent of its prewar human assets, but the rate of destruction of physical assets was even higher at 25 per cent or more. When the lost assets of both kinds are valued at replacement cost and prewar prices, it transpires that aggregate war losses amounted to a minimum of 22 per cent of the Soviet Union's prewar broad (physical and human) capital stock.

The evidence available, although somewhat heterogeneous in character, also suggests that the supply-side shocks to the Soviet population, fixed capital, and GNP resulting from World War II were persistent in character, and that their effects on postwar levels of the aggregate variables were never made up; the prewar trend path was not regained within any relevant historical time-horizon.[31]

Series for GNP per head before and after World War II are hard to interpret given the breaks in data, but a plausible reading suggests again a persistent shock amounting to 11 per cent of prewar GNP per head. Given the scale of asset losses reported above, it appears that less than one quarter of this loss can be explained by losses of physical and human capital per head and changes in dependency. The otherwise unexplained loss amounts to about 7 per cent of GNP per head.[32]

On the other hand, productivity series (GNP per worker, industry value added per worker and per hour worked) support the hypothesis of a productivity loss which was long lived but not indefinitely persistent. One plau-

Table 7.13. *Soviet losses of physical and human*
assets during World War II (billion rubles at
prewar prices and per cent)

	Billion rubles 1	% 2
(A) Loss of physical assets		
Prewar assets	2,263	
War losses	566	25
(B) Loss of human assets		
Prewar assets	1,489–1,515	
War losses	268–294	18–19
(C) Loss of combined assets		
Prewar assets	3,753–3,778	
War losses	834–860	22–23

Note:
The methodology for this calculation follows that set out by
Broadberry and Howlett in chapter 2. The percentage figure
for physical asset losses represents a conservative correction
of the official figure of 30 per cent. The range of figures for
human asset losses arises from our uncertainty as to how
net Soviet emigration is treated in the underlying
demographic estimates. Net emigration should be excluded
from war *deaths*, but not from war *losses* (since emigrants,
although alive, are lost to the economy).
Source: Harrison (1996a), table 7.3.

sible interpretation is that World War II was associated with a considerable
negative shock followed by an acceleration which made good most of the
initial loss over a period of twenty to thirty years. More precisely, if we
model the postwar acceleration as recovery to a long-run 'normal' trend,
then the half-life of the wartime shock is computed at nine to ten years
(altenatively, it was not until the mid-1970s that roughly 90 per cent of the
effect of the war had worn off).[33]
    Whichever way we read the Soviet record, on an international compari-
son it appears that the Soviet Union was the only one of the victors to suffer
a significant, long-lasting economic setback from World War II (the evidence for other countries is reviewed in chapter 1). From this point of view
the impact of the war on the Soviet economy was far more consistent with
the experience of the vanquished countries than with the experience of the
victors, Britain and the United States.

The institutional legacy

The war did not only affect the size and growth of the Soviet economy, but also affected institutions and systems. The Soviet economic and social system was not radically altered by the war. Indeed, to a superficial glance, the systemic changes attributable to the war were much less in the Soviet Union than in Germany, Japan, France, or Great Britain. Within the framework of broad continuity in the political and ownership systems, however, the war left permanent traces. Most obviously, the defence industry complex emerged from World War II with tremendous prestige, and permanently increased power to command national resources in peacetime. After an initial postwar demobilization, the Soviet defence industry began to grow again in the context of the US nuclear threat and the outbreak of the Korean War.

Militarization of the postwar Soviet economy was not inevitable. The war had also given rise to new currents favouring both international and domestic relaxation, with less civilian discipline and sacrifice, and more emphasis on openness and the peaceful use of resources. The evolution of the war raised questions about the wisdom of the Soviet Union's prewar leadership, Stalin's role, and whether it was really necessary to renew military competition with former wartime Allies. However, this mood lacked public expression, and remained underground for a decade after 1945. It finally emerged under Khrushchev in the theme of 'peaceful coexistence', but by now it was in a permanently weakened form; this explains much of the failure of moves towards an effective model of socialist reform after 1955.

In contrast, the postwar military-industrial élite was entrenched in its positions, with victory lending legitimacy to conservative tendencies strengthening authoritarian rule and favouring the continuation of a militarized economy. Consequently, Soviet postwar economic development was permanently distorted by a heavy peacetime defence burden. During World War II the Soviet economy showed itself capable of mobilizing resources for military use on a scale normally characteristic of economies at much higher income levels. The same remained true in the peacetime era which followed.

Lessons of the war took practical forms which also tended to consolidate the wartime structures of the defence industry complex. In 1941, a heavy price had been paid for lack of peacetime preparedness. In the postwar years a high level of economic preparedness was sought in order to avoid any lengthy conversion period in the opening phase of the next war. This necessarily implied large peacetime commitment of resources to the army and defence industry complex, for combat-ready stocks of weapons, and for reserve production capacities which could quickly be brought into operation at need.

The war was also held to have illustrated the virtues of vertically integrated, large-scale production, in order to supply a mass army with low-cost munitions. Before World War II, defence plants were heavily concentrated in the western and southern regions of European USSR, often relying on far-flung sources of materials and components. As a result of World War II the centre of gravity of the Soviet defence industry was shifted hundreds of kilometres eastward to the Urals and western Siberia. There, huge evacuated factories and new self-sufficient workplace communities were grafted onto remote rural localities. A further result was that defence industry was increasingly concentrated on Russian Federation territory.

After the war, despite some westward reverse evacuation, the new war economy of the Urals and Siberia was kept in existence. Weapons factories of the remote interior were developed into closed, self-sufficient 'company towns' forming giant, vertically integrated production systems; their existence was a closely guarded secret, and they were literally taken off the map.

The war and postwar sclerosis

Continuity from wartime success to postwar consolidation of the Soviet defence industry complex was guaranteed by the ideological and political institutions of Soviet patriotism and party guidance.

'Party guidance' was embodied in the coalescence of party and state hierarchies. The state hierarchy, which transmitted the orders of government via the ministerial system to the economy's productive agencies, was paralleled at every level by a party hierarchy with its own apparatus designed for formulating goals, monitoring progress, and solving problems, giving life to the dead hand of government bureaucracy. In defence industry the interests of society became absolutely identified with those of the party.

Julian Cooper has shown that personnel were selected for careers within the closed world of the defence industry complex, on the basis of industrial experience and professional competence combined with political qualifications, moving between party and state posts (and sometimes combining them).[34] Imbued with party-mindedness, these officials ensured the implementation of party policies, and this also secured the privileged position of military-economic interests.

'Soviet patriotism' was also embodied in the defence industry complex. Soviet patriotism meant unified control from Moscow over all the shared resources of the all-Union state, regardless of particular ethnic, national and republican boundaries and interests. The principle of Soviet patriotism gave Soviet leaders the unchallenged right to mobilize resources towards common military-economic goals of the party and state. This in turn guaranteed the privileges of the defence industry complex.

Soviet patriotism was explicitly multinational, but within the Soviet brotherhood of nations the Russians were accorded a special place – 'elder brother' to the rest. This special place reflected the Russians' historic colonizing role within limits of the old empire, with the Russian capital of Moscow as its centre. In wartime Russia national military pride and great-power traditions were strengthened by the Russians' special role in repelling the German invader after the loss of the non-Russian republics in the west, and by the terrible demographic cost of the war to the Russian people.

Despite the multinational ethic of Soviet patriotism, it was ethnic Russians who dominated the leadership of the postwar defence industry complex.[35] The privileged position of the defence industry, led by Russians and located largely on Russian territory, was entrenched by the war. This made a major contribution to postwar avoidance of military-civilian conflict. The defence industry was protected from criticism, and its leaders found little need to take an active political role. Its key position became obvious in two ways: in privileged resource allocation (defence spending on weapons), and in the extraordinary continuity and influence of its leadership. The 'Brezhnev generation' dominated Soviet political life through the 1960s, 1970s, and 1980s. The core of this generation was the leadership of the Soviet defence industry complex, men (and they were exclusively *men*) who gained office in the last years before World War II, proved themselves in wartime, and retained their hold on the levers of power until dying in office many decades later.[36]

Conclusion

For forty years, the Soviet historiography of World War II was dominated by unthinking triumphalism. 'Why have the victors in the war lost the peace?' is a new question for Russians, at least in public.[37] Of course, this is a question which does not have a deterministic answer – the Soviet economy did not collapse at the end of the 1980s because of its success in mobilizing against Germany at the beginning of the 1940s. Without a successful Soviet war effort, Germany would probably have succeeded in establishing a colonial empire in eastern Europe, and the whole course of global history would have changed. Nonetheless, there are some aspects of the Soviet war effort which, in hindsight, may have something to tell us about the vicissitudes of Soviet postwar experience.

Among the war's effects were confirmation or entrenchment of certain aspects of the Soviet economic system which were already present before the war. Thus, the mobilization capacity of the Soviet economy was already visible before the war in the campaigns to 'build socialism' through the mass collectivization of peasant farming, rapid public-sector industrialization and urbanization, and so on. The war confirmed the high mobilization capacity of the Soviet economic system and showed that it could be used just as effectively for military purposes as for peacetime goals. This meant that the Soviet economy devoted the same high proportion of national resources to the war as other much more highly developed market economies without collapsing.

In the postwar period, the Soviet economy continued to carry a very large defence burden, much higher in proportion to GNP than the burdens carried by the main NATO powers. Whether or not this resulted in a dynamic loss to the Soviet growth rate (a subject on which economists find it hard to agree), there was certainly a substantial static loss to Soviet consumers over many years.[38]

In the same spirit the war entrenched a production system based on mass-production technology under centralized management for national goals, rather than on flexible production for consumer markets. The mass-production system was already being built before the war, but in the teeth of craft resistance. Arguably, the war was one factor which allowed the obstacles of conservatism to be swept aside (others included the prewar Stakhanov movement, the purges, and so on).[39]

Finally, the war entrenched a generation of leaders associated with the defence industry and defence issues – the 'Brezhnev generation'. These leaders were selected from the cohort promoted to positions of authority in the last phase of the prewar purges, in 1938–40. Those who survived the purges, the war, Stalin's last years, and the post-Stalin transition, were considered to have proved themselves. Once they were young and innovative, but having fought their way to the top of the Stalinist political system in their youth, they became unwilling in old age to contemplate new upheavals. The war had taught them the wrong lessons. Unable to adapt to new times, they made an important contribution to the system's long-term decay.

Notes

1 Gatrell, Harrison (1993).
2 Harrison (1990), 587.
3 Harrison (1988).
4 Harrison (1996a), appendix A.
5 See also Millar (1980).

6 In 1942 farming households saved 13.7 billion rubles, nearly two-fifths of their cash incomes, while non-farm households' accumulated savings fell (GARF, f. 687, op. 48, d. 5726, l. 183).

7 GARF, f. 3922/4372, op. 4, d. 115, ll. 50–3. For further discussion, see Harrison (1995).

8 Wheatcroft, Davies (1985).

9 Harrison (1985), 23–25.

10 Davies (1984, 1993).

11 Bergson (1953), 7–9n.

12 Khanin (1991), 14–28.

13 Wiles (1962), 226.

14 For recent discussion of the Gerschenkron effect and other issues, see Wheatcroft and Davies (1994).

15 Harrison (1993); Wheatcroft and Davies (1994).

16 Harrison (1995).

17 For full results see Harrison (1996a).

18 Raymond Powell, the pioneer of wartime Soviet GNP estimates, was forced to rely principally on these unreliable official index numbers of branch output; see Powell (1968).

19 A similar process was noted in Germany, and accounted for much of the belated surge of German war production between 1941 and 1944; see Overy (1994).

20 These alternative measures correspond with the concepts of '(I) national utilization', and '(II) domestic finance' of resources supplied to the war effort, outlined by the present author in Harrison (1988), 183–4. The figures given here supersede the somewhat higher wartime percentages reported in ibid., 184, table 3, which were based on crudely adjusted official data and guesswork.

21 Kaldor (1946), Klein (1959).

22 See Moskoff (1990), Barber and Harrison (1991).

23 Arutiunian (1970), Nove (1985).

24 Harrison (1996a), ch. 5.

25 Rybakovskii (1989), 96. Rybakovskii's own estimate (27–28 million) was little more than the new Goskomstat figures which were soon to appear.

26 Andreev, Darskii and Khar'kova (1990), 26–7.

27 Ellman and Maksudov (1994), 672.

28 Figures reported by Krivosheev (1993) are reviewed by Maksudov (1993).

29 For more detail, see Barber and Harrison (1991), 86–9.

30 This is not the first attempt to assess the war's long-run economic impact. See for example Millar, Linz (1978), Linz (1980, 1985).

31 On the persistence of the demographic shock, see Ellman and Maksudov (1994), 674. Moorsteen and Powell (1966), 243, investigating capital losses, and Syme (1994), investigating GNP losses, found by different means a permanent or near permanent shock to the levels of these variables (according to Moorsteen and Powell's figures the capital stock would have regained its prewar growth path after 140 years), with the loss represented by six to seven years' growth.

32 Harrison (1996a), appendix N.

33 Harrison (1996b).
34 Cooper (1988), 174–5.
35 Ibid., 176.
36 Crowfoot and Harrison (1990).
37 Hence the title of a recent article by Andrei Illarionov (1995): 'Pochemu pobediteli v voine proigrali mir?'
38 For a sceptical view of the growth effects of the defence burden see Easterly and Fischer (1995).
39 See for example Siegelbaum (1988).

References

Archives

GARF: Gosudarstvennyi Arkhiv Rossiiskoi Federatsii (State Archive of the Russian Federation).
RGAE: Rossiiskii Gosudarstvennyi Arkhiv Ekonomiki (Russian State Economics Archive).

Books, articles, and working papers

Andreev, E., Darskii, L., and Khar'kova, T. (1990), 'Otsenka liudskikh poter' v period Velikoi Otechestvennoi voiny', *Vestnik statistiki*, no. 10, 25–7.
Arutiunian, Iu. V. (1970), *Sovetskoe krest'ianstvo v gody Velikoi Otechestvennoi voiny* (2nd edn), Moscow.
Barber, J., and Harrison, M. (1991), *The Soviet home front, 1941–5: a social and economic history of the USSR in World War II*, London.
Bergson, A. (1953), *Soviet national income and product in 1937*, New York.
Cooper, J. M. (1988), 'The élite of the defence industry complex', in Lane, D., ed., *Élites and political power in the USSR*, Aldershot.
Crafts, N. F. R., and Mills, T. C. (1995), 'Europe's golden age: an econometric investigation of changing trend rates of growth', in van Ark, B., and Crafts, N. F. R., eds., *Quantitative aspects of Europe's postwar growth*, Cambridge.
Crowfoot, J., and Harrison, M. (1990), 'The USSR Council of Ministers under late Stalinism, 1945–1954: its production branch composition and the requirements of national economy and policy', *Soviet Studies*, vol. 42(1), 39–58.
Davies, R. W. (1984), 'Capital investment and capital stock in the USSR, 1928–1940: Soviet and western estimates', in Davies, R. W., ed., *Soviet investment for planned industrialisation, 1929–1937: Policy and practice*, Berkeley, CA.
——— (1993), 'Soviet military expenditure and the armaments industry, 1929–33: a reconsideration', *Europe-Asia Studies*, vol. 45(4), 577–608.
Easterly, W., and Fischer, S. (1995), 'The Soviet economic decline', *World Bank Economic Review*, vol. 9(3), 341–71.
Ellman, M., and Maksudov, S. (1994), 'Soviet deaths in the Great Patriotic War: a note', *Europe-Asia Studies*, vol. 46(4), 671–80.

Gatrell, P., and Harrison. M. (1993), 'The Russian and Soviet economy in two World Wars', *Economic History Review*, vol. 46(3), 425–52.

Harrison, M. (1985), *Soviet planning in peace and war, 1938–1945*, Cambridge.

(1988), 'Resource mobilization for World War II: the U.S.A., U.K., U.S.S.R., and Germany, 1938–1945', *Economic History Review*, vol. 41, 171–92.

(1990), 'The volume of Soviet munitions output, 1937–1945', *Journal of Economic History*, vol. 50, 569–90.

(1993), 'Soviet economic growth since 1928: the alternative statistics of G. I. Khanin', *Europe-Asia Studies*, vol. 45, 141–67.

(1995), 'Soviet national accounting for World War II: an inside view', in J. M. Cooper, M. Perrie, and E. A. Rees, eds., *Soviet history, 1917–1953: essays in honour of R. W. Davies*, London and Basingstoke, 219–42.

(1996a), *Accounting for war: Soviet production, employment, and the defence burden, 1940–1945*, Cambridge.

(1996b), 'Trends in Soviet labour productivity, 1928–1985: what the record shows', University of Warwick, Department of Economics, Working Paper Series no. 9605.

Illarionov, A. N. (1995), 'Pochemu pobediteli v voine proigrali mir?', *Segodnia*, 2 July.

Kaldor, N. (1946), 'The German war economy', *Review of Economic Studies*, vol. 13, 33–52.

Khanin, G. I. (1991), *Dinamika ekonomicheskogo razvitiia SSSR*, Novosibirsk.

Klein, B. H. (1959), *Germany's economic preparations for war*, Cambridge, MA.

Krivosheev, G. F., ed. (1993), *Grif sekretnosti sniat. Poteri Vooruzhennykh Sil SSSR v voinakh, boevykh deistviiakh i voennykh konfliktakh*, Moscow.

Linz, S. J. (1980), 'Economic origins of the Cold War? an examination of the carryover costs of World War II to the Soviet people', Ph.D. dissertation, University of Illinois at Urbana-Champaign.

(1985), 'World War II and Soviet economic growth, 1940–1953', in Linz, S. J., ed., *The impact of World War II on the Soviet Union*, Totowa, NJ, 11–38.

Maksudov, S. (1993), 'O frontovykh poteriakh Sovetskoi Armii v gody Vtoroi Mirovoi voiny', *Svobodnaia mysl'*, no. 10, 117–19.

Millar, J. R. (1980), 'Financing the Soviet effort in World War II', *Soviet Studies*, vol. 32(1), 106–23.

Millar, J. R., and Linz, S. J. (1978), 'The cost of World War II to the Soviet people: a research note', *Journal of Economic History*, vol. 38(4).

Moorsteen, R., and Powell, R. P. (1966), *The Soviet capital stock, 1928–1962*, Homewood, IL.

Moskoff, W. (1990), *The bread of affliction: the food supply in the USSR during World War II*, Cambridge.

Nove, A. (1985), 'The Soviet peasantry in World War II', in Linz, S. J., ed., *The impact of World War II on the Soviet Union*, Totowa, NJ.

Overy, R. J. (1994), *War and economy in the Third Reich*, Oxford.

Plotnikov, K. N. (1955), *Ocherki istorii biudzheta sovetskogo gosudarstva*, Moscow.

Powell, R. P. (1968), 'The Soviet capital stock and related series for the war years', in *Two supplements to Richard Moorsteen and Raymond P. Powell, The Soviet capital stock, 1928–1962*, Yale University, The Economic Growth Center.

Rybakovskii, L. (1989), 'Dvadtsat' millionov ili bol'she?', *Politicheskoe obozrenie*, no. 10, 96–8.

Siegelbaum, L. H. (1988), *Stakhanovism and the politics of productivity in the USSR, 1935–1941*, Cambridge.

Syme, T. (1994), appendix to Harrison, M., 'Russian and Soviet economic growth reassessed in the light of new growth theory', University of Warwick, Department of Economics, Working Paper Series, no. 9404.

Wheatcroft, S. G., and Davies, R. W. (1994), 'The crooked mirror of Soviet economic statistics', in Davies, R. W., Harrison, M., and Wheatcroft, S. G., eds., *The economic transformation of the Soviet Union, 1913–1945*, Cambridge, 24–37.

Wheatcroft, S. G., and Davies, R. W., eds. (1985), *Materials for a balance of the Soviet national economy, 1928–1930*, Cambridge.

Wiles, P. J. D. (1962), *The political economy of communism*, Oxford.

Index

Printed in the United States
By Bookmasters